IRISH LITERATURE
THE EIGHTEENTH CENTURY

A NEW ANNOTATED ANTHOLOGY OF EIGHTEENTH AND NINETEENTH CENTURY IRISH LITERATURE

Major new book series which demonstrates the growth, variety and achievement of Irish writing in the eighteenth and nineteenth centuries. Covering prose, poetry and drama, the volumes not only contain work by major authors but also include less obvious material gleaned from sources such as letters, diaries, court reports, newspapers and journals.

Irish Literature
The Eighteenth Century
An Annotated Anthology
Edited and Introduced by
A. Norman Jeffares and
Peter van de Kamp

Irish Literature in the Eighteenth Century illustrates not only the impressive achievement of the great writers—Swift, Berkeley, Burke, Goldsmith and Sheridan—but also shows the varied accomplishment of others, providing unexpected, entertaining examples from the pens of the less well known. Here are examples of the witty comic dramas so successfully written by Susannah Centlivre, Congreve, Steele, Farquhar and Macklin. There are serious and humorous essayists represented, including Steele, Lord Orrery, Thomas Sheridan and Richard Lovell Edgeworth. Beginning with Gulliver's Travels, fiction includes John Amory's strange imaginings, Sterne's stream of consciousness, Frances Sheridan's insights, Henry Brooke's sentimentalities and Goldsmith's charm. Poetry ranges from the classical to the innovative. Graceful lyrics, anonymous jeux d'esprit, descriptive pieces, savage satires and personal poems are written by very different poets, among them learned witty women, clergymen and drunken ne'er-do-wells. Politicians, notably Grattan and Curran, produced eloquent speeches; effective essays and pamphlets accompanied political activity. Personal letters and diaries—such as the exuberant Dorothea Herbert's Recollections—convey the changing ethos of this century's literature, based on the classics and moving to an increasing interest in the translation of Irish literature. This book conveys its fascinating liveliness and rich variety.

Irish Literature
The Nineteenth Century
Volume I
An Annotated Anthology
Edited and Introduced by
A. Norman Jeffares and
Peter van de Kamp

'*This anthology is a superlative achievement and for at least a generation is sure to be the outstanding work in its field. Jeffares and van de Kamp bring to their task a fine blend of scholarship, good judgment and innovation. And they have produced a fascinating collection of Irish writing which scholars, students and general readers will find both inviting and accessible.*'

James H. Murphy, President of The Society for the
Study of
Nineteenth-Century Ireland

This, the first of three volumes, spans the first third of the nineteenth century. It documents Ireland's significant literary contribution to an age of invention, with Thomas Moore's romantic Melodies, Maria Edgeworth's regional fiction, and Charles Maturin's voyeuristic Gothic stories. It witnesses the rise of a quest for authenticity—mapping and transmuting the Gaelic past (in Hardiman's *Irish Minstrelsy*, Petrie's essay on the round towers, and O'Curry's research into Irish manuscripts) and faithfully depicting the real Ireland (in the first-hand accounts of Mary Leadbeater, William Hamilton Maxwell, Asenath Nicholson, the peasant fiction of William Carleton and the Catholic fiction of the Banim brothers). In Jonah Barrington's Sketches it records the demise of the rollicking squirearchy, while in the stories of Lover it portrays the rise of the stage Irishman. But it also offers a selection from political documents and speeches, and from popular writings which were imprinted on the Irish consciousness. These are contextualised by historical documents, and by Irish forays into European Romanticism.

Irish Literature
The Nineteenth Century
Volume II

An Annotated Anthology
Edited and Introduced by
A. Norman Jeffares and
Peter van de Kamp

The second of the three volumes, roughly spans the middle decades of the nineteenth century, a period dominated by the enormity of the Great Famine. Its terror is recorded in first-hand accounts and in the powerless yet forceful reactions which this cataclysmic event engendered in such writers as John Mitchel (who in his *Jail Journal* pits the self against the state). This volume documents the rise of cultural nationalism, in the work of the contributors to *The Nation* (Davis, Mangan, Lady Wilde), and the response of Unionist intelligentsia in the *Dublin University Magazine*. It juxtaposes the authentic Gaelic voice in translation (Ferguson and Walsh) against the haunting intensity of Mangan and the non-conformism of his fellow inauthenticator 'Father Prout'. It witnesses the stage Irishman in Lever's fiction being placed on Boucicault's popular podium, in his reworking of Gerald Griffin's account of *The Colleen Bawn*. It records the rise of Fenianism (in such writers as Charles Kickham), and it sees Ireland taking stock (in the work of W.E.H. Lecky). It notes the emergence of a new literary confidence in the works of Sigerson and Todhunter. It extends well beyond examinations of Irish identity, not only in encapsulating popular writing, but also by incorporating writers of Irish descent who investigated different cultures.

Irish Literature
The Nineteenth Century
Volume III
An Annotated Anthology
Edited and Introduced by
A. Norman Jeffares and
Peter van de Kamp

The last of the three volumes, roughly spans the last thirty years of the nineteenth century, a period which saw the emergence of the Land League, the dynamiting campaign of the Fenians, and the rise and fall of Charles Stewart Parnell. It witnessed changes in all literary genres. Standish James O'Grady conveyed a sense of heroic excitement in his affirmation of Gaelic Ireland's literary heritage. Douglas Hyde promoted Irish language and culture through his foundation of the Gaelic League. Writers affiliated with the Irish Literary Society tried to re-energise Young Ireland's ideals of cultural nationalism. Under the aegis of Ireland's literary renaissance a new interest in Celticism became manifest. The year after the publication of Allingham's *Collected Poems* W.B. Yeats's *The Wanderings of Oisin* marked the emergence of Irish mythology and legend in an elegant, sensuous and highly influential manner. With Wilde, Shaw, Martyn and George Moore he expanded Ireland's aesthetic horizons; as Yeats introduced French *Symbolisme* in *The Secret Rose* and *The Wind Among the Reeds*, Oscar Wilde preached the paradoxes of decadence, Shaw uncovered society's hypocrisies, while Martyn embraced Ibsen's social realism, and Moore combined Zola's naturalism with the synaesthesia of Totalkunst. Major writers combined to form Ireland's National Theatre. Pioneers such as Lafcadio Hearn were exploring different cultures, which were to influence European literature and drama. The last decades of the nineteenth century were a powerfully creative period, rich in its literary collaborations, and profoundly impressive in its vitality.

IRISH LITERATURE
THE EIGHTEENTH CENTURY

Irish Literature
The Eighteenth Century

Editors

A. NORMAN JEFFARES
AND
PETER VAN DE KAMP

IRISH ACADEMIC PRESS
DUBLIN • PORTLAND, OR

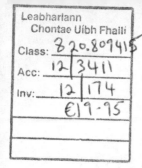
First published in 2006 by
IRISH ACADEMIC PRESS
44 Northumberland Road, Dublin 4, Ireland

and in the United States of America by
IRISH ACADEMIC PRESS
c/o ISBS, Suite 300
920 NE 58th Avenue
Portland, Oregon 97213-3786

Website: www.iap.ie

British Library Cataloguing in Publication Data
An entry is available on request

ISBN 0-7165-2799-5 (cloth)
ISBN 0-7165-2804-5 (paper)

Library of Congress Cataloging-in-Publication Data
An entry is available on request

Printed by MPG Books Ltd, Bodmin Cornwall

Contents

Contents

Contents

NOTE ON TEXT

Where possible original spellings, syntax and punctuation have been retained. The editors have, however, made a small number of necessary textual corrections which do not impair the authenticity of the original text.

Alexander Norman (Derry) Jeffares (11 August 1920–1 June 2005)

On the morning of 1 June, Derry passed away peacefully in his sleep. The night before he had sent an ambulance home, and had gone to bed. He died in harness: on 30 May we had finished correcting the proofs of the nineteenth-century anthology, Vol. One; not long before he had submitted his final contribution to our joint venture, the introduction to the last volume. His part of our mammoth task was completed (as always he was ahead of me in getting things done). And Derry was going to allow himself to take off that coat of armour: intending our anthologies to be the last of his 'academic' publications, he had started writing his memoirs, which, in style, he called his 'anecdotes'. Derry's final full stop marked the end of an incredibly distinguished academic career, which had been set in motion when as a schoolboy editor of sixteen he had called on W.B. Yeats, a former pupil of the Erasmus Smith High School in Dublin, asking him for a poem for *The Erasmian*, the school magazine (Yeats sent him home, but a week later he submitted 'What Then'). That schoolboy would become renowned for his extensive work on Yeats, and on the eighteenth-century Irish literature for which he shared Yeats's love, but his many publications were to extend beyond the field of Irish studies, to include English, Commonwealth and American literature (he championed Walt Whitman). I asked Derry years ago how many books he had published; he replied, under his breath, 'Well, over two hundred.' He was the general editor of various series of texts, including *A Review of English Literature*, the influential *Writers and Critics* series of monographs, and of the *York Notes*. He edited the refreshing journals *AREL* and *ARIEL*. His enterprising spirit took him to three continents; first to Groningen in post-War Holland—when he left there to take up a lectureship at Edinburgh University he had to assure the Dutch Queen that he could support his wife Jeanne (an assurance he kept all his life, aided by mutual reliance: she vetted anything he wrote, and he couldn't understand scholars who baulked at that criterion). He was to hold chairs in Adelaide, Leeds, where he was known as the king-maker, transforming the university to a remarkable centre of excellence, and Stirling, taking a very active part in Scottish arts as chairman of PEN Scotland, of Book Trust Scotland, and vice chairman of the Scottish Arts Council. He was also a member of the Arts Council of Great Britain, Fellow of the Royal Society of Literature, of the Royal Society of Edinburgh and the Australian Academy of the Humanities, Honorary Fellow of Trinity College, Dublin, and honorary Doctor of the Universities of Stirling and Lille.

Derry *had* become a legend in his lifetime. He took considerable pleasure from my relaying to him the question asked by several people what it was like to work with his grandson. Collaborating with him, daily, for years, was always great fun, and deserves hyperbole, for his generosity was unparagoned in academe, his energy unequalled, his sense of humour, his bonhomie, infectious. He was really looking forward to the launch of these books; seeing them into publication without him is a lonely enterprise.

Peter van de Kamp,Tralee, July 2005

Foreword

This anthology of Irish literature in the eighteenth century is a tale of two countries (England and Ireland), two cities (London and Dublin), two cultures and two languages (English and Irish). Only an editor, or editors, with a profound understanding of enormous political complexities shaping the relationship (sometimes the non-relationship) between England and Ireland could have created this brilliant, surprising, comprehensive anthology. For almost sixty years, Professor A. N. Jeffares has been an outstanding scholar, critic and teacher of Irish literature, not only in Ireland, England and Scotland, but all over the world. Since his death I appreciate even more and more the depth and range of his achievements and the strength and laughing magic of his personality. His co-editor here, Dr Peter van de Kamp, has been steadily building an impressive reputation as a scholar and critic of Irish writing over the past decades. Derry Jeffares and Peter van de Kamp make a formidable combination and have given us a collection which will last as long as readers pay attention to the literature of that fascinating century.

In Ireland, it was a century of opposites: wealth and poverty, elegance and ugliness, tyranny and slavery, violence and the search for peace, education and ignorance, sophisticated style and congested filth, beautiful architecture and squalid, reeking hut-homes, order and lawlessness – these are some of the features of life in Ireland, and perhaps especially in Dublin, in the eighteenth century. This anthology, demonstrating the encyclopaedic knowledge of Professor Jeffares and the vigorous research prowess of Peter van de Kamp, outlines, in a lucid, learned and elegant manner, the ways in which the above-mentioned opposites and many more, worked to produce a literature that is unique for the beautifully clear and candid ways it captured the massive contradictions and complexities of life in Ireland during that time. And so we get to read fascinating extracts from the work of famous writers such as Jonathan Swift, George Berkeley, Oliver Goldsmith, Edmund Burke, Maria Edgeworth, Richard Lovell Edgworth, as well as a host of dramatists including William Congreve, George Farquhar, Richard Brinsley Sheridan and Sir Richard Steele.

These are some of the famous writers, but this anthology also gives us generous and revealing selections from writers forgotten or unheard of for a long time; these selections will surprise and delight readers for their energy, insights and candid powers of expression. I am thinking especially of letters, extracts from plays, diaries, songs, poems, ballads, comic pieces of various kinds, memoirs, theological meditations, political statements, essays and some wonderful translations. There is freedom of utterance here, a stylish abandon, a controlled enthusiasm and energy heart-warmingly free of tight-lipped, self-protecting inhibitionism. This anthology frequently feels like an epic exercise in intellectual and emotional freedom, achieved through clear vision and the most subtle and effective stylistic and technical skills. An entire century is revealed. Readers will experience a unique journey through history, politics and day-to-day living when they immerse themselves in this collection. It's the kind of book that deepens in richness and revelation the more it is read. A truly monumental achievement.

BRENDAN KENNELLY

June 2005

Acknowledgements

These volumes grew out of a suggestion made by Prof. Augustine Martin in 1983 to produce a series of Irish Readers. We should like to acknowledge our indebtedness to Prof. Terence Brown (Trinity College, Dublin), Peter Costello (Dublin), Prof. Jacques Chuto (University of Paris XII), Prof. Anne Crookshank (Trinity College, Dublin), Prof. Adèle Crowder (Queen's University, Kingston), Prof. Christopher Crowder (Queen's University, Kingston), Prof. Warwick Gould (University of London), Prof. John Kelly (University of Oxford), Prof. Brendan Kennelly (Trinity College, Dublin), Dr Peter Liebregts (University of Leiden), Sarah Mahaffy, Daphne Maxwell, Dr James H. Murphy (de Paul University, Chicago), Dr Neil Murphy (Nanyang University, Singapore), Prof. Ellen Shannon-Mangan (Astoria, Oregon), Prof. Colin Smythe, Dr Bruce Stewart (University of Ulster), Dr Wim Tigges (University of Leiden), Prof. Loreto Todd (University of Ulster) and Deirdre Toomey.

The librarians of the Athenaeum, the National Library of Ireland, Trinity College, Dublin, Trinity College, Cambridge, University College, Dublin, the University of St. Andrews, the University of Stirling, and of the Institute of Technology, Tralee were indispensable in making material available to us. We should particularly like to thank Siobhan O'Callaghan for her unstinting efforts to get us more than just the books and journals we wanted, and Joanne Ball for her help in tracing and proffering images for our covers.

Introduction

I THE ACHIEVEMENT

To survey the achievement of Irish writing in English and translations of Irish literature in the eighteenth century is to realise what a wide range of human experience is involved. It is expressed brilliantly in so many different ways by so many very different individuals.

The chronology of Irish writing in the century begins with William Congreve's masterpiece *The Way of the World* (1700), the swan song of Restoration comedy, and ends with the emergence of romantic expression given mellifluity in the poems and songs of Tom Moore. It is, however, a century to be celebrated for profound philosophical, aesthetic and political thought, since it is renowned for the writings of Jonathan Swift, George Berkeley and Edmund Burke, a century too when drama took on a new tone in the comedies of George Farquhar, Oliver Goldsmith and Richard Brinsley Sheridan, while many Irish dramatists such as Richard Steele and Hugh Kelly pursued more sentimental modes and others continued, like Arthur Murphy and Susannah Centlivre, to write comedies of manners in the Restoration manner.

Sentimentality had also found expression, in Henry Brooke's novel *The Fool of Quality*. The novel form suited many authors, Thomas Amory, Laurence Sterne, Frances Sheridan and Oliver Goldsmith making their own unique contributions to the genre. Just as the progress of poetry moved from the Augustan tones of Thomas Parnell, whose poems were edited by Pope, to more personal Irish tones – those of, say, George Ogle or Thomas Dermody – so towards the close of the century there came an interest in and interpretation of Gaelic bardic and musical culture and antiquities in the hands of Charles O'Conor, Joseph Cooper Walker, Charlotte Brooke and Edward Bunting.

The essay, effectively employed earlier by Swift and Steele for political, social and moral ends, reached a new achievement in the attractive apparent detachment and whimsical humour of Goldsmith in *The Citizen of the World; or, Letters from a Chinese Philosopher, Residing in London to his Friends in the East*. It is harder now to appreciate fully the oratory of Irish statesmen and politicians from printed versions of

1

their speeches, but Burke, Sheridan, Henry Flood, Henry Grattan, John Philpot Curran and Theobald Wolfe Tone at times produced powerful effects upon their audiences whether in their speeches or in their political writings. These reflect in the early part of the century a reaction against the complexities of the seventeenth century, an adoption of the easy familiar style found in the essayists, appealing to the well-educated through a straightforward approach. This, however, became intricate, almost involuted, even at times pedantic in the latter part of the century, sometimes redeemed by an oratorical and spell-binding appeal – Sheridan's theatrical experience and capacity for emotional appeal held his audience for long periods as he attacked Warren Hastings, whereas Burke, when addressing the House of Commons, could occasionally very quickly empty it.

There are many excellent minor writers to be discovered in the different genres. Irish authors, for instance, were prolific in comedies, farces and comic operas; more serious subjects were pursued by John Toland, William King, Peter Browne and Philip Skelton; many minor poets flourished, including Swift with his wide range of subjects, and the lighter verses of his Irish circle of jesting friends; there were ballads and popular songs; diaries, lively anonymous memoirs, essays and letters; all these add up to interpretations of complex, changing societies both in Ireland and in England, both affected and influenced by Irish writers. With some rhetorical oversimplification and not a little truth Yeats, ignoring the politics and the poverty, described the eighteenth century as 'that one Irish century that escaped from darkness and confusion'.

II THE WRITERS AND THEIR WORK BRIEFLY SURVEYED

Jonathan Swift

Swift is Ireland's first great writer in English, shaped by his personal desire to be treated like a lord, by his powerful intellect and capacity for irony and invention, and by the political realities of his time. Short of money as a student, he, like most of the Fellows and undergraduates, fled from Ireland when James II's Lord Deputy's troops occupied Trinity College, Dublin, as part of a policy of giving power to Catholics. In England Swift experienced in the elegant ambience of Moor Park, Sir William Temple's home in Surrey, the world of diplomacy and the court while acting as Sir William's secretary, for Temple had been a very successful ambassador abroad and had many influential friends, including the king.

There Swift read voraciously, writing *The Battle of the Books* (1704), a lively mock-heroic praising the ancients. But the anonymous *A Tale of a Tub* (1704) gave still more scope for his intellectual energy. Adopting in it the persona of a 'modern' (whose views would have been the opposite of his own) Swift illuminated the distortions of Christianity as practised by the Roman Catholics, the Anglicans and the Presbyterians, his book highly irreverent, overflowing with wit, parody, irony, ridicule, paradox, and surprise. Of this allegory in which a father (God) leaves three coats to his sons, Peter (the Roman Catholic Church), Martin (the Anglican, the Protestant established Church) and Jack (the Nonconformist Churches), in his will (the Bible) which obviously they interpret differently, Swift is reputed to have said when rereading it in later life 'Good God, what a genius I had when I wrote that book.'

On his emergence from the sheltered life of Moor Park Swift found the need for a different style of writing. No less aggressive, no less energetic, he became more aware of his audience: he had to learn how to persuade. When he went to London (first in 1707, then from 1710 to 1714) to represent the Church of Ireland, which he valued the more having taken orders and felt isolated in his first two parishes, his scanty congregations surrounded by Presbyterians in the North and by Catholics in the South, he was soon in a position of political power and prestige through the influential effect of his writings. He swayed the decisions of the Tory ministry; his writings in *The Examiner* and in pamphlets were invaluable to them; indeed he helped to stop a war. He had rapidly learned how to penetrate his targets with the right amount of explosive satire.

In London Swift enjoyed the intellectual stimulus and the good company of his fellow wits in the Scriblerus Club. He formed close friendships, not least with Pope, Arbuthnot and Gay. When he returned to Dublin as Dean of St Patrick's Cathedral – a return to what he called ironically his banishment, for he had been disappointed in his hopes of preferment in England – he missed being at the centre of things and decided he would keep out of politics in Ireland.

This, however, was a vain hope. He was disgusted by the human misery of poverty in Ireland and by the lack of order in the country. Remedies for this had been put forward in William Petty's (1623–87) *The Political Anatomy of Ireland* (1691) which argued for transfer of population and a single government, its members decided proportionally, and, more vigorously, in William Molyneux's (1656-98)

The Case of Ireland's being bound by acts of Parliament in England, Stated (1698) in which Molyneux's view was that Ireland had its own parliament in Dublin and owed allegiance to the King but not to the Westminster parliament, a rejection, in effect, of colonial status for Ireland.

Swift did not regard Ireland as a depending kingdom. 'Were not', he asked, 'the people of Ireland born as *Free* as these of *England*?' They had not forfeited their freedom, their Parliament was as representative as that of England; they were subjects of the same king; they had the same God as their protector. He ended with a fierce, heartfelt question: 'Am I a *Free-man* in *England,* and do I become a *Slave* in six hours by crossing the Channel?' To him it seemed that the Irish were not helping themselves, and he began his powerful political pamphleteering, something not without very real danger. The printer of his *Proposals for Universal Use of Irish Manufactures* (1720) was prosecuted, and both Swift and his printer risked severe punishment in 1722 when the *Drapier's Letters* destroyed any likelihood of a proposed copper coinage being made for Ireland by William Wood, an English ironmaster.

These letters purported to be written by a Dublin shopkeeper – yet another case of Swift adopting a persona – and they were full of Swift's sense of the absurd as he contemplated the likely effects of Wood's halfpence were they to be put in circulation. Through these letters and their effect Swift attained fame in Ireland as a popular patriot, was known as 'The Drapier' and bonfires were lit to welcome him home from one of the two last visits he made to England. His pessimism emerged in *A Short View of the State of Ireland* (1727–8) and then came his devastating *A Modest Proposal for Preventing the Children of the Poor in Ireland from being Burdensome, and for making them beneficial* (1722).

In this Swift puts forward his argument as though he were some kind of social economist, giving his outrageous solution a matter-of-fact air with careful calculations and apparent practical objectivity. This was an expression of his *saeva indignatio,* his fierce anger at work, his imagination let loose with an energy that verges on the grotesque. This imagination shaped his best known work, *Gulliver's Travels* (1726) which in the supposed Captain Gulliver's four voyages does more than parody the successful genre of the traveller's tale, for humanity is regarded from four points of view, the last where man is contrasted with the Houyhnhnms, the rational horses who expel Gulliver for his apparent likeness to the Yahoos; he was 'a creature who though capable of reason was not rational.' The irony of the last book has unduly disturbed critics who underestimate the subtleties and complexities of Swift's irony – and his superb sense of humour, black though it may be at times, so evident in the last images of Gulliver returned home but now unable to endure his wife or children, – 'the very smell of them was intolerable' – and taking refuge with the horses in his stable.

Swift's humour irradiates much of the *Journal to Stella*, those often playful, often concerned letters he wrote from London to Esther Johnson, whom he called Stella, and her friend Rebecca Dingley. Stella was his closest friend; their friendship had begun at Moor Park when she was eight and he twenty-two. He wrote poems to her on her birthdays; she and Rebecca Dingley had moved to Dublin, and his letters convey something of the affectionate teasing, the badinage they exchanged. One of his most haunting poems tells of his despair when his ship was stuck in Holyhead by contrary winds and she was gravely ill in Dublin. A more risky and ultimately damaging friendship was the one between himself and the vivacious Vanessa, Esther Vanhomrigh, another young girl he had educated, but who had, despite his strong and repeated advice, followed him from London to Ireland. His poem *Cadenus and Vanessa* treats their relationship somewhat wryly.

Swift's poems reflect many aspects of his personality: extremes of tension and relaxation shape them; fierce indignation at political pretence and public hypocrisy often expressed with aggressive vehemence or else affectionate, often amused appreciation of friends, addressed with conversational ease. He could also record the cries of street vendors – his prose shows that he was also interested in conversation and his directions to servants are the result of sharp observations – and the poems could express his dislike of bodily decay in such poems as 'A Beautiful Young Nymph going to Bed', 'The Lady's Dressing Room' or 'Strephon and Chloe' which record comic differences between appearance and reality and are, perhaps, a means of purging his disgust, by expressing it very directly, at the coarser aspects of eighteenth century life: the smells, the dirt, the putrefaction. Of his poems probably the best known is 'Verses on the Death of Dr Swift, D.S.P.D.,' its neat and invasive wit at the service alike of moral judgement and the raillery that could sometimes lighten his darker moments of depression.

Swift was educated in Ireland, and Irish life, with its lively speech, influenced by Gaelic usage, and with its often exuberant humour, deeply influenced him, as did the religious and political complexities of life in Ireland. Aware early in life of the gap between his ambition and achievement, he was also aware of the gap between his theories of what it meant to be a protestant – he cared deeply about Christianity and the Church though he did not curb his ironic wit in defending them – and the reality of his own position in Ireland, something brought home to him by his heady experience of political power in a more orderly and much wealthier England.

His sense of difference – metaphysical almost in the tensions it created – a free man in England, who wished to be equally free in Ireland – left him in a mid-channel attitude, a state affecting many other Irish writers, detached from English ways, critical of them, yet desirous of being treated as equals.

George Berkeley

George Berkeley, who went to Kilkenny College a little after Swift, was luckier in his subsequent days at Trinity College, Dublin, since the College had settled back into a more normal state after the Williamite victory in 1690. Berkeley became a Fellow in 1703, three years after taking his B.A. and was later to become Dean of Derry (1724) and then Bishop of Cloyne (1734). In England in 1713 he became friendly with Swift, Pope, Addison and Steele. After travelling in Europe he lived in Rhode Island for 3 years, having gone to America hoping to found a college in Bermuda, his hopes dashed when the funds promised by Walpole's government did not materialise.

Berkeley had begun to develop his immaterialist philosophy, writing his Notebooks (now known as his *Philosophical Commentaries*) in 1707, his *New Theory of Vision* appearing in 1709. In his Notebooks (no 696) he wrote to warn his reader against plausible, empty, fallible words. The reader should, he argued, regard them as occasions of bringing into his mind determined significations; if they fell short of this then they were 'Gibberish Jargon and deserve not the name of Language.' In this desire for clarity of expression he resembled Swift, who, as his Dublin bookseller and publisher, Faulkner, recorded, had the proofs of his *Works* read aloud not only to himself but to two menservants, altering and emending until they understood fully, at which point he would say, 'This will do; for I write to the vulgar more than the learned.'

Another point of similarity, in each case when these writers had settled back in Ireland, was Berkeley's identification of himself with the economic needs of the country, just as Swift had urged economic and political independence upon the Dublin parliament. But earlier in his life he had written firmly in his *Commentaries* on several occasions 'We Irish men differ from mathematicians and others who think categorically', and he was to echo the views of Molyneux and Swift about the need for fair economic treatment of Ireland by England. He realised too that self-help was necessary (some of his aims were achieved in the establishment of the Dublin Society in 1730 to improve 'husbandry, manufactures and other useful arts.' The society, to become the Royal Dublin Society in 1750, took over an art school after 1739 which trained many Irish painters).

Berkeley's philosophical works, *An Essay towards a New Theory of Vision* (1709, 1710, 1732), *A Treatise concerning the Principles of Human Knowledge* (1710, 1734) and *Three Dialogues between Hylas and Philonous* (1713, 1725, 1734) were marked by the lucidity he valued; they were gracefully written and he mastered the dialogue form very effectively. In *Alciphron* (1732) he opposed the ideas of freethinkers, drawing parallels between the language of religion and that of science. In *The Analyst* he attacked Newton's views and reacted against Locke's ideas also, thinking scepticism and atheism would result from Locke's distinction between primary and secondary qualities of bodies. This book was a rigorous defence of Christian principles.

Berkeley believed that there were only minds and ideas in the universe, minds perceiving, and ideas (and sensations) being perceived. Physical objects exist in being perceived, he thought, because they have the qualities we perceive them to possess. This is an idealistic view that the physical world of objects depends upon the mind observing it. God gives us the sensations that make up the physical world; so God is their source, and we are in touch with him since he is infinite mind; thus we can be aware of his existence and can perceive correctly and accurately the physical world: it is real. Existence consists in being perceived. His thought and his ideas are still studied, still effective; he remains Ireland's greatest philosopher.

The Dramatists

Another kind of Irishness was exhibited by the dramatists. The first Irish theatre, opened in 1637 in Werburgh Street, Dublin, under the patronage of the Lord Lieutenant, Thomas Wentworth, the Earl of Strafford, and managed by John Ogilby, lasted only four years – till the 1641 war – but was replaced by the Theatre Royal, the Smock Alley Theatre, in 1662. This theatre flourished and many Irish dramatists, actors and actresses got their training there. But London was their magnet. Irish writers were drawn there, seeking from the established order of audiences, managers, and the critics greater fame and fortune, even the chance of patronage, such as the official posts which came to

Congreve and Steele and Orrery's commission in his regiment that came to Farquhar. What had they to offer the English audiences? Quite simply, they knew how to entertain, how to supply skilfully woven plots, to surprise with witty dialogue, all this in a tradition running from Congreve to Oscar Wilde and George Bernard Shaw. It was one of emigrant playwrights, who knew how to question established ideas while holding up mirrors to the English establishment.

With the exception of some late seventeenth century works such as Nahum Tate's adaption of *King Lear* (1687), Thomas Southerne's *Isabella; or, The Fatal Marriage* (1694) and *Oroonoko* (1695), and Congreve's *The Mourning Bride* (1697), these expatriate Irish writers avoided tragedy. Henry Brooke, admittedly, wrote *Gustavus Vasa* (1739), which, though acted in Dublin, was prohibited in England as political in intent, the villain resembling the Prime Minister, Sir Robert Walpole. But those Irish dramatists who crossed the Irish Sea found ample comic material in their observation of English social life and manners.

William Congreve

This observation often became a critical contemplation. For instance, Congreve (1670-1729) was educated in Ireland, but is often thought by Irish critics to have accepted the conventions – and standards – of English Restoration comedies. It was certainly something for which he was attacked by the Rev. Jeremy Collier in his *Short View of the Immorality and Profaneness of the English Stage* (1698). He defended himself (not very effectively) by arguing that satirical representation of well-bred people was allowable if their manners were ridiculous and that the author's own ideas should not be confused with those of the foolish people he exposes on the stage. Though his plays, in the manner of his English predecessors, concentrated upon money and marriage while depicting the conflicts of youth and age, problems of inheritance and debts, intrigues pursued with intelligence, flippant views of marriages, deceits, and contrasts between sophisticated city and naïve country ways, he did depict beneath the persiflage of *Love for Love* (1695) a tempered idealism rather than fashionable flippancy about marriage, for Valentine and Angelica realise that a civilised marriage needs more than witty gallantry to make it work. And in *The Way of the World* (1700) contemporary attitudes to marriage do not satisfy Millamant and Mirabel who aim at a marriage that will last and lead to a lasting happiness. She is cautious about committing herself; he realises she must find freedom in marriage as must he, a freedom based upon their respect for each other, upon their intellectual equality, and a realistic awareness of the dangers of marriage as well as its potential blessings.

George Farquhar

Farquhar (1677-1707) was more innovative as well as reflecting the altering, more moral views of English society. Not only had Jeremy Collier fired a telling broadside into the immorality of current comedies at the end of the seventeenth century, but the theatre audience itself was changing, no longer delighting in an anti-Puritan permissiveness, however witty and polished. Middle class writers were coming into evidence now. Farquhar moved his two most successful comedies *The Recruiting Officer* (1706) and *The Beaux Stratagem* (1707) from the city to the country. There he presented kinder attitudes; although the plot of the *Recruiting Officer* revolves around marriage, the characters do care for and are tolerant of each other; their conversations, while often humorous and full of repartee, do not echo the straining after wit and epigram, nor the absurdity of caricature, nor yet the shock effect of blatant immorality provided by Restoration comedy: the country life Farquhar portrays is very different from that of the London drawing rooms and taverns.

The play arose out of his own experience of army life; as Lieutenant Farquhar of the Grenadiers he had been recruiting in Lichfield and Shrewsbury in 1704 for the Earl of Orrery's regiment. It could be argued that Farquhar's own matrimonial experience might have prompted the sympathetic exploration of incompatibility in *The Beaux Stratagem* – he had been led to believe his wife had an income of £700 a year which proved to be untrue – which echoes the arguments of Milton's *The Doctrine and Discipline of Divorce* (1643) and ends most unusually and unexpectedly with the Sullens, husband and wife, agreeing to part for ever. This play emphasises the difference between city and country very effectively by bringing two fortune-hunting gallants from London into a gallery of memorable country characters.

Farquhar developed a new kind of hero in some of his plays, a dashing man somewhat on the make with a devil-may-care charm, and probably founded on his own personality. Having fought at the Battle of the Boyne on the victorious Williamite side at the age of twelve he displayed an aggressive, roistering side of his character as an undergraduate at Trinity College, abandoning further study there for the career of an actor at the Smock Alley Theatre; this career he also abandoned when he accidentally wounded a fellow actor on stage, going to London, on the advice of his friend the actor Robert Wilks, to write comedies. The main character in his first play *Love and a Bottle* (1693), Roebuck, obviously had an autobiographical basis; 'a compound of practical rake and speculative gentleman', ebullient, wild, but of a lively, cheerful, warm-hearted disposition. Sir Harry Wildair in *The Constant Couple* (1699) is a more mature and equally exuberant but more attractive character – Farquhar himself was growing up, though his amorous temperament led him into various scrapes. Plume, the generous-minded, and perhaps surprisingly sensitive recruiting officer, reflected the kindly reception Farquhar had received when recruiting in Lichfield and Shropshire, and his time there probably provided much of the detail of country life portrayed in the inn and in the Sullens' household in *The Beaux Stratagem*. For instance, Boniface the innkeeper was modelled on a local landlord in Lichfield, Count Bellair upon the French prisoners held there, and Scrub upon a servant of Sir Thomas Biddulph. This use of autobiographical experience was something that can be expected of the Irish comic writers who were able not only to view the English scene detachedly but to make dramatic use of their own role in it, a role perhaps at times uneasy or insecure but successfully masked by an ability to use it to amuse an audience in what becomes an artistic if at times exaggerated way, a need that may even demand some self-mockery.

Oliver Goldsmith

The same capacity for self-mockery was typical of Oliver Goldsmith (1728-74). It prevails in his comedies *The Good Natur'd Man* (1768), a self-portrait if ever there was, and especially in *She Stoops to Conquer* (1773) where the arrival of the heroes in what they take to be a country inn leads to their treating their host and his family in a cavalier fashion, something based on Goldsmith's own embarrassing experience when a young man; he mistook a country house for an inn, where he did himself very well only to discover his mistake the next morning when he called for the reckoning. Goldsmith's comedies are full of his particular sense of fun, which has lasted well. *She Stoops to Conquer* is still popular in our time.

Richard Brinsley Sheridan

Sheridan was another author who drew very closely on his own experiences in setting *The Rivals* (1775) in Bath. While using the conventional conflicts between youth and age in the Absolutes, father and son, and while poking fun at the polite society he observed in Bath – the romantic and silly Lydia Languish reading light novels from the circulating library, Bob Acres, the countrified and sometimes clumsy opposite of the elegant Anthony Absolute and, of course, the inimitable Mrs Malaprop – Sheridan reflected his family life in the city, with an autocratic father, with his own romantic elopement with the talented and beautiful singer Eliza Linley and with the two duels that arose out of his attachment to her. The elopement and marriage also influenced *The Duenna* (1775) while the contrast between his own character and that of his brother Charles obviously suggested the central theme of *The School for Scandal* (1777), the contrasting natures of the Surface brothers, Charles and Joseph. He probably drew his inspiration for Mrs Malaprop from Mrs Tryfort, a character in his mother's play *A Journey to Bath*.

In *The School for Scandal* Sheridan used some of the classic ingredients of Restoration comedy: lovers kept apart, mistaken identity, mockery of the country girl in town life and, especially, the exposure of hypocrisy. He had a special skill in that. Witness how convincingly in this masterpiece he has the suitably named scandalmongers, Mrs Candour, Sir Benjamin Backbite and Lady Sneerwell, build up the absurd story of a duel between Charles Surface and Sir Peter Teazle: Sir Peter wounded by a small sword, by a bullet in his thorax. The increasingly circumstantial detail makes the affair more credible until its utter untruth is demonstrated by Sir Peter's appearance, unharmed physically if psychologically disturbed.

Sheridan transcended the established elements in his skilfully unfolded plot by being humorous without becoming coarse, by portraying intrigue without becoming cynically amoral. But like Goldsmith he feared the effects of sentimental comedy. He showed how a comedy could be funny, could include the ridiculous and could be successfully satirical without the failing of sentimentality, something of which Goldsmith and he were so highly critical. Goldsmith's essay on sentimental comedy and his preface to *The Good Natur'd Man* reveal his hope that too much refinement would not banish humour and character from the stage – French comedy had become, he thought, so elevated and sentimental that it had 'not only banished humour and Molière from the stage' but 'banished all spectators too'. Sheridan wrote a new prologue for *The Rivals* on its second successful production, casting ridicule on the Sentimental Muse, and in *The*

Critic he mocked Cumberland (who had contributed many sentimental comedies to the contemporary stage) as Sir Fretful Plagiary.

Sir Richard Steele

Sentimental comedy, however, had proved an effective counterweight to those comedies attacked by Collier. It began just before the turn of the century and was given its fullest expression in Steele's *The Conscious Lovers* (1722). Here are no aristocrats, no wits, ridiculing the citizens, the cits. Instead Steele puts in the mouth of Mr Sealand the merchant a smug speech of self-praise, in which he describes merchants as 'gentry grown into the world in this last century' who now regard themselves 'as honourable and almost as useful as the landed class that had thought themselves so much above us.'

Steele was successful in capturing the new bourgeois middle class audience with such a play. He had, after all, been helping to shape its attitudes and beliefs in *The Tatler* (1709–1711) and *The Spectator* (1711–12) and after them in *The Guardian* and *The Englishman*. These were journals which had considerable influence, Steele creating the characters of Sir Andrew Freeport, representing commerce in the small club of equals which included Sir Roger de Coverley typifying the country gentry, Will Honeycomb the town and Captain Sentry the army. When an army officer himself Steele had displayed moral courage in writing *The Christian Hero* (1707) with its missionary zeal for reform which made him decidedly unpopular with his fellow officers. He had, however, a good sense of humour which ran through his comedies, and this humour informed the satire of his later journals, which show he knew the need to avoid priggishness.

The Stage Irishman and the Irish Gentleman

Among the targets Steele denounced in *The Christian Hero* and elsewhere was duelling. Farquhar, too, had queried conventional attitudes to this in *The Constant Couple* (1699) where Sir Harry Wildair despises convention in refusing to fight a duel, giving some commonsense reasons for doing so. Duelling, however, did not disturb some of Sheridan's characters. Sir Lucius O'Trigger, driven on by his code of honour, is positively addicted to it. Yet Sheridan was satirising the whole concept of duelling in the final scenes of the *The Rivals*, and mocking its appeal as a subject for scandal in *The School for Scandal*. In Sir Lucius O'Trigger Sheridan was creating an Irish gentleman, possibly drawing on his father,

Thomas Sheridan's (1719–1788) *Captain O'Blunder* (1754), a farce, significantly retitled *The Brave Irishman*, where the hero (whose pronunciation is mocked and whose speech contains many Gaelic words) pursues love affairs in London. He is gullible but loveable and generous: 'gentle as a dove', and outside the norm of military characters.

O'Blunder has, however, some of the attributes of the stage Irishman, a character designed to amuse English audiences, especially when in servant or footman roles. An early example of this is the servant Teague in Farquhar's *The Twin Rivals*, who is given to uttering Irish bulls (it is worth reading the amusing *Essay on Irish Bulls* (1802) by Maria Edgeworth and her father which satirises English attitudes of refusing to take the Irish seriously). This kind of comic character persisted on the stage.

The Irish playwrights differed in their treatment of the stage Irishman. For instance, Charles Macklin, following on Thomas Sheridan's *Captain O'Blunder*, created in *Love à la Mode* (1759) Sir Callaghan O'Brallaghan, another forerunner of Sir Lucius O'Trigger. Macklin founded his character on an Irish officer in the Prussian service whom he had met in a tavern near Covent Garden. His Sir Callaghan is an Irish gentleman, a man of honour, given to witty speeches. His liveliness was continued in Macklin's *The True-Born Irishman: or, The Irish Fine Lady* (1762), Macklin well conscious of the differences between Irish and English concepts of the gentleman.

Hugh Kelly (1739–1777) in the preface to *The School for Wives* (1773) offered a criticism of the tendency to portray Irish gentlemen as having an overquick sense of honour, an overreadiness to draw their swords when they thought themselves injured. To make them proud of a barbarous propensity to duelling, to make them delight in an effusion of blood was, he argued, to reproach them unjustly. This desire to present a more favourable view of Irish manners and morals was continued by John O'Keeffe (1747-1833), now known for his *Wild Oats* (1792), yet another reaction against sentimental comedy. He was a prolific writer of farces and comic operas and in the lively dialogue of *The Poor Soldier* (1783) and, especially in *The Wicklow Gold Mines; or, the Lads from the Hills* (1796), he was appealing to Irish more than English audiences.

The Range of Irish Drama

The range of drama continuously provided by Irish writers throughout the eighteenth century was wide, then. To name but a few of those successful in their day there are plays such as Arthur Murphy's (1727-

1805) *The Way to Keep Him* (1760; revised 1761) couched in the classical tradition of the comedy of manners; or plays such as Charles Macklin's *The Man of the World* (1781) attacking political corruption; or comic operas such as Isaac Bickerstaff's *Love in a Village* (1761); or sentimental comedies such as Hugh Kelly's *False Delicacy* (1760); and cleverly constructed plays such as Frances Sheridan's (1724-16) *The Discovery* (1763) and *The Dupe* (1763).

Laurence Sterne

Laurence Sterne (1713–68), the supreme practitioner of sensibility in the novel, had long enough time in Ireland to realise – apart from something he shared with many Irish writers, the contrast between genteel poverty and rich relatives, and hence the crucial problem of how ambition's aims could be achieved, and the limitations of genteel poverty overcome – that the role of talk as the cheapest means of entertainment was vital.

The Life of Tristram Shandy, Gentleman (1759–1767) demonstrates that he regarded writing as a different form of conversation, in which he shared with his readers his stream of consciousness, his self-investigation which echoed Swift's sermon, on 'The Difficulty of knowing Oneself'. Sterne's career was in the Church, but preferment 'was long coming'; success in the novel came instead and he became famous. *Tristram Shandy* is about what Sterne found moving or laughable: he responded to almost every emotional stimulus; his idiosyncratic humour records the absurdity of human behaviour, including his own, for the investigation of sentimentality is blended with ironic self-mockery:

'My good friend, quoth I – as sure as I am I – and you are you – And who are you? said he – Don't puzzle me; said I.'

So, apart from such jokes as those of the hot chestnuts, of Uncle Toby's encounter with the widow Wadman, of Mrs Shandy's inability to follow her husband's intellectual theorising – indeed of her query at the moment of Tristram's procreation as to whether Mr Shandy had remembered to wind the clock, there is here a cavalier treatment of the novel form. Sterne parodies it with virtuosity; his innovative skill results in blank pages, asterisks, and diagrams as well as the varying speed of narration which ambles reflectively or records immediate reactions, instant recording of emblems taking the reader completely into the writer's confidence. This blend of spontaneity and deliberation brings us the immediacy of conversation.

Sterne is never dull. His humour as well as his sensitivity to emotions (of others as well as his own) makes *A Sentimental Journey Through France and Italy* (1768) memorable. Suffering from tuberculosis Sterne spent two years (1702–64) travelling in France and Italy in search of health. His hectic intensity, reflecting his illness, marked his *Journal to Eliza* (published after his death as *Yorick to Eliza* (1775)) in which 'a poor sick-headed, sick-hearted Yorick' conveyed his feelings for Elizabeth Draper whom he had met in London and known for but two months before she sailed back to Bombay to her husband. The *Journal* was written under the shadow of illness just as he had composed the opening books of *Tristram Shandy* under the strains imposed by the deaths of his mother and uncle, and by his wife's mental breakdown. He had published *The Sermons of Mr Yorick* (1760–69) and was reputed to have been a good pastor in Yorkshire, where he had three livings, the third at Coxwold which became 'Shandy Hall'. Sterne, however, remained always ready to cry, like one of his characters, *Voila un persiflage*!

Goldsmith as man of letters

Goldsmith grew up in an Irish country rectory inheriting his own great generosity from his father, who may have been the model for the impractical, idealistic and highly likeable parson portrayed with mild irony in *The Vicar of Wakefield* (1766), an excellent story drawing upon human responses. In it Goldsmith uses an equivalent of the Gaelic present habitual tense to create the continuity of pastoral content – an effective miniaturisation – which is rudely shattered by the disasters which strike the vicar's family. The novel overflows with Goldsmith's sense of anticlimax, absurdity and something not wit nor perhaps even humour but fun: we can still enjoy the happy ending, based upon European ideas of the family and, of course, the genuineness of the vicar, whose unworldly goodness has stood up to the testing of misfortunes.

Goldsmith wanted to make people laugh, but he also broke through eighteenth-century conventions in his two main poems. In *The Traveller* (1704) he meditates on loneliness, and the attraction of home for the wanderer. His is persuasive and powerful poetry, transcending the orthodoxies of the heroic couplet. It stemmed from Goldsmith's grand tour of the continent begun with 'a guinea in his pocket, one shirt to his back and a flute in his hand' in which he was reputed to have paid his way by debating in universities as well as playing his flute in less intellectual company. His reflections in *An*

Enquiry into the Present State of Polite Learning in Europe (1759) show his discerning observation.

The Deserted Village (1770), his second long poem, also deals with the nostalgia of the exile. His comments in the *Chinese Letters* on England reflect both admiration and some resentment at its wealth and the authority of its great men (points made in Letter LVII). *The Deserted Village* deals with depopulation, scaling down the erstwhile village life in a way that conveys Goldsmith's affection for its contentment as he contrasts it with the emptiness of the depopulated countryside. The vignettes of the smith, the village schoolmaster and the preacher 'passing rich on forty pounds a year' are the stuff of homely memories, conveyed with poignancy and given an air of spontaneity, which is achieved by Goldsmith's skill in altering the tone, as, for instance, in the passage beginning

> Ill fares the land, to hastening ills a prey,
> While wealth accumulates, and men decay....

He could achieve elegance in shorter poems, the 'Stanzas on Woman', for example, or 'Retaliation', a generous reply to the teasing of his friends.

Goldsmith gave up doctoring at the insistence of his friends: he then had to earn his living by writing and so he wrote histories of England, of Greece and of Rome; he also wrote sensitive biographies of Richard Nash who made Bath fashionable, and of Voltaire. And his *History of the Earth and Animated Nature* can still be read with pleasure. And there was an impressive flow of hack writing: Introductions, Prefaces, Criticism, Compilations. It is well to remember Dr Johnson's Latin epitaph for the monument in Westminster Abbey which included the phrase that there was almost no form of literature that Goldsmith had not put his hand to and that whatever he had attempted he had made elegant.

Burke: political philosopher

Edmund Burke (1729–97), after graduating from Trinity College, Dublin, read law at the Middle Temple in London. His first book, *A Vindication of Natural Society* appeared in 1756, the next year he published the *Philosophical Enquiry into the Origin of our Ideas of the Sublime and Beautiful*, begun when he was nineteen; it was regarded by Dr Johnson as an example of 'true criticism.' Burke maintained that the sublime and the beautiful, though blended at times, were nonetheless very different, the one involved in pain, the other in pleasure. Thus the sublime includes the vast, the dark and rugged, the solid, massive and gloomy, whereas beauty includes the small, the smooth and the polished, the clear, light and delicate. His aesthetic theories were poised between the Augustans' emphasis on reason and the Romantics' innovation, the emotional involvement of the self.

Though he abandoned the idea of a literary career, becoming an MP in 1765, Burke wrote prose that was rational and persuasive, employing a good deal of irony; in this he resembled Swift, and it is probable that both writers found in irony a sophisticated, almost double way of seeing things, rather than completely accepting the assumptions of their contemporaries. Burke's views on the way the American colonies should be treated, for instance, were arguments in favour of conciliation. In his speech of 22 March 1775 he put forward his views of how an Empire should be organised politically; he was practical in favouring what he called systematic indulgence; rights should not be insisted upon: central control could delegate decisions to local governments which would naturally be different in different regions. The colonists, he reminded his fellow MPs, drew their ideas on liberty and on taxation from the ideas and principles of England.

In his *Letter from a Distinguished English Commoner to a Peer in Ireland* (1783) Burke was voicing his desire to see the franchise extended to Catholics in Ireland. His views on the need for this were soon sharpened by his contemplation of affairs in France, expressed in his *Reflections on the Revolution in France* (1790). Here he stresses his desire for stability; he wanted, as he had said in his speech on conciliation with America, all government to be founded upon compromise; he disliked 'this continual talk of resistance and revolution, or the practice of making the extreme medicine of the constitution its daily bread.' Here is his irony at work, for such talk could render 'the habit of society dangerously valetudinarian'.

His view of parliament was idealistic; he was essentially a gradualist. Aware of the need to make law certain he was also sensitive to the need to reform the criminal code. Society, he thought, was a contract, a continuity. Beneath the measured, careful, stately eloquence of his *Reflections* there is a deep emotional commitment, an instinctive horror of what the new revolutionary cycle could introduce when passion, political passion, turned into the savagery of recurring revenge, reprisal and repression. His *Thoughts on the Prospect of a Regicide Peace in a Series of Letters* (1796) articulates his instinctive apprehension, indeed his horror of the anarchy that revolution would create.

Burke knew his Irish history, and his irony increased as his disillusion deepened. His letters to Sir Hercules Langrishe (1792 and 1795) and to his son Richard (1793) indicate his continuing anxiety about the stability of Ireland. If the Catholics were not integrated in the political system there would be a danger of revolution. He attacked the protestant Ascendancy, the Irish House of Commons in Dublin, and yet went on to say he supported the Established Church in both England and Ireland; it was, he told his son, 'a great link towards holding fast the connexion of religion with the state; and for keeping these two islands in their present critical independence of constitution, in a close connexion of *opinion and affection*'.

Burke's son died in 1794 and public events seemed menacing. Radical agitation was rife in England – the first part of Paine's *The Rights of Man* (1781) was written as a reply to Burke's *Reflections on the Revolution in France* (1790) – and Ireland was discontented. The Irish Catholics, however, he was convinced, were by nature conservative and if emancipated would support anti-Jacobinism in Ireland. His second letter to Sir Hercules Langrishe put these points very clearly: 'The worst of the matter is this: you are partly leading men on, partly driving into Jacobinism that description of your people whose religious principles – church polity, and habitual discipline – might make them an invincible dyke against that inundation.' The Irish administration seemed inflexible, inimical to change and politicians in England were complacent, possessed of a 'profound security'. After the conciliatory Lord Lieutenant, Earl Fitzwilliam, appointed in January 1795, was dismissed on 23 February of the same year, events in Ireland seemed to be moving inexorably towards an outbreak of violence. The United Irishmen, suppressed in 1794, became a radical secret society; the draconian repressive measures pursued by the army under General Lake, accentuated by the near success of the French in landing a force in West Cork, were counterproductive and were followed by the outbreak of insurrection in 1798, Wolfe Tone's nationalism having replaced the early economic concerns of Grattan's parliament.

Burke's prophetic despair had found expressive utterance in his *Letter to a Noble Lord* written a year before he died in 1797. This is well worth reading; it contains a dignified justification of his life, an explanation of his policies and of his confidence in the constitution which he had worked to strengthen and for which he had a feeling of affection. He was a traditionalist who had a large view of life, of Empire, founded upon the revolution of 1688, one harbouring diversity of local governments and cultures, as well as of a Europe which had, he was convinced, to guard against doctrinaire thought, against those abstract theories which could lead to a revolution of an entirely new kind threatening all the order he treasured. Fundamentally he believed in law, but he was flexible enough, pragmatic enough in his love of liberty to prefer peace to abstract truth.

The rediscovery of the Gaelic tradition

In the last quarter of the century an interest in the antiquities and history of Ireland developed. One of the pioneers of the period, a friend of the blind harper Turlough Carolan, and founder of the first Catholic Association, Charles O'Conor (1710–90) of Belanagare, Co Roscommon, published *Dissertations on the Ancient History of Ireland* (1753), and the need to preserve Irish annals and manuscripts was stressed in Sylvester O'Halloran's (1728–1807) *Insula Sacra* (1770). A skilled Limerick medical man, who had studied in Paris and Leyden, an authority on surgical subjects, he wrote a *General History of Ireland* (1774) – reading this book later triggered off the interest of Standish O'Grady (1846–1928) whose writings had such an influence in the late nineteenth century. Joseph Cooper Walker (1761–1810) who wrote a life of Turlough Carolan in 1786, published his *Historical Memoirs of the Irish Bards* (1786); though he had not a deep knowledge of Irish, he gave a chronological account of Irish poetry and music. One of the founder members of the Royal Irish Academy in 1785, he drew inspiration from other enthusiastic Celtic scholars; besides O'Conor and O'Halloran, he knew Charles Vallancey and Bishop Percy. Percy's *Reliques of Ancient English Poetry* (3 vols, 1765) greatly influenced the work of another of Walker's friends, Charlotte Brooke (?1740–1793), the eldest daughter of Henry Brooke, the novelist and man of letters. Her *Reliques of Irish Poetry* (1789) is prefaced by an encomium of Irish poetry. She wrote separate introductions and notes for the different sections of the book, and provided the originals of the poems she translated, thinking her English versions did not convey the forceful effect of the Irish. A modest person, she was encouraged not only by her father but by Walker and was advised by O'Halloran and Theophilus O'Flanagan (1764-1814), a native Irish speaker from Co Clare, a Trinity College graduate who edited *Transactions* (1808), a volume produced by the Dublin Gaelic society.

Another pioneering scholar was Edward Bunting (1773–1843), a musicologist and organist who collected and transcribed airs from the nine harpers who were present at the famous Harpers' Festival in

Belfast in 1792. He went on to collect airs in Ulster, Munster and Connaught for his *General Collection of the Ancient Music of Ireland* (1796), its sixty-six airs expanded by seventy-seven extra airs in the second edition of 1809. Yet more airs, a hundred and twenty, some collected by that gifted artist, archaeologist and antiquarian George Petrie (1790–1866), appeared in *The Ancient Music of Ireland* (1840). Bunting inspired Thomas Moore's popular *Irish Melodies*, the music being adapted from Bunting's original versions by Sir John Stevenson. Bunting's work also influenced Robert Emmet (1778–1803), who imagined himself at the head of 20,000 men marching to an air which he heard sung by Moore. Bunting was an invaluable conserver of Irish airs that might otherwise have vanished completely.

Much was achieved in eighteenth century Ireland. Many vast and dignified houses such as Castletown House, constructed so confidently in Co Kildare, or the elegantly proportioned Russborough House, or Carlton, graced the countryside, matched by such town houses in Dublin, as Powerscourt House, Belvedere House, Clonmell House and Alborough House. In Dublin the professional classes had fine squares of town houses, Fitzwilliam, Merrion or Mountjoy, to occupy, or else had their houses in the spacious streets encouraged by the Wide Streets Commission established in 1758. There were fine public buildings: the Parliament House in College Green was designed by one of the MPs, Sir Edward Lovett Pearce. Facing it is the great Palladian West Front of Trinity College (built 1755–59) and behind it the Chapel and Examination Hall, all designed by Sir William Chambers, the Viceregal Lodge in the Phoenix Park, St George's Church in Hardwicke Street, the superb Casino at Malahide, and, on the Liffey, Gandon's Custom House (begun in 1781) and his majestic Four Courts (begun in 1786). This is but to name but a few of the better-known urban buildings of the period.

The gentry enjoyed conviviality; they graced their lives with the work of Irish silversmiths, furniture makers, glassmakers, bookbinders, stonemasons and workers in plaster and stucco. Theatres were built in many cities. Irish-trained artists produced portraits, family groups, pictures of houses, landscapes, horses and dogs given their places in portraits of their owners. Among the artists were Hugh Douglas Hamilton, Robert Healy, Nathaniel Hone, Thomas Hickey, James Barry and George Barret (both of them friends of Edmund Burke in London), Jonathan Fisher, Thomas Roberts and Nathaniel Grogan. James Barry (1711–1806) was probably most in tune with the neo-classic aesthetic world in which so many Anglo-

Irish were at home – for this flourishing of the arts took place in the period of the Ascendancy parliament, Grattan's parliament.

Grattan queried the basis of this Ascendancy himself. Like Burke in England, he saw the need for change. His large vision was not shared by his fellow politicians. As Burke argued in England on behalf of Catholic emancipation, of admitting Irish Catholics into 'a general harmony', so Grattan asked on 25 February 1782 whether the Irish parliament was to be 'a protestant settlement or an Irish nation?' Yet although on the 16th of the following April he was hopeful enough, optimistic enough to praise his fellow members for having 'moulded the jarring elements of their country into a nation', all of his efforts came too late. Too little was achieved and by 1795 Burke confessed that his sanguine hopes were blasted. The private parallel to the public situation lies in Wolfe Tone's (1765–98) *Journal*. There he recorded the delights of pleasant picnics in Dublin by the seaside: this was the period when he could write in a cool measured way in his *Argument on behalf of the Catholics of Ireland* (1791). He did not see the peaceful Revolution of 1782 as in any way final though Grattan had then proclaimed Ireland's liberty as a nation. His optimism still surfaced, however, even after the storms of 1796 had ruined the French plans of landing troops in Ireland. It was not until the failure of the 1798 landings that he came to the sombre realisation of the military failure of what had become his revolutionary hopes for Irish independence.

This century in Ireland is interwoven with the thoughts of writers. They do not only include the three main ones – Swift with his 'Do I become a slave in six hours by crossing the Channel?', Berkeley with his 'We Irish men do not think so' and Burke, in his still faintly hopeful mood of 1792, with his 'It is known, I believe, that the greater, as well as the sounder part of our excluded countrymen, have not adopted the wild ideas, and wilder engagement, which have been held out to them; but have rather chosen to hope small and safe concessions from the legal power, than boundless objects from trouble and confusion.' – but there are a variety of others committed in varying degrees to the subject matter of Ireland: poets, playwrights, novelists, composers of ballads and songs, philosophers, theologians and writers of sermons, historians, politicians, orators and polemicists, antiquarians, translators, diarists, inventors, writers of memoirs and letters. Their writing usually echoes the unobtrusive, deceptively plain classical outlines of the many small houses built during the century throughout the Irish countryside: they remind us that such houses, like the literature, were meant to last.

NAHUM TATE (1652–1715)

The son of a Presbyterian clergyman, he was born in Dublin and educated at Trinity College, Dublin. A dramatist and poet as well as editor and translator, he was largely known for his adaptations of Elizabethan plays, notably his *The History of King Lear* (1681) where he departed from Shakespeare, marrying Cordelia to Edgar, restoring two thirds of his kingdom to Lear and removing the part of the Fool. His version was played on the English stage until the mid-19th century. He wrote the libretto for Purcell's *Dido and Aeneas* (1689) and, with Nicholas Brady (1659-1726), a native of Cork who held church livings in Stratford-upon-Avon and London, he wrote *A New Version of the Psalms* (1659). His hymn included here appeared in the *Supplement* (1763) to that work. He became Poet Laureate in 1692; reappointed on the accession of Queen Anne he was also appointed Historiographer Royal. He died in debt in London in 1715.

While Shepherds Watched Their Flocks By Night

While Shepherds watched their flocks by night,
All seated on the ground,
The angel of the Lord came down,
And glory shone around.

'Fear not,' said he, for mighty dread
Had seized their troubled mind;
'Glad tidings of great joy I bring
To you and all mankind.

'To you, in David's town, this day
Is born of David's line,
The Saviour, who is Christ the Lord,
And this shall be the sign:

'The heavenly babe you there shall find
To human view displayed,
All meanly wrapped in swaddling bands,
And in a manger laid.'

Thus spake the seraph; and forthwith
Appeared a shining throng
Of angels, praising God, who thus
Addressed their joyful song:

'All glory be to God on high,
And to the earth be peace;
Goodwill henceforth from Heaven to men
Begin and never cease.'

The Penance

Nymph Fanaret, the gentlest maid
That ever happy swain obeyed,
(For what offense I cannot say)
A day and night, and half a day,
Banished her shepherd from her sight:
His fault for certain was not slight,
Or sure this tender judge had ne'er
Imposed a penance so severe.
And lest he should anon revoke
What in her warmer rage she spoke,
She bound the sentence with an oath,
Protested by her Faith and Troth,
Nought should compound for his offence
But the full time of abstinence.
Yet when his penance-glass was run,
His hours of castigation done,
Should he defer one moment's space
To come and be restored to grace,
With sparkling threat'ning eye she swore
That failing would incense her more
Than all his trespasses before.

SUSANNAH CENTLIVRE (?1667-1723)

Susannah Freeman was probably born in Co. Tyrone. Orphaned, she was brought up by relatives at Holbeach in Lincolnshire. She ran off at fifteen, living, disguised as a boy, with Anthony Hammond at the University of Cambridge. Her first two husbands were each killed in duels; she then married a French chef in 1707. She wrote eighteen plays and farces, sometimes anonymously, disliking the bias of many who were averse to anything written by women. Her most popular plays were comedies of manners with complex plots in which the women are often independently minded and outwit bullying parents or guardians. The best known were *The Busy Body* (1710), *The Wonder! Or A Woman Keeps a Secret* (1714) and *A Bold Stroke for a Wife* (1718). The excerpt here, from *The Wonder! Or A Woman Keeps a Secret*, illustrates Isabella's dislike of the marriage planned for her. Don Felix in this play was David Garrick's favourite role.

From *The Wonder! Or A Woman Keeps a Secret.*

ACT I. SCENE I.

Enter Isabella *and* Inis *her Maid.*

INIS.　　　For Goodness sake, madam, where are you going in this Pet?

ISABELLA　Any where to avoid Matrimony; the Thoughts of a Husband is as terrible to me as the Sight of a Hobgoblin.

INIS　　　Ay, of an old Husband; but if you may chuse for yourself, I fancy Matrimony would be no such frightful thing to you.

ISABELLA　You are pretty much in the right, *Inis*; but to be forc'd into the Arms of an Ideot, a sneaking, snivling, drivling, avaricious Fool, who has neither Person to please the Eye, Sense to charm the Ear, nor Generosity to supply those Defects. Ah, *Inis!* what pleasant Lives Women lead in *England*, where Duty wears no Fetter but Inclination: the Custom of our Country inslaves us from our very Cradles, first to our Parents, next to our Husbands, and when Heaven is so kind to rid us of both these, our Brothers still usurp Authority, and expect a blind Obedience from us; so that Maids, Wives, or Widows, we are little better than Slaves to the Tyrant Man; therefore to avoid their Power, I resolve to cast myself into a Monastery.

INIS.　　　That is, you'll cut your own Throat to avoid another's doing it for you. Ah, Madam, those Eyes tell me you have no Nun's flesh about you; a Monastery, quotha! Where you'll wish yourself in the Green Sickness in a Month.

ISABELLA　What care I, there will be no Man to plague me.

INIS　　　No, nor what's much worse, to please you neither. Ad'slife, madam, you are the first Woman that ever despair'd in a Christian Country – Were I in your Place

ISABELLA　Why, what would your Wisdom do if you were?

INIS.　　　I'd imbark with the first fair Wind with all my Jewels, and seek my Fortune on t'other side the Water; no Shore can treat you worse than your own; there's ne'er a Father in *Christendom* should make me marry any Man against my Will.

ISABELLA I am too great a coward to follow your Advice. I must contrive some way to avoid *Don Guzman*, and yet stay in my own Country.

Enter Don Lopez.

LOPEZ (*Aside.*) Must you so, Mistress? but I shall take Care to prevent you.
Isabella, whither are you going, my Child.

ISABELLA Ha! My Father! to Church, Sir.

INIS. (*Aside.*) The old Rogue has certainly over-heard her.

LOPEZ Your Devotion must needs be very strong, or your Memory, very weak, my Dear; why, Vespers are over for this night; come, come, you shall have a better Errand to Church than to say your Prayers there. *Don Guzman* is arriv'd in the River, and I expect him ashore Tomorrow.

ISABELLA Ha, To-morrow!

LOPEZ He writes me Word, that his Estate in *Holland* is worth 12000 Crowns a Year, which, together with what he had before, will make thee the happiest Wife in *Lisbon*.

ISABELLA And the most unhappy Woman in the World. Oh Sir! If I have any Power in your Heart, if the Tenderness of a Father be not quite extinct, hear me with Patience.

LOPEZ No Objection against the Marriage, and I will hear whatever thou hast to say.

ISABELLA That's torturing me on the Rack, and forbidding me to groan; upon my Knees I claim the privilege of Flesh and Blood.

[*Kneels.*

LOPEZ I grant it, thou shalt have an Arm full of Flesh and Blood To-morrow; Flesh and Blood, quotha; Heaven forbid I should deny thee Flesh and Blood, my Girl.

ISABELLA (*Aside.*) Do not mistake, Sir; the fatal Stroke which separates Soul and Body, is not more terrible to the Thoughts of Sinners, than the Name of *Guzman* to my Ear.

LOPEZ Puh, Puh; you lye, you lye.

ISABELLA My frighted heart beats hard against my Breast, as if it fought a Passage to your Feet, to beg you'd change your Purpose.

LOPEZ A very pretty Speech, this; if it were turn'd into blank Verse, it would serve for a *Tragedy*; why, thou hast more Wit than I thought thou hadst, Child. I fancy this was all *extempore*, I don't believe thou did'st ever think of one Word on't before.

INIS   Yes, but she has, my Lord, for I have heard her say the same Things a thousand Times.

LOPEZ   How, how? What do you top your second-hand Jests upon your Father, Hussy, who knows better what's good for you than you do yourself? remember 'tis your Duty to obey.

ISABELLA   (*Rising.*) I never disobey'd before, and wish I had not Reason now; but nature has got the better of my Duty, and makes me loath the harsh Commands you lay.

LOPEZ   Ha, ha, very fine! Ha, ha.

ISABELLA   Death itself would be more welcome.

LOPEZ   Are you sure of that?

ISABELLA   I am your Daughter, my Lord, and can boast as strong a Resolution as yourself; I'll die before I'll marry *Guzman*.

LOPEZ   Say you so? I'll try that presently. (*Draws.*) Here let me see with what Dexterity you can breathe a Vein now (*offers her his Sword.*) The Point is pretty sharp, 'twill do your Business I warrant you.

INIS.   Bless me, Sir, What do you mean to put a Sword into the Hands of a desperate Woman?

LOPEZ   Desperate, ha, ha, ha, you see how desperate she is; what art thou frighted little *Bell*? ha!

ISABELLA   I confess I am startled at your Morals, Sir.

LOPEZ   Ay, ay, Child, thou hadst better take the Man, he'll hurt thee the least of the two.

ISABELLA   I shall take neither, Sir; Death has many Doors, and when I can live no longer with Pleasure, I shall find one to let him in at without your Aid.

LOPEZ   Say'st thou so, my dear *Bell*? Ods, I'm afraid thou art a little Lunatick, *Bell*. I must take care of thee Child, (*takes hold of her, and pulls out of his pocket a Key*) I shall make bold to secure thee, my Dear: I'll see if Locks and Bars can keep thee till *Guzman* comes; go, get you into your Chamber.

> *There I'll your boasted Resolution try,*
> *And see who'll get the better, you or I.*

> [*Pushes her in, and locks the Door.*

JONATHAN SWIFT (1667–1745)

Born a posthumous child in Dublin and educated at Kilkenny College and Trinity College, Dublin, Swift left Dublin in 1689 like many other Protestants alarmed by the politics of the Earl of Tyrconnel, James II's viceroy. He acted as secretary to Sir William Temple, a retired diplomat, at Moor Park in Surrey where he met Esther Johnson, whom he called Stella and who became his close lifelong friend. Ordained in Dublin, he was appointed to the parish of Kilroot in Northern Ireland. He returned to Moor Park, and, after Temple's death, became vicar of Laracor in Co. Meath.

In London to renegotiate a remission of taxes for the clergy of the Church of Ireland, he became friendly with Addison and Steele, writing pieces for *The Tatler*. Swift's letters to Stella and her companion Rebecca Dingley, who had moved to Dublin, convey his lively life in London, where he had begun to write on behalf of the Tories, editing *The Examiner* and becoming a friend of the Ministers who came to power in 1710, Robert Harley and Henry St. John. From 1710 to 1714 Swift was at the centre of affairs, writing various essays, including *The Conduct of the Allies*, an impressively influential pamphlet. His other friends included Pope, Gay and Arbuthnot, members of the Scriblerus Club, which they formed in 1713.

Swift failed to get a post in England – the Queen was reputed to have been disturbed by his *A Tale of a Tub* (1704), in which he satirises the perversion of Christian sects – he deprecated fundamentalism. He was appointed Dean of St Patrick's Cathedral in Dublin in 1714. In London he had become friendly with Esther Vanhomrigh, whom he called Vanessa. Against his advice she followed him to Ireland, living in Dublin and then in Celbridge Abbey until her early death in 1723. Their troubled friendship is described in Swift's long poem 'Cadenus and Vanessa'. Swift took some time to recover from his depression – he had been suffering severe bouts of Ménière's disease– and made new, younger friends in Ireland, among them Thomas Sheridan and Patrick Delany, and then found it impossible to keep out of Irish politics. His *Proposal for the Universal Use of Irish Manufacture* (1720) was followed by the *Drapier's Letters*, the first published in 1724. These so influenced public opinion that the government was forced to abandon a proposal for the minting of a large amount of copper coins. His ebullient jocularity and wit informed many of the poems he wrote in the 1720s while he was writing his masterpiece, *Gulliver's Travels*, and his devastating propaganda pamphlet, *A Modest Proposal* (1729), in which his fierce anger, *saeva indignatio*, was given its head, his rage at the poverty of Ireland. He could be appealingly direct in his poems to his friends who shared his delight in raillery, the spirit of the bagatelle; and both his poetry and his prose are clear, precise and powerful. A master of invention and irony, often assuming the persona of an innocent observer or narrator, fiercely independent himself, he defended the established Anglican tradition and fought for an independent Ireland with its parliament in Dublin parallel to that in Westminster, owing allegiance to the King in a partnership established in the 'Glorious Revolution' of 1688.

The Humble Petition of Frances Harris
(1699)

To their Excellencies
The Lords Justices of Ireland.
The humble petition of Frances Harris,
Who must starve, and die a maid if it miscarries.

Humbly showeth

That I went to warm myself in Lady Betty's chamber,
    because I was cold;
And I had in a purse seven pounds, four shillings and six pence
    (besides farthings) in money and gold;
So, because I had been buying things for my Lady last night,
I was resolved to tell my money, to see if it was right.
Now you must know, because my trunk has a very bad lock,
Therefore all the money I have (which, God knows,
    is a very small stock)
I keep in my pocket, tied about my middle, next my smock.
So, when I went to put up my purse, as God would have it, my
    smock was unripped;
And instead of putting it into my pocket, down it slipped:
Then the bell rung, and I went down to put my Lady to bed;
And, God knows, I thought my money was as safe as
    my maidenhead.
So, when I came up again, I found my pocket feel very light;
But when I searched, and missed my purse, Lord! I thought I
    should have sunk outright.
Lord! Madam, says Mary, how d'ye do? Indeed, said I, never
    worse:
But pray, Mary, can you tell what I have done with my purse?
Lord help me, said Mary, I never stirred out of this place:
Nay, said I, I had it in Lady Betty's chamber, that's a plain case.
So Mary got me to bed, and covered me up warm;
However, she stole away my garters, that I might do myself
    no harm.
So I tumbled and tossed all night, as you may very well think;
But hardly ever set my eyes together, or slept a wink.
So I was a-dreamed, methought, that I went and searched the
    folks round;

And in a corner of Mrs Duke's box, tied in a rag, the money
    was found.
So next morning we told Whittle, and he fell a-swearing;
Then my dame Wadgar came, and she, you know, is thick
    of hearing:
Dame, said I, as loud as I could bawl, do you know what
    a loss I have had?
Nay, said she, my Lord Collway's folks are all very sad,
For my Lord Dromedary comes a Tuesday without fail;
Pugh! said I, but that's not the business that I ail.
Says Cary, says he, I have been a servant this five and twenty years,
    come spring,
And in all the places I lived, I never heard of such a thing.
Yes, says the steward, I remember when I was at my
    Lord Shrewsbury's,
Such a thing as this happened, just about the time of
    gooseberries.
So I went to the party suspected, and I found her full of grief;
(Now, you must know, of all things in the world, I hate
    a thief.)
However, I was resolved to bring the discourse slily about;
Mrs Duke, said I, here's an ugly accident has happened out;
'Tis not that I value the money three skips of a louse;
But the thing I stand upon, is the credit of the house;
'Tis true, seven pounds, four shillings, and six pence, makes a great
    hole in my wages;
Besides, as they say, service is no inheritance in these ages.
Now, Mrs Duke, you know, and everybody understands,
That though 'tis hard to judge, yet money can't go without hands.
The devil take me, said she (blessing herself), if ever I saw't!
So she roared like a Bedlam,[1] as though I had called her
    all to naught;
So you know, what could I say to her any more:
I e'en left her, and came away as wise as I was before.
Well: but then they would have had me gone to the
    cunning-man:
No, said I, 'tis the same thing, the chaplain will be here anon.
So the chaplain came in. Now the servants say he is my
    sweetheart,

---

1 *a Bedlam*: a mad person, a Bedlamite, an inmate of Bethlehem Hospital in London.

Because he's always in my chamber, and I always take
    his part;
So, as the Devil would have it, before I was aware, out I
    blundered,
Parson, said I, can you cast a nativity, when a body's
    plundered?
(Now you must know, he hates to be called 'Parson'
    like the devil.)
Truly, says he, Mrs Nab, it might become you to be more
    civil:
If your money be gone, as a learned Divine says, d'ye see,
You are no text for my handling, so take that from me:
I was never taken for a conjurer before, I'd have you to know.
Lord! said I, don't be angry, I am sure I never thought you so:
You know, I honour the cloth, I design to be a parson's wife;
I never took one in your coat for a conjurer in all my life.
With that, he twisted his girdle at me like a rope, as who
    should say,
Now you may go hang yourself for me; and so went away.
Well; I thought I should have swooned: Lord, said I, what
    shall I do?
I have lost my money; and I shall lose my true-love too!
So, my lord called me; Harry, said my lord, don't cry,
I'll give something towards thy loss; and says my Lady,
    so will I.
Oh! but, said I, what if, after all, the chaplain won't come to?
For that, he said (an't please your Excellencies) I must
    petition you.

The premises tenderly considered, I desire your Excellencies'
    protection:
And that I may have a share in next Sunday's collection:
And over and above, that I may have your Excellencies' letter,
With an order for the chaplain aforesaid; or instead of
    him a better.
And then your poor petitioner, both night and day,
Or the chaplain (for 'tis his trade) as in duty bound, shall
    ever pray.

Jonathan Swift

From *A Tale of a Tub*

[Swift wrote this about 1697; it was published in 1704. In it Peter represents the Pope and the Roman Catholic Church; Martin, Luther and the Church of England; and Jack, Calvin and dissenting Protestantism. The coats are the doctrine and faith of Christianity, the will is the New Testament.]

[*THE HISTORY OF CHRISTIANITY*]

Once upon a time, there was a man who had three sons by one wife, and all at a birth, neither could the midwife tell certainly which was the eldest. Their father died while they were young, and upon his deathbed, calling the lads to him, spoke thus:

'Sons, because I have purchased no estate, nor was born to any, I have long considered of some good legacies to bequeath you; and at last, with much care as well as expense, have provided each of you (here they are) a new coat. Now, you are to understand, that these coats have two virtues contained in them: one is, that with good wearing, they will last you fresh and sound as long as you live; the other is, that they will grow in the same proportion with your bodies, lengthening and widening of themselves, so as to be always fit. Here, let me see them on you before I die. So, very well; pray children, wear them clean, and brush them often. You will find in my will (here it is) full instructions in every particular concerning the wearing and management of your coats, wherein you must be very exact to avoid the penalties I have appointed for every transgression or neglect, upon which your future fortunes will entirely depend. I have also commanded in my will, that you should live together in one house like brethren and friends, for then you will be sure to thrive, and not otherwise.'

Here the story says, this good father died, and the three sons went all together to seek their fortunes.

I shall not trouble you with recounting what adventures they met for the first seven years, any farther than by taking notice, that they carefully observed their father's will, and kept their coats in very good order; that they travelled through several countries, encountered a reasonable quantity of giants, and slew certain dragons.

Being now arrived at the proper age for producing themselves, they came up to town and fell in love with the ladies, but especially three, who about that time were in chief reputation: the Duchess d'Argent, Madame de Grands Titres, and the Countess d'Orgueil. On their first appearance, our three adventurers met with a very bad reception, and soon with great sagacity guessing out the reason, they quickly began to improve in the good qualities of the town: they writ, and rallied, and rhymed, and sung, and said, and said nothing: they drank, and fought, and whored, and slept, and swore, and took snuff: they went to new plays on the first night, haunted the chocolate-houses, beat the watch, lay on bulks, and got claps: they bilked hackney-coachmen, ran in debt with shopkeepers, and lay with their wives; they killed bailiffs, kicked fiddlers down stairs, eat at Locket's, loitered at Will's, they talked of the drawing-room and never came there; dined with lords they never saw; whispered a duchess, and spoke never a word; exposed the scrawls of their laundress for billets-doux of quality; came ever just from court and were never seen in it; attended the Levee *sub dio*;[1] got a list of peers by heart in one company, and with great familiarity retailed them in another. Above all, they constantly attended those Committees of Senators who are silent in the House, and loud in the Coffee-House, where they nightly adjourn to chew the cud of politics, and are encompassed with a ring of disciples who lie in wait to catch up their droppings. The three brothers had acquired forty other qualifications of the like stamp too tedious to recount, and by consequence were justly reckoned the most accomplished persons in town. But all would not suffice and the ladies aforesaid continued still inflexible. To clear up which difficulty I must, with the reader's good leave and patience, have recourse to some points of weight, which the authors of that age have not sufficiently illustrated.

For about this time it happened a sect arose whose tenets obtained and spread very far, especially in the *grand monde* and among everybody of good fashion. They worshipped a sort of idol who, as their doctrine delivered, did daily create men by a kind of manufactory operation. This idol they placed in the highest parts of the house, on an altar erected about three foot. He was shewn in the posture of a Persian emperor, sitting on a superficies with his legs interwoven under him. This god had a goose for his ensign, whence it is that some learned men pretend to deduce his original from Jupiter Capitolinus. At his left hand, beneath the altar, Hell seemed to open, and catch at the animals the idol was creating; to prevent which, certain of his priests hourly flung in pieces of the uninformed mass or substance,

---

1 *sub dio*: outside.

and sometimes whole limbs already enlivened, which that horrid gulf insatiably swallowed, terrible to behold. The goose was also held a subaltern divinity or *deus minorum gentium*,[1] before whose shrine was sacrificed that creature whose hourly food is human gore, and who is in so great renown abroad for being the delight and favourite of the Ægyptian Cercopithecus. Millions of these animals were cruelly slaughtered every day to appease the hunger of that consuming deity. The chief idol was also worshipped as the inventor of the yard and needle, whether as the god of seamen or on account of certain other mystical attributes, hath not been sufficiently cleared.

The worshippers of this deity had also a system of their belief which seemed to turn upon the following fundamentals. They held the universe to be a large suit of clothes, which invests everything: that the earth is invested by the air; the air is invested by the stars; and the stars are invested by the *primum mobile*. Look on this globe of earth, you will find it to be a very complete and fashionable dress. What is that which some call land, but a fine coat faced with green? or the sea, but a waistcoat of water-tabby. Proceed to the particular works of the creation, you will find how curious Journeyman Nature hath been, to trim up the vegetable beaux; observe how sparkish a periwig adorns the head of a beech and what a fine doublet of white satin is worn by the birch. To conclude from all, what is man himself but a micro-coat, or rather a complete suit of clothes with all its trimmings? As to his body, there can be no dispute; but examine even the acquirements of his mind, you will find them all contribute in their order towards furnishing out an exact dress. To instance no more: is not religion a cloak, honesty a pair of shoes worn out in the dirt, self-love a surtout, vanity a shirt, and conscience a pair of breeches which, though a cover for lewdness as well as nastiness, is easily slipt down for the service of both?

These *postulata*[2] being admitted it will follow in due course of reasoning that those beings which the world calls improperly suits of clothes are in reality the most refined species of animals; or to proceed higher, that they are rational creatures, or men. For is it not manifest that they live, and move, and talk, and perform all other offices of human life? Are not beauty, and wit, and mien, and breeding, their inseparable proprieties? In short, we see nothing but them, hear nothing but them. Is it not they who walk the streets, fill up parliament-,

---

1 *deus minorum gentium*: god of lesser tribes.
2 *postulata*: assumptions.

coffee-, play-, bawdy-houses? 'Tis true indeed, that these animals which are vulgarly called suits of clothes, or dresses, do according to certain compositions, receive different appellations. If one of them be trimmed up with a gold chain, and a red gown, and a white rod, and a great horse, it is called a Lord-Mayor; if certain ermines and furs be placed in a certain position we style them a Judge; and so an apt conjunction of lawn and black satin we entitle a Bishop.

Others of these professors, though agreeing in the main system, were yet more refined upon certain branches of it, and held that man was an animal compounded of two dresses, the natural and the celestial suit, which were the body and the soul; that the soul was the outward, and the body the inward clothing; that the latter was *ex traduce*,[1] but the former of daily creation and circumfusion. This last they proved by scripture, because in them we live, and move, and have our being; as likewise by philosophy, because they are all in all, and all in every part. Besides, said they, separate these two, and you will find the body to be only a senseless unsavoury carcase. By all which it is manifest, that the outward dress must needs be the soul.

To this system of religion were tagged several subaltern doctrines which were entertained with great vogue; as particularly, the faculties of the mind were deduced by the learned among them in this manner: embroidery was sheer wit; gold fringe was agreeable conversation; gold lace was repartee; a huge long periwig was humour; and a coat full of powder was very good raillery; all which required abundance of *finesse* and *delicatesse* to manage with advantage, as well as a strict observance after times and fashions.

I have with much pains and reading, collected out of ancient authors this short summary of a body of philosophy and divinity, which seems to have been composed by a vein and race of thinking, very different from any other systems either ancient or modern. And it was not merely to entertain or satisfy the reader's curiosity but rather to give him light into several circumstances of the following story; that knowing the state of dispositions and opinions in an age so remote, he may better comprehend those great events which were the issue of them. I advise therefore the courteous reader to peruse with a world of application, again and again, whatever I have written upon this matter. And so leaving these broken ends, I carefully gather up the chief thread of my story and proceed.

These opinions therefore were so universal, as well as the practices

---

1 *ex traduce*: begotten by parents.

of them, among the refined part of court and town, that our three brother-adventurers as their circumstances then stood were strangely at a loss. For, on the one side, the three ladies they addressed themselves to (whom we have named already) were ever at the very top of the fashion, and abhorred all that were below it but the breadth of a hair. On the other side, their father's will was very precise, and it was the main precept in it with the greatest penalties annexed, not to add to, or diminish from their coats one thread without a positive command in the will. Now the coats their father had left them were, 'tis true, of very good cloth and, besides, so neatly sewn, you would swear they were all of a piece, but at the same time very plain, and with little or no ornament. And it happened that before they were a month in town, great shoulder-knots came up. Straight, all the world was shoulder-knots; no approaching the ladies' *ruelles* without the quota of shoulder-knots. 'That fellow,' cries one, 'has no soul; where is his shoulder-knot?' Our three brethren soon discovered their want by sad experience, meeting in their walks with forty mortifications and indignities. If they went to the playhouse, the door-keeper showed them into the twelve-penny gallery. If they called a boat, says a waterman, 'I am first sculler.' If they stepped to the Rose to take a bottle, the drawer would cry, 'Friend, we sell no ale.' If they went to visit a lady, a footman met them at the door with, 'Pray send up your message.' In this unhappy case they went immediately to consult their father's Will, read it over and over, but not a word of the shoulder-knot. What should they do? What temper should they find? Obedience was absolutely necessary, and yet shoulder-knots appeared extremely requisite. After much thought one of the brothers who happened to be more book-learned than the other two, said, he had found an expedient. ''Tis true,' said he, 'there is nothing here in this Will, *totidem verbis*,[1] making mention of shoulder-knots, but I dare conjecture we may find them inclusive, or *totidem syllabis*.'[2] This distinction was immediately approved by all, and so they fell again to examine the will. But their evil star had so directed the matter that the first syllable was not to be found in the whole writing. Upon which disappointment, he who found the former evasion took heart and said, 'Brothers, there is yet hopes; for though we cannot find them *totidem verbis*, nor *totidem syllabis*, I dare engage we shall make them out, *tertio modo*, or *totidem literis*.'[3] This discovery was also highly

---

1 *totidem verbis*: in so many words.
2 *totidem syllabis*: in so many syllables.
3 *tertio modo*, or *totidem literis*: a third way, in so many letters.

commended, upon which they fell once more to the scrutiny, and soon picked out S,H,O,U,L,D,E,R, when the same planet, enemy to their repose, had wonderfully contrived that a K was not to be found. Here was a weighty difficulty! But the distinguishing brother (for whom we shall hereafter find a name) now his hand was in, proved by a very good argument, that K was a modern, illegitimate letter, unknown to the learned ages, nor anywhere to be found in ancient manuscripts. ''Tis true,' said he, 'the word *Calendæ* hath in Q.V.C.[1] been sometimes writ with a K, but erroneously, for in the best copies it has been ever spelt with a C. And by consequence it was a gross mistake in our language to spell 'knot' with a K'; but that from henceforward he would take care it should be writ with a C. Upon this all farther difficulty vanished; shoulder-knots were made clearly out to be *jure paterno*[2] and our three gentlemen swaggered with as large and as flaunting ones as the best.

But, as human happiness is of a very short duration, so in those days were human fashions upon which it entirely depends. Shoulder-knots had their time, and we must now imagine them in their decline; for a certain lord came just from Paris with fifty yards of gold lace upon his coat, exactly trimmed after the court fashion of that month. In two days all mankind appeared closed up in bars of gold lace: whoever durst peep abroad without his compliment of gold lace, was as scandalous as a [eunuch], and as ill received among the women. What should our three knights do in this momentous affair? They had sufficiently strained a point already in the affair of shoulder-knots. Upon recourse to the Will nothing appeared there but *altum silentium*.[3] That of the shoulder-knots was a loose, flying, circumstantial point; but this of gold lace seemed too considerable an alteration without better warrant. It did *aliquo modo essentiæ adhærere*,[4] and therefore required a positive precept. But about this time it fell out that the learned brother aforesaid had read *Aristotelis Dialectica*, and especially that wonderful piece *de Interpretatione*, which has the faculty of teaching its readers to find out a meaning in everything but itself, like commentators on the Revelations, who proceed prophets without understanding a syllable of the text. 'Brothers,' said he, 'you are to be informed that of wills *duo sunt genera*, nuncupatory and scriptory;[5]

---

1 *Q.V.C.: Quibusdam veteribus codicibus*: some ancient manuscript.
2 *jure paterno*: by fatherly law.
3 *altum silentium*: deep silence.
4 *aliquo modo essentæ adhærere*: somehow belong to the essence.
5 *duo ... scriptory*: there are two kinds, oral and written.

that in the scriptory will here before us, there is no precept or mention about gold lace, *concediture*; but, *si idem affirmetur de nuncupatorio, negatur.*[1] For brothers, if you remember, we heard a fellow say when we were boys, that he heard my father's man say, that he heard my father say, that he would advise his sons to get gold lace on their coats, as soon as ever they could procure money to buy it.' 'By G – , that is very true,' cries the other. 'I remember it perfectly well,' said the third. And so without more ado they got the largest gold lace in the parish, and walked about as fine as lords.

A while after there came up all in fashion a pretty sort of flame-coloured satin for linings, and the mercer brought a pattern of it immediately to our three gentlemen, 'An please your worships,' said he, 'my Lord C[lifford]; and Sir J[ohn] W[aters] had linings out of this very piece last night; it takes wonderfully, and I shall not have a remnant left enough to make my wife a pin-cushion, by to-morrow morning at ten o'clock.' Upon this, they fell again to rummage the Will, because the present case also required a positive precept, the lining being held by orthodox writers to be of the essence of the coat. After long search they could fix upon nothing to the matter in hand except a short advice of their father's in the Will, to take care of fire, and put out their candles before they went to sleep. This, though a good deal for the purpose and helping very far towards self-conviction, yet not seeming wholly of force to establish a command; and being resolved to avoid farther scruple, as well as future occasion for scandal, says he that was the scholar, 'I remember to have read in wills of a codicil annexed, which is indeed a part of the will, and what it contains hath equal authority with the rest. Now, I have been considering of this same will here before us, and I cannot reckon it to be complete, for want of such a codicil. I will therefore fasten one in its proper place very dexterously. I have had it by me some time; it was written by a dog-keeper of my grandfather's, and talks a great deal (as good luck would have it) of this very flame-coloured satin.' The project was immediately approved by the other two; an old parchment scroll was tagged on according to art, in the form of a codicil annexed, and the satin bought and worn.

Next winter, a player, hired for the purpose by the corporation of fringe-makers, acted his part in a new comedy all covered with silver fringe, and according to the laudable custom, gave rise to that fashion. Upon which, the brothers consulting their father's Will, to their

---

1 *si idem … negatur*: I agree; but I deny the same of the oral.

great astonishment found these words; 'Item, I charge and command my said three sons to wear no sort of silver fringe upon or about their said coats,' etc., with a penalty in case of disobedience, too long here to insert. However, after some pause the brother so often mentioned for his erudition, who was well skilled in criticisms, had found in a certain author which he said should be nameless, that the same word which in the will is called fringe, does also signify a broomstick, and doubtless ought to have the same interpretation in this paragraph. This, another of the brothers disliked, because of that epithet silver, which could not, he humbly conceived, in propriety of speech be reasonably applied to a broom-stick; but it was replied upon him that this epithet was understood in a mythological and allegorical sense. However, he objected again, why their father should forbid them to wear a broom-stick on their coats, a caution that seemed unnatural and impertinent; upon which he was taken up short, as one that spoke irreverently of a mystery which doubtless was very useful and significant, but ought not to be over-curiously pried into or nicely reasoned upon. And in short, their father's authority being now considerably sunk, this expedient was allowed to serve as a lawful dispensation for wearing their full proportion of silver fringe.

A while after was revived an old fashion, long antiquated, of embroidery with Indian figures of men, women, and children. Here they had no occasion to examine the Will. They remembered but too well how their father had always abhorred this fashion; that he made several paragraphs on purpose importing his utter detestation of it, and bestowing his everlasting curse to his sons, whenever they should wear it. For all this, in a few days they appeared higher in the fashion than anybody else in town. But they solved the matter by saying that these figures were not at all the same with those that were formerly worn and were meant in the will. Besides, they did not wear them in that sense as forbidden by their father, but as they were a commendable custom, and of great use to the public. That these rigorous clauses in the will did therefore require some allowance, and a favourable interpretation, and ought to be understood *cum grano salis*.[1]

But fashions perpetually altering in that age, the scholastic brother grew weary of searching further evasions and solving everlasting contradictions. Resolved, therefore, at all hazards to comply with the modes of the world, they concerted matters together, and agreed unanimously to lock up their father's Will in a strong box, brought

---

1 *cum grano salis*: with a grain of salt.

out of Greece or Italy (I have forgot which) and trouble themselves no further to examine it, but only refer to its authority whenever they thought fit. In consequence whereof, a while after it grew a general mode to wear an infinite number of points, most of them tagged with silver: upon which, the scholar pronounced *ex cathedra*[1] that points were absolutely *jure paterno*, as they might very well remember. 'Tis true indeed, the fashion prescribed somewhat more than were directly named in the Will; however, that they as heirs-general of their father had power to make and add certain clauses for public emolument, though not deducible, *totidem verbis*, from the letter of the will, or else *multa absurda sequerentur.*[2] This was understood for canonical, and therefore on the following Sunday they came to church all covered with points.

The learned brother, so often mentioned, was reckoned the best scholar in all that or the next street to it; insomuch as, having run something behind-hand with the world, he obtained the favour from a certain lord, to receive him into his house, and to teach his children. A while after the lord died, and he, by long practice of his father's Will, found the way of contriving a deed of conveyance of that house to himself and his heirs; upon which he took possession, turned the young squires out, and received his brothers in their stead.

A Description of a City Shower
(1710)

Careful observers may foretell the hour
(By sure prognostics) when to dread a shower:
While rain depends, the pensive cat gives o'er
Her frolics and pursues her tail no more.
Returning home at night, you'll find the sink
Strike your offended sense with double stink.
If you be wise, then go not far to dine:
You'll spend in coach-hire more than save in wine.
A coming shower your shooting corns presage,
Old aches throb, your hollow tooth will rage.
Sauntering in coffee-house is Dulman seen;
He damns the climate and complains of spleen.
    Meanwhile the South, rising with dabbled wings,

---

1 *ex cathedra*: by (papal) authority.
2 *multa absurda sequerentur*: many absurdities would follow.

A sable cloud athwart the welkin flings,
That swilled more liquor than it could contain
And, like a drunkard, gives it up again.
Brisk Susan whips her linen from the rope,
While the first drizzling shower is borne aslope:
Such is that sprinkling which some careless quean
Flirts on you from her mop, but not so clean:
You fly, invoke the gods; then turning, stop
To rail; she singing, still whirls on her mop.
Not yet the dust had shunned the unequal strife,
But, aided by the wind, fought still for life,
And wafted with its foe by violent gust,
'Twas doubtful which was rain and which was dust.
Ah! where must needy poet seek for aid
When dust and rain at once his coat invade?
Sole coat, where dust cemented by the rain
Erects the nap, and leaves a mingled stain.

Now in contiguous drops the flood comes down,
Threatening with deluge this devoted town.
To shops in crowds the daggled females fly,
Pretend to cheapen goods but nothing buy.
The Templar spruce, while every spout's abroach,
Stays till 'tis fair, yet seems to call a coach.
The tucked-up sempstress walks with hasty strides,
While streams run down her oiled umbrella's sides.
Here various kinds by various fortunes led
Commence acquaintance underneath a shed.
Triumphant Tories and desponding Whigs
Forget their feuds, and join to save their wigs.
Boxed in a chair the beau impatient sits,
While spouts run clattering o'er the roof by fits;
And ever and anon with frightful din
The leather sounds; he trembles from within.
So when Troy chairmen bore the wooden steed,
Pregnant with Greeks, impatient to be freed,
(Those bully Greeks, who, as the moderns do,
Instead of paying chairmen, run them through),
Laocoön[1] struck the outside with his spear,

---

1 *Laocoön*: A reference to Virgil, *Aeneid* II. 40–56, where Laocoon hurls his spear at the side of the wooden horse containing the Greeks. He is unable to persuade the Trojans of the danger the horse represents.

And each imprisoned hero quaked for fear,
   Now from all parts the swelling kennels flow,
And bear their trophies with them as they go:
Filth of all hues and odors seem to tell
What street they sailed from, by their sight and smell.
They, as each torrent drives with rapid force
From Smithfield or St. Pulchre's shape their course;
And in huge confluent join at Snow Hill ridge,
Fall from the conduit prone to Holborn Bridge.
Sweepings from butchers stalls, dung, guts, and blood,
Drowned puppies, stinking sprats, all drenched in mud,
Dead cats, and turnip tops come tumbling down the flood.

From *the Journal to Stella*
LETTER 14

LONDON, Jan. 16, 1710–11

O faith, young women, I have sent my letter N.13 without one crumb of an answer to any of MD's[1]; there's for you now; and yet Presto[2] ben't angry faith, not a bit, only he will begin to be in pain next Irish post, except he sees MD's little handwriting in the glass frame at the bar of St James's Coffee-house, where Presto would never go but for that purpose. Presto is at home, God help him, every night from six till bed time, and has as little enjoyment or pleasure in life at present as any body in the world, although in full favour with all the Ministry. As hope saved, nothing gives Presto any sort of dream of happiness but a letter now and then from his own dearest MD. I love the expectation of it; and when it does not come, I comfort myself, that I have it yet to be happy with. Yes, faith, and when I write to MD, I am happy too; it is just as if methinks you were here, and I prating to you, and telling you where I have been: Well, says you, 'Presto, come, where have you been to-day? come, let's hear now.' And so then I answer; Ford and I were visiting Mr Lewis and Mr Prior; and Prior has given me a fine

---

1 *MD's*: 'My Dear', or 'My Dears', pet name for Stella – Hester or, as she called herself, Esther – Johnson, (1681–1728) and her friend Rebecca Dingley. The letters contain the 'little language', or code, in which Swift disguised playful and affectionate addresses to Stella and Dingley. It was suppressed or 'edited' in early printed texts, and may have been teasing imitation of Stella's speech as a small child.
2 *Presto*: Swift himself.

Plautus, and then Ford would have had me dine at his lodgings, and so I would not; and so I dined with him at an eating-house; which I have not done five times since I came here; and so I came home, after visiting Sir Andrew Fountaine's mother and sister, and Sir Andrew Fountaine is mending, though slowly.

17. I was making, this morning, some general visits, and at twelve I called at the coffee-house for a letter from MD; so the man said he had given it to Patrick;[1] then I went to the Court of Requests and Treasury to find Mr. Harley,[2] and, after some time spent in mutual reproaches, I promised to dine with him; I stayed there till seven, then called at Sterne's and Leigh's to talk about your box, and to have it sent by Smyth. Sterne says he has been making inquiries, and will set things right as soon as possible. I suppose it lies at Chester, at least I hope so, and only wants a lift over to you. Here has little Harrison been to complain, that the printer I recommended to him for his Tatler is a coxcomb; and yet to see how things will happen; for this very printer is my cousin, his name is Dryden Leach; did you never hear of Dryden Leach, he that prints the Postman? He acted Oroonoko,[3] he's in love with Miss Cross.—Well, so I came home to read my letter from Stella, but the dog Patrick was abroad; at last he came, and I got my letter; I found another hand had superscribed it; when I opened it, I found it written all in French, and subscribed Bernage: faith, I was ready to fling it at Patrick's head. Bernage tells me he had been to desire your recommendation to me to make him a captain; and your cautious answer, 'That he had as much power with me as you,' was a notable one; if you were here, I would present you to the ministry as a person of ability. Bernage should let me know where to write to him; this is the second letter I have had without any direction; however, I beg I may not have a third, but that you will ask him, and send me how I shall direct to him. In the mean time, tell him that if regiments are to be raised here, as he says, I will speak to George Granville, Secretary at War, to make him a captain; and use what other interest I conveniently can. I think that is enough, and so tell him, and don't trouble me with his letters, when I expect them from MD; do you hear, young women? write to Presto.

---

1 *Patrick*: Swift's servant.
2 *Mr Harley*: Robert Harley (1661–1724), Secretary of State 1704–1708, formed a Tory administration in 1710. He became the first Earl of Oxford in 1711. Dismissed in 1714, he was impeached and released after two years' imprisonment in the Tower of London.
3 *Oroonoko*: the main figure in Southerne's tragedy *Oroonoko*, produced in 1695, based on Aphra Behn's novel *Oroonoko, or the History of the Royal Slave* (?1678); stimulated by her experiences in Surinam, it was the first expression in English writing of sympathy for oppressed negroes.

18. I was this morning with Mr Secretary St. John,[1] and we were to dine at Mr Harley's alone, about some business of importance; but there were two or three gentlemen there. Mr. Secretary and I went together from his office to Mr. Harley's, and thought to have been very wise; but the deuce a bit: the company stayed, and more came, and Harley went away at seven, and the Secretary and I stayed with the rest of the company till eleven; I would then have had him come away; but he was in for't; and though he swore he would come away at that flask, there I left him. I wonder at the civility of these people; when he saw I would drink no more, he would always pass the bottle by me, and yet I could not keep the toad from drinking himself, nor he would not let me go neither, nor Masham, who was with us. When I got home, I found a parcel directed to me; and opening it, I found a pamphlet written entirely against myself, not by name, but against something I writ: it is pretty civil, and affects to be so, and I think I will take no notice of it; 'tis against something written very lately; and indeed I know not what to say, nor do I care; and so you are a saucy rogue for losing your money to-day at Stoyte's; to let that bungler beat you, fy, Stella, an't you ashamed? well, I forgive you this once, never do so again; no, noooo. Kiss and be friends, sirrah.—Come, let me go sleep; I go earlier to bed than formerly; and have not been out so late these two months; but the secretary was in a drinking humour. So good-night, myownlittledearsaucyinsolentrogues.

Stella's Birthday

(1725)

As, when a beauteous nymph decays,
We say, she's past her dancing days;
So, poets lose their feet by time,
And can no longer dance in rhyme.
Your annual bard had rather chose
To celebrate your birth in prose;
Yet, merry folks, who want by chance
A pair to make a country dance,

---

1 *Mr Secrectary St. John*: Henry St. John (1678–1751), created first Viscount Bolingbroke, shared the leadership of the Tory party with Harley. He negotiated the Treaty of Utrecht in 1713. Plotting a Jacobite restoration when Queen Anne died, he was dismissed and fled to the continent. Returning to England in 1723, he failed to be readmitted to political life and lived from 1735 to 1742 in France.

Call the old housekeeper, and get her
To fill a place, for want of better;
While Sheridan is off the hooks,
And friend Delany at his books,
That Stella may avoid disgrace,
Once more the Dean supplies their place.
Beauty and wit, too sad a truth,
Have always been confined to youth;
The god of wit, and beauty's queen,
He twenty-one, and she fifteen:
No poet ever sweetly sung,
Unless he were like Phoebus, young;
Nor ever nymph inspired to rhyme,
Unless, like Venus, in her prime.
At fifty-six, if this be true,
Am I a poet fit for you?
Or at the age of forty-three,
Are you a subject fit for me?

Adieu bright wit, and radiant eyes;
You must be grave, and I be wise.
Our fate in vain we would oppose,
But I'll be still your friend in prose:
Esteem and friendship to express,
Will not require poetic dress;
And if the muse deny her aid
To have them *sung*, they may be *said*.

But, Stella, say, what evil tongue
Reports you are no longer young?
That Time sits with his scythe to mow
Where erst sat Cupid with his bow;

That half your locks are turned to grey;
I'll ne'er believe a word they say.
'Tis true, but let it not be known,
My eyes are somewhat dimmish grown;
For nature, always in the right,
To your decays adapts my sight,
And wrinkles undistinguished pass,
For I'm ashamed to use a glass;

And till I see them with these eyes,
Whoever says you have them, lies.

No length of time can make you quit
Honour and virtue, sense and wit,
Thus you may still be young to me,
While I can better hear than see;
Oh, ne'er may fortune show her spite,
To make me deaf, and mend my sight.

A Modest Proposal

FOR PREVENTING THE CHILDREN OF POOR PEOPLE IN IRELAND FROM BEING A BURDEN TO THEIR PARENTS OR COUNTRY, AND FOR MAKING THEM BENEFICIAL TO THE PUBLIC

(1729)

It is a melancholy object to those who walk through this great town, or travel in the country, when they see the streets, the roads, and cabin-doors crowded with beggars of the female sex, followed by three, four, or six children, all in rags, and importuning every passenger for an alms. These mothers, instead of being able to work for their honest livelihood, are forced to employ all their time in strolling, to beg sustenance for their helpless infants who, as they grow up, either turn thieves for want of work, or leave their dear Native Country to fight for the Pretender in Spain, or sell themselves to the Barbadoes.

I think it is agreed by all parties that this prodigious number of children, in the arms, or on the backs, or at the heels of their mothers, and frequently of their fathers, is in the present deplorable state of the kingdom, a very great additional grievance; and therefore whoever could find out a fair, cheap, and easy method of making these children sound useful members of the commonwealth would deserve so well of the public, as to have his statue set up for a preserver of the nation.

But my intention is very far from being confined to provide only for the children of professed beggars, it is of a much greater extent, and shall take in the whole number of infants at a certain age, who are born of parents in effect as little able to support them as those who demand our charity in the streets.

As to my own part, having turned my thoughts for many years upon this important subject, and maturely weighed the several schemes of other projectors, I have always found them grossly mistaken in the computation. It is true a child just dropped from its dam may be supported by her milk for a solar year with little other nourishment, at most not above the value of two shillings, which the mother may certainly get, or the value in scraps, by her lawful occupation of begging. And it is exactly at one year old that I propose to provide for them in such a manner as, instead of being a charge upon their parents, or the parish, or wanting food and raiment for the rest of their lives, they shall, on the contrary contribute to the feeding and partly to the clothing, of many thousands.

There is likewise another great advantage in my scheme, that it will prevent those voluntary abortions, and that horrid practice of women murdering their bastard children, alas! too frequent among us, sacrificing the poor innocent babes, I doubt more to avoid the expense than the shame, which would move tears and pity in the most savage and inhuman breast.

The number of souls in this kingdom being usually reckoned one million and a half, of these I calculate there may be about two hundred thousand couple whose wives are breeders, from which number I subtract thirty thousand couples who are able to maintain their own children, although I apprehend there cannot be so many under the present distresses of the kingdom, but this being granted, there will remain an hundred and seventy thousand breeders. I again subtract fifty thousand for those women who miscarry, or whose children die by accident, or disease within the year. There only remain one hundred and twenty thousand children of poor parents annually born. The question therefore is, how this number shall be reared and provided for, which, as I have already said, under the present situation of affairs is utterly impossible by all the methods hitherto proposed: for we can neither employ them in handicraft, or agriculture; we neither build houses (I mean in the country) nor cultivate land; they can very seldom pick up a livelihood by stealing till they arrive at six years old, except where they are of towardly parts, although I confess they learn the rudiments much earlier, during which time, they can however be properly looked upon only as probationers, as I have been informed by a principal gentleman in the County of Cavan, who protested to me that he never knew above one or two instances under the age of six, even in a part of the kingdom so renowned for the quickest proficiency in that art.

I am assured by our merchants that a boy or a girl, before twelve years old, is no saleable commodity; and even when they come to this age, they will not yield above three pounds, or three pounds and half-a-crown at most on the Exchange, which cannot turn to account either to the parents or the kingdom, the charge of nutriment and rags having been at least four times that value.

I shall now therefore humbly propose my own thoughts, which I hope will not be liable to the least objection.

I have been assured by a very knowing American of my acquaintance in London, that a young healthy child well nursed, is at a year old a most delicious, nourishing, and wholesome food, whether stewed, roasted, baked, or boiled, and I make no doubt that it will equally serve in a fricassee, or a ragoust.

I do therefore humbly offer it to public consideration, that of the hundred and twenty thousand children, already computed, twenty thousand may be reserved for breed, whereof only one fourth part to be males, which is more than we allow to sheep, black-cattle, or swine; and my reason is that these children are seldom the fruits of marriage, a circumstance not much regarded by our savages; therefore one male will be sufficient to serve four females. That the remaining hundred thousand may at a year old be offered in the sale to the persons of quality and fortune, through the kingdom, always advising the mother to let them suck plentifully in the last month, so as to render them plump and fat for a good table. A child will make two dishes at an entertainment for friends, and when the family dines alone the fore or hind quarter will make a reasonable dish, and seasoned with a little pepper or salt will be very good boiled on the fourth day, especially in winter.

I have reckoned upon a medium, that a child just born will weigh 12 pounds, and in a solar year, if tolerably nursed, increaseth to 28 pounds.

I grant this food will be somewhat dear, and therefore very proper for landlords, who, as they have already devoured most of the parents, seem to have the best title to the children.

Infants' flesh will be in season throughout the year, but more plentiful in March, and a little before and after; for we are told by a grave author, an eminent French physician,[1] that fish being a prolific diet, there are more children born in Roman Catholic countries about nine months after Lent, than at any other season; therefore, reckoning a year after Lent, the markets will be more glutted than usual, because the number of Popish infants is at least three to one in this kingdom, and therefore it will have one other collateral advantage by lessening the number of Papists among us.

I have already computed the charge of nursing a beggar's child (in

---

1 *an eminent physician*: François Rabelais (c. 1494–1559) author of *Gargantua and Pantagruel*.

which list I reckon all cottagers, labourers, and four fifths of the farmers) to be about two shillings per annum, rags included, and I believe no gentleman would repine to give ten shillings for the carcass of a good fat child, which, as I have said, will make four dishes of excellent nutritive meat, when he hath only some particular friend, or his own family to dine with him. Thus the Squire will learn to be a good landlord, and grow popular among his tenants, the mother will have eight shillings net profit, and be fit for work till she produces another child.

Those who are more thrifty (as I must confess the times require) may flay the carcass; the skin of which, artificially dressed, will make admirable gloves for ladies, and summer boots for fine gentlemen.

As to our City of Dublin, shambles may be appointed for this purpose in the most convenient parts of it, and butchers we may be assured will not be wanting, although I rather recommend buying the children alive, and dressing them hot from the knife, as we do roasting pigs.

A very worthy person, a true lover of his country, and whose virtues I highly esteem, was lately pleased in discoursing on this matter, to offer a refinement upon my scheme. He said that many gentlemen of this kingdom, having of late destroyed their deer, he conceived that the want of venison might be well supplied by the bodies of young lads and maidens not exceeding fourteen years of age, nor under twelve, so great a number of both sexes in every country being now ready to starve for want of work and service; and these to be disposed of by their parents if alive, or otherwise by their nearest relations. But with due deference to so excellent a friend and so deserving a patriot, I cannot be altogether in his sentiments; for as to the males, my American acquaintance assured me from frequent experience that their flesh was generally tough and lean, like that of our schoolboys, by continual exercise, and their taste disagreeable, and to fatten them would not answer the charge. Then as to the females, it would, I think, with humble submission, be a loss to the public, because they soon would become breeders themselves. And besides, it is not improbable that some scrupulous people might be apt to censure such a practice (although indeed very unjustly) as a little bordering upon cruelty; which, I confess, hath always been with me the strongest objection against any project, however so well intended.

But in order to justify my friend, he confessed that this expedient was put into his head by the famous Psalmanazar,[1] a native of the island

---

1 *Psalmanazar*: George Psalmanazar (?1679–1763), a Frenchman and friend of Samuel Johnson; he posed as a Formosan and wrote *An Historical and Geographical Description of Formosa* (1704), containing accounts of cannibalism and infanticide.

Formosa, who came from thence to London above twenty years ago, and in conversation told my friend, that in his country when any young person happened to be put to death, the executioner sold the carcass to persons of quality, as a prime dainty; and that in his time the body of a plump girl of fifteen, who was crucified for an attempt to poison the emperor, was sold to his Imperial Majesty's Prime Minister of State, and other great mandarins of the Court, in joints from the gibbet, at four hundred crowns. Neither indeed can I deny, that if the same use were made of several plump young girls in this town, who without one single groat to their fortunes, cannot stir abroad without a chair, and appear at the playhouse and assemblies in foreign fineries which they never will pay for, the kingdom would not be the worse.

Some persons of a desponding spirit are in great concern about that vast number of poor people who are aged, diseased, or maimed, and I have been desired to employ my thoughts what course may be taken to ease the nation of so grievous an encumbrance. But I am not in the least pain upon that matter because it is very well known that they are every day dying and rotting, by cold and famine, and filth, and vermin, as fast as can be reasonably expected. And as to the young labourers, they are now in as hopeful a condition. They cannot get work, and consequently pine away for want of nourishment, to a degree that if at any time they are accidentally hired to common labour, they have not strength to perform it; and thus the country and themselves are happily delivered from the evils to come.

I have too long digressed, and therefore shall return to my subject. I think the advantages by the proposal which I have made are obvious and many, as well as of the highest importance.

For first, as I have already observed, it would greatly lessen the number of Papists, with whom we are yearly over-run, being the principal breeders of the nation as well as our most dangerous enemies, and who stay at home on purpose with a design to deliver the kingdom to the Pretender, hoping to take their advantage by the absence of so many good Protestants, who have chosen rather to leave their country than stay at home and pay tithes against their conscience to an Episcopal curate.

Secondly, The poorer tenants will have something valuable of their own, which by law may be made liable to distress, and help to pay their landlord's rent, their corn and cattle being already seized, and money a thing unknown.

Thirdly, Whereas the maintenance of an hundred thousand children, from two years old and upwards, cannot be computed at less than ten shillings a piece per annum, the nation's stock will be thereby increased fifty thousand pounds per annum, besides the profit of a new dish introduced to the tables of all gentlemen of fortune in the kingdom who have any refinement in taste; and the money will circulate among ourselves, the goods being entirely of our own growth and manufacture.

Fourthly, The constant breeders, beside the gain of eight shillings sterling per annum by the sale of their children, will be rid of the charge of maintaining them after the first year.

Fifthly, This food would likewise bring great custom to taverns, where the vintners will certainly be so prudent as to procure the best receipts for dressing it to perfection, and consequently have their houses frequented by all the fine gentlemen, who justly value themselves upon their knowledge in good eating; and a skilful cook, who understands how to oblige his guests, will contrive to make it as expensive as they please.

Sixthly, this would be a great inducement to marriage, which all wise nations have either encouraged by rewards, or enforced by laws and penalties. It would increase the care and tenderness of mothers toward their children, when they were sure of a settlement for life to the poor babes, provided in some sort by the public to their annual profit instead of expense. We should see an honest emulation among the married women, which of them could bring the fattest child to the market. Men would become as fond of their wives, during the time of their pregnancy, as they are now of their mares in foal, their cows in calf, or sows when they are ready to farrow; nor offer to beat or kick them (as is too frequent a practice) for fear of a miscarriage.

Many other advantages might be enumerated. For instance, the addition of some thousand carcasses in our exportation of barrelled beef; the propagation of swine's flesh and improvement in the art of making good bacon, so much wanted among us by the great destruction of pigs, too frequent at our tables, which are no way comparable in taste or magnificence to a well-grown, fat yearling child, which roasted whole will make a considerable figure at a Lord Mayor's feast, or any other public entertainment. But this and many others I omit, being studious of brevity.

Supposing that one thousand families in this city would be constant customers for infants' flesh, besides others who might have it at merry-meetings, particularly weddings and christenings, I compute that Dublin would take off annually about twenty thousand carcasses, and the rest of the kingdom (where probably they will be sold somewhat cheaper) the remaining eighty thousand.

I can think of no one objection that will possibly be raised against this proposal, unless it should be urged that the number of people will be thereby much lessened in the kingdom. This I freely own, and it was indeed one principal design in offering it to the world. I desire the reader will observe, that I calculate my remedy for this one individual Kingdom of Ireland, and for no other that ever was, is, or, I think, ever can be upon earth. Therefore let no man talk to me of other expedients; of taxing our absentees at five shillings a pound; of using neither clothes, nor household furniture, except what is our own growth and manufacture; of utterly rejecting the materials and instruments that promote foreign luxury; of curing the expensiveness of pride, vanity, idleness, and gaming in our women; of introducing a vein of parsimony, prudence, and temperance; of learning to love our Country, wherein we differ even from Laplanders, and the inhabitants of Topinamboo;[1] of quitting our animosities and factions, nor act any longer like the Jews, who were murdering one another at the very moment their city was taken; of being a little cautious not to sell our country and consciences for nothing; of teaching landlords to have at least one degree of mercy towards their tenants; lastly of putting a spirit of honesty, industry and skill into our shopkeepers, who, if a resolution could now be taken to buy only our native goods, would immediately unite to cheat and exact upon us in the price, the measure, and the goodness, nor could ever yet be brought to make one fair proposal of just dealing, though often and earnestly invited to it.

Therefore I repeat, let no man talk to me of these and the like expedients, till he hath at least a glimpse of hope that there will ever be some hearty and sincere attempt to put them in practice.

But as to myself, having been wearied out for many years with offering vain, idle, visionary thoughts, and at length utterly despairing of success, I fortunately fell upon this proposal, which as it is wholly new, so it hath something solid and real, of no expense and little trouble, full in our own power, and whereby we can incur no danger in disobliging England. For this kind of commodity will not bear exportation, the flesh being of too tender a consistence to admit a long continuance in salt, although perhaps I could name a country which would be glad to eat up our whole nation without it.

After all, I am not so violently bent upon my own opinion as to reject any offer proposed by wise men, which shall be found equally innocent, cheap, easy and effectual. But before something of that kind shall be advanced in contradiction to my scheme, and offering a better, I desire

---

1 *Topinamboo*: a region in Brazil.

the author, or authors, will be pleased maturely to consider two points. First, as things now stand, how they will be able to find food and raiment for an hundred thousand useless mouths and backs. And secondly, there being a round million of creatures in human figure throughout this kingdom, whose whole subsistence put into a common stock would leave them in debt two millions of pounds sterling, adding those who are beggars by profession, to the bulk of farmers, cottagers, and labourers with their wives and children, who are beggars in effect; I desire those politicians who dislike my overture and may perhaps be so bold to attempt an answer, that they will first ask the parents of these mortals, whether they would not at this day think it a great happiness to have been sold for food at a year old, in the manner I prescribe; and thereby have avoided such a perpetual scene of misfortunes as they have since gone through, by the oppression of landlords, the impossibility of paying rent without money or trade, the want of common sustenance, with neither house nor clothes to cover them from the inclemencies of the weather, and the most inevitable prospect of entailing the like or greater miseries upon their breed for ever.

I profess, in the sincerity of my heart, that I have not the least personal interest in endeavouring to promote this necessary work, having no other motive than the public good of my country, by advancing our trade, providing for infants, relieving the poor, and giving some pleasure to the rich. I have no children, by which I can propose to get a single penny; the youngest being nine years old, and my wife past child-bearing.

The Description of an Irish Feast

(1720)

TRANSLATED ALMOST LITERALLY OUT OF THE ORIGINAL IRISH[1]

> O'Rourk's noble fare
> > Will ne'er be forgot,
> By those who were there,
> > Or those who were not.
> His revels to keep,
> > We sup and we dine,
> On seven score sheep,

---

1 *The Description of an Irish Feast*: The poem (of 96 lines) by Hugh MacGauran, 'Plearaca na Ruarcach', was set to music by the blind poet and composer Turlough Carolan (1670–1738). Tradition has it that Swift admired him and entertained him at the Deanery.

Fat bullocks and swine.
Usquebagh[1] to our feast
  In pails was brought up,
An hundred at least,
  And a madder[2] our cup.
O there is the sport,
  We rise with the light,
In disorderly sort,
  From snoring all night.
O how was I tricked,
  My pipe it was broke,
My pocket was picked,
  I lost my new cloak.
I'm rifled, quoth Nell,
  Of mantle and kercher,
Why then fare them well,
  The de'il take the searcher.
Come, harper, strike up,
  But first by your favour,
Boy, give us a cup;
  Ay, this has some savour:
O'Rourk's jolly boys
  Ne'er dreamt of the matter,
Till roused by the noise,
  And musical clatter,
They bounce from their nest,
  No longer will tarry,
They rise ready dressed,
  Without one *Ave Mary*.
They dance in a round,
  Cutting capers and ramping,
A mercy the ground
  Did not burst with their stamping,
The floor is all wet
  With leaps and with jumps,
While the water and sweat,
  Splish, splash in their pumps.
Bless you late and early,
  Laughlin O' Enagin,

---

1 *Usquebagh*: whiskey (from the Irish *uiscebeatha*, the water of life).
2 *a madder*: a wooden vessel, usually square in shape.

By my hand, you dance rarely,
   Margery Grinagin.
Bring straw for our bed,
   Shake it down to the feet,
Then over us spread,
   The winnowing sheet.
To show, I don't flinch,
   Fill the bowl up again,
Then give us a pinch
   Of your sneezing, a *Yean*.[3]
Good Lord, what a sight,
   After all their good cheer,
For people to fight
   In the midst of their beer:
They rise from their feast,
   And hot are their brains,
A cubit at least
   The length of their *skenes*.
What stabs and what cuts,
   What clattering of sticks,
What strokes on the guts,
   What bastings and kicks!
With cudgels of oak,
   Well hardened in flame,
An hundred heads broke,
   An hundred struck lame.
You churl, I'll maintain
   My father built Lusk,
The castle of Slane,
   And Carrickdrumrusk:
The Earl of Kildare,
   And Moynalta, his brother,
As great as they are,
   I was nursed by their mother.
Ask that of old Madam,
   She'll tell you who's who,
As far up as Adam,
   She knows it is true,
Come down with that beam,
   If cudgels are scarce,

---

3 *Yean*: another Irish word for a woman.

A blow on the wame,
 Or a kick on the arse.

A Pastoral Dialogue
(?1729)

A nymph and swain, Sheelah and Dermot hight,
Who wont to weed the court of Gosford knight,
While each with stubbed knife removed the roots
That raised between the stones their daily shoots;
As at their work they sat in counterview,
With mutual beauty smit, their passion grew.
Sing, heavenly Muse, in sweetly flowing strain,
The soft endearments of the nymph and swain.

DERMOT

My love to Sheelah is more firmly fixed
Than stronger weeds that grow these stones betwixt:
My spud[1] these nettles from the stones can part;
No knife so keen to weed thee from my heart.

SHEELAH

My love for gentle Dermot faster grows
Than yon tall dock that rises to thy nose.
Cut down the dock, 'twill sprout again; but O!
Love rooted out, again will never grow.

DERMOT

No more that briar thy tender leg shall rake:
(I spare the thistle for Sir Arthur's sake.)
Sharp are the stones, take thou this rushy mat;
The hardest bum will bruise with sitting squat.

SHEELAH

Thy breeches, torn behind, stand gaping wide;
This petticoat shall save thy dear backside;
Nor need I blush, although you feel it wet;
Dermot, I vow, 'tis nothing else but sweat.

1 *spud*: a knife or weeding tool.

DERMOT

At an old stubborn root I chanced to tug,
When the Dean threw me this tobacco plug:
A longer ha'porth never did I see;
This, dearest Sheelah, thou shalt share with me.

SHEELAH

In at the pantry door this morn I slipped,
And from the shelf a charming crust I whipped;
Dennis was out, and I got hither safe;
And thou, my dear, shalt have the biggest half.

DERMOT

When you saw Tady at long-bullets[1] play,
You sat and loused him all a sunshine day.
How could you, Sheelah, listen to his tales,
Or crack such lice as his betwixt your nails?

SHEELAH

When you with Oonagh stood behind a ditch,
I peeped, and saw you kiss the dirty bitch.
Dermot, how could you touch those nasty sluts!
I almost wish this spud were in your guts.

DERMOT

If Oonagh once I kissed, forbear to chide;
Her aunt's my gossip by my father's side:
But, if I ever touch her lips again,
May I be doomed for life to weed in rain.

SHEELAH

Dermot, I swear, though Tady's locks could hold
Ten thousand lice, and every louse was gold,
Him on my lap you never more should see;
Or may I lose my weeding-knife – and thee.

DERMOT

O, could I earn for thee, my lovely lass,
A pair of brogues to bear thee dry to mass!

---

1 *long-bullets*: or long-bowls, a skittle game akin to ninepins.

But see where Norah with the sowens[1] comes –
Then let us rise, and rest our weary bums.

From Gulliver's Travels
(1726)

[Lemuel Gulliver, a ship's surgeon, describes his experiences in various unknown lands.]

[GULLIVER'S ARRIVAL IN LILLIPUT]

...On the fifth of *November*, which was the beginning of summer in those parts, the weather being very hazy, the seamen spied a rock, within half a cable's length of the ship; but the wind was so strong, that we were driven directly upon it, and immediately split. Six of the crew, of whom I was one, having let down the boat into the sea, made a shift to get clear of the ship, and the rock. We rowed by my computation about three leagues, till we were able to work no longer, being already spent with labour while we were in the ship. We therefore trusted ourselves to the mercy of the waves, and in about half an hour the boat was overset by a sudden flurry from the north. What became of my companions in the boat, as well as of those who escaped on the rock, or were left in the vessel, I cannot tell; but conclude they were all lost. For my own part, I swam as fortune directed me, and was pushed forward by wind and tide. I often let my legs drop, and could feel no bottom: but when I was almost gone, and able to struggle no longer, I found myself within my depth; and by this time the storm was much abated. The declivity was so small, that I walked near a mile before I got to the shore, which I conjectured was about eight a-clock in the evening. I then advanced forward near half a mile, but could not discover any sign of houses or inhabitants; at least I was in so weak a condition, that I did not observe them. I was extremely tired, and with that, and the heat of the weather, and about half a pint of brandy that I drank as I left the ship, I found myself much inclined to sleep. I lay down on the grass, which was very short and soft, where I slept sounder than ever I remember to have done in my life, and, as I reckoned, above nine hours; for when I awakened, it was just daylight. I attempted to rise, but was not able to stir: for as I happened to

---

1 *sowens*: food made of oatmeal or sometimes of the shellings of oats.

lie on my back, I found my arms and legs were strongly fastened on each side to the ground; and my hair, which was long and thick, tied down in the same manner. I likewise felt several slender ligatures across my body, from my armpits to my thighs. I could only look upwards; the sun began to grow hot, and the light offended my eyes. I heard a confused noise about me, but in the posture I lay, could see nothing except the sky. In a little time I felt something alive moving on my left leg, which advancing gently forward over my breast, came almost up to my chin; when bending my eyes downwards as much as I could, I perceived it to be a human creature not six inches high, with a bow and arrow in his hands, and a quiver at his back. In the mean time, I felt at least forty more of the same kind (as I conjectured) following the first. I was in the utmost astonishment, and roared so loud, that they all ran back in a fright; and some of them, as I was afterwards told, were hurt with the falls they got by leaping from my sides upon the ground. However, they soon returned, and one of them, who ventured so far as to get a full sight of my face, lifting up his hands and eyes by way of admiration, cried out in a shrill but distinct voice, *Hekinah Degul*: the others repeated the same words several times, but I then knew not what they meant. I lay all this while, as the reader may believe, in great uneasiness: at length, struggling to get loose, I had the fortune to break the strings, and wrench out the pegs that fastened my left arm to the ground; for, by lifting it up to my face I discovered the methods they had taken to bind me; and, at the same time, with a violent pull, which gave me excessive pain, I a little loosened the strings that tied down my hair on the left side, so that I was just able to turn my head about two inches. But the creatures ran off a second time, before I could seize them; whereupon there was a great shout in a very shrill accent, and after it ceased, I heard one of them cry aloud, *Tolgo Phonac*; when in an instant I felt above a hundred arrows discharged on my left hand, which pricked me like so many needles; and besides they shot another flight into the air, as we do bombs in Europe, whereof many, I suppose, fell on my body (though I felt them not) and some on my face, which I immediately covered with my left hand. When this shower of arrows was over, I fell a groaning with grief and pain, and then striving again to get loose, they discharged another volley larger than the first, and some of them attempted with spears to stick me in the sides; but, by good luck, I had on me a buff jerkin, which they could not pierce. I thought it the most prudent method to lie still, and my design was to continue so till night, when, my left hand being already loose, I could easily free myself: and as for the inhabitants, I had reason to believe I might be a match for the greatest armies they could bring against me, if they were all of the same size with him that I saw. But fortune disposed otherwise of me. When the people observed I was quiet, they discharged no more arrows: But, by the noise I heard, I knew their Numbers increased; and about four yards from me, over-against my right ear, I heard a knocking for above an hour, like that of people at work; when turning my head that way, as well as the pegs and strings would permit me, I saw a stage erected about a foot and a half from the ground, capable of holding four of the inhabitants, with two or three ladders to mount it: from whence one of them, who seemed to be a person of quality, made me a long speech, whereof I understood not one syllable. But I should have mentioned, that before the principal person began his oration, he cried out three times *Langro Dehul san* (these words and the former were afterwards repeated and explained to me). Whereupon immediately about fifty of the inhabitants came, and cut the strings that fastened the left side of my head, which gave me the liberty of turning it to the right, and of observing the person and gesture of him that was to speak. He appeared to be of a middle age, and taller than any of the other three who attended him, whereof one was a page that held up his train, and seemed to be somewhat longer than my middle finger; the other two stood one on each side to support him. He acted every part of an orator, and I could observe many periods of threatenings, and others of promises, pity and kindness. I answered in a few words, but in the most submissive manner, lifting up my left hand and both my eyes to the sun, as calling him for a witness; and being almost famished with hunger, having not eaten a morsel for some hours before I left the ship, I found the demands of nature so strong upon me, that I could not forbear showing my impatience (perhaps against the strict rules of decency) by putting my finger frequently on my mouth, to signify that I wanted food. The *Hurgo* (for so they call a great lord, as I afterwards learned) understood me very well. He descended from the stage, and commanded that several ladders should be applied to my sides, on which above an hundred of the inhabitants mounted, and walked towards my mouth, laden with baskets full of meat, which had been provided, and sent thither by the King's orders upon the first intelligence he received of me. I observed there was the flesh of several animals, but could not distinguish them by the taste. There were shoulders, legs and loins, shaped like those of mutton, and very well dressed, but smaller than the wings of a lark. I eat them by two or three at a mouthful, and took three loaves at a time, about the bigness of musket bullets. They supplied me as fast as they could, showing a thousand marks of wonder and astonishment at my bulk and appetite. I then made another sign that I wanted drink. They found by my eating that a small quantity would not suffice me, and being a most ingenious people, they slung up with great dexterity one of their largest hogsheads, then rolled it towards my hand, and beat out the top; I drank it off at a draught, which I might well do, for it hardly held half a pint, and tasted like a small wine of Burgundy, but much more delicious. They brought me a second hogshead, which I drank in the same manner, and made signs for more, but they had none to give me. When I had performed these wonders, they shouted for joy, and danced upon my breast, repeating several times as they did at first, *Hekinah Degul*. They made me a sign that I should throw down the two hogsheads, but first warned the people below to stand out of the way, crying aloud, *Borach Mivola*, and when they saw the vessels in the air, there was a universal shout of *Hekinah Degul*. I confess I was often tempted while they were passing backwards and forwards on my body, to seize forty or fifty of the first that came in my reach, and dash them against the ground. But the remembrance of what I had felt, which probably might not be the worst they could do, and the promise of honour I made them, for so I interpreted my submissive behaviour, soon drove out these imaginations. Besides, I now considered myself as bound by the laws of hospitality to a people who had treated me with so much expense and magnificence. However, in my thoughts I could not sufficiently wonder at the intrepidity of these diminutive mortals, who durst venture to mount and walk upon my body, while one of my hands was at liberty, without trembling at the very sight of so prodigious a creature as I must appear to them. After some time, when they observed that I made no more demands for meat, there appeared before me a person of high rank from his Imperial Majesty. His Excellency having mounted on the small of my right leg, advanced forwards up to my face, with about a dozen of his retinue. And producing his credentials under the signet royal, which he applied close to my eyes, spoke about ten minutes, without any signs of anger, but with a kind of determinate resolution; often pointing forwards, which, as I afterwards found, was towards the capital city, about half a mile distant, whither it was agreed by his Majesty in council that I must be conveyed. I answered in few words, but to no purpose, and made a sign with my hand that was loose, putting it to the other (but over his Excellency's head, for fear of hurting him or his train) and then to my own head and body, to signify that I desired my liberty. It appeared that he understood me well enough, for he shook his head by way of disapprobation, and held his hand in a posture to show that I must be carried as a prisoner. However, he made other signs to let me understand that I should have meat and drink enough, and very good treatment. Whereupon I once more thought of attempting to break my bonds, but again, when I felt the smart of their arrows upon my face and hands, which were all in blisters, and many of the darts still sticking in them, and observing likewise that the number of my enemies increased, I gave tokens to let them know that they might do with me what they pleased. Upon this the *Hurgo* and his train withdrew with much civility and chearful countenances. Soon after I heard a general shout, with frequent repetitions of the words, *Peplom Selan*, and I felt great numbers of the people on my left side relaxing the cords to such a degree that I was able to turn upon my right, and to ease myself with making water; which I very plentifully did, to the great astonishment of the people, who conjecturing by my motions what I was going to do, immediately opened to the right and left on that side to avoid the torrent which fell with such noise and violence from me. But before this, they had daubed my face and both my hands with a sort of ointment very pleasant to the smell, which in a few minutes removed all the smart of their arrows. These circumstances, added to the refreshment I had received by their victuals and drink, which were very nourishing, disposed me to sleep. I slept about eight hours, as I was afterwards assured; and it was no wonder, for the physicians, by the Emperor's order, had mingled a sleeping potion in the hogsheads of wine.

It seems that upon the first moment I was discovered sleeping on the ground after my landing, the Emperor had early Notice of it by an express, and determined in council that I should be tied in the manner I have related (which was done in the night while I slept), that plenty of meat and drink should be sent me, and a machine prepared to carry me to the capital city.

This resolution perhaps may appear very bold and dangerous, and I am confident would not be imitated by any Prince in Europe on the like occasion; however, in my opinion, it was extremely prudent, as well as generous. For supposing these people had endeavoured to kill me with their spears and arrows while I was asleep, I should certainly have awakened with the first sense of smart, which might so far have roused my rage and strength, as to have enabled me to break the strings wherewith I was tied; after which, as they were not able to make resistance, so they could expect no Mercy.

[*In his second voyage Gulliver arrives in Brobdingnag, a land peopled by giant beings. He gets on well with the Royal family who treat him as a kind of pet.*]

[*GULLIVER PRAISES ENGLAND TO THE KING OF BROBDINGNAG*]

He was perfectly astonished with the historical account I gave him of our affairs during the last century; protesting it was only a heap of conspiracies, rebellions, murders, massacres, revolutions, banishments, the very worst effects that avarice, faction, hypocrisy, perfidiousness, cruelty, rage, madness, hatred, envy, lust, malice, and ambition, could produce.

His Majesty in another audience was at the pains to recapitulate the sum of all I had spoken, compared the questions he made with the answers I had given; then taking me into his hands, and stroking me gently, delivered himself in these words, which I shall never forget, nor the manner he spoke them in: 'My little friend *Grildrig*, you have made a most admirable panegyric upon your country. You have clearly proved that ignorance, idleness, and vice are the proper ingredients for qualifying a legislator; that laws are best explained, interpreted, and applied by those whose interest and abilities lie in perverting, confounding, and eluding them. I observe among you some lines of an institution, which, in its original might have been tolerable, but these half erased, and the rest wholly blurred and blotted by corruptions. It doth not appear from all you have said, how any one perfection is required toward the procurement of any one station among you, much less that men are ennobled on account of their virtue, that priests are advanced for their piety or learning, soldiers, for their conduct or valour, judges for their integrity, senators for the love of their country, or counsellors for their wisdom. As for yourself, (continued the King) who have spent the greatest part of your life in travelling, I am well disposed to hope you may hitherto have escaped many vices of your country. But, by what I have gathered from your own relation, and the answers I have with much pains wringed and extorted from you, I cannot but conclude the bulk of your natives, to be the most pernicious race of little odious vermin that nature ever suffered to crawl upon the surface of the earth.'

Nothing but an extreme love of truth could have hindered me from concealing this part of my story. It was in vain to discover my resentments, which were always turned into ridicule; and I was forced to rest with patience while my noble and beloved country was so injuriously treated. I am heartily sorry as any of my readers can possibly be, that such an occasion was given: but this prince happened to be so curious and inquisitive upon every particular, that it could not consist either with gratitude or good manners to refuse giving him what satisfaction I was able. Yet thus much I may be allowed to say in my own vindication, that I artfully eluded many of his questions, and gave to every point a more favourable turn, by many degrees than the strictness of truth would allow. For, I have always borne that laudable partiality to my own country, which Dionysius Halicarnassensis[1] with so much justice recommends to an historian: I would hide the frailties and deformities of my political mother, and place her virtues and beauties in the most advantageous light. This was my sincere endeavour in those many discourses I had with that monarch, although it unfortunately failed of success.

But, great allowances should be given to a King who lives wholly secluded from the rest of the world, and must therefore be altogether unacquainted with the manners and customs that most prevail in other nations: the want of which knowledge will ever produce many prejudices, and a certain narrowness of thinking, from which we and the politer countries of Europe are wholly exempted. And it would be hard indeed, if so remote a prince's notions of virtue and vice were to be offered as a standard for all mankind.

To confirm what I have now said, and further to show the miserable effects of a confined education, I shall here insert a passage, which will hardly obtain belief. In hopes to ingratiate myself farther into his Majesty's favour, I told him of an invention, discovered between three and four hundred years ago, to make a certain powder, into an heap of which the smallest spark of fire falling, would kindle the whole in a moment, although it were as big as a mountain, and make it all fly up in the air together, with a noise and agitation greater than thunder. That a proper quantity of this powder rammed into a hollow tube of brass or iron, according to its bigness, would drive a ball of iron or lead with such violence and speed as nothing was able to sustain its force. That the largest balls thus discharged would not only destroy whole ranks of an army at once, but batter the strongest walls to the ground, sink down ships with a thousand men in each, to the bottom of the sea; and when linked together by a chain, would cut

---

1 *Dionysius Halicarnassensis*: Greek orator and historian who wrote *Antiquitates Romanæ*, which covered Roman History up to the first Punic war; he taught at Rome from 30–8BC.

through masts and rigging, divide hundreds of bodies in the middle, and lay all waste before them. That we often put this powder into large hollow balls of iron, and discharged them by an engine into some city we were besieging, which would rip up the pavements, tear the houses to pieces, burst and throw splinters on every side, dashing out the brains of all who came near. That I knew the ingredients very well, which were cheap, and common; I understood the manner of compounding them, and could direct his workmen how to make those tubes of a size proportionable to all other things in his Majesty's kingdom, and the largest need not be above a hundred foot long; twenty or thirty of which tubes, charged with the proper quantity of powder and balls, would batter down the walls of the strongest town in his dominions in a few hours, or destroy the whole metropolis, if ever it should pretend to dispute his absolute commands. This I humbly offered to his Majesty as a small tribute of acknowledgment, in return of so many marks that I had received of his royal favour and protection.

The King was struck with horror at the description I had given of those terrible engines, and the proposal I had made. He was amazed how so impotent and grovelling an insect as I (these were his expressions) could entertain such inhuman ideas, and in so familiar a manner as to appear wholly unmoved at all the scenes of blood and desolation which I had painted as the common effects of those destructive machines, whereof, he said, some evil genius, enemy to mankind, must have been the first contriver. As for himself, he protested, that although few things delighted him so much as new discoveries in art or in nature, yet he would rather lose half his kingdom, than be privy to such a secret, which he commanded me, as I valued any life, never to mention any more.

A strange effect of narrow principles and short views! that a prince possessed of every quality which procures veneration, love, and esteem; of strong parts, great wisdom, and profound learning, endued with admirable talents for government, and almost adored by his subjects, should, from a nice unnecessary scruple, whereof in Europe we can have no conception, let slip an opportunity put into his hands, that would have made him absolute master of the lives, the liberties, and the fortunes of his people. Neither do I say this with the least intention to detract from the many virtues of that excellent King, whose character I am sensible will on this account be very much lessened in the opinion of an English reader: but, I take this defect among them to have risen from their ignorance, by not having hitherto reduced politics into a science, as the more acute wits of Europe have done. For, I remember very well, in a discourse one day with the King, when I happened to say there were several thousand books among us written upon the art of government, it gave him (directly contrary to my intention) a very mean opinion of our understandings. He professed both to abominate and despise all mystery, refinement, and intrigue, either in a prince or a minister. He could not tell what I meant by secrets of state, where an enemy or some rival nation were not in the case. He confined the knowledge of governing within very narrow bounds; to common sense and reason, to justice and lenity, to the speedy determination of civil and criminal causes; with some other obvious topics which are not worth considering. And, he gave it for his opinion, that whoever could make two ears of corn, or two blades of grass to grow upon a spot of ground where only one grew before, would deserve better of mankind, and do more essential service to his country, than the whole race of politicians put together.

The learning of this people is very defective, consisting only in morality, history, poetry, and mathematics, wherein they must be allowed to excel. But, the last of these is wholly applied to what may be useful in life, to the improvement of agriculture, and all mechanical arts; so that among us it would be little esteemed. And as to ideas, entities, abstractions, and transcendentals, I could never drive the least conception into their heads....

[*In his third voyage Gulliver arrives in the Kingdom of Lugnagg and learns of the Struldbruggs.*]

One day in much good company I was asked by a person of quality, whether I had seen any of their *Struldbruggs*, or immortals. I said I had not; and desired he would explain to me what he meant by such an appellation applied to a mortal creature. He told me that sometimes, though very rarely, a child happened to be born in a family, with a red circular spot in the forehead, directly over the left eyebrow, which was an infallible mark that it should never die. The spot, as he described it, was about the compass of a silver threepence, but in the course of time grew larger, and changed its colour; for at twelve years old it became green, so continued till five and twenty, then turned to a deep blue; at five and forty it grew coal black, and as large as an English shilling, but never admitted any farther alteration. He said these births were so rare, that he did not believe there could be above eleven hundred *Struldbruggs* of both sexes in the whole kingdom, of which he computed about fifty in the metropolis, and, among the rest a young girl born about three years ago. That these productions were not peculiar to any family but a mere effect of chance, and the children of the *Struldbruggs* themselves were equally mortal with the rest of the people.

I freely own myself to have been struck with inexpressible delight upon hearing this account: and the person who gave it me happening to understand the *Balnibarbian* language, which I spoke very well, I could not forbear breaking out into expressions perhaps a little too extravagant. I cried out, as in a rapture: 'Happy nation where every child hath at least a chance for being immortal! Happy people who enjoy so many living examples of ancient virtue, and have masters ready to instruct them in the wisdom of all former ages! But happiest, beyond all comparison, are those excellent *Struldbruggs*, who, born exempt from that universal calamity of human nature, have their minds free and disengaged, without the weight and depression of spirits caused by the continual apprehensions of death.' I discovered my admiration that I had not observed any of these illustrious persons at court: the black spot on the forehead being so remarkable a distinction that I could not have easily overlooked it; and it was impossible that his Majesty, a most judicious prince, should not provide himself with a good number of such wise and able counsellors. Yet perhaps the virtue of those reverend sages was too strict for the corrupt and libertine manners of a court. And we often find by experience that young men are too opinionated and volatile to be guided by the sober dictates of their seniors. However, since the King was pleased to allow me access to his royal person, I was resolved upon the very first occasion to deliver my opinion to him on this matter freely and at large by the help of my interpreter; and whether he would please to take my advice or no, yet in one thing I was determined, that his Majesty having frequently offered me an establishment in this country, I would with great thankfulness accept the favour, and pass my life here in the conversation of those superior beings the *Struldbruggs*, if they would please to admit me.

The gentleman to whom I addressed my discourse, because (as I have already observed) he spoke the language of *Balnibarbi*, said to me with a sort of a smile, which usually ariseth from pity to the ignorant, that he was glad of any occasion to keep me among them, and desired my permission to explain to the company what I had spoke. He did so, and they talked together for some time in their own language, whereof I understood not a syllable, neither could I observe by their countenances what impression my discourse had made on them. After a short silence the same person told me that his friends and mine (so he thought fit to express himself) were very much pleased with the judicious remarks I had made on the great happiness and advantages of immortal life, and they were desirous to know in a particular manner, what scheme of living I should have formed to myself, if it had fallen to my lot to have been born a *Struldbrugg*.

I answered, it was easy to be eloquent on so copious and delightful a subject, especially to me who have been often apt to amuse myself with visions of what I should do if I were a king, a general, or a great lord; and upon this very case I had frequently run over the whole system how I should employ myself, and pass the time if I were sure to live for ever.

That, if it had been my good fortune to come into the world a *Struldbrugg*, as soon as I could discover my own happiness by understanding the difference between life and death, I would first resolve by all arts and methods whatsoever to procure myself riches; in the pursuit of which by thrift and management, I might reasonably expect in about two hundred years to be the wealthiest man in the kingdom. In the second place, I would from my earliest youth apply myself to the study of arts and sciences, by which I should arrive in time to excel all others in learning. Lastly I would carefully record every action and event of consequence that happened in the public, impartially draw the characters of the several successions of princes, and great ministers of state, with my own observations on every point. I would exactly set down the several changes in customs, language, fashions of dress, diet, and diversions. By all which acquirements, I should be a living treasury of knowledge and wisdom, and certainly become the oracle of the nation.

I would never marry after threescore, but live in a hospitable manner, yet still on the saving side. I would entertain myself in forming and directing the minds of hopeful young men, by convincing them from my own remembrance, experience and observation, fortified by numerous examples, of the usefulness of virtue in public and private life. But, my choice and constant companions should be a set of my own immortal brotherhood; among whom I would elect a dozen from the most ancient down to my own contemporaries. Where any of these wanted fortunes, I would provide them with convenient lodges round my own estate, and have some of them always at my table, only mingling a few of the most valuable among you mortals, whom length of time would harden me to lose with little or no reluctance, and treat your posterity after the same manner, just as a man diverts himself with the annual succession of pinks and tulips in his garden, without regretting the loss of those which withered the preceding year.

These *Struldbruggs* and I would mutually communicate our observations and memorials through the course of time, remark the several gradations by which corruption steals into the world, and oppose it in every step, by giving perpetual warning and instruction to mankind; which, added to the strong influence of our own example, would probably prevent that continual degeneracy of human nature so justly complained of in all ages.

Add to all this, the pleasure of seeing the various revolutions of states and empires, the changes in the lower and upper world, ancient cities in ruins, and obscure villages become the seats of kings; famous rivers lessening into shallow brooks, the ocean leaving one coast dry, and overwhelming another; the discovery of many countries yet unknown; barbarity overrunning the politest nations, and the most barbarous become civilized. I should then see the discovery of the longitude, the perpetual motion, the universal medicine, and many other great inventions, brought to the utmost perfection.

What wonderful discoveries should we make in astronomy, by outliving and confirming our own predictions, by observing the progress and return of comets, with the changes of motion in the sun, moon, and stars.

I enlarged upon many other topics which the natural desire of endless life and sublunary happiness could easily furnish me with. When I had ended, and the sum of my discourse had been interpreted as before to the rest of the company, there was a good deal of talk among them in the language of the country, not without some laughter at my expense. At last the same gentleman who had been my interpreter said he was desired by the rest to set me right in a few mistakes which I had fallen into through the common imbecility of human nature, and upon that allowance was less answerable for them. That, this breed of *Struldbruggs* was peculiar to their country, for there were no such people either in *Balnibarbi* or Japan, where he had the honour to be ambassador from his Majesty, and found the natives in both those kingdoms very hard to believe that the fact was possible, and it appeared from my astonishment when he first mentioned the matter to me, that I received it as a thing wholly new, and scarcely to be credited. That in the two kingdoms above mentioned, where during his residence he had conversed very much, he observed long life to be the universal desire and wish of mankind. That whoever had one foot in the grave, was sure to hold back the other as strongly as he could. That the oldest had still hopes of living one day longer, and looked on death as the greatest evil, from which nature always prompted him to retreat; only in this island of *Luggnagg* the appetite for living was not so eager, from the continual example of the *Struldbruggs* before their eyes.

That the system of living contrived by me was unreasonable and unjust, because it supposed a perpetuity of youth, health, and vigour, which no man could be so foolish to hope, however extravagant he may be in his wishes. That the question therefore was not whether a man would choose to be always in the prime of youth, attended with prosperity and health, but how he would pass a perpetual life under all the usual disadvantages which old age brings along with it. For although few men will avow their desires of being immortal upon such hard conditions, yet in the two kingdoms before-mentioned of *Balnibarbi* and Japan, he observed that every man desired to put off death for sometime longer, let it approach ever so late, and he rarely heard of any man who died willingly, except he were incited by the extremity of grief or torture. And he appealed to me whether in those countries I had travelled as well as my own, I had not observed the same general disposition.

After this preface he gave me a particular account of the *Struldbruggs* among them. He said they commonly acted like mortals, till about thirty years old, after which by degrees they grew melancholy and dejected, increasing in both till they came to four-score. This he learned from their own confession; for otherwise, there not being above two or three of that species born in an age, they were too few to form a general observation by. When they came to four-score years, which is reckoned the extremity of living in this country, they had not only all the follies and infirmities of other old men, but many more which arose from the dreadful prospects of never dying. They were not only opinionative, peevish, covetous, morose, vain, talkative, but incapable of friendship, and dead to all natural affection, which never descended below their grandchildren. Envy and impotent desires are their prevailing passions. But those objects against which their envy seems principally directed, are the vices of the younger sort, and the deaths of the old. By reflecting on the former they find themselves cut off from all possibility of pleasure; and whenever they see a funeral, they lament and repine that others have gone to a harbour of rest, to which they themselves never can hope to arrive. They have no remembrance of any thing but what they learned and observed in their youth and middle age, and even that is very imperfect. And for the truth or particulars of any fact it is safer to depend on common traditions than upon their best recollections. The least miserable among them appear to be those who turn to dotage, and entirely lose their understandings; these meet with more pity and assistance, because they want many bad qualities which abound in others.

If a *Struldbrugg* happen to marry one of his own kind, the marriage is dissolved of course by the courtesy of the kingdom, as soon as the younger of the two comes to be four-score. For the law thinks it a reasonable indulgence, that those who are condemned without any fault of their own to a perpetual continuance in the world, should not have their misery doubled by the load of a wife.

As soon as they have completed the term of eighty years, they are looked on as dead in law; their heirs immediately succeed to their estates, only a small pittance is reserved for their support, and the poor ones are maintained at the public charge. After that period they are held incapable of any employment of trust or profit, they cannot purchase lands or take leases, neither are they allowed to be witnesses in any cause, either civil or criminal, not even for the decision of meres[1] and bounds.

At ninety they lose their teeth and hair; they have at that age no distinction of taste, but eat and drink whatever they can get, without relish or appetite. The diseases they were subject to still continue without increasing or diminishing. In talking they forget the common appellation of things, and the names of persons, even of those who are their nearest friends and relations. For the same reason they never can amuse themselves with reading, because their memory will not serve to carry them from the beginning of a sentence to the end; and by this defect they are deprived of the only entertainment whereof they might otherwise be capable.

The language of this country being always upon the flux, the *Struldbruggs* of one age do not understand those of another, neither are they able after two hundred years to hold any conversation (farther than by a few general words) with their neighbours the mortals, and thus they lie under the disadvantage of living like foreigners in their own country.

This was the account given me of the *Struldbruggs*, as near as I can remember. I afterwards saw five or six of different ages, the youngest not above two hundred years old, who were brought to me at several

---

1 *meres*: boundaries or boundary markers.

times by some of my friends; but although they were told that I was a great traveller, and had seen all the world, they had not the least curiosity to ask me a question; only desired I would give them *Slumskudask*, or a token of remembrance, which is a modest way of begging, to avoid the law that strictly forbids it, because they are provided for by the public, although indeed with a very scanty allowance.

They are despised and hated by all sorts of people; when one of them is born, it is reckoned ominous, and their birth is recorded very particularly; so that you may know their age by consulting the registry, which however hath not been kept above a thousand years past, or at least hath been destroyed by time or public disturbances. But the usual way of computing how old they are, is by asking them what kings or great persons they can remember, and then consulting history; for infallibly the last prince in their mind did not begin his reign after they were four-score years old.

They were the most mortifying sight I ever beheld, and the women more horrible than the men. Besides the usual deformities in extreme old age, they acquired an additional ghastliness in proportion to their number of years, which is not to be described, and among half a dozen I soon distinguished which was the eldest, although there was not above a century or two between them.

The reader will easily believe, that from what I had heard and seen, my keen appetite for perpetuity of life was much abated. I grew heartily ashamed of the pleasing visions I had formed, and thought no tyrant could invent a death into which I would not run with pleasure from such a life. The king heard of all that had passed between me and my friends upon this occasion, and rallied me very pleasantly, wishing I could send a couple of *Struldbruggs* to my own country, to arm our people against the fear of death; but this it seems is forbidden by the fundamental laws of the kingdom, or else I should have been well content with the trouble and expense of transporting them.

I could not but agree that the laws of this kingdom relating to the *Struldbruggs* were founded upon the strongest reasons, and such as any other country would be under the necessity of enacting in the like circumstances. Otherwise, as avarice is the necessary consequent of old age, those immortals would in time become proprietors of the whole nation, and engross the civil power, which, for want of abilities to manage, must end in the ruin of the public.

[Gulliver's final voyage took him to the land of the Houyhnhms (the name echoes the neighing 'hwee-nim'). These are horse-like rational creatures who rule over the Yahoos, savage creatures who have human form.]

As I ought to have understood human nature much better than I supposed it possible for my master [a Houyhnhm] to do, so it was easy to apply the character he gave of the *Yahoos* to myself and my countrymen, and I believed I could yet make farther discoveries from my own observation. I therefore often begged his favour to let me go among the herds of *Yahoos* in the neighbourhood, to which he always very graciously consented, being perfectly convinced that the hatred I bore those brutes would never suffer me to be corrupted by them; and his honour ordered one of his servants, a strong sorrel nag, very honest and goodnatured, to be my guard, without whose protection I durst not undertake such adventures. For I have already told the reader how much I was pestered by these odious animals upon my first arrival. And I afterwards failed very narrowly three or four times of falling into their clutches, when I happened to stray at any distance without my hanger. And I have reason to believe they had some imagination that I was of their own species, which I often assisted myself, by stripping up my sleeves, and showing my naked arms and breasts in their sight, when my protector was with me. At which times they would approach as near as they durst, and imitate my actions after the manner of monkeys, but ever with great signs of hatred, as a tame jackdaw with cap and stockings is always persecuted by the wild ones, when he happens to be got among them.

They are prodigiously nimble from their infancy; however, I once caught a young male of three years old, and endeavoured by all marks of tenderness to make it quiet; but the little imp fell a squalling and scratching, and biting with such violence, that I was forced to let it go, and it was high time, for a whole troop of old ones came about us at the noise, but finding the cub was safe (for away it ran) and my sorrel nag being by, they durst not venture near us. I observed the young animal's flesh to smell very rank, and the stink was somewhat between a weasel and a fox, but much more disagreeable. I forgot another circumstance (and perhaps I might have the reader's pardon, if it were wholly omitted) that while I held the odious vermin in my hands, it voided its filthy excrements of a yellow liquid substance, all over my clothes; but by good fortune there was a small brook hard by, where I washed myself as clean as I could, although I durst not come into my master's presence, until I were sufficiently aired.

By what I could discover, the *Yahoos* appear to be the most unteachable of all animals, their capacities never reaching higher than to draw or carry burthens. Yet I am of opinion, this defect ariseth chiefly from a perverse, restive disposition. For they are cunning, malicious, treacherous and revengeful. They are strong and hardy, but of a cowardly spirit, and, by consequence, insolent, abject, and cruel. It is observed, that the red-haired of both sexes are more libidinous and mischievous than the rest, whom yet they much exceed in strength and activity.

The *Houyhnhnms* keep the *Yahoos* for present use in huts not far from the house; but the rest are sent abroad to certain fields, where they dig up roots, eat several kinds of herbs, and search about for carrion, or sometimes catch weasels and *Luhimuhs* (a sort of wild rat) which they greedily devour. Nature hath taught them to dig deep holes with their nails on the side of a rising ground, wherein they lie by themselves, only the kennels of the females are larger, sufficient to hold two or three cubs.

They swim from their infancy like frogs, and are able to continue long under water, where they often take fish, which the females carry home to their young. And upon this occasion, I hope the reader will pardon my relating an odd adventure.

Being one day abroad with my protector the sorrel nag, and the weather exceeding hot, I entreated him to let me bathe in a river that was near. He consented, and I immediately stripped myself stark naked, and went down softly into the stream. It happened that a young female *Yahoo* standing behind a bank saw the whole proceeding, and inflamed by desire, as the nag and I conjectured, came running with all speed, and leaped into the water within five yards of the place where I bathed. I was never in my life so terribly frightened; the nag was grazing at some distance, not suspecting any harm. She embraced me after a most fulsome manner; I roared as loud as I could, and the nag came galloping towards me, whereupon she quitted her grasp with the utmost reluctancy, and leaped upon the opposite bank, where she stood gazing and howling all the time I was putting on my clothes.

This was matter of diversion to my master and his family, as well as of mortification to myself. For now I could no longer deny that I was a real *Yahoo*, in every limb and feature, since the females had a natural propensity to me as one of their own species: neither was the hair of this brute of a red colour, (which might have been some excuse for an appetite a little irregular) but black as a sloe, and her countenance did not make an appearance altogether so hideous as the rest of the kind; for, I think, she could not be above eleven years old.

Having lived three years in this country, the reader I suppose will expect that I should, like other travellers, give him some account of the manners and customs of its inhabitants, which it was indeed my principal study to learn.

As these noble *Houyhnhnms* are endowed by nature with a general disposition to all virtues, and have no conceptions or ideas of what is evil in a rational creature, so their grand maxim is, to cultivate reason, and to be wholly governed by it. Neither is reason among them a point problematical as with us, where men can argue with plausibility on both sides of a question; but strikes you with immediate conviction; as it must needs do where it is not mingled, obscured or discoloured by passion and interest. I remember it was with extreme difficulty that I could bring my master to understand the meaning of the word opinion, or how a point could be disputable; because reason taught us to affirm or deny only where we are certain; and beyond our knowledge we cannot do either. So that controversies, wranglings, disputes, and positiveness in false or dubious propositions are evils unknown among the *Houyhnhnms*. In the like manner when I used to explain to him our several systems of natural philosophy, he would laugh that a creature pretending to reason, should value itself upon the knowledge of other people's conjectures, and in things where that knowledge, if it were certain, could be of no use. Wherein he agreed entirely with the sentiments of Socrates, as Plato delivers them; which I mention as the highest honour I can do that prince of philosophers. I have often since reflected what destruction such a doctrine would make in the libraries of Europe; and how many paths to fame would be then shut up in the learned world.

Friendship and benevolence are the two principal virtues among the *Houyhnhnms*, and these not confined to particular objects, but universal to the whole race. For a stranger from the remotest part is equally treated with the nearest neighbour, and wherever he goes, looks upon himself as at home. They preserve decency and civility in the highest degrees, but are altogether ignorant of ceremony. They have no fondness for their colts or foals, but the care they take in educating them proceeds entirely from the dictates of reason. And I observed my master to show the same affection to his neighbour's issue that he had for his own. They will have it that nature teaches them to love the whole species, and it is reason only that maketh a distinction of persons, where there is a superior degree of virtue.

When the matron *Houyhnhnms* have produced one of each sex, they no longer accompany with their consorts, except they lose one of their issue by some casualty, which very seldom happens: but in such a case they meet again. Or when the like accident befalls a person whose wife is past bearing, some other couple bestow him one of their own colts, and then go together again until the mother is pregnant. This caution is necessary to prevent the country from being overburdened with numbers. But the race of inferior *Houyhnhnms*, bred up to be servants is not so strictly limited upon this article. These are allowed to produce three of each sex, to be domestics in the noble families.

In their marriages they are exactly careful to choose such colours as will not make any disagreeable mixture in the breed. Strength is chiefly valued in the male, and comeliness in the female, not upon the account of love, but to preserve the race from degenerating; for where a female happens to excel in strength, a consort is chosen with regard to comeliness. Courtship, love, presents, jointures, settlements, have no place in their thoughts; or terms whereby to express them in their language. The young couple meet and are joined, merely because it is the determination of their parents and friends: it is what they see done every day, and they look upon it as one of the necessary actions of a rational being. But the violation of marriage, or any other unchastity, was never heard of: and the married pair pass their lives with the same friendship and mutual benevolence that they bear to all others of the same species, who come in their way; without jealousy, fondness, quarrelling, or discontent.

In educating the youth of both sexes, their method is admirable, and highly deserves our imitation. These are not suffered to taste a grain of oats, except upon certain days, till eighteen years old; nor milk, but very rarely; and in summer they graze two hours in the morning, and as long in the evening, which their parents likewise observe, but the servants are not allowed above half that time, and a great part of their grass is brought home which they eat at the most convenient hours, when they can be best spared from work.

Temperance, industry, exercise and cleanliness are the lessons equally enjoined to the young ones of both sexes; and my master thought it monstrous in us to give the females a different kind of education from the males, except in some articles of domestic management; whereby, as he truly observed, one half of our natives were good for nothing but bringing children into the world; and to trust the care of our children to such useless animals, he said, was yet a greater instance of brutality....

[*GULLIVER'S RETURN TO HIS HOME*]

[*Expelled by the Houyhnhms as a danger to society he has been rescued against his wishes by some Portuguese sailors whose captain takes him to Lisbon and persuades him to take a passage to England.*]

My wife and family received me with great surprise and joy, because they concluded me certainly dead; but I must freely confess the sight of them filled me only with hatred, disgust, and contempt, and the more by reflecting on the near alliance I had to them. For, although since my unfortunate exile from the *Houyhnhnm* country I had compelled myself to tolerate the sight of *Yahoos*, and to converse with Don Pedro de Mendez, yet my memory and imagination were perpetually filled with the virtues and ideas of those exalted *Houyhnhnms*. And when I began to consider, that by copulating with one of the *Yahoo*-species I had become a parent of more, it struck me with the utmost shame, confusion and horror.

A soon as I entered the house, my wife took me in her arms, and kissed me, at which, having not been used to the touch of that odious animal for so many years, I fell into a swoon for almost an hour. At the time I am writing it is five years since my last return to England: during the first year I could not endure my wife or children in my presence, the very smell of them was intolerable, much less could I suffer them to eat in the same room. To this hour they dare not presume to touch my bread, or drink out of the same cup, neither was I ever able to let one of them take me by the hand. The first money I laid out was to buy two young stone-horses[1] which I keep in a good stable, and next to them, the groom is my greatest favourite; for I feel my spirits revived by the smell he contracts in the stable. My horses understand me tolerably well; I converse with them at least four hours every day. They are strangers to bridle or saddle, they live in great amity with me, and friendship to each other.

---

1 *stone-horses*: ungelded horses, stallions.

An Epigram on Scolding
(1746)

Great folks are of a finer mould;
Lord! how politely they can scold;
While a coarse English tongue will itch,
For whore and rogue; and dog and bitch.

Verses Made for the Women Who Cry Apples, etc.
(1746)

APPLES

Come buy my fine wares,
   Plums, apples, and pears,
   A hundred a penny,
   In conscience too many,
   Come, will you have any;
My children are seven,
I wish them in heaven,
My husband's a sot,
With his pipe and his pot,
Not a farthing will gain 'em,
And I must maintain 'em.

ASPARAGUS

   Ripe 'sparagrass,
   Fit for lad or lass,
   To make their water pass:
   O, 'tis a pretty picking
   With a tender chicken.

ONIONS

   Come, follow me by the smell,
   Here's delicate onions to sell,
   I promise to use you well.
They make the blood warmer,
You'll feed like a farmer:

For this is every cook's opinion,
No savoury dish without an onion;
But lest your kissing should be spoiled,
Your onions must be thoroughly boiled;
    Or else you may spare
    Your mistress a share,
The secret will never be known;
    She cannot discover
    The breath of her lover,
But think is as sweet as her own.

OYSTERS

    Charming oysters I cry,
    My masters come buy,
    So plump and so fresh,
    So sweet is their flesh,
    No Colchester oyster,
    Is sweeter and moister,
    Your stomach they settle,
    And rouse up your mettle,
    They'll make you a dad
    Of a lass or a lad;
    And Madam your wife
They'll please to the life;
Be she barren, be she old,
Be she slut, or be she scold,
Eat my oysters, and lie near her
She'll be fruitful, never fear her.

HERRINGS

    Be not sparing,
    Leave off swearing,
    Buy my herring
    Fresh from Malahide,
    Better ne'er was tried.
Come eat 'em with pure fresh butter and mustard,
Their bellies are soft, and as white as a custard.
Come, sixpence a dozen to get me some bread,
Or, like my own herrings, I soon shall be dead.

ORANGES

Come, buy my fine oranges, sauce for your veal,
And charming when squeezed in a pot of brown ale.
Well roasted, with sugar and wine in a cup,
They'll make a sweet bishop[1] when gentlefolks sup.

Early Disappointments Recollected by Swift

FROM SWIFT'S LETTER TO CHARLES FORD, 12 NOVEMBER 1708

I formerly used to envy my own Happiness when I was a Schoolboy, the delicious Holidays, the Saterday afternoon, and the charming Custards in a blind Alley; I never considered the Confinement ten hours a day, to Nouns and Verbs, the Terror of the Rod, the bloddy Noses, and broken Shins.

FROM THOMAS SHERIDAN, *THE LIFE OF THE REV. DR JONATHAN SWIFT* (1784)

When I was a schoolboy at Kilkenny, and in the lower form, I longed very much to have a horse of my own to ride on. One day I saw a poor man leading a very mangy lean horse out of the town to kill him for the skin. I asked the man if he would sell him, which he readily consented to upon my offering him somewhat more than the price of the hide, which was all the money I had in the world. I immediately got on him, to the great envy of some of my school fellows, and to the ridicule of others, and rode him about the town. The horse soon tired, and laid down. As I had no stable to put him into, nor any money to pay for his sustenance, I began to find out what a foolish bargain I had made, and cried heartily for the loss of my cash; but the horse dying soon after upon the spot gave me some relief.

FROM SWIFT'S LETTER TO VISCOUNT BOLINGBROKE AND ALEXANDER POPE, 5 APRIL 1729

I never wake without finding life a more insignificant thing than it was the day before: which is one great advantage I get by living in

---

1 *bishop*: a mulled wine drunk with oranges and lemon and sugar (probably derived from the Dutch *bisschop*).

this country, where there is nothing I shall be sorry to lose; but my greatest misery is recollecting the scene of twenty years past, and then all on a sudden dropping into the present. I remember when I was a little boy, I felt a great fish at the end of my line which I drew up almost on the ground, but it dropt in, and the disappointment vexeth me to this very day, and I believe it was the type of all my future disappointments.

Verses on the Death of Dr Swift, D.S.P.D.
(1739)

Dans l'adversité de nos meilleurs amis nous trouvons quelque chose, qui ne nous deplaist pas.[1]

As Rochefoucauld[2] his maxims drew
From Nature, I believe 'em true:
They argue no corrupted mind
In him; the fault is in mankind.

This maxim more than all the rest
Is thought too base for human breast;
'In all distresses of our friends
'We first consult our private ends,
'While nature kindly bent to ease us,
'Points out some circumstance to please us'.

If this perhaps your patience move
Let reason and experience prove.

We all behold with envious eyes,
Our equal raised above our size;
Who would not at a crowded show,
Stand high himself, keep others low?
I love my friend as well as you,
But would not have him stop my view;

---

1 *Dans l'adversité ... deplaist pas*: 'In the adversity of our best friends, we find something that doth not displease us' (Rochefoucauld, *Maximes supprimées* No. 18).
2 *Rochefoucauld*: duc François de la Rochefoucauld (1613–1680), French author of the *Reflexions ou sentences et maximes morales* (1665).

Then let him have the higher post;
I ask but for an inch at most.

　　If in a Battle you should find,
One, whom you love of all mankind,
Had some heroic action done,
A champion killed, or trophy won;
Rather than thus be overtopped,
Would you not wish his laurels cropped?

　　Dear honest Ned is in the gout,
Lies racked with pain, and you without:
How patiently you hear him groan!
How glad the case is not your own!

　　What poet would not grieve to see,
His brethren write as well as he?
But rather than they should excel,
He'd wish his rivals all in hell.

　　Her end when emulation misses,
She turns to envy, stings and hisses:
The strongest friendship yields to pride,
Unless the odds be on our side.

　　Vain humankind! Fantastic race!
Thy various follies, who can trace?
Self-love, ambition, envy, pride,
Their empire in our hearts divide:
Give others riches, power, and station,
'Tis all on me a usurpation.
I have no title to aspire;
Yet, when you sink, I seem the higher.
In POPE,[1] I cannot read a Line,
But with a sigh, I wish it mine:
When he can in one couplet fix
More sense than I can do in six:
It gives me such a jealous fit,
I cry, 'Pox take him, and his wit.'

---

1 *Pope*: Alexander Pope (1688–1744), English poet and satirist.

Why must I be outdone by GAY,[1]
In my own humorous biting way?

ARBUTHNOTT[2] is no more my friend,
Who dares to irony pretend;
Which I was born to introduce,
Refined it first, and showed its use.

ST. JOHN,[3] as well as PULTENEY[4] knows,
That I had some repute for prose;
And till they drove me out of date,
Could maul a minister of state:
If they have mortified my pride,
And made me throw my pen aside;
If with such talents heaven hath blest 'em,
Have I not reason to detest 'em?

To all my foes, dear fortune, send
Thy gifts, but never to my friend:
I tamely can endure the first,
But, this with envy makes me burst.

Thus much may serve by way of proem,
Proceed we therefore to our poem.

The time is not remote, when I
Must by the course of nature die:
When I foresee my special friends,
Will try to find their private ends:
Though it is hardly understood,
Which way my death can do them good;
Yet thus, methinks, I hear 'em speak;
'See, how the Dean begins to break:
Poor Gentleman, he droops apace,

---

1 *Gay*: John Gay (1685–1732), English poet and dramatist.
2 *Arbuthnot*: John Arbuthnot (1667–1735), Scottish physician and satirist.
3 *St. John*: Henry St John (1678–1751), Viscount Bolingbroke, who shared the leadership of the Tory party with Robert Harley, 1st Earl of Oxford. He negotiated the Treaty of Utrecht in 1713 and was plotting a Jacobite rebellion when Queen Anne died; this led to his dismissal and subsequent exile in France.
4. *Pulteney*: William Pulteney (1684–1764), statesman, Secretary-at-War (1714) and First Lord of the Treasury (1746).

You plainly find it in his face:
That old vertigo in his head,
Will never leave him, till he's dead:
Besides, his memory decays,
He recollects not what he says;
He cannot call his friends to mind;
Forgets the place where last he dined:
Plies you with stories o'er and o'er,
He told them fifty times before.
How does he fancy we can sit,
To hear his out-of-fashioned wit?
But he takes up with younger folks,
Who for his wine will bear his jokes:
Faith, he must make his stories shorter,
Or change his comrades once a quarter:
In half the time, he talks them round;
There must another set be found.

   'For Poetry, he's past his prime,
He takes an hour to find a rhyme:
His fire is out, his wit decayed,
His fancy sunk, his Muse a jade.
I'd have him throw away his pen;
But there's no talking to some men.'

   And, then their tenderness appears,
By adding largely to my years:
'He's older than he would be reckoned,
And well remembers *Charles* the Second.[1]

   'He hardly drinks a pint of wine;
And that, I doubt, is no good sign.
His stomach too begins to fail:
Last year we thought him strong and hale;
But now, he's quite another thing;
I wish he may hold out till Spring.'

   Then hug themselves, and reason thus;
'It is not yet so bad with us.'

---

1 *Charles the Second*: Charles II (1630–1685), King of Great Britain and Ireland.

In such a case they talk in tropes,
And, by their fears express their hopes:
Some great misfortune to portend,
No enemy can match a friend;
With all the kindness they profess,
The merit of a lucky guess,
(When daily 'Howd'y's' come of course,
And servants answer: 'Worse and worse')
Would please 'em better than to tell,
That, GOD be praised, the Dean is well.
Then he who prophesied the best,
Approves his foresight to the rest:
'You know, I always feared the worst,
And often told you so at first:'
He'd rather choose that I should die,
Than his prediction prove a lie.
Not one foretells I shall recover;
But, all agree, to give me over.

Yet should some neighbour feel a pain,
Just in the parts, where I complain;
How many a message would he send?
What hearty prayers that I should mend?
Enquire what regimen I kept;
What gave me ease, and how I slept?
And more lament, when I was dead,
Than all the snivellers round my bed.

My good companions, never fear,
For though you may mistake a year;
Though your prognostics run too fast,
They must be verified at last.

'Behold the fatal day arrive!
How is the Dean? He's just alive.
Now the departing prayer is read:
He hardly breathes. The Dean is dead.
Before the passing-bell begun,
The news through half the town has run.
O, may we all for Death prepare!
What has he left? And who's his heir?

I know no more than what the news is,
'Tis all bequeathed to public uses.
To public use! A perfect whim!
What had the public done for him!
'Mere envy, avarice, and pride!
'He gave it all: – But first he died.
'And had the Dean, in all the nation,
'No worthy friend, no poor relation?
'So ready to do strangers good,
'Forgetting his own flesh and blood?

Now Grub-Street[1] Wits are all employed;
With elegies, the town is cloyed:
Some paragraph in every paper,
To *curse* the *Dean*, or *bless* the *Drapier*.[2]

The doctors tender of their fame,
Wisely on me lay all the blame:
'We must confess his case was nice;
But he would never take advice:
Had he been ruled, for ought appears,
He might have lived these twenty years:
For when we opened him we found,
That all his vital parts were sound.'

From Dublin soon to London spread,
'Tis told at Court, the Dean is dead.

Kind Lady Suffolk[3] in the spleen,
Runs laughing up to tell the Queen.
The Queen, so gracious, mild, and good,
Cries, 'Is he gone? 'Tis time he should.
He's dead you say; why let him rot;
I'm glad the medals were forgot.

---

1 *Grub-Street*: Dr Johnson described it in his Dictionary as near Moorfields in London, 'much inhabited by writers of small histories, dictionaries, and temporary poems, whence any mean production is called *grubstreet*.'
2 *the Drapier*: under the name of 'M. B.' a Dublin Drapier, Swift had published five letters urging the people of Ireland to resist granting a patent to William Wood to mint halfpence for Ireland.
3 *Lady Suffolk*: Henrietta Howard, Countess of Suffolk (?1687–1797), Bedchamber Woman to Princess Caroline and mistress of the Prince of Wales.

I promised them, I own; but when?
I only was the princess then;
But now as consort of the King,
You know 'tis quite a different thing.

Now, Chartres[1] at Sir Robert's levee,[2]
Tells, with a sneer, the tidings heavy:
'Why, is he dead without his shoes?'[3]
(Cries Bob) 'I'm sorry for the news;
Oh, were the wretch but living still,
And in his place my good friend Will;[4]
Or, had a mitre on his head
Provided Bolingbroke were dead.'

Now Curll[5] his shop from rubbish drains;
Three genuine tomes of Swift's remains.
And then to make them pass the glibber,
Revised by *Tibbalds, Moore, and Cibber.*[6]
He'll treat me as he does my betters.
Publish my will, my life, my letters.
Revive the libels born to die;
Which POPE must bear, as well as I.

Here shift the scene, to represent
How those I love, my death lament.
Poor POPE will grieve a month; and GAY
A week; and ARBUTHNOTT a day.

ST. JOHN himself will scarce forbear,
To bite his pen, and drop a tear.

---

1 *Chartres*: Colonel Francis Chartres (1675–1732), Scottish landlord. He had tried to bribe his way into Parliament in 1727. A debauchee, usurer and gambler, he was convicted of rape in 1730 but was released from prison, through, it was suggested, Walpole 's intervention.
2 *Sir Robert's levee*: A reference to Sir Robert Walpole (1676–1745). In 1712 he was expelled from the House of Commons and sent to the Tower of London for alleged corruption, but after the accession of George I he became Chancellor of the Exchequer and First Lord of the Treasury. He was a Whig, a shrewd and unscrupulous manipulator.
3 *without his shoes*: a slang phrase for being hanged.
4 *Will*: William Pulteney.
5 *Curll*: Edmund Curll (1675–1747), bookseller and pamphleteer, known for his literary frauds and indecent publications.
6 *Tibbalds, Moore, and Cibber*: Lewis Theobald (1688–1744), dramatist, poet, and editor of Shakespeare (King of the Duncis in Pope's *The Dunciad*); James Moore Smythe (1702–1734), poetaster and playwright; Colley Cibber (1671-1757), actor, playwright and singularly undeserving poet laureate (he succeeded Theobald as 'King Dunce').

The rest will give a shrug and cry,
'I'm sorry; but we all must die.'
Indifference clad in wisdom's guise,
All fortitude of mind supplies:
For how can stony bowels melt,
In those who never pity felt;
When *we* are lashed, *they* kiss the rod;
Resigning to the Will of God.

　　The fools, my juniors by a year,
Are tortured with suspense and fear.
Who wisely thought my age a screen,
When death approached, to stand between:
The screen removed, their hearts are trembling,
They mourn for me without dissembling.

　　My female friends, whose tender hearts
Have better learned to act their parts.
Receive the news in doleful dumps,
'The Dean is dead, (*and what is trumps?*)
Then Lord have mercy on his Soul.
(*Ladies, I'll venture for the vole.*[1])
Six Deans they say must bear the pall.
(*I wish I knew what King to call.*)'
'Madam, your husband will attend
The funeral of so good a friend.'
'No Madam, 'tis a shocking sight,
And he's engaged tomorrow night!
My Lady Club would take it ill,
If he should fail her at quadrille.
He loved the Dean. (*I lead a heart.*)
But dearest friends, they say, must part.
His time was come, he ran his race;
We hope he's in a better place.'

　　Why do we grieve that friends should die?
No loss more easy to supply.
One year is past; a different scene;
No further mention of the Dean;

---

1 *the vole*: in the card game quadrille, to win all the tricks.

Who now, alas, no more is missed,
Than if he never did exist.
Where's now this favourite of Apollo?
Departed; and his works must follow:
Must undergo the common fate;
His kind of wit is out of date.
Some country squire to Lintot[1] goes,
Inquires for SWIFT in Verse and Prose:
Says Lintot, 'I have heard the name:
He died a year ago.' The same.
He searcheth all his shop in vain;
'Sir you may find them in Duck Lane:[2]
I sent them with a load of books,
Last Monday to the pastry-cook's.
To fancy they could live a year!
I find you're but a stranger here.
The Dean was famous in his time;
And had a kind of knack at rhyme:
His way of writing now is past;
The town hath got a better taste:
I keep no antiquated stuff;
But, spick and span I have enough.
Pray, do but give me leave to show 'em;
Here's Colley Cibber's birthday poem.
This ode you never yet have seen,
By Stephen Duck,[3] upon the Queen.
Then, here's a letter finely penned
Against the *Craftsman*[4] and his friend;
It clearly shows that all reflection
On ministers, is disaffection.
Next, here's Sir Robert's Vindication.
And Mr Henly's[5] last oration:
The hawkers have not got 'em yet,
Your honour please to buy a set?

---

1 *Lintot*: Bernard Lintot (1675–1736), bookseller, who published several of Pope's works, including his translations of Homer.
2 *Duck Lane*: where second-hand books were sold.
3 *Stephen Duck*: 'the thresher poet' (1705–1756), a farm-labourer whose verses incurred the favour of Queen Caroline.
4 the *Craftsman*: a paper founded by Bolingbroke and Pulteney in 1726 to discredit Walpole.
5 *Mr Henly*: Rev. John Henley (1692–1756), an Independent preacher known as 'Orator Henley', who defended Walpole in *The Hyp Doctor.*

'Here's Woolston's Tracts,⁶ the twelfth Edition;
'Tis read by every politician:
The country members, when in town,
To all their boroughs send them down:
You never met a thing so smart;
The courtiers have them all by heart:
Those maids of honour (who can read)
Are taught to use them for their creed.
The reverend author's good intention,
Hath been rewarded with a pension:
He doth an honour to his gown,
By bravely running priestcraft down:
He shows, as sure as GOD'S in Gloucester,
That Jesus was a grand impostor:
That all his miracles were cheats,
Performed as jugglers do their feats:
The Church had never such a writer:
A shame, he hath not got a mitre!

Suppose me dead; and then suppose
A club assembled at the Rose;
Where from discourse of this and that,
I grow the subject of their chat:
And, while they toss my name about,
With favour some, and some without;
One quite indifferent in the cause,
My character impartial draws:

'The Dean, if we believe report,
Was never ill received at court:
As for his works in verse and prose,
I own myself no judge of those:
Nor, can I tell what critics thought 'em;
But, this I know, all people bought 'em;
As with a moral view designed
To cure the vices of mankind:
His vein, ironically grave,
Exposed the fool, and lashed the knave:

---

1 *Woolston's Tracts*: Rev. Thomas Woolston (1670–1733) a freethinker who was tried for
blasphemy in 1729.

To steal a hint was never known,
But what he writ was all his own.

   'He never thought an honour done him,
Because a duke was proud to own him:
Would rather slip aside, and choose
To talk with wits in dirty shoes:
Despis'd the fools with stars and garters,
So often seen caressing Chartres:
He never courted men in station,
Nor persons held in admiration;
Of no man's greatness was afraid,
Because he sought for no man's aid.
Though trusted long in great affairs,
He gave himself no haughty airs:
Without regarding private ends,
Spent all his credit for his friends:
And only chose the wise and good;
No flatterers; no allies in blood;
But succoured virtue in distress,
And seldom failed of good success;
As numbers in their hearts must own,
Who, but for him, had been unknown.

   'With princes kept a due decorum,
But never stood in awe before 'em:
And to her Majesty, GOD bless her,
Would speak as free as to her dresser,
She thought it his peculiar whim,
Nor took it ill as come from him.
He followed David's lesson just,
"In Princes never put thy trust."
And, would you make him truly sour;
Provoke him with a slave in power:
The Irish Senate, if you named,
With what Impatience he declaimed!
Fair LIBERTY was all his cry;
For her he stood prepared to die;
For her he boldly stood alone;
For her he oft exposed his own.
Two Kingdoms just as factions led,

Had set a price upon his head;
But, not a Traitor could be found,
To sell him for six-hundred pound.[1]

'Had he but spared his tongue and pen,
He might have rose like other men:
But, Power was never in his thought;
And, wealth he valued not a groat:
Ingratitude he often found,
And pitied those who meant the wound:
But, kept the tenor of his mind,
To merit well of humankind:
Nor made a sacrifice of those
Who still were true, to please his foes.
He laboured many a fruitless hour
To reconcile his friends in power;
Saw mischief by a faction brewing,
While they pursued each other's ruin.
But, finding vain was all his care,
He left the Court in mere despair.

'And, oh! how short are human schemes!
Here ended all our golden dreams.
What ST. JOHN's skill in state affairs,
What ORMONDE's valour,[2] OXFORD's cares,[3]
To save their sinking country lent,
Was all destroyed by one event.[4]
Too soon that precious life was ended,
On which alone, our weal depended.
When up a dangerous faction starts,
With wrath and vengeance in their hearts:
By solemn league and covenant bound,
To ruin, slaughter, and confound;
To turn religion to a fable,

---

1 *six-hundred pound*: the House of Lords offered a £300 reward for identifying the author of the *Public Spirit of the Whigs*, while in Ireland the same sum was offered for the identification of the author of *The Drapier's Fourth Letter*.
2 *Ormonde's valour*: James Butler, Duke of Ormonde (1665–1745), a Jacobite who joined William of Orange and fought at the Battle of the Boyne. He succeeded Marlborough as Captain-General. He went into exile in France in 1714.
3. *Oxford's cares*: Robert Harley, 1st Earl of Oxford, was the founder of the South Sea Company (of the South Sea Bubble).
4 *destroyed by one event*: Queen Anne died on 1 August 1714.

And make the government a Babel:
Pervert the law, disgrace the gown,
Corrupt the senate, rob the crown;
To sacrifice old England's glory,
And make her infamous in story.
When such a tempest shook the land,
How could unguarded virtue stand?

'With horror, grief, despair the Dean
Beheld the dire destructive scene:
His Friends in exile, or the Tower,[1]
Himself within the frown of power;
Pursu'd by base envenomed pens,
Far to the land of slaves and fens;[2]
A servile race in folly nursed,
Who truckle most, when treated worst.

'By innocence and resolution,
He bore continual persecution;
While numbers to preferment rose;
Whose merits were, to be his foes.
When, *ev'n his own familiar friends*
Intent upon their private ends,
Like renegadoes now he feels,
Against him lifting up their heels.

'The Dean did by his pen defeat
An infamous destructive cheat.
Taught fools their interest how to know;
And gave them arms to ward the blow.
Envy hath owned it was his doing,
To save that helpless land from ruin,
While they who at the steerage stood,
And reaped the profit, sought his blood.

'To save them from their evil fate,
In him was held a crime of state.
A wicked monster on the bench,[3]
Whose fury blood could never quench;

---

1 *in exile, or the tower*: see notes on Harley and St John.
2 *land of slaves and fens*: Ireland.
3 *monster on the bench*: William Whitshed (1656–1727), Chief Justice of the King's Bench in Ireland; when the jury acquitted Edward Waters of sedition for printing Swift's anonymous pamphlet *Proposal for the Universal Use of Irish Manufacture*, he sent the jury back nine times.

As vile and profligate a villain,
As modern Scroggs,[1] or old Tressilian;[2]
Who long all justice had discarded,
Nor feared he GOD, *nor man regarded*;
Vowed on the Dean his rage to vent,
And make him of his zeal repent;
But Heaven his innocence defends,
The grateful people stand his friends:
Not strains of law, nor judges' frown,
Nor topics brought to please the crown,
Nor witness hired, nor jury picked,
Prevail to bring him in convict.

'In exile with a steady heart,
He spent his life's declining part;
Where, folly, pride, and faction sway,
Remote from ST. JOHN POPE, and GAY.

'His Friendship there to few confined,
Were always of the middling kind:
No fools of rank, a mongrel breed,
Who fain would pass for lords indeed:
Where titles give no right or power,
And peerage is a withered flower,
He would have held it a disgrace,
If such a wretch had known his face.
On rural squires, that kingdom's bane,
He vented oft his wrath in vain:
Biennial squires, to market brought;
Who sell their souls and votes for naught;
The nation stripped, go joyful back,
To rob the church, their tenants rack,
Go snacks with thieves and rapparees,[3]
And; keep the peace, to pick up fees
In every job to have a share,
A gaol or barrack to repair;
And turn the tax for public roads
Commodious to their own abodes.

---

1 *Scroggs*: William Scroggs (?1623–1683), Lord Chief Justice (1678–1681); he was impeached in 1680 and removed from office.
2 *Tressilian*: Sir Robert Tressilian, Chief Justice at the time of the Peasants' Revolt, hanged in 1388 by the lords appellant.
3 *rapparees*: 18th century Irish Jacobite irregulars, called after their weapons *rapaire* in Irish, or half-pikes. The term came to mean bandits or highwaymen.

'Perhaps I may allow the Dean
Had too much Satire in his vein;
And seemed determined not to starve it,
Because no age could more deserve it.
Yet, malice never was his aim;
He lashed the vice but spared the name.
No individual could resent,
Where thousands equally were meant.
His Satire points at no defect,
But what all mortals may correct;
For he abhorred that senseless tribe,
Who call it humour when they jibe:
He spared a hump or crooked nose,
Whose owners set not up for beaux.
True genuine dullness moved his pity,
Unless it offered to be witty.
Those, who their ignorance confessed,
He ne'er offended with a jest;
But laughed to hear an idiot quote,
A Verse from Horace, learned by rote.

'He knew an hundred pleasant stories,
With all the turns of Whigs and Tories:
Was cheerful to his dying day,
And friends would let him have his way.

'He gave the little wealth he had,
To build a house for fools and mad:[1]
And showed by one satiric touch,
No nation wanted it so much:
That kingdom he hath left his debtor,
I wish it soon may have a better.'

---

1 *a house for fools and mad*: St Patrick's Hospital, founded in 1757.

JOHN TOLAND (1670-1722)

Born in Inishowen, Co. Donegal, a native Irish speaker, he was educated at the Universities of Glasgow and Leyden, the Franciscan College at Prague and the University of Oxford. He departed from Roman Catholicism, writing *Christianity Not Mysterious* (1696) in which he argued for a rational religion. This book aroused considerable opposition, especially from churchmen and philosophers in Ireland, and Toland had to leave the country in 1697. He wrote a life of Milton in 1698 and edited his prose works; he travelled to Berlin in 1702, publishing various political and theological pamphlets. His knowedge of Irish led to his idiosyncratic *History of the Druids* (1726), also known as *A Critical History of the Celtic Religion and Learning*. His interest in Celtic antiquity influenced his awareness of the need for a Dictionary of Irish, for an exploration of the relationship between Irish and Welsh and for the systematic collection of Irish manuscripts as a basis for any serious study of Irish history.

From *A Critical History of the Celtic Religion and Learning* (1726)

...whether, besides the language and traditions of the Irish, or the monuments of stone and other materials which the country affords, there yet remain any Literary records truly antient and unadulterated, whereby the History of the Druids, with such other points of antiquity, may be retriev'd, or at least illustrated? This is a material question, to which I return a clear and direct answer; that not onely there remain very many antient Manuscripts undoubtedly genuine, besides such as are forg'd, and greater numbers interpolated, several whereof are in Ireland itself, some here in England, and others in the Irish Monasteries abroad; but that, notwithstanding the long state of barbarity in which that nation hath lain, and after all the rebellions and wars with which the kingdom has been harrass'd; they have incomparably more antient materials of that kind for their history, to which even their Mythology is not unserviceable, than either the English, or the French, or any other European nation, with whose Manuscripts I have any acquaintance. Of these I shall one day give a catalogue, marking the places where they now ly, as many as I know of them; but not meaning every Transcript of the same Manuscript, which wou'd be endless, if not impossible. In all conditions the Irish have been strangely sollicitous, if not in some degree superstitious, about preserving their books and parchments; even those of them which are so old, as to be now partly or wholly unintelligible. Abundance, thro' over care have perished under ground, the concealer not having skill, or wanting searcloth and other proper materials for preserving them. The most valuable pieces, both in verse and prose, were written by their Heathen ancestors; whereof some indeed have been interpolated after the prevailing of Christianity, which additions or alterations are nevertheless easily distinguish'd: and in these books the rites and formularies of the Druids, together with their Divinity and Philosophy; especially their two grand doctrines of the eternity and incorruptibility of the universe, and the incessant Revolution of all beings and forms, are very specially, tho' sometimes very figuratively, express'd. Hence their Allanimation and Transmigration.[1] Why none of the natives have hitherto made any better use of these treasures; or why both they, and such others as have written concerning the History of Ireland, have onely entertain'd the world with the fables of it, as no country wants a fabulous account of its original, or the succession of its Princes, why the modern Irish Historians, I say, give us such a medley of relations, unpick'd and unchosen, I had rather any man else shou'd tell. The matter is certainly ready, there wants but will or skill for working of it; separating the Dross from the pure Ore, and distinguishing counterfeit from sterling coin. This in the meantime is undeniable, that learned men in other places, perceiving the same dishes to be eternally serv'd up at every meal, are of opinion that there is no better fare in the country while those things have been conceal'd from them by the ignorant or the lazy, that would have added no small ornament even to their classical studies....

WILLIAM CONGREVE (1670-1779)

Although he was born at Bardsey, a village outside Leeds, Congreve grew up in Ireland. His father became commander of the garrison at Youghal, Co. Cork in 1674 before serving at Carrickfergus and then joining the Duke of Ormonde's regiment at Kilkenny. William was moulded by his education at Kilkenny College, and subsequently at Trinity College, Dublin. His friendships at school and university with Swift and Joseph Keally were lifelong; he probably also formed friendships with actors in Dublin. The family left Ireland as a result of the English Revolution, Congreve's father returning in 1690 as agent for Richard Boyle, Earl of Cork. This position enabled him to send William to the Middle Temple in London, where he began to move in literary circles, publishing his novel *Incognita* in 1692. His comedy *The Old Batchelor* was very successful in 1693; it was followed by another comedy, *The Double*

---

1 *Allanimation and Transmigration*: These terms stand for the eternity of the Universe and the perpetual mutations of Being.

Dealer, that year. *Love for Love*, staged in 1695, was followed by a tragedy, *The Mourning Bride*, in 1697 – the most profitable of his plays. His career as a dramatist virtually ended with *The Way of the World* (1700), a brilliant play though in a genre which was falling out of fashion. He held various public posts but was short of money until 1705, when he became commissioner of wine licences. A Whig, through Swift's influence he was not turned out of office when the Tories came to power in 1710, the year his *Works* were published in three volumes. He became relatively wealthy when the Whigs returned to power in 1714, being given an office in Customs and appointed Secretary of Jamaica. He left a small legacy to the actress Mrs Bracegirdle, with whom he had had a close friendship earlier, while the rest went to the Duchess of Marlborough, a close and caring friend until his death. He was thought to have been the father of her second daughter Mary. His latter days were plagued by gout and failing sight, though, as Gay told Swift, he never lost anything of his cheerful temper.

From *The Way of the World*
(1700)
ACT IV, SCENE I.

SIR WILLFULL Your servant, then with your leave I'll return to my company.

[*Exit*

MILLAMANT Aye, aye, ha, ha, ha.
'Like Phœbus sung the no less am'rous boy.'

Enter Mirabell.

MIRABELL – 'Like Daphne she as lovely and as coy.'[1] Do you lock yourself up from me, to make my search more curious? Or is this pretty artifice contrived, to signify that here the chase must end, and my pursuit be crowned, for you can fly no further.–

MILLAMANT Vanity! No – I'll fly and be followed to the last moment, though I am upon the very verge of matrimony; I expect you should solicit me as much as if I were wavering at the grate of a monastery, with one foot over the threshold. I'll be solicited to the very last, nay and afterwards.

MIRABELL What, after the last?

MILLAMANT Oh, I should think I was poor and had nothing to bestow, if I were reduced to an inglorious ease; and freed from

---

1 '*Like Daphne ... coy.*': Mirabell completes the couplet begun by Millamant: it is from Edmund Waller's (1606–87) 'The Story of Phoebus and Daphne, Applied'.

the agreeable fatigues of solicitation.

MIRABELL But do not you know, that when favours are conferred upon instant and tedious solicitation, that they diminish their value, and that both the giver loses the grace, and the receiver lessens his pleaure?

MILLAMANT It may be in things of common application; but never sure in love. Oh, I hate a lover, that can dare to think, he draws a moment's air, independent on the bounty of his mistress. There is not so impudent a thing in nature, as the saucy look of an assured man, confident of success. The pedantic arrogance of a very husband, has not so pragmatical an air. Ah! I'll never marry, unless I am first made sure of my will and pleasure.

MIRABELL Would you have 'em both before marriage? Or will you be contented with the first now, and stay for the other till after grace?

MILLAMANT Ah don't be impertinent – My dear liberty, shall I leave thee? My faithful solitude, my darling contemplation must I bid you then adieu? Ay-h adieu – my morning thoughts, agreeable wakings, indolent slumbers, all ye *douceurs*,[1] ye *someils du matin*[2] adieu – I can't do this, 'tis more than impossible – positively Mirabell, I'll lie abed in a morning as long as I please.

MIRABELL Then I'll get up in a morning as early as I please.

MILLAMANT Ah! Idle creature, get up when you will – and d'ye hear, I won't be called names after I'm married; positively I won't be called names.

MIRABELL Names!

MILLAMANT Aye, as wife, spouse, my dear, joy, jewel, love, sweetheart and the rest of that nauseous cant, in which men and their wives are so fulsomely familiar, – I shall never bear that, – good Mirabell don't let us be familiar or fond, nor kiss before folks, like my Lady Fadler and Sir Francis: nor go to Hyde Park together the first Sunday in a new chariot, to provoke eyes and whispers; and then never to be seen together again; as if we were proud of one another the first week, and ashamed of one another for ever after. Let us never visit together, nor go to a play together, but let us be very strange and well bred: let us be strange as if

---

1 *douceurs*: pleasures.
2 *Someils du matin*: day-dreams.

we had been married a great while; and as well bred as if we were not married at all.

MIRABELL   Have you any more conditions to offer? Hitherto your demands are pretty reasonable.

MILLAMANT   Trifles, – as liberty to pay and receive visits to and from whom I please, to write and receive letters, without interrogatories or wry faces on your part. To wear what I please; and choose conversation with regard only to my own taste; to have no obligation upon me to converse with wits that I don't like, because they are your acquaintance; or to be intimate with fools, because they may be your relations. Come to dinner when I please, dine in my dressing room when I'm out of humour without giving a reason. To have my closet inviolate; to be sole empress of my tea-table, which you must never presume to approach without first asking leave. And lastly, wherever I am, you shall always knock at the door before you come in. These articles subscribed, if I continue to endure you a little longer, I may by degrees dwindle into a wife.

MIRABELL   Your bill of fare is something advanced in this latter account. Well, have I liberty to offer conditions – that when you are dwindled into a wife, I may not be beyond measure enlarged into a husband?

MILLAMANT   You have free leave; propose your utmost, speak and spare not.

MIRABELL   I thank you. *Imprimis*[1] then, I covenant that your acquaintance be general; that you admit no sworn confident, or intimate of your own sex; no she-friend to screen her affairs under your countenance and tempt you to make trial of a mutual secrecy. No decoy-duck to wheedle you a fop – scrambling to the play in a mask – then bring you home in a pretended fright, when you think you shall be found out. – And rail at me for missing the play, and disappointing the frolic which you had to pick me up and prove my constancy.

MILLAMANT   Detestable *Imprimis*! I go to the play in a mask!

MIRABELL   *Item*, I article, that you continue to like your own face, as long as I shall. And while it passes current with me, that you endeavour not to new coin it. To which end, togeth-

---

1 *Imprimis*: in the first place (from the Latin phrase, *in primis*).

er with all vizards for the day, I prohibit all masks for the night, made of oiled-skins and I know not what – hog's bones, hare's-gall, pig-water, and the marrow of a roasted cat. In short, I forbid all commerce with the gentlewoman in what-d'ye-call-it Court. *Item*, I shut my doors against all bawds with baskets and pennyworths of muslin, china, fans, atlasses, &c. – *Item* when you shall be breeeding –

MILLAMANT   Ah! Name it not.

MIRABELL   Which may be presumed, with a blessing on our endeavours –

MILLAMANT   Odious endeavours!

MIRABELL   I denounce against all straight-lacing, squeezing for a shape, till you mould my boy's head like a sugar-loaf; and instead of a man-child, make me the father of a crooked-billet. Lastly to the dominion of the tea-table, I submit. – But with *proviso*, that you exceed not in your province; but restrain yourself to native and simple tea-table drinks, as tea, chocolate and coffee. As likewise to genuine and, authorized tea-table talk, – such as mending of fashions, spoiling reputations, railing at absent friends, and so forth – but that on no account you encroach upon the men's prerogative, and presume to drink healths, or toast fellows; for prevention of which; I banish all foreign forces, all auxiliaries to the tea-table, as orange-brandy, all aniseed, cinnamon, citron and Barbadoes waters, together with ratafia and the most noble spirit of clary, – but for cowslip-wine, poppy-water and all dormitives, those I allow, – these provisos admitted, in other things I may prove a tractable and complying husband.

MILLAMANT   O horrid provisos! Filthy strong waters! I toast fellows, odious men! I hate your odious provisos.

MIRABELL   Then we're agreed. Shall I kiss your hand upon the contract? And here comes one to be a witness to the sealing of the deed.

Enter Mrs. Fainall.

MILLAMANT   Fainall, what shall I do? Shall I have him? I think I must have him.

MRS FAINALL   Aye, aye, take him, take him, what should you do?

MILLAMANT   Well then – I'll take my death I'm in a horrid fright – Fainall, I shall never say it – well – I think – I'll endure you.

MRS FAINALL Fie, fie, have him, have him, and tell him so in plain
terms: for I am sure you have a mind to him.

MILLAMANT Are you? I think I have – and the horrid man looks as if
he thought so too – Well, you ridiculous thing you, I'll
have you, – I won't be kissed, nor I won't be thanked –
Here kiss my hand though – so hold your tongue now,
and don't say a word.

MRS FAINALL Mirabell, there's a necessity for your obedience; – you
have neither time to talk nor stay. My mother is coming;
and in my conscience if she should see you, would fall
into fits, and maybe not recover time enough to return to
Sir Rowland, who as Foible tells me is in a fair way to
succeed. Therefore spare your ecstasies for another occasion, and slip down the back stairs, where Foible waits to
consult you.

MILLAMANT Aye, go, go. In the meantime I suppose you have said
something to please me.

MIRABELL I am all obedience.

[Exit Mirabell

MRS FAINALL Yonder Sir Willfull's drunk; and so noisy that my mother has been forced to leave Sir Rowland to appease him;
but he answers her only with singing and drinking – what
they have done by this time I know not. But Petulant and
he were upon quarreling as I came by.

MILLAMANT Well, if Mirabell should not make a good husband, I am
a lost thing; – for I love him violently.

MRS FAINALL So it seems, when you mind not what's said to you, – If
you doubt him, you had best take up with Sir Willfull.

MILLAMANT How can you name that superannuated lubber, foh!

[Exit Mirabell

Song

False tho' you've been to me and Love,
　　I nere can take revenge,
(So much your wondrous beautys move)
　　Tho' I resent your change.

In hours of bliss we oft have met,
　　They could not allways last;
And tho' the present I regret,

I still am Gratefull for the past.

But think not, Iris, tho' my breast
 A gen'rous flame has warm'd
You ere again could make me blest,
 Or charm as one you charm'd.

Who may your future favours own
 May future change forgive;
In Love, the first deceit alone
 Is what you never can retrieve.

A Hue and Cry after Fair Amoret

Fair Amoret is gone astray –
 Pursue and seek her, ev'ry lover;
I'll tell the signs by which you may
 The wand'ring Shepherdess discover.

Coquette and coy at once her air,
 Both studied, tho' both seem neglected;
Careless she is, with artful care,
 Affecting to seem unaffected.

With skill her eyes dart ev'ry glance,
 Yet change so soon you'd never suspect them,
For she'd persuade they wound by chance,
 Tho' certain aim and art direct them.

She likes herself, yet others hates
 For that which in herself she prizes;
And, while she laughs at them, forgets
 She is the thing that she despises.

Song

I tell thee, Charmion, could I time retrieve,
And could again begin to love and live,
To you I should my earliest offering give;
I know my eyes would lead my heart to you,
And I should all my vows and oaths renew,

But to be plain, I never would be true.
For by our weak and weary truth, I find,
Love hates to centre in a point assigned,
But runs with joy the circle of the mind.
Then never let us chain what should be free,
But for relief of either sex agree,
Since women love to change, and so do we.

SIR RICHARD STEELE (1672-1729)

Richard Steele, soldier, author and politician, born in Dublin, was educated at the Charterhouse and subsequently at Merton College, Oxford. He enrolled in the Life Guards as a trooper in 1694, then was commissioned in the Coldstream Guards. He severely wounded another Irishman in a duel in 1700, displaying in *The Christian Hero* (1701) a reaction against the irregularity of army life and arguing that gentlemanly virtues should be based upon Christian values. He wrote three comedies which departed from Restoration comedy's cynical attitudes. He became gazetteer in 1707 and began to edit a periodical, the *Tatler*, in 1709 with the help of Addison, his friend and schoolfellow. They collaborated in the *Spectator* (1711-12), which was followed by the *Guardian* (1713). *The Englishman* (1713-14) was more concerned with politics than with the earlier journals' social comedy. Steele's political career fluctuated; elected MP in 1713, he was expelled from the House of Commons the next year. On the accession of George I, however, his fortunes improved. He became supervisor of the Drury Lane Theatre, and was knighted in 1715. But his Drury Lane patent was later revoked and he was estranged from Addison. His last play *The Conscious Lovers* (1722) was the first outstandingly successful sentimental comedy. He returned to Wales for the last five years of his life because of financial problems.

From the *Spectator*. No. 2 [*The Club*] (Friday, March 2, 1711)

> *... Ast Alii sex*
> *Et plures uno conclamant ore.*
> Juvenal[1]

The first of our society is a gentleman of Worcestershire, of an ancient descent, a baronet, his name Sir Roger de Coverley. His great grandfather was inventor of that famous country dance which is called after

---

1 *Ast Alii ... ore*: Juvenal, *Satires*, 7.167-8: 'Six and more cry out with one voice'.

him. All who know that shire are very well acquainted with the parts and merits of Sir Roger. He is a gentleman that is very singular in his behaviour, but his singularities proceed from his good sense, and are contradictions to the manners of the world, only as he thinks the world is in the wrong. However, this humour creates him no enemies, for he does nothing with sourness or obstinacy; and his being unconfined to modes and forms, makes him but the readier and more capable to please and oblige all who know him. When he is in town he lives in Soho Square: it is said he keeps himself a bachelor by reason he was crossed in love, by a perverse beautiful widow of the next county to him. Before this disappointment, Sir Roger was what you call a fine gentleman, had often supped with my Lord Rochester and Sir George Etherege,[1] fought a duel upon his first coming to town, and kicked bully Dawson in a public coffee-house for calling him youngster. But being ill-used by the above-mentioned widow, he was very serious for a year and a half; and though, his temper being naturally jovial, he at last got over it, he grew careless of himself and never dressed afterwards; he continues to wear a coat and doublet of the same cut that were in fashion at the time of his repulse, which, in his merry humours, he tells us, has been in and out twelve times since he first wore it. 'Tis said Sir Roger grew humble in his desires after he had forgot this cruel beauty, insomuch that it is reported he has frequently offended in point of chastity with beggars and gypsies: but this is looked upon by his friends rather as matter of raillery than truth. He is now in his fifty-sixth year, cheerful, gay, and hearty, keeps a good house both in town and country, a great lover of mankind; but there is such a mirthful cast in his behaviour, that he is rather beloved than esteemed: his tenants grow rich, his servants look satisfied, all the young women profess love to him, and the young men are glad of his company; when he comes into a house he calls the servants by their names, and talks all the way up stairs to a visit. I must not omit that Sir Roger is a Justice of the *Quorum*; that he fills the chair at a quarter session with great abilities, and three months ago gained universal applause, by explaining a passage in the Game Act.

The gentleman next in esteem and authority among us is another bachelor, who is a member of the Inner Temple, a man of great probity, wit, and understanding; but he has chosen his place of residence rather to obey the direction of an old humoursome father than in pur-

---

1 *my Lord Rochester and Sir George Etherege*: John Wilmot, 2nd Earl of Rochester (1648–1680), a libertine and poet, known for *A Satire against Mankind*. Sir George Etherege (?1634–1691) wrote several Restoration comedies. Both were known as court wits.

suit of his own inclinations. He was placed there to study the laws of the land, and is the most learned of any of the house in those of the stage. Aristotle and Longinus are much better understood by him than Littleton or Coke.[1] The father sends up every post questions relating to marriage articles, leases, and tenures, in the neighbourhood; all which questions he agrees with an attorney to answer and take care of in the lump: he is studying the passions themselves, when he should be inquiring into the debates among men which arise from them. He knows the argument of each of the Orations of Demosthenes[2] and Tully,[3] but not one case in the reports of our own courts. No one ever took him for a fool, but none, except his intimate friends, know he has a great deal of wit. This turn makes him at once both disinterested and agreeable: as few of his thoughts are drawn from business, they are most of them fit for conversation. His taste of books is a little too just for the age he lives in; he has read all, but approves of very few. His familiarity with the customs, manners, actions, and writings of the ancients, makes him a very delicate observer of what occurs to him in the present world. He is an excellent critic, and the time of the play, is his hour of business; exactly at five he passes through New-Inn, crosses through Russell Court, and takes a turn at Will's till the play begins; he has his shoes rubbed and his periwig powdered at the barber's as you go into the Rose. It is for the good of the audience when he is at the play, for the actors have an ambition to please him.

The person of next consideration is Sir Andrew Freeport, a merchant of great eminence in the city of London: a person of indefatigable industry, strong reason, and great experience. His notions of trade are noble and generous, and (as every rich man has usually some sly way of jesting, which would make no great figure were he not a rich man) he calls the sea the British Common. He is acquainted with commerce in all its parts, and will tell you that it is a stupid and barbarous way to extend dominion by arms; for true power is to be got by arts and industry. He will often argue, that if this part of our trade were well cultivated, we should gain from one nation; and if another, from another. I have heard him prove, that diligence makes more lasting acquisitions than valour, and that sloth has ruined more nations than the sword. He

---

1 *Littleton or Coke*: Sir Thomas Littleton (1422–1481), author of a treatise on *Tenures* (1574); Sir Edward Coke (1552–1634), known for his eleven volumes of *Reports* (1600–1615) and his *Institutes* (1628–1644), the first part of which was a commentary on Littleton's *Tenures*. They were the principal authorities on real property for a considerable time.
2 *Demosthenes*: Demosthenes (c. 383–322 BC), the greatest of the Greek orators.
3 *Tully*: Marcus Tullius Cicero (106–40 BC), the Roman orator whose speeches included the Verrines and the Philippics. Both men played a prominent part in politics.

abounds in several frugal maxims, among which the greatest favourite is, 'A penny saved is a penny got.' A general trader of good sense is pleasanter company than a general scholar; and Sir Andrew having a natural unaffected eloquence, the perspicuity of his discourse gives the same pleasure that wit would in another man. He has made his fortunes himself; and says that England may be richer than other kingdoms, by as plain methods as he himself is richer than other men; though at the same time I can say this of him, that there is not a point in the compass but blows home a ship in which he is an owner.

Next to Sir Andrew in the Club-room sits Captain Sentry, a gentleman of great courage, good understanding, but invincible modesty. He is one of those that deserve very well, but are very awkward at putting their talents within the observation of such as should take notice of them. He was some years a captain, and behaved himself with great gallantry in several engagements and at several sieges; but having a small estate of his own, and being next heir to Sir Roger, he has quitted a way of life in which no man can rise suitably to his merit, who is not something of a courtier as well as a soldier. I have heard him often lament, that in a profession where merit is placed in so conspicuous a view, impudence should get the better of modesty. When he has talked to this purpose I never heard him make a sour expression, but frankly confess that he left the world because he was not fit for it. A strict honesty and an even regular behaviour are in themselves obstacles to him that must press through crowds who endeavour at the same end with himself, the favour of a commander. He will however in this way of talk excuse generals for not disposing according to men's desert, or inquiring into it: For, says he, that great man who has a mind to help me, has as many to break through to come at me, as I have to come at him; therefore he will conclude, that the man who would make a figure, especially in a military way, must get over all false modesty, and assist his patron against the importunity of other pretenders by a proper assurance in his own vindication. He says it is a civil cowardice to be backward in asserting what you ought to expect, as it is a military fear to be slow in attacking when it is your duty. With this candour does the gentleman speak of himself and others. The same frankness runs through all his conversation. The military part of his life has furnished him with many adventures, in the relation of which he is very agreeable to the company; for he is never over-bearing, though accustomed to command men in the utmost degree below him; nor ever too obsequious, from an habit of obeying men highly above him.

But that our society may not appear a set of humourists unacquainted with the gallantries and pleasures of the age, we have amongst us the gallant Will. Honeycomb, a gentleman who according to his years should be in the decline of his life, but having ever been very careful of his person, and always had a very easy fortune, time has made but very little impression, either by wrinkles on his forehead, or traces in his brain. His person is well turned, of a good height. He is very ready at that sort of discourse with which men usually entertain women. He has all his life dressed very well, and remembers habits as others do men. He can smile when one speaks to him, and laughs easily. He knows the history of every mode, and can inform you from which of the French King's wenches our wives and daughters had this manner of curling their hair, that way of placing their hoods; whose frailty was covered by such a sort of a petticoat, and whose vanity to show her foot made that part of the dress so short in such a year. In a word, all his conversation and knowledge has been in the female world: as other men of his age will take notice to you what such a minister said upon such and such an occasion, he will tell you when the Duke of Monmouth danced at Court such a woman was then smitten, another was taken with him at the head of his troop in the Park. In all these important relations, he has ever about the same time received a kind glance or a blow of a fan from some celebrated beauty, mother of the present Lord such-a-one. If you speak of a young Commoner that said a lively thing in the House, he starts up, 'He has good blood in his veins; Tom Mirabell begot him, the rogue cheated me in that affair; that young fellow's mother used me more like a dog than any woman I ever made advances to.' This way of talking of his very much enlivens the conversation among us of a more sedate turn; and I find there is not one of the company but myself, who rarely speak at all, but speaks of him as of that sort of man who is usually called a well-bred fine gentleman. To conclude his character, where women are not concerned, he is an honest worthy man.

I cannot tell whether I am to account him whom I am next to speak of, as one of our company; for he visits us but seldom, but when he does it adds to every man else a new enjoyment of himself. He is a clergyman, a very philosophic man, of general learning, great sanctity of life, and the most exact good breeding. He has the misfortune to be of a very weak constitution, and consequently cannot accept of such cares and business as preferments in his function would oblige him to: he is therefore among divines what a chamber-counsellor is among lawyers. The probity of his mind, and the integrity of his life, create him followers, as being eloquent or loud advances others. He seldom introduces the subject he speaks upon; but we are so far gone in years that he observes, when he is among us, an earnestness to have him fall on some divine topic, which he always treats with much authority, as one who has no interests in this world, as one who is hastening to the object of all his wishes, and conceives hope from his decays and infirmities. These are my ordinary companions.

Some Letters to Mary Scurlock

(1707-1708)[1]

BEFORE THEIR MARRIAGE

1707 [August]
Ld Sunderland's Office.

Madam

With what language shall I addresse my Lovely Fair to acquaint Her with the Sentiments of an Heart she delights to Torture? I have not a minute's Quiet out of Y^r sight and when I'me with You, You Use me with so much distance, that I am still in a State of Absence heightened with a View of the Charms which I am deny'd to Approach. In a word You must give Me either a Fan, a Mask or a Glove, you have Wore or I cannot Live, otherwise You must expect I'le Kiss Your hand, or when I next sit by You Steal Your Handkerchief. You Your self are too Great a Bounty to be receiv'd at Once therefore I must be prepar'd by degrees least the Mighty Gift distract Me with Joy. Dear Mrs. Scurlock I'me tir'd with calling You by that name therefore Say the day in which Youle take that of, Madam, Y^r Most Obedient Most devoted Hu^{bl} Ser^{nt}

RICH^d STEELE

Saturday-night [August 30, 1707]

Dear, Lovely Mrs. Scurlock

I have been in very Good company, where your Health, under the Character of the Woman I lov'd best has been often drank. So that I may say I am Dead Drunk for Your sake, which is more yⁿ I dye for you.

Y^{rs}
R: STEELE

---

1 Letters to Mary Scurlock: Steele met her in 1707 or in December 1706, at the funeral of his first wife. She lived from 1678 to 1718.

S^{nt} James's Coffee-house, Sep^{br} 1st, 1707

Madam,

It is the hardest thing in the World to be in Love and yet attend businesse. As for Me, all who speake to Me find Me out, and I must Lock my self up, or other people will do it for Me.

A Gentleman ask'd Me this Morning what news from Lisbon, and I answer'd, She's Exquisitely handsome. Another desir'd to know when I had been last at Hampton-Court, I reply'd Twill be on Tuesday come se'nnight. Prithee Allow Me at least to Kisse Your hand before that day, that my mind may be in some Composure. Oh Love!

A thousand Torments dwell about Thee,

Yet who would Live to Live without Thee?

Methinks I could write a Volume to You, but all the Language on earth would fail in saying how much, and with what disinterested passion, I am Ever Y^{rs},

RICH^{d} STEELE

Sep^{br}2^{d}, 1707 between One and Two.

Dear Creature

Ever since sev'n this morning I have been in Company, but have stole a moment to Pour out the fullnesse of my thoughts, and complain to You of the interruption that Impertinent amusement call'd businesse has giv'n Me amidst my Contemplation on the best of Women, and the most Agreeable object that ever Charm'd the Heart of Man.

I am, Dearest Lovelyest Creature
Eternally Thine,
R: STEELE

AFTER THEIR MARRIAGE
(*which took place on 9 September 1707*)

May 19th, 1708
Ld Sunderland's Office
11 of Clock.

Dear Prue

I desire of You to gett the Coach and y^{r} Self ready as soon as You can conveniently and call for Me here from Whence We will go and Spend some time together in the fresh Air in free Conference. Let my best Periwigg be put in the Coach Box and my New Shoes for 'tis a Comfort to [be] well dress'd in agreeable Company. You are Vitall Life to

Y^r Oblig'd Affectionate Husband & Humble Ser^{nt}

Richd Steele

Sep^{br} 19th, 1708, five in the Evening.

Dear Prue

I send you seven-pen'orth of Wall nutts at five a penny Which is the greatest proof I can give you at present of my being with my whole Heart

Y^{rs}

Richd Steele

The Love-Sick Maid

From place to place forlorn I go,
With downcast eyes a silent shade:
Forbidden to declare my woe;
To speak, till spoken to, afraid.

My inward pangs, my secret grief,
My soft consenting looks betray:
He loves, but gives me no relief:
Why speaks not he who may?

Why, Lovely Charmer, Tell me Why

Why, lovely charmer, tell me why
So very kind, and yet so shy?
Why does that cold forbidding air
Give damps of sorrow and despair?
Or why that smile my soul subdue,
And kindle up my flames anew?

In vain you strive with all your art,
By turns to freeze and fire my heart;
When I behold a face so fair,
So sweet a look, so soft an air,
My ravished soul is charmed all o'er,
I cannot love thee less nor more.

GEORGE FARQUHAR (?1677–1707)

Born near Derry, the son of a clergyman, Farquhar was an undergraduate at Trinity College, Dublin from 1694, having reputedly fought at the Battle of the Boyne in 1690. He acted in the Smock Alley Theatre in Dublin but accidentally stabbed another actor and left for London. There his first play, *Love and a Bottle* (1698), proved successful at Drury Lane, and he followed it with several other plays including *The Constant Couple* (1699) and *Sir Harry Wildair* (1701).

Farquhar married a widow with three daughters, joined the army in 1704, but sold his commission two years later to meet his rising debts. He then wrote *The Recruiting Officer* (1706) and *The Beaux Stratagem* (1707), dying just as the latter became a success. His last two plays mark a shift away from the city-centred comedies popular after the Restoration of Charles II in 1660. These two plays, being set in the country, reflect Farquhar's interest in local people, his sympathy for ill-matched couples and his often exuberant sense of fun.

Thus Damon Knocked at Celia's Door

Thus Damon knocked at Celia's door,
Thus Damon knocked at Celia's door,
He sighed and begged and wept and swore,
The sign was so, she answered no,
The sign was so, she answered no, no, no no.

Again he sighed, again he prayed,
No, Damon, no, no, no, no, no, I am afraid;
Consider, Damon, I'm a maid,
Consider, Damon, no, no, no, no, no, no, no, I'm a Maid.

At last his sighs and tears made way,
She rose and softly turned the key;
Come in, said she, but do not, do not stay,
I may conclude, you will be rude;
But if you are you may:
I may conclude, you will be rude,
But if you are you may.

From *The Beaux Stratagem*
(1707)

ACT II.

SCENE I.—A gallery in Lady Bountiful's house

Mrs Sullen and Dorinda meeting.

DORINDA   Morrow, my dear sister; are you for church this morning?

MRS SULLEN Anywhere to pray; for heaven alone can help me: but, I think, Dorinda, there's no form of prayer in the liturgy against bad husbands.

DORINDA   But there's a form of law in Doctors' Commons;[1] and I swear, sister Sullen, rather than see you thus continually discontented, I would advise you to apply to that: for besides the part that I bear in your vexatious broils, as being sister to the husband, and friend to the wife; your example gives me such an impression of matrimony, that I shall be apt to condemn my person to a long vacation all its life – But supposing, Madam, that you brought it to a case of separation, what can you urge against your husband? My brother is, first, the most constant man alive.

MRS SULLEN The most constant husband, I grant ye.

DORINDA   He never sleeps from you.

MRS SULLEN No, he always sleeps with me.

DORINDA   He allows you a maintenance suitable to your quality.

MRS SULLEN A maintenance! do you take me, Madam, for an hospital child, that I must sit down, and bless my benefactors for meat, drink, and clothes? As I take it, Madam, I brought your brother ten thousand pounds, out of which, I might expect some pretty things, called pleasures.

DORINDA   You share in all the pleasures that the country affords.

MRS SULLEN Country pleasures! racks and torments! Dost think, child, that my limbs were made for leaping of ditches, and clambering over stiles; or that my parents wisely foreseeing my future happiness in country pleasures, had early instructed me in the rural accomplishments of drinking fat ale, playing at whisk, and smoking tobacco with my husband; or of spreading of plasters, brewing of diet-drinks, and stilling rosemary-water, with the good old gentlewoman my mother-in-law?

DORINDA   I'm sorry, Madam, that it is not more in our power to

---

1 *Doctors' Commons*: London College of Doctors of Law, where advocates dealt, *inter alia*, with divorces.

divert you; I could wish, indeed, that our entertainments were a little more polite, or your taste a little less refined: but, pray, Madam, how came the poets and philosophers that laboured so much in hunting after pleasure, to place it at last in a country life?

MRS SULLEN Because they wanted money, child, to find out the pleasures of the Town: did you ever see a poet or philosopher worth ten thousand pound; if you can show me such a man, I'll lay you fifty pounds you'll find him somewhere within the weekly bills.[1] Not that I disapprove rural pleasures, as the poets have painted them; in their landscape every Phillis has her Coridon[2], every murmuring stream, and every flowery mead gives fresh alarms to love. – Besides, you'll find, that their couples were never married: – but yonder I see my Coridon, and a sweet swain it is, heaven knows! – Come, Dorinda, don't be angry, he's my husband, and your brother; and, between both, is he not a sad brute?

DORINDA I have nothing to say to your part of him, you're the best judge.

MRS SULLEN O sister, sister! if ever you marry, beware of a sullen, silent sot, one that's always musing, but never thinks: – there's some diversion in a talking blockhead; and since a woman must wear chains, I would have the pleasure of hearing 'em rattle a little. – Now you shall see, but take this by the way; – he came home this morning at his usual hour of four, wakened me out of a sweet dream of something else, by tumbling over the tea-table, which he broke all to pieces; after his man and he had rolled about the room like sick passengers in a storm, he comes flounce into bed, dead as a salmon into a fishmonger's basket; his feet cold as ice, his breath hot as a furnace, and his hands and his face as greasy as his flannel night-cap. – O matrimony! – He tosses up the clothes with a barbarous swing over his shoulders, disorders the whole economy of my bed, leaves me half naked, and my whole night's comfort is the tuneable serenade of that wakeful nightingale, his nose. – O the pleasure of counting the melancholy clock by a snoring husband! –But now, sister, you shall see how hand-

---

1 *the weekly bills*: The Weekly Bills of Mortality, issued from 1583 to 1837. Mrs Sullen is saying the 'poet or philosopher' will be found in London.
2 *Phillis … Coridon*: generic proper names in pastoral poetry for a shepherd and his sweetheart.

somely, being a well-bred man, he will beg my pardon.
Enter Sullen.

SULLEN   My head aches consumedly.

MRS SULLEN   Will you be pleased, my dear, to drink tea with us this
                morning? It may do your head good.

SULLEN   No.

DORINDA   Coffee, brother?

SULLEN   Psha!

MRS SULLEN   Will you please to dress, and go to church with me? the
                air may help you.

SULLEN   Scrub.

                                                                    [*Calls.*

Enter Scrub.

SCRUB   Sir.

SULLEN   What day o' th' week is this?

SCRUB   Sunday, an't please your worship.

SULLEN   Sunday! Bring me a dram, and d'ye hear, set out the veni-
                son-pasty and a tankard of strong beer upon the hall-
                table, I'll go to breakfast.

                                                                    [*Going.*

DORINDA   Stay, stay, brother, you shan't get off so; you were very
                naughty last night, and must make your wife reparation;
                come, come, brother, won't you ask pardon?

SULLEN   For what?

DORINDA   For being drunk last night.

SULLEN   I can afford it, can't I?

MRS SULLEN   But I can't, Sir.

SULLEN   Then you may let it alone.

MRS SULLEN   But I must tell you, Sir, that this is not to be borne.

SULLEN   I'm glad on't.

MRS SULLEN   What is the reason, Sir, that you use me thus inhumanely?

SULLEN   Scrub?

SCRUB   Sir.

SULLEN   Get things ready to shave my head.

                                                                    [*Exit.*

MRS SULLEN   Have a care of coming near his temples, Scrub, for fear
                you meet something there that may turn the edge of your
                razor.—[*Exit* Scrub.] Inveterate stupidity! did you ever
                know so hard, so obstinate a spleen as his? O sister, sister!

    I shall never ha' good of the beast till I get him to Town; London, dear London is the place for managing and breaking a husband.

DORINDA   And has not a husband the same opportunities there for humbling a wife?

MRS SULLEN No, no, child, 'tis a standing maxim in conjugal discipline, that when a man would enslave his wife, he hurries her into the country; and when a lady would be arbitrary with her husband, she wheedles her booby up to Town. A man dare not play the tyrant in London, because there are so many examples to encourage the subject to rebel. O Dorinda! Dorinda! A fine woman may do anything in London: O' my conscience, she may raise an army of forty thousand men.

DORINDA   I fancy, sister, you have a mind to be trying your power that way here in Lichfield; you have drawn the French count to your colours already.

MRS SULLEN The French are a people that can't live without their gallantries.

DORINDA   And some English that I know, sister, are not averse to such amusements.

MRS SULLEN Well, sister, since the truth must out, it may do as well now as hereafter; I think, one way to rouse my lethargic sottish husband, is, to give him a rival; security begets negligence in all people, and men must be alarmed to make 'em alert in their duty: women are like pictures, of no value in the hands of a fool, till he hears men of sense bid high for the purchase.

DORINDA   This might do, sister, if my brother's understanding were to be convinced into a passion for you; but, I fancy there's a natural aversion on his side; and I fancy, sister, that you don't come much behind him, if you dealt fairly.

MRS SULLEN I own it, we are united contradictions, fire and water: but I could be contented, with a great many other wives, to humour the censorious mob, and give the world an appearance of living well with my husband, could I bring him but to dissemble a little kindness to keep me in countenance.

DORINDA   But how do you know, sister, but that, instead of rousing your husband by this artifice to a counterfeit kindness, he should awake in a real fury?

MRS SULLEN Let him: – if I can't entice him to the one, I would provoke him to the other.

DORINDA   But how must I behave myself between ye?

MRS SULLEN You must assist me.

DORINDA   What, against my own brother?

MRS SULLEN He's but half a brother, and I'm your entire friend: if I go
a step beyond the bounds of honour, leave me; till then,
I expect you should go along with me in everything, while
I trust my honour in your hands, you may trust your
brother's in mine. The count is to dine here today.

DORINDA   'Tis a strange thing, sister, that I can't like that man.

MRS SULLEN You like nothing, your time is not come; love and death
have their fatalities, and strike home one time or other: –
you'll pay for all one day, I warrant ye. – But come, my
lady's tea is ready, and 'tis almost church time.

[*Exeunt.*

SCENE II—A ROOM IN BONIFACE'S INN

Enter Aimwell dressed, and Archer.

AIMWELL   And was she the daughter of the house?

ARCHER   The landlord is so blind as to think so; but I dare swear
she has better blood in her veins.

AIMWELL   Why dost think so?

ARCHER   Because the baggage has a pert *je ne sais quoi*, she reads
plays, keeps a monkey, and is troubled with vapours.

AIMWELL   By which discoveries I guess that you know more of her.

ARCHER   Not yet, faith, the lady gives herself airs, forsooth, nothing under a gentleman.

AIMWELL   Let me take her in hand.

ARCHER   Say one word more o' that, and I'll declare myself, spoil
your sport there, and everywhere else; look ye, Aimwell,
every man in his own sphere.

AIMWELL   Right; and therefore you must pimp for your master.

ARCHER   In the usual forms, good Sir, after I have served myself. –
But to our business: – You are so well dressed, Tom, and
make so handsome a figure, that I fancy you may do execution in a country church; the exterior part strikes first,
and you're in the right to make that impression
favourable.

AIMWELL   There's something in that which may turn to advantage;
the appearance of a stranger in a country church draws as

many gazers as a blazing star; no sooner he comes into the cathedral, but a train of whispers runs buzzing round the congregation in a moment; – *who is he? whence comes he? do you know him?* – Then I, Sir, tips me the verger with half a crown; he pockets the simony, and inducts me into the best pew in the church, I pull out my snuff-box, turn myself round, bow to the bishop, or the dean, if he be the commanding officer; single out a beauty, rivet both my eyes to hers, set my nose a-bleeding by the strength of imagination, and show the whole church my concern, by my endeavouring to hide it; after the sermon, the whole town gives me to her for a lover, and by persuading the lady that I am a-dying for her, the tables are turned, and she in good earnest falls in love with me?

ARCHER   There's nothing in this, Tom, without a precedent; but instead of riveting your eyes to a beauty, try to fix 'em upon a fortune, that's our business at present.

AIMWELL   Pshaw, no woman can be a beauty without a fortune. – Let me alone, for I am a marksman.

ARCHER   Tom.

AIMWELL   Aye.

ARCHER   When were you at church before, pray?

AIMWELL   Um – I was there at the coronation.[1]

ARCHER   And how can you expect a blessing by going to church now?

AIMWELL   Blessing! Nay, Frank, I ask but for a wife.

[*Exit.*

ARCHER   Truly, the man is not very unreasonable in his demands.

[*Exit at the opposite door.*

JOHN WINSTANLEY (?1678-1750)

Little is known of Winstanley's life. The poem included here suggests he may have been an undergraduate at Trinity College, Dublin, the 'College-bottle' being one with the College seal on it, and the 'Burgersdiscius' referring to the logic textbook used in the College at the time. Winstanley died in Dublin in 1750, his *Poems* appearing the next year. He described himself as '*a Doctor tho without Degrees*', as Apollo's and the Muses' licensed doctor.

---

1 *the coronation*: Queen Anne's coronation, in 1702.

An Inventory of the Furniture of a Collegian's Chamber

Imprimis[1], there's a *Table* blotted;
A tatter'd *Hanging* all besnotted;
A *Bed* of Flocks, as one may rank it,
Reduc'd to *Rug*, and half a *Blanket*;
A *Tinder-box*, as People tell us;
A broken-winded pair of *Bellows*.
A pair of *Tongs*, bought from a Broker,
A *Fender*, and a rusty *Poker*.
A *Penny-pot*, and *Bason*, this
Design'd for Water, that for Piss.
A *Trencher*, and a *College-bottle*
Riding on *Locke*, or *Aristotle*:
A smutty *Ballad*, musty *Libel*,
A *Burgersdiscius*, and a *Bible*:
A *Prayer-book*, he seldom handles;
Item, a Pound of *Farthing-candles*.
A rusty *Fork*, a blunted *Whittle*,
To cut his *Table*, and his *Vittle*.
There is likewise a pair of *Breeches*,
But patch'd, and fallen in the Stitches.
Item, a *Surplice*, not unmeeting
Either for *Chappel*, or for *Sheeting*,
Hung up in Study very little,
Plaister'd with Cobwebs, Ink, and Spittle,
With lofty *Prospect*, all so pleasing,
And *Sky-light window* without Glazing.
Item, if I am not mistaken,
A *Mouse-trap*, with a Bit of *Bacon*.
A *Candlestick*, without a *Snuffer*,
Whereby his Fingers often suffer;
And *Chairs* a couple, (I forgot 'em)
But each of them without a *Bottom*.
A *Bottle-Standish*, *Pen* unmended,
His inventory thus is ended.

---

1 *Imprimis*: in the first place (from the Latin phrase, in primis), originally used to introduce an itemised list (such as an inventory).

THOMAS PARNELL (1679-1718)

Born in Dublin, Parnell was educated at Trinity College, Dublin, and ordained into the Church of Ireland, becoming a minor canon of St Patrick's Cathedral, Dublin and then archdeacon of Clogher in 1706 before being presented to the Vicarage of Finglas in 1716. A protégé of Swift and a member of the Scriblerus Club in London, he was valued for his wit and the quality of his writing; he contributed papers to the *Spectator* and the *Guardian* and helped Pope with his translation of Homer's *Iliad*. After the death of his wife in 1711 he lived in some retirement in Ireland drinking excessively. He died at Chester on his way back to Ireland after visiting old friends in London, Pope publishing his *Poems on Several Occasions* (1722); his *Posthumous Works* appeared in 1758. His work contributed to the late Augustan churchyard poetry; 'The Hermit', 'A Nightpiece on Death' and his 'Hymn to Contentment' show his easy versification and versatility.

Song

My days have been so wondrous free,
    The little birds that fly
With careless ease from tree to tree,
    Were but as blest as I.

Ask gliding waters, if a tear
    Of mine increased their stream?
Or ask the flying gales, if e'er
    I lent one sigh to them?

But now my former days retire,
    And I'm by beauty caught;
The tender chains of sweet desire
    Are fixed upon my thought.

An eager hope within my breast
    Does every doubt control,
And charming Nancy stands confessed
    The favourite of my soul.

Ye nightingales, ye twisting pines,
    Ye swains that haunt the grove,
Ye gentle echoes, breezy winds!
    Ye close retreats of love—

With all of nature, all of art,

    Assist the dear design;
Oh teach a young, unpracticed heart
    To make her ever mine!

The very thought of change I hate,
    As much as of despair;
Nor ever covet to be great,
    Unless it be for her.

'Tis true, the passion in my mind
    Is mix'd with soft distress;
Yet while the fair I love is kind,
    I cannot wish it less.

Song

When thy beauty appears,
In its graces and airs,
All bright as an angel new dropt from the sky;
At distance I gaze, and am awed by my fears
So strangely you dazzle my eye!

But when without art,
Your kind thoughts you impart,
When your love runs in blushes through every vein;
When it darts from your eyes, when it pants in
    your heart,
Then I know you're a woman again.

There's a passion and pride
In our sex, she replied,
And thus (might I gratify both) I would do;
Still an angel appear to each lover beside,
But still be a woman to you.

A Night-Piece on Death

By the blue taper's trembling light,
No more I waste the wakeful night,
Intent with endless view to pore
The schoolmen and the sages o'er:
Their books from wisdom widely stray,

Or point at best the longest way.
I'll seek a readier path, and go
Where wisdom's surely taught *below*.

How deep yon azure dyes the sky!
Where orbs of gold unnumbered lie,
While through their ranks in silver pride
The nether crescent seems to glide.
The slumb'ring breeze forgets to breathe;
The lake is smooth and clear beneath,
Where once again the spangled show
Descends to meet our eyes below.
The grounds which on the right aspire,
In dimness from the view retire:
The left presents a place of graves,
Whose wall the silent water laves.
That steeple guides thy doubtful sight
Among the vivid gleams of night.
There pass with melancholy state,
By all the solemn heaps of fate,
And think, as softly-sad you tread
Above the venerable dead,
Time was, like thee they life possessed,
And time shall be, that thou shalt rest.

Those graves, with bending osier bound,
That nameless heave the crumbled ground,
Quick to the glancing thought disclose
Where *Toil* and *Poverty* repose.

The flat smooth stones that bear a name,
The chisels slender help to fame,
(Which e'er our set of friends decay
Their frequent steps may wear away),
A *middle race* of mortals own,
Men, half ambitious, all unknown.

The marble tombs that rise on high,
Whose dead in vaulted arches lie,
Whose pillars swell with sculptured stones,
Arms, angels, epitaphs, and bones,
These (all the poor remains of state)
Adorn the *rich*, or praise the *great*;
Who while on earth in fame they live,
Are senseless of the fame they give.

Ha! while I gaze, pale *Cynthia* fades,

The bursting earth unveils the shades!
All slow, and wan, and wrapped with shrouds,
They rise in visionary crowds,
And all with sober accent cry,
Think, mortal, what it is to die.

　　Now from yon black and fun'ral yew,
That bathes the charnel house with dew,
Methinks I hear a *voice* begin;
(Ye ravens, cease your croaking din,
Ye tolling clocks, no time resound
O'er the long lake and midnight ground)
It sends a peal of hollow groans,
Thus speaking from among the bones:

　　When men my scythe and darts supply,
How great a *King* of *Fears* am I!
They view me like the last of things:
They make, and then they dread, my stings.
Fools! if you less provoked your fears,
No more my spectre-form appears.
Death's but a path that must be trod,
If man would ever pass to God:
A port of calms, a state of ease
From the rough rage of swelling seas.

　　Why then thy flowing sable stoles,
Deep pendent cypress, mourning poles,
Loose scarfs to fall athwart thy weeds,
Long palls, drawn hearses, covered steeds,
And plumes of black, that as they tread,
Nod o'er the 'scutcheons of the dead?

　　Nor can the parted body know,
Nor wants the soul, these forms of woe:
As men who long in prison dwell,
With lamps that glimmer round the cell,
Whene'er their suffering years are run,
Spring forth to greet the glitt'ring sun:
Such joy, though far transcending sense,
Have pious souls at parting hence.
On earth, and in the body placed,
A few, and evil, years they waste:
But when their chains are cast aside,
See the glad scene unfolding wide,
Clap the glad wing, and tower away
And mingle with the blaze of day.

GEORGE BERKELEY (1685-1753)

Born at Dysart Castle, Co. Kilkenny, Berkeley was educated at Kilkenny College, and Trinity College, Dublin, where he became a Fellow in 1707. An idealist philosopher (his *Philosophical Commentaries* contains this entry: 'mem: that I was sceptical distrustful at 8 years old and consequently by nature disposed for these new Doctrines'), his *Essay towards a New Theory of Vision* (1709) was followed by *The Principles of Human Knowledge* (1710), the immaterialism of both of which were better received when he put them in *Three Dialogues between Hylas and Philonous* (1713). He spent some time in London, befriended by Swift, Addison, Steele, Arbuthnot and Pope. He travelled in Italy, became Dean of Derry in 1724, and in 1729 went to Rhode Island, hoping to establish a missionary college in Bermuda. Established in Newport he found the promised government funding for the project was not forthcoming and returned in 1731. He then wrote several books including his *Theory of Vision Vindicated* (1733) and *The Analyst* (1734), a work on mathematics which confuted the views of free-thinking mathematicians. Appointed Bishop of Cloyne in 1734, he was disturbed by the poverty of Ireland, and the three parts of his *The Querist* (1735, 1736 and 1737) reflected his concern and proposed some remedies. In *Siris: a Chain of Philosophical Reflexions and Inquiries concerning the Virtue of Tar-Water* (1744) he incorporated various metaphysical reflections and speculations as well as arguing the benefits of tar-water. Berkeley believed that knowledge can be explained by our perceptions, his doctrine of immaterialism resting on the belief that objects do not exist outside our perception of them.

From *Treatise concerning the Principles of Human Knowledge* (1710)

1 It is evident to any one who takes a survey of the objects of human knowledge, that they are either ideas actually imprinted on the senses, or else such as are perceived by attending to the passions and operations of the mind, or lastly ideas formed by help of memory and imagination, either compounding, dividing, or barely representing those originally perceived in the aforesaid ways. By sight I have the ideas of light and colours with their several degrees and variations. By touch I perceive, for example, hard and soft, heat and cold, motion and resistance, and of all these more and less either as to quantity or degree. Smelling furnishes me with odours; the palate with tastes, and hearing conveys sounds to the mind in all their variety of tone and composition. And as several of these are observed to accompany each other, they come to be marked by one name, and so to be reputed as one thing. Thus, for example, a certain colour, taste, smell, figure and consistence having

been observed to go together, are accounted one distinct thing, signified by the name *apple*. Other collections of ideas constitute a stone, a tree, a book, and the like sensible things; which, as they are pleasing or disagreeable, excite the passions of love, hatred, joy, grief, and so forth.

2 But besides all that endless variety of ideas or objects of knowledge, there is likewise something which knows or perceives them, and exercises divers operations, as willing, imagining, remembering, about them. This perceiving, active being is what I call *mind, spirit, soul,* or *my self.* By which words I do not denote any one of my ideas, but a thing entirely distinct from them, wherein they exist, or, which is the same thing, whereby they are perceived; for the existence of an idea consists in being perceived.

3 That neither our thoughts, nor passions, nor ideas formed by the imagination, exist without the mind, is what every body will allow. And it seems no less evident that the various sensations or ideas imprinted on the sense, however blended or combined together (that is, whatever objects they compose) cannot exist otherwise than in a mind perceiving them. I think an intuitive knowledge may be obtained of this, by any one that shall attend to what is meant by the term *exist* when applied to sensible things. The table I write on, I say, exists, that is, I see and feel it; and if I were out of my study I should say it existed, meaning thereby that if I was in my study I might perceive it, or that some other spirit actually does perceive it. There was an odour, that is, it was smelled; there was a sound, that is to say, it was heard; a colour or figure, and it was perceived by sight or touch. This is all that I can understand by these and the like expressions. For as to what is said of the absolute existence of unthinking things without any relation to their being perceived, that seems perfectly unintelligible. Their *esse* is *percipi*,[1] nor is it possible they should have any existence out of the minds or thinking things which perceive them.

4 It is indeed an opinion strangely prevailing amongst men, that houses, mountains, rivers, and in a word all sensible objects have an existence natural or real, distinct from their being perceived by the understanding. But with how great an assurance and acquiescence soever this principle may be entertained in the world; yet whoever shall find in his heart to call it in question, may, if I mistake not, perceive it to involve a manifest contradiction. For what are the forementioned objects but the things we perceive by sense, and what do we perceive besides our own ideas or sensations; and is it not plainly

---

1 *Esse is percipi*: Berkeley's subjective principle: their existence consists in being perceived.

repugnant that any one of these or any combination of them, should exist unperceived?...

25 All our ideas, sensations, notions, or the things which we perceive, by whatsoever names they may be distinguished, are visibly inactive—there is nothing of Power or Agency included in them. So that one idea or object of thought cannot produce or make any alteration in another.—To be satisfied of the truth of this, there is nothing else requisite but a bare observation of our ideas. For, since they and every part of them exist only in the mind, it follows that there is nothing in them but what is perceived: but whoever shall attend to his ideas, whether of sense or reflection, will not perceive in them any power or activity; there is, therefore, no such thing contained in them. A little attention will discover to us that the very being of an idea implies passiveness and inertness in it, insomuch that it is impossible for an idea to do anything, or, strictly speaking, to be the cause of anything: neither can it be the resemblance or pattern of any active being, as is evident from sect. 8. Whence it plainly follows that extension, figure, and motion cannot be the cause of our sensations. To say, therefore, that these are the effects of powers resulting from the configuration, number, motion, and size of corpuscles, must certainly be false.

26 We perceive a continual *succession* of ideas; some are anew excited, others are changed or totally disappear There is therefore some Cause of these ideas, whereon they depend, and which produces and changes them. That this cause cannot be any quality, or idea, or combination of ideas is clear from the preceding section. It must therefore be a substance; but it has been shewn that there is no corporeal or material substance: it remains therefore that the cause of ideas is an incorporeal active substance or Spirit.

27 A Spirit is one simple, undivided, active being—as it *perceives* ideas it is called the *Understanding*, and as it *produces* or otherwise *operates* about them it is called the *Will*. Hence there can be no *idea* formed of a soul or spirit; for, all ideas whatever, being passive and inert, (vid. sect 25,) cannot represent unto us, by way of image or likeness, that which acts. A little attention will make it plain to any one that to have an idea which shall be *like* that active principle of motion and change of ideas is absolutely impossible. Such is the nature of Spirit, or that which acts, that it cannot be of itself perceived, but only by the effects which it produceth.—If any man shall doubt of the truth of what is here delivered, let him but reflect and try if we can frame the idea of any Power or Active Being; and whether he has ideas of two principal powers, marked by the names *Will* and *Understanding*,

distinct from each other, as well as from a third idea of Substance or Being in general, with a relative notion of its supporting or being the subject of the aforesaid powers—which is signified by the name Soul or Spirit. This is what some hold; but, so far as I can see, the words *will*, *soul*, *spirit*, do not stand for different ideas, or, in truth, for any idea at all, but for something which is very different from ideas, and which, being an Agent, cannot be like unto, or represented by, any idea whatsoever. Though it must be owned at the same time that we have some *notion* of soul, spirit, and the operations of the mind; such as willing, loving, hating—inasmuch as we know or understand the meaning of these words.

28 I find I can excite ideas in my mind at pleasure, and vary and shift the scene as oft as I think fit. It is no more than willing, and straightway this or that idea arises in my fancy; and by the same power it is obliterated and makes way for another. This making and unmaking of ideas doth very properly denominate the mind active. This much is certain and grounded on experience: but when we talk of unthinking agents, or of exciting ideas exclusive of Volition, we only amuse ourselves with words.

29 But, whatever power I may have over my own thoughts, I find the ideas actually perceived by Sense have not a like dependence on my will. When in broad daylight I open my eyes, it is not in my power to choose whether I shall see or no, or to determine what particular objects shall present themselves to my view; and so likewise as to the hearing and other senses, the ideas imprinted on them are not creatures of my will. There is therefore some *other* Will or Spirit that produces them.

30 The ideas of Sense are more strong, lively, and distinct than those of the Imagination; they have likewise a steadiness, order, and coherence, and are not excited at random, as those which are the effects of human wills often are, but in a regular train or series—the admirable connexion whereof sufficiently testifies the wisdom and benevolence of its Author. Now the set rules or established methods wherein the Mind we depend on excites in us the ideas of sense, are called the *laws of nature*; and these we learn by experience, which teaches us that such and such ideas are attended with such and such other ideas, in the ordinary course of things.

31 This gives us a sort of foresight which enables us to regulate our actions for the benefit of life. And without this we should be eternally at a loss; we could not know how to act anything that might procure us the least pleasure, or remove the least pain of sense. That food nourishes, sleep refreshes, and fire warms us; that to sow in the seedtime is

the way to reap in the harvest; and in general that to obtain such or such ends, such or such means are conducive—all this we know, not by discovering any *necessary connexion* between our ideas, but only by the *observation* of the settled laws of nature, without which we should be all in uncertainty and confusion, and a grown man no more know how to manage himself in the affairs of life than an infant just born.

32 And yet this consistent uniform working, which so evidently displays the goodness and wisdom of that Governing Spirit whose Will constitutes the laws of nature, is so far from leading our thoughts to Him, that it rather sends them wandering after second causes For, when we perceive certain ideas of Sense constantly followed by other ideas, and we know this is not of our own doing, we forthwith attribute power and agency to the ideas themselves, and make one the cause of another, than which nothing can be more absurd and unintelligible. Thus, for example, having observed that when we perceive by sight a certain round luminous figure we at the same time perceive by touch the idea or sensation called heat, we do from thence conclude the sun to be the *cause* of heat. And in like manner perceiving the motion and collision of bodies to be attended with sound, we are inclined to think the latter the *effect* of the former.

33 The ideas imprinted on the Senses by the Author of nature are called *real things*: and those excited in the Imagination being less regular, vivid, and constant, are more properly termed *ideas*, or *images of things*, which they copy and represent. But then our sensations, be they never so vivid and distinct, are nevertheless ideas; that is, they exist in the mind, or are perceived by it, as truly as the ideas of its own framing. The ideas of Sense are allowed to have more reality in them, that is, to be more strong, orderly, and coherent than the creatures of the mind; but this is no argument that they exist without the mind. They are also less dependent on the spirit, or thinking substance which perceives them, in that they are excited by the will of another and more powerful Spirit; yet still they are *ideas*, and certainly no idea, whether faint or strong, can exist otherwise than in a mind perceiving it.

America or The Muse's Refuge
A Prophecy

The Muse, disgusted at an age and clime,
Barren of every glorious theme,
In distant lands now waits a better time,
Producing subjects worthy fame:

In happy climes, where from the genial sun
    And virgin earth such scenes ensue,
The force of art by nature seems outdone,
    And fancied beauties by the true:

In happy climes the seat of innocence,
    Where nature guides and virtue rules,
Where men shall not impose for truth and sense,
    The pedantry of courts and schools:

There shall be sung another golden age,
    The rise of empire and of arts,
The good and great inspiring epic rage,
    The wisest heads and noblest hearts.

Not such as Europe breeds in her decay;
    Such as she bred when fresh and young,
When heav'nly flame did animate her clay,
    By future poets shall be sung.

Westward the course of empire takes its way;
    The four first acts already past,
A fifth shall close the drama with the day;
    Time's noblest offspring is the last.

Siris and a letter about tar-water

[In *Siris* Berkeley moved on from his initial medical descriptions to metaphysical speculation; the treatise begins with tar-water and ends with the Holy Trinity. His biographer and editor, A.A. Luce, has argued in his *Life* that those who have followed the theory of the ether since Berkeley's day will be loth to call Berkeley's speculations altogether baseless and absurd: 'He had found a cheap and safe medicinal substance which cured, or helped to cure, disease; and in the science of his days, not entirely obsolete yet, he found speculative reasons for the virtue of the cure'. Berkeley made modest claims for the cure and the reasons why it worked, treading, as his biographer remarks, on a few professional corns, but, against the ridicule of his own period and that of later days, fair-minded readers will, Professor Luce suggests, set the silent gratitude of the countless poor and indeed of public men in the eighteenth century.]

Siris: A Chain of Philosophical Reflexions and Inquiries, &c.

(1744)

For Introduction to the following piece, I assure the reader that nothing could, in my present situation, have induced me to be at the pains of writing it, but a firm belief that it would prove a valuable present to the public. What entertainment soever the reasoning or notional part may afford the Mind, I will venture to say, the other part seemeth so surely calculated to do good to the Body that both must be gainers. For, if the lute be not well tuned, the musician fails of his harmony. And, in our present state, the operations of the mind so far depend on the right tone or good condition of its instrument, that anything which greatly contributes to preserve or recover the health of the Body is well worth the attention of the Mind. These considerations have moved me to communicate to the public the salutary virtues of Tar-water; to which I thought myself indispensably obliged by the duty every man owes to mankind. And, as effects are linked with their causes, my thoughts on this low but useful theme led to farther inquiries, and those on to others; remote perhaps and speculative, but I hope not altogether useless or unentertaining.

1. In certain parts of America, Tar-water is made by putting a quart of cold water to a quart of tar, and stirring them well together in a vessel, which is left standing till the tar sinks to the bottom. A glass of clear water, being poured off for a draught, is replaced by the same quantity of fresh water, the vessel being shaken and left to stand as before. And this is repeated for every glass, so long as the tar continues to impregnate the water sufficiently, which appears by the smell and taste. But, as this method produceth tar-water of a nauseous kind, and different degrees of strength, I choose to make it in the following manner: Pour a gallon of cold water on a quart of tar, and stir, work, and mix them thoroughly together, with a wooden ladle or flat stick, for the space of five or six minutes; after which the vessel must stand close covered and unmoved three days and nights, that the tar may have full time to subside; and then the clear water, having been first carefully skimmed without shaking the vessel, is to be poured off, and kept in bottles well stopped for use; no more being made from the same tar, which may still serve for common uses.

2. The cold infusion of tar hath been used in some of our Colonies, as a preservative or preparative against the small-pox; which foreign practice induced me to try it in my own neighbourhood, when the

small-pox raged with great violence. And the trial fully answered my expectation; all those within my knowledge who took the tar-water having either escaped that distemper, or had it very favourably. In one family there was a remarkable instance of seven children, who came all very well through the small-pox, except one young child which could not be brought to drink tar-water as the rest had done.

3. Several were preserved from taking the small-pox by the use of this liquor; others had it in the mildest manner; and others, that they might be able to take the infection, were obliged to intermit drinking the tar-water. I have found it may be drunk with great safety and success for any length of time, and this not only before, but also during the distemper. The general rule for taking it is:—about half a pint night and morning, on an empty stomach; which quantity may be varied, according to the case and the age of the patient, provided it be always taken on an empty stomach, and about two hours before or after a meal. For children and squeamish persons it may be made weaker, or given little and often; more water or less stirring makes it weaker, as less water or more stirring makes it stronger. It should not be lighter than French, nor deeper coloured than Spanish white wine. If a spirit be not very sensibly perceived on drinking, either the tar has been bad, or already used, or the tar-water carelessly made or kept. Particular experience will best shew how much and how strong the stomach can bear, and what are the properest times for taking it. I apprehend no danger from excess in the use of this medicine.

A Letter by the Author of Siris To the Reverend Dr. Hales,
ON THE
BENEFIT OF TAR-WATER IN FEVERS,
FOR CATTLE AS WELL AS THE HUMAN SPECIES

To one gallon of fresh tar, pour six gallons of cold water; stir and work them strongly together, with a large flat stick, for the space of one full hour; let the whole stand six or eight hours, that the tar may subside; then scum it, and pour off the water, whereof three gallons warm are to be given the first day, two the second, and one the third day, at equal intervals, the dose not being less than a pint, nor more than a quart; and the beast being all that time, and for two or three days after, kept warm and nourished, if it will not eat hay, with mash or gruel.

I believe this course will rarely fail of success, having often observed fevers in human kind to have been cured by a similar method. But, as in fevers it often throws out pustules or ulcers on the surface of the body, so in beasts it may be presumed to do the like; which ulcers, being anointed with a little tar, will, I doubt not, in a short time, dry up and disappear.

By this means the lives of infected cattle may be preserved at the expense of a gallon of tar for each. A thing which I repeat and inculcate, not only for the sake of the cattle and their owners, but also for the benefit of mankind in general, with regard to a fever; which terrible subduer and destroyer of our species, I have constantly found to be itself easily subdued by tar-water. Nevertheless, though in most other cases I find the use of this medicine hath generally obtained, yet in this most dangerous and frequent case, where its aid is most wanted, and at the same time most sure, I do not find that the use thereof has equally obtained abroad in the world.

It grieves me to think that so many thousands of our species should daily perish, by a distemper which may be easily cured by a remedy so ready at hand, so easy to take, and so cheap to purchase, as tar-water, which I never knew to fail when copiously drank in any sort of fever. All this I say after more than a hundred trials, in my own family and neighbourhood.

But, whatever backwardness people may have to try experiments on themselves or their friends, yet it is hoped that they may venture to try them on their Cattle, and that the success of such trials in fevers of brutes (for a fever it plainly is) may dispose them to probable hopes of the same success in their own species.

Experiments, I grant, ought to be made with caution, and yet they may be made, and actually are made every day on probable reasons and analogy. Thus, for instance, because I knew that tar-water was cordial and diaphoretic, and yet no inflamer, I ventured to give it in every stage of the small-pox, though I had never heard of its being given otherwise than as a preservative against that distemper; and the success answered my expectation.

If I can but introduce the general use of tar-water for this murrain, which is in truth a fever, I flatter myself this may pave the way for its general use in all fevers whatever.

A murrain among cattle hath been sometimes observed to be the forerunner of the Plague among men. If that should prove the present case (which God forbid) I would earnestly recommend the copious drinking of warm tar-water, from the very first appearance of the symptoms of such plague. I do also recommend it to be tried in like manner against the bite of a mad dog, when other approved remedies are not at hand.

From *The Querist*

(1752)

29. What makes a wealthy people? Whether mines of gold and silver are capable of doing this? And whether the negroes, amidst the gold sands of Afric, are not poor and destitute?

30. Whether there be any virtue in gold or silver, other than as they set people at work, or create industry?...

32. Whether if there was no silver or gold in the kingdom, our trade might not, nevertheless, supply bills of exchange, sufficient to answer the demands of absentees in England or elsewhere?

33. Whether current bank notes may not be deemed money? And whether they are not actually the greater part of the money of this kingdom?

34. Provided the wheels move, whether it is not the same thing, as to the effect of the machine, be this done by the force of wind, or water, or animals?

35. Whether power to command the industry of others be not real wealth? And whether money be not in truth tickets or tokens for conveying and recording such power, and whether it be of great consequence what materials the tickets are made of?...

134. Whether, if there was a wall of brass a thousand cubits high round this kingdom, our natives might not nevertheless live cleanly and comfortably, till the land, and reap the fruits of it?...

461. Whether to oil the wheels of commerce be not a common benefit? And whether this be not done by avoiding fractions and multiplying small silver?...

475. As wealth is really power, and coin a ticket conveying power, whether those tickets which are the fittest for that use ought not to be preferred?...

477. Whether the public is not more benefited by a shilling that circulates than a pound that lies dead?...

480. Whether facilitating and quickening the circulation of power to supply wants be not the promoting of wealth and industry among the lower people? And whether upon this the wealth of the great doth not depend?...

570. Whether means are not so far useful as they answer the end? And whether, in different circumstances, the same ends are not obtained by different means?...

572. Whether, therefore, it would not be highly expedient if our

money were coined of peculiar values, best fitted to the circumstances and uses of our own country; and whether any other people could take umbrage at our consulting our own convenience, in an affair entirely domestic, and that lies within ourselves?

From *Philosophical Commentaries, generally called the Commonplace Book*

P
There are men who say there are insensible extensions, there are others who say the Wall is not white, the fire is not hot &c We Irish men cannot attain to these truths.

The Mathematicians there are insensible lines,

all angles

X
about these they harangue, these cut in a point, at these are divisible ad infinitum. We Irish men can con- ceive ~~no such thing~~ no such lines.

w^t

X
The Mathematicians talk of ~~something~~ they call a point, this they ~~they~~ say is not altogether nothing nor is it downright something, now we Irish men are apt to think something & nothing are next neighbours....

+
How could I venture thoughts into the world, before I knew the[y] would be of use to the world? and how could I know that till I had try'd how the[y] suited other men's ideas.

+
I Publish not this so much for anything else as to know whether other men have the same Ideas as we Irishmen, this is my end and not to be inform'd as to my own Particular.

+
The Materialist & Nihilarians need not be of a party.

PATRICK DELANY (1685-1768)

Delany was educated at Trinity College, where he became a Fellow. A popular preacher, he received many benefices: Chancellor of St Patrick's Cathedral,

Dublin in 1730, and Dean of Down in 1744. In Dublin he established himself in Delville, and made this elegant house known for its hospitality. His second wife, Mrs Pendarves, whom he married in 1743, established its fine garden—her connections had led to his Deanship. Delany's guests included Swift, who thought him the best wit in Ireland. He wrote controversially on various subjects, including polygamy and Jewish religion and customs. He produced a two volume *Life and Writings of King David* (1740-42) and his *Observations upon Lord Orrery's Remarks on the Life and Writings of Dr Jonathan Swift** (1752) were based on his personal knowledge of a friend; he had testified earlier to his admiration for the Dean in his poem *News from Parnassus* (1721). He founded several Dublin papers and published *Social Duties of Life* (15 sermons) in 1744, to which he added 5 sermons on vice in 1747. This passage is taken from his *Eighteen Discourses* (1766).

[*Of Gaming*]
(1766)

... For first, all gaming for any thing considerable, is founded upon avarice: and is if not a direct, yet (what is much worse) a deliberate violation, of the tenth commandment: and therefore in this respect, it is perhaps the vice of all others, most inexcusable: in crimes of other kinds; surprise, inattention, and violence of passion, altho' they cannot wholly excuse the committal, yet doubtless they alleviate much of the guilt. But here, all these pretences are taken away. And men are so far from being under the influence of any of these alleviating circumstances, that nothing is more notorious than their proceeding to the practice of this vice, with the utmost caution and coolness of judgment. And we are told, that it is in contests of this kind, as in war: he that hath most presence of mind, and is least embarrassed, is generally most successful.

Besides the deliberate impiety of this vice, it were worth while to consider also, the folly of it. For what can be more absurd, than for any man in his senses, without any necessity, to put it to the chance of a die, whether his house, his money, or his estate, shall be his own, or another man's? So that nothing but a desperate state of affairs, can ground the least appearance of a reasonable plea for such a practice. And even in that case, if the property of a third person can any way be hazarded by the risk we run; then is great dishonesty added to great impudence. And therefore suppose there were no impiety in this practice, yet such is the folly and danger of it, that you scarce invent a case where it would be pardonable even upon the score of stupidity: unless you could suppose a fool of wealth, so immensely rich, that losses of that kind could not affect the main of his fortune, but that supposition is impossible. Since it is evident, that no fortune can be so large, and inexhaustible, as to be able to supply an extravagance of this kind. There is no fund adequate to gameing: nor can you imagine any condition of life so immensely affluent, as may not be exhausted, by an extravagance of this kind, in one hour.

Well, but men may limit themselves in this extravagance: and resolve never to exceed a certain sum: true, men may easily make such resolutions; but the difficulty is, how to keep them: when losses, and ill luck have fretted their spirits, and inflamed their blood, to such a degree, that they have lost the thoughts of every thing, but recovery, and revenge, and I dare say, if it were possible to make an estimate of such resolutions, not one in ten thousand of them hath ever been kept. Nay is it not madness, to expect, that men in so raving, and distracted a condition, as losing gamesters, are often observed to be; that will not stick to abuse their best friends; will swear a thousand vain oaths in a breath; profane, nay blaspheme the sacred name of GOD, without regret; to expect that creatures in that condition, should regard resolutions of caution, and prudence; is an extravagance of folly, almost equal to theirs. And indeed, such is the distraction, and extravagance of men in that condition; that I know nothing more likely to deter any man of reflection, either from entering into such a course of life, or continuing in it; than a calm observation of that series of distractions, which if I am well informed (for I thank GOD I speak not by experience) tear the breast of a losing gamester, in the course of a few hours. The ravings of a fever, and the pangs of a convulsion, are nothing to them. Nay in all appearance, they are the liveliest emblems of the torments of hell! made up of a wild mixture of fury, and anguish, regret and despair! so that if nothing but the philosophy of life, were concerned in this practice; a man of common prudence would avoid it, as a pestilence; as the greatest bane, to the peace, and tranquillity of life.

But it may be urged, that there are men of such cool and calm tempers, as never to be ruffled, or heated, either into any discomposure of their temper, or disturbance of their understanding on such occasions. And therefore, these men seem to be an exception, to all the prohibitions of prudence, that lie against gaming. In answer to this, it cannot I believe be denied, that there are such men in the world: but then I believe it cannot well be denied, that they are men of the worst characters in it. They are men, who have studied all the arts of fraud, and villany of every kind, in perfection. Black, saturnine, deliberate villains, who lay themselves out by all the wiles of flattery, wine, seduction, and deceit, to draw the unwary into their snares: and when they once get them there, destroy them without remorse. They are to the light unthinking part of the world, what the spider is to the fly: they wait with cool, deliberate, unwearied patience, till they get their prey within their nest, and then drain out their vitals without remorse; or to speak more properly, enjoy their dying complaints. One would imagine the psalmist had this scene in view, in his description of those hardened miscreants, whose snares, and nets, are spread for the innocent. *He lieth in wait to catch or* (as I think might better be translated) *seize the poor:* (that is the poor deluded mortals that fall into his snares) *he doth seize the poor, when he draweth him into his net. In his secret places doth he murder the innocent.* Forgetting, that *god beholdeth all his ungodliness and wrong:* and will in his own time repay it, with dreadful vengeance. And therefore well doth St. *Paul* admonish, I *Thess.* iv. 6, That *no man go beyond, and defraud his brother in any matter: because that the Lord is the avenger of all such.*

But still it may be urged, that some men can play with so much prudence, and temper, as never to engage for more than trifles; consequently to be perfectly unconcerned at any inconsiderable loss that may ensue. True, some men doubtless can do so, and to such, playing for trifles, may doubtless be as innocent, as any other Amusement whatsoever. But how few of these are there in the world in comparison of those, who begin with trifles, and warmed with their losses, are carried on by degrees, to boundless extravagance? and even of those, who can lose with temper, how many are there, to whom, money and time so spent can become an agreeable reflection? and to whom, it would not have been infinitely more satisfactory upon reflection, to have employed that time, to the attainment of some good purpose in life; or that trifle to the relief of the poor. Which, however inconsiderable to the loser, might, to them, be of the last consequence? and therefore, altho' gaming in a low and temperate manner, may possibly be numbered among the innocent diversions of life; yet probably it is the most dangerous, and, to the eye of reason, the least desirable of them all.

And if this practice be liable to all these objections and difficulties, under the conduct of the greatest prudence, and calmness of temper, in the best company, and in all the alleviating circumstances that can possibly attend it; how infinitely detestable, and abominable must it be, in all its deformity? in places of public resort, and in the society of the most profligate, and abandoned part of mankind: for such beyond all question, are the herd of common gamesters. Men of desperate fortunes, no education, no principles, no conscience, no science (except that of defrauding all they deal with, by all the low arts of deceit, and perjury) engaged in such practices, as naturally tend to create quarrels, and contentions, with all their horrid consequences. And lead men into riots, and excesses of every kind. For surely, of these may it be strictly said, what *Solomon* observeth of the wicked, in the ivth chapt. of his Proverbs. *They sleep not, except they have done mischief: and they cause some to fall. For they eat the bread of wickedness, and drink the wine of violence.* And therefore, for men of liberal education, and good morals, men of any valuable character, to mix with such a herd, would be an argument of more desperate folly, than for a man in sound health, to throw himself into a pest house: inasmuch as the corruption of the mind, is of vastly worse consequence, than the infection of the body. And how hard it will be to avoid such corruption, from such society, is easy to conceive. *Can a man touch pitch, and not be defiled therewith?*[1] And therefore, *Solomon* adviseth, not only, not to enter into the path of the wicked, but carefully to avoid it. *Avoid it, pass not by it, turn from it, and pass away.*[2]

It may be urged in the last place, in behalf of gaming, that many men have raised their fortunes by it. And that since it is not expressly forbidden in the scriptures, it may be practised without sin. To this I answer, that altho' there be no express prohibition of it, in scripture, yet is it plainly implied in the tenth commandment. And as to the other part of the objection, it is notorious, that a thousand fortunes are ruined by it, for one that is raised. So that in this respect, a particular curse seems to attend it. And surely it is little less than madness, to propose to establish your fortune, by any method, where the odds are in fact so greatly against you. Besides, that gaming is not in the number of those arts, by which GOD Almighty hath ordained that the good things of this world should be acquired: for these, are the natural effects of honesty, and industry, in the improvement, and application of our best abilities, both of body and mind. And if GOD Almighty had made them ordinarily the purchase of chance, and vice, and idleness; he had destroyed the right order of things; and substituted the worst means in the room of the best: and consequently, taken away much, from the wisdom and beauty of his own establishment.

If then you would avoid a deliberate if not a direct violation, of the tenth commandment; together with infinite disquiet, and distraction; and the severe reflections of time, and fortune ill spent: if you would shun the society of the vilest, and most abandoned part of mankind,

---

1 Ecclesiastes 13. 1.
2 Proverbs 4. 15.

and the double ruin of soul and body, consequent to such a commerce: if ye would act consistently with those laws of GOD and man, that are the rules of your duty, and that wise order of things, established by the divine wisdom, for the attainment of the good things of this world; renounce that impious, that absurd, that detestable practice of gaming.

THOMAS SHERIDAN (1687-1738)

Sheridan, the grandson of Donnchadh Siordain, who became the Rev. Dennis Sheridan and helped Bishop Bedell with his translation of the Bible into Irish, was born in Co. Cavan. His uncles Thomas and William both became Bishops. Sheridan, through his marriage, regained the house and lands at Quilca, Co. Cavan, original Sheridan property which had been confiscated for the family loyalty to James II. Swift celebrated the somewhat chaotic household at Quilca, where he and Stella sometimes stayed, in various poems. Sheridan graduated from Trinity College, Dublin in 1710/11; he took orders (D.D. in 1726) and established a successful school in Capel Street, Dublin ('I am famous', he wrote, 'for giving the best advice and following the worst'). An excellent classical scholar, he wrote a good Latin grammar and his pupils performed Greek tragedies in Greek. He was given a living at Ringcurran, Co. Cork in 1725 and lost the possibility of future patronage through an injudicious sermon. In 1730 he was able to exchange his Cork parish for one in Co. Meath, nearer Quilca. Five years later he became Headmaster of the Royal School in Cavan. A good translator, notably of Persius and Juvenal, he enjoyed writing comic verse and exchanged many jesting verse letters with Swift. They shared a common education, were High Churchmen, and enjoyed 'base trifles'; both were inveterate punsters. They differed, however, in their attitudes to money, Swift almost obsessively careful, Sheridan notoriously careless in financial matters. Sheridan's lack of judgment often belied his essential good nature and good humour. They began *The Intelligencer* in 1728, a weekly paper which gave 'two or three of us', Swift later remarked, 'a chance to indulge our fancy by writing a personal commentary.'

To the *Dean*, when in England, in 1726

You will excuse me, I suppose,
For sending rhyme instead of prose,
Because hot weather makes me lazy,
To write in metre is more easy.

While you are trudging London town,
I'm strolling Dublin, up and down;
While you converse with lords and dukes,

I have their betters here, my books:
Fix'd in an elbow chair at ease,
I chuse companions as I please.
I'd rather have one single shelf,
Than all my friends, except your self;
For after all that can be said,
Our best acquaintance, are the dead.
While you're in raptures with Faustina,
I'm charm'd at home, with our Sheelina;
While you are starving there in state,
I'm cramming here with butcher's meat:
You say, when with those Lords you dine,
They treat you with the best of wine;
Burgundy, Cyprus, and Tockay,
Why so can we, as well as they.
No reason, my dear Dean,
But you should travel home again.
What tho' you mayn't in Ireland hope,
To find such folk as Gay and Pope:
If you with rhymers here would share,
But half the wit, that you can spare;
I'd lay twelve eggs, that in twelve days,
You'd make a doz'n of Popes and Gays.

Our weather's good, our sky is clear,
We've ev'ry joy, if you were here;
So lofty, and so bright a skie,
Was never seen by *Ireland's-Eye!*
I think it fit to let you know,
This week I shall to Quilca go;
To see McFayden's horny brothers,
First suck, and after bull their mothers.
To see alas, my wither'd trees!
To see what all the country sees!
My stunted quicks,[1] my famish'd beeves,
My servants such a pack of thieves;
My shatter'd firs, my blasted oaks,
My house in common to all folks:
No cabbage for a single snail,

---

1 *quicks*: quick or quickset hedge, especially of hawthorn.

My turnips, carrots, parsnips, fail;
My no green pease, my few green sprouts,
My mother always in the pouts:
My horses rid, or gone astray,
My fish all stol'n, or run away:
My mutton lean, my pullets old,
My poultry starv'd, the corn all sold.

A man come now, from Quilca says,
They've stolen the locks from all your keys:
But what must fret and vex me more,
He says, they stole the keys before.
They've stol'n the knives from all the forks,
And half the cows from half the sturks;[1]
Nay more, the fellow swears and vows,
They've stol'n the sturks from half the cows.
With many more accounts of woe,
Yet tho' the devil be there, I'll go:
'Twixt you and me, the reason's clear,
Because, I've more vexation here.

From *The Intelligencer*, 2
(1728)

[The visit of Swift and Sheridan to the South East of Ireland and their experiences in Gorey, Co. Wexford]

Occusare capro, cornu ferit ille, caveto
Virgil, *Eclogue* IX l. 25[2]

My design, in Writing this *Paper*, being chiefly to expose such *Barbarians*, who think themselves exempt from those Laws of *Hospitality*, which have, through all Ages and Countries, been observed by the best and most distinguished part of Mankind; I hope I shall, *even in my own Country*, find Persons enough, to joyn with me in a hearty detestation of a certain *Country-Squire*, at the Relation of the following *Fact*, which I shall tell without the least Aggravation, or Partiality.

---

1 *sturks*: stirks.
2 *Occusare ... caveto*: 'Take care not to meet a he-goat, he butts with his horn.' This is a reference to Abel Ram, the landlord of Gorey, which he represented in the Irish House of Commons (1692–1740).

Two *Clergy-men*, of some Distinction, Travelling to the Country for their Health, happened to set up together in a small Village, which was under the Dominion of a certain *Animal*, dignified with a *brace of Titles*, that of a *Militia-Collonel*, and a *Squire*. One of these Gentlemen standing in the Street, and observing *a Coach-man* driving his *Coach and four Horses* furiously against him, turned into the close Passage between his *Inn* and the *Sign-post*, but the *Coach-man*, instead of driving through the middle of the Street, which was the usual and most commodious way, turned short, and Drove full upon the Gentleman, without any Notice, so that he was on a sudden enclosed between the *fore-horses*, and if his Friend and another Gentleman, who were in the middle of the Street, had not suddenly cryed out to stop the *Coach*, he must have unavoidably been trodden under the Horses Feet, and his Body bruised to Death by the Wheels running over him. His Friend who saw with Terror what had like to have befallen him, full of Indignation, repaired immediately to the aforesaid *Squire* or *Collonel* (to whom he was told the *Equipage* belonged) with a Complaint against his *Coach-man*. But the *Squire* instead of expressing any Concern, or offering any Redress, sent the Doctor away with the following Answer. *Sir, I have a great Regard for your Cloath, and have sent my Coach-man to ask your Friend's Pardon; for one of your Servants this moment, told me what had happened.* But, Sir, said the *Doctor*, do you think *that is sufficient*? I dare venture to affirm, if the like had befallen you, within the Liberties of my Friend, and you were brought to the same Danger by his Servant, he would not only have him Punished, but at the same time, he would discharge him his Service. Sir, (said the *Collonel*) *I tell you again, that I have sent my Coach-man to ask his Pardon, and I think that is enough*, which he spoke with some sturdiness; and well he might; for he had two *Cannons* at his Back. Good God, said the *Doctor* to himself, (when had got out of Gun-shot) what a *Hottentot* have I been talking to! who so little values the Life of a Gentleman, and as it happen'd that very Gentleman, to whom the Nation had in a particular manner been obliged. Back he went full of Resentment, for the slighting Treatment his Friend met with, and very Candidly reported all that passed; who being a Man of a different spirit from that wretched *Collonel*, ordered one of his Servants to Write the following Letter.

SIR,

My Master commanded me to tell you, That if you do not punish and turn off that Villain your Coach-man, he will think there was

*a Design upon his Life, I put this in Writing for fear of mistakes,
I am your humble Servant to command*

A.R.

The Superscription was, FOR SQUIRE WETHER, *or some such
Name*.

This *Letter* was delivered, and away went the *Travellers*. They had
not Rode far, before they fell into the Company of a Gentleman, a
degree above the common Level, and who seemed to be a Man of
Candor and Integrity, which encouraged them to recount what had
happened. He said in Answer, that they had a narrow escape; and it was
a Wonder that the whole Town did not fall upon them at once, and
worry them; for the People there, had little or no *Devotion*, besides
what was engaged to the *Squire*, as an effect of the Terrors, they lay
under from their *Landlord*, who Rode them all down, as poor as his
Fox-hunters. After this he took occasion with great Modesty, and
Decency, to draw his *Character*, which was to the following purpose.
That the *Squire* had about *fifteen hundred Pounds* a Year, and lived in a
long White-Barn; where no Man living was one *Farthing* the better for
him. That his *Piety* consisted in Six *Psalms* every Day after Dinner, without one Drop of Wine. That he had once reduced a certain *Reverend
Dean*, plumper than any two of his *Brethren*, to be as slender about the
Waste as a Weazle by a Fortnight Scouring of bad Ale, to which the
Dean was not accustomed. That his *hospitality* was within the enclosure
of a *Rampart*, with a Draw-bridge. That if any Gentleman was admitted by chance, his entertainment was *lean Salt-beef, sour Beer*, and
Muddy Ale. That his *Charity* was as much upon the catch as a *Pick-
pocket*; for his method was to bring others to erect *Charity-Schools*, by
promising his Assistance, and so leaving them in the Lurch.

That without the least Tincture of Learning, he was a great pretender to *Oratory* and *Poetry*, and eminently bad at both, which (I hope
I shall be excused the Digression) brings to my Memory a Character,
given by *Julius Capitolinus* of the Emperor *VERUS. Melior quidem
Orator fuisse dicitur, quam Poeta; imo (ut verius dicam) pejor Poeta
quam Rhetor*, (viz.) *He was a better Orator than Poet, but, to speak the
thing more properly, He was a viler Poet than an Orator*. But to give you
a Specimen of his *Genius*, I shall repeat an *Epigram* of his own
Composition (and I am very sure it is every Line his own, without any
help) which is drawn by a Sign-Dawber on the Cross-board of a Ferry-
boat, in Characters that have hitherto stood the Fury of all Weathers.

All you that are
To Andrew *Heir,*
And you that him attend
Shall Ferry'd be,
Oe'r Carrick *free,*
For Blank's *the Boatman's Friend.*

The behaviour of this *Squire* being of the most Savage kind, I think my self obliged out of the tender Regard, which I bear to all Strangers, and Travellers, to animadvert upon him in as gentle a manner as the occasion will allow. And therefore I shall first lay down a few Postulatums. *That every Travelling-Gentleman is presumed to be under the Protection of the Governing-Mayor, Sovereign, Portriff, or Squire of the Town or Village, which he happens to make his Stage. That the Laws of Humanity, Hospitality and Civility, oblige him, if there be no Accommodation in the Publick Houses, fit for a Person of Distinction, to invite him to his own, or to supply the Deficiencies as well as he can. That if any Insult or Injury be offered either to such a stranger, or his Servants, the Squire is obliged to justify, vindicate, and espouse their Cause.* This was the method observed among the civilized People of the old *Jewish,* and *Heathen* World; Where we find some of the *Patriarchs* themselves condescending to wash the Feet of such Travellers, as they entertained. And so sacred was the Regard for Strangers among the *Heathens,* that they dignifyed their Supreme GOD with the Title of *Jupiter Hospitalis.* Nothing was thought so monstrous as to offer any Violence to Sojourners among them, which was so religiously observed, that it became the glory of the most distinguished Heroes, to destroy and extirpate such as were remarkable for their Cruelty to Strangers. This it was, which added so much glory to the character of *Theseus,* for the Punishments he inflicted on *Sisiphus, Procrustes,*[1] &c. It was owing likewise to a generous

---

1 *Theseus ... Procrustes*: Theseus was a legendary hero of Attica, and champion of the oppressed; son of Aegeus, king of Athens, and Aethra, daughter of the king of Troezen, on reaching maturity, he was sent to his father in Athens by his mother. Among his heroic deeds along the way was the slaying of Procrustes, 'the Stretcher' (he used to stretch his victim's limbs to match the size of the bed onto which he tied them – or cut their limbs to size). He slew the Minotaur in the labyrinth at Crete, conquered the Amazons, whose queen he married, took part in the Calydonian hunt and the search for the Golden Fleece. Some sources claim he killed the wily Sisyphus, founder of Corinth, who robbed travellers and hurled them into the sea. Sisyphus hated his brother Salmonneus, and asked the Delphic Oracle how he could kill him. It told him to have children by Salmoneus' daughter Tyro. She bore him two, but killed them when she heard of the oracle; this caused him to commmit an impious act: in some versions of the legend (there are many) he was punished by having to push a large boulder up a steep hill in Hades; whenever it neared the top it rolled down and he had to spend eternity pushing it up again.

Indignation, That *Hercules* threw *Diomede* (The *Collonel* and *Squire* of that Age) to be devoured by those Horses,¹ which he fed with the Flesh of poor Travellers, and I find upon enquiry that they were *Coach-Horses* too. I shall make no farther remark upon this, nor Application, but say to the Squire, That it is very happy for him the present Age has not one *Hercules* left, or a Week would not pass, before he should feel the weight of that *Heroe's Club*, or be thrown by way of Reprizal under his own *Horses* feet. And I may farther add, that in this whole Kingdom, from one end of it to the other, another *Squire* could not be found, who would behave himself in the same manner to the same Person; but Hundreds, who on the Contrary, would have given all the Satisfaction, that Gentlemen of Justice, Humanity, and common Benevolence ought to do, upon the like accident, although they had never seen him before. I confess this *Paper* contains nothing besides a dry Fact, and a few occasional Observations upon it. But in the former I told my READERS, that Facts would be the chief part of the *Entertainment*, I meant to give them. If what I have said, may have any Effect on the Person concerned, (to whom care shall be taken to send this Account) or if it helps to revive the old spirit of *Hospitality* among us, or at least begets a Detestation of the like inhuman *Usage* in others; one part of my design is answered. However, it cannot be unseasonable to expose Malice, Avarice, Brutality, and Hypocrisie, wherever we find it.

From The Intelligencer, 13
(1729)

Sermo datur cunctis, animi sapientia paucis.

Cato²

There is one kind of Conversation, which every one Aims at, and every one almost fails in; It is that of *Story-telling*. I know not any thing which engages our Attention with more Delight, when a Person has a sufficient stock of Talents Necessary for it, such as *Good Sense, True Humour, a clear Head, a ready Command of Language*, and *a Variety of proper Gesture*, to give Life and Spirit to what he says. If any of these be wanting, the Listners, instead of being diverted, are made very uneasy; but if the Person be utterly Void of them all, as it

---

1 *Hercules ... Horses*: Hercules tamed the steeds of Diomede, which devoured the flesh of men.
2 *Sermo datur cunctis, animi sapientia paucis*: The art of conversation is given to all, but a wise spirit to few.

is very often the Case, he becomes a Nuissance to the Company, and they are so long upon the Rack as he speaks. It has sometimes fallen to my Lot, that a Man whom I never offended, has laid me under the Persecution of a long Story, and Compelled me to hear, what neither concerned himself, nor me, nor indeed any Body else, and at the same time, he was as much in earnest, as if both our Lives and Fortunes, and the Felicity of the whole Kingdom depended upon what he said. A Humour very unaccountable! That a Man shall be letting off Words for an hour or two, with a very innocent Intention, and after he has done his best, only makes me uneasy, and himself Contemptible.

This natural Infirmity in Men, is not only confined to *Story-telling*, but it appears likewise in every Essay whatsoever of their Intellectuals. As for Instance; If one of these be a Preacher of GOD's Word, by far fetched Criticisms, numerous Divisions, and Sub-divisions, incoherent Digressions, tedious Repetitions, useless Remarks, Weak Answers to strong Objections, Inferences to no Premises, tedious Exhortations, and many other Methods of Protraction, he shall draw you out a Discourse for an hour and a quarter, unequally dispensing Opium and Edification to his Flock, there being seven Sleepers for one Hearer. If he be a Lawyer, he shall, by an uncommon Way of Amusement, run away with a Subject, which might be explained in two Minutes, and Dilate upon it two hours, with such a Volubility of Tongue, such Affluence of Expression, with something so like a good Style, and manner of Thinking, that the Judges and Jury, attend with as much Gravity, as if there were a continued Chain of true Reasoning, and solid Argument. If he be a Member of the Upper or Lower House, he does not proceed four Sentences, before the Rest know where to have him an hour hence; in the mean time they Divert one another, in talking of matters indifferent, till the Gentleman has done. I could give many more Instances, but that I think these sufficient for my present purpose; beside, least I should incur the like Reproach my self, I must in a few Words, divide the *Story-tellers*, into *the short, the long, the marvellous, the Insipid,* and *the Delightful.*

The short Story-teller is he, who tells a great deal in few Words, engages your Attention, pleases your Imagination, or quickly excites your Laughter. Of this Rank were *Xenophon, Plutarch, Macrobius,* among the Ancients. *Ex. gr.*

When the *Nephelai* of *Aristophanes,* a Satyr upon *Socrates* was Acting, his Friends desired him to retire, and hide behind them. No said *Socrates,* I will stand up here, where I may be seen; for now I think my self like a good Feast, and that every one has share of me. *vid. Feast of Xenophon.*

Brasidas the Famous *Lacedemonian* General caught a *Mouse*. It bit him, and by that means made its escape. *O Jupiter*, said he, what Creature so Contemptible, but may have it's Liberty if it will Contend for it. *vid. Plutarch, de profect, virtut.*

Diogenes, having sailed to *Chios*, while it was under the Dominion of the *Persians*, said in a full Assembly, the Inhabitants were Fools for Erecting a Colledge, and building Temples, since the *Persians* would not allow them the privilege of making their own *Priests*, but sent them over the most Illiterate of their *Magi*.

Augustus while he was encamped with his Army, some where near *Mantua*, was disturbed three Nights successively, by the hooting of an *Owl*. Proclamation was made to the Soldiers, that whoever caught the Offender, (so that he might be brought to Justice,) should have an ample reward for his pains. Every one was Loyally engaged in the pursuit of this *Bird*. At last, one more Vigilant than the rest, found him in a Hollow-tree, so brought him in Triumph to the Emperor, who saw him with the greatest Joy, but gave the Soldier a sum of Money, so far below his Expectation, that he let the *Owl* fly away that Instant, so true a Sense of Liberty, ran through the very meanest of the *Romans*. *Macrob. Sat.*

The *long Story-teller* is one, who tells little or nothing in a great number of Words; for this, many among the Moderns are famous, particularly the *French*. And among our selves in this Kingdom we have a vast Number of the better sort. As well as I can recollect there are six Deans, four Judges, six and thirty Councellors at Law, sixty five Attorneys, some few Fellows of the College, every Alderman through the whole Nation, except one, all old Gentlemen, and Ladies, without exception, five of the College of Physicians, three or four Lords, two hundred Squires, and some few People of distinction beside.

I shall here insert a fragment of a long Story, by way of example, containing 129 Words, which might have been said in these ten following, *viz. Nine Years ago I was to Preach for a Friend.*

I remember once, I think it was about seven Years ago – No I lye – It was about nine Years ago; for it was just when my Wife was Lying in of *Dicky*, I remember particularly the Mid-wife would have had me stay to keep her company, and it was the heaviest Day of Storm and Rain, that I ever saw before, or since, but because I engaged to Preach for a very Worthy Friend of mine, who lived about twenty Miles off, and this being *Saturday*, I could not defer it to the next Morning, though I had an excellent Nag, which could have Rid it in three hours, I bought him of a Neighbour one Mr. *Masterson*, yet because I would not put my Friend in a fright &c. Thus far he went in one Minute. The Story lasted an Hour, so that upon a fair computation he Spoke 7740 Words, instead of 600, by which means he made use of 7140 more than he had occasion for. If a right application were made of this hint, which I have given, it would be of admirable Effect in the dispatch of publick business, as well as private conversation, nay in the very Writing of Books, for which I refer the reader to the *Fable of the Bees*, and the two Elaborate Treatises, Written by the Learned Mr. *H———n*.

The marvellous, is he, who is fond of telling such things as no Man alive, who has the least use of his reason, can believe. This humour prevails very much in Travellers, and the Vain glorious, but is very pardonable, because no Man's Faith is imposed upon, or if it should be so, no ill consequence attends it. And beside, there is some kind of Amusement in seeing a Person seriously extravagant, expecting another should give Credit to what he knows impossible for the greatest Dunce to Swallow.

One of these, who had. travelled to *Damascus*, told his Company, that the *Bees* of that Country were as big as *Turkies*. Pray Sir, said a Gentleman (begging pardon for the Question) How large were the Hives? The same size with Ours, replied the Traveller. Very strange, said the other. But how got they into their Hives? That is none of my business, I Gad let them look to that.

Another, who had Travelled as far as *Persia*, spoke to his Man *John*, as he was returning home, telling him, how Necessary it was, that a Traveller should draw things beyond the Life, or else, he could not hope for that respect from his Country-Men, which otherwise he might have. But at the same time, *John*, said he, wheresoever I shall Dine, or Sup, keep you close to my Chair, and if I do very much exceed the bounds of Truth, Punch me behind, that I may correct my self. It happened on a Day, that he Dined with a Certain Gentleman, who shall be Nameless, where he affirmed, that he saw a *Monkey* in the Island *Borneo*, which had a Tail three-score Yards long. *John* punched him. I am certain it is fifty at least. *John* punched again. I believe to speak within compass, for I did not measure it, it must have been forty. *John* gave him tother Touch. I remember it lay over a Quick-set hedge, and therefore could not be less than thirty. *John* at him again. I could take my Oath it was twenty. This did not satisfy *John*. Upon which the Master turned about in a Rage and said, Damn you for a Puppy, would you have the *Monkey* without any Tail at all?

Did not the famous Dr. *Burnet*, whose History[1] is much of the same stamp with his Travels, affirm that he saw an *Elephant* play at Ball? And that grave Gentleman *Ysbrant Ides*,[2] in his Travels through *Muscovy to China*, assures us, that he saw *Elephants*, which were taught to low like *Cows*, to yell like *Tigers*, and to mimick the sounding of a Trumpet; but their highest Perfection, as he relates it, was that of singing like Canary birds. However this is not so marvellous (for *Pliny* relates Wonderful things of their Docility) as what a Gentleman told a full Company in my hearing within this fortnight. That he had seen a Show at *Bristol*, which was a *Hare*, taught to stand upon her hind-legs and bow to all the Company, to each Person in particular, with a very good Grace, and then proceed to beat several Marches on the Drum. After this a *Dog* was set upon the Table. His Master, the *Show-man*, made many grievous Complaints against him, for High Crimes, and Misdemeanors. The *Hare* nits her Brows, kindles her Eyes like a Lady, falls in a Passion, attacks the *Dog* with all her Rage and Fury, as if she had been his Wife, Scratches, bites, and cuffs him round the Table, till the Spectators had enough for their Money.

There is a certain Gentleman, now in *Ireland*, most remarkably fond of the marvellous (but this through Vanity) who among an infinite number of the like Rarities, affirms, that he has a *Carp*, in a Pond by itself, which has for twenty Years past, supplyed him and his Friends, with a very good Dish of Fish, when they either came to Dine, or Sup with him. And the manner of it is thus. The Cook-maid goes with a large Kitchin-knife, which has a Whistle in its handle; she no sooner blows it, but the *Carp* comes to the Sluice and turns up its Belly, till she cuts out as much as she has occasion for, and then away it scuds. The Chasm is filled in a Day or two, and the *Carp* is as sound as a *Roach*, ready for the Knife again. Now, if he and his Cook-maid took the most solemn Oath to the truth of this, or the most sanctified *Quaker* should say YEA to it, which is made equal to any Prelate's Oath, I would no more give Credit to them, than I would to the *Collonel* who said he was at the Battle of *Landen*, where his Majesty King *William*, of Glorious Memory, lost the Day. And this *Collonel*, being in the utmost Confusion, fled among the rest. He Swore he had Galloped above two miles, after his Horses Head was Shot off, by a Cannon-ball, which he should not have missed, if the poor Creature had not stooped at a River side to Drink.

---

1 *Dr. Burnet – History*: Bishop Burnet's *History of my Own Time* is a major source for the political history of the late seventeenth and early eighteenth century.
2 Ysbrant Ides: Everard Ysbrant Ides wrote a collection of *Travels to China* (1691–1696).

I should be glad to spend an Evening with half a dozen Gentlemen of this uncommon Genius, for I am certain they would improve upon one another, and thereby I might have an Oportunity of observing how far the Marvellous could be carried, or whether it has any bounds at all.

The insipid, who may not unfitly be called Soporifick, is one who goes plodding on in a heavy dull Relation of unimportant Facts. You Shall have an Account from such a Person of every Minute Circumstance, which happened in the Company where he has been, what he did, and what they did, what they said, and what he said, with a Million of trite Phrases, with an *and so* beginning every Sentence. And *to make a long Story short*. And *as I was saying*, with many more expletives of equal Signification. It is a most dreadful thing, when Men have neither the Talent of speaking, nor the Discretion of holding their Tongues, and that, of all People, such as are least qualified, are commonly the most earnest in this way of Conversation.

The Delightful Story-teller is one, who speaks not a Word too much, or too little; who can, in a very careless manner, give a great deal of pleasure to others, and desires rather to Divert, than be Applauded; who shews good understanding, and a delicate turn of Wit in every thing which comes from him; who can entertain his Company better with the History of a Child and its *Hobby-horse*, than one of the *Soporificks* can with an Account of *Alexander*, and *Bucephalus*. Such a Person is not unlike a bad Reader who makes the most ingenious Piece his own, that is, Dull and Detestable, by only coming through his Mouth. But to return to the Delightful *Story-teller*, I cannot describe him by any Words so well, as his own, and therefore take the following Story to shew him in the most agreeable light.

A Mountebank in Leicester-Fields had drawn a huge Assembly about him; among the rest a Fat unwieldy Fellow, half stifled in the Press, would be every fit Crying out Lord! what a filthy Crowd is here! pray good People give Way a little! bless me! what a Devil has raked this Rable[1] together? Zounds what squeezing is this! Honest Friend remove your Elbow. At last a Weaver, that stood next him, could hold no longer. A Plague confound you, said he, for an Over grown Sloven; and who, in the Devil's Name, helps to make up the Crowd half so much as your self? Don't you consider (with a Pox) that you take up more room with that Carcass than any five here? Is not the Place as fit

---

1 *Rable*: obsolete form of *rabble*.

for us, as for you? bring your own Guts to a reasonable Compass (and be Damnd) and then I'll engage we shall have room enough for us all.

This I have transcribed from a most Celebrated Author, with great pleasure, and do earnestly recommend it to my Country-men, as the true standard of *Story-telling*, both as to Style, and Manner, and every thing requisite not only to please the Hearer, but to gain his favour and Affection. And for the Time to come, be it Enacted, that if any person of what Rank soever, shall presume to exceed Six Minutes in a Story, to *hum* or *haw*, use *hyphens* between his Words, or Digressions, or offers to engage the Company to hear another Story when he has done, or speaks one Word more than is Necessary, or is a Stammerer in his Speech, that then it shall, and may be lawful for any one of the said Company, or the whole Company together, to pull out his, hers or their Watches to make use of broad hints, or innuendoes for him the said *Story-teller*, to break off, although abruptly, otherwise he is to have a Glove, or Handkerchief, crammed into his Mouth for the first default, and for the second, to be kicked out of Company.

MARY BARBER (1690-1757)

A poet ('Sapphira'), she was probably born in Dublin and married a draper. Swift raised money for her *Poems on Several Occasions* (1734) and presented her with the manuscript of his *Polite Conversations* (1738), which brought her some income. She suffered from rheumatism and did not write much in later years.

Advice to her Son on Marriage

From *The Conclusion of a Letter to the Rev. Mr C—*

When you gain her Affection, take care to preserve it;
Lest others persuade her, you do not deserve it.
Still study to heighten the Joys of her Life;
Not treat her the worse, for her being your wife.
If in Judgment she errs, set her right, without Pride:
'Tis the Province of insolent fools, to deride.
A Husband's first Praise, is a Friend and Protector
Then change not these Titles, for Tyrant and Hector.
Let your person be neat, unaffectedly clean,
Tho' alone with your Wife the whole Day you remain.
Chuse Books, for her study, to fashion her mind,

To emulate those who excell'd of her Kind.
Be Religion the principal Care of your Life,
As you hope to be blest in your Children and Wife:
So you, in your Marriage, shall gain its true end;
And find, in your Wife, a Companion and Friend.

THOMAS AMORY (?1691-1788)

A mory was brought up in Ireland (and may possibly have been born on his father's estate in Co. Clare). He does not seem to have studied at Trinity College, Dublin, as he claimed he had; he mentions knowing several distinguished contemporary Irish writers, among them Toland, Swift and Berkeley. He moved to England in the mid 1750s, living at Hounslow and Westminster. He wrote two novels, the first, *Memoirs of Several Ladies of Great Britain* (1755), was intended to be the first volume of a series which would include a miscellany of his interests in travel, in Unitarian beliefs, medicine (he had had some medical training) antiquities and nature. This novel, centred on Mrs Marinda Benlow, dealt with a community of learned women sequestered on a 'Green Island' to the west of St. Kilda in the midst of luxuriant vegetation. The manuscript of Amory's *The Ancient and Present State of Great Britain* was accidentally burnt, so that he is known for his novels, full of arcane learning, marital history and fantasy. In *The Life and Opinions of John Buncle, Esq.* (1756; 1766) Amory and his eponymous hero are often confused: the novel exhibits an early interest in Ireland's language, history and blend of gaelic and Anglo-Irish culture.

From *The Life and Opinions of John Buncle, Esq.* (1756; 1766)

... On then I went at all hazards, and in a tedious manner was forced to creep the way: but to make some amends, the prospects from the hills were fine, and things very curious occurred. Groups of crests of mountains appeared here and there, like large cities with towers and old Gothic edifices, and from caverns in their sides torrents of water streamed out, and tumbled in various courses to the most delightful vales below. In some of the vast hills there were openings quite through, so as to see the sun, at the end of three or four thousand yards; and in many of them were sloping caverns, very wonderful to behold.

I found in one of them, near the top of a very high mountain, a descent like steps of stairs, that was in breadth and height like the aisle of a church, for three hundred yards, and then ended at a kind of door, or small arched opening, that was high enough for a tall man to walk into a grand room which it led to. This chamber was a square of seventeen yards, and had an arched roof about twenty high. The stone of it was a green marble, not earthy and opaque, but pure and crystalline, which made it appear very beautiful, as the walls were as smooth as if the best polish had made them so. There was another opening or door at the other side of this chamber, and from it likewise went a descent like steps, but the downward passage here was much steeper than the other I had come to, and the opening not more than one third as wide and high; narrowing gradually to the bottom of the sloping road, till it ended in a round hole, a yard and a quarter every way. I could see the day at the opening below, though it seemed at a great distance from me, and as it was not dangerous to descend, I determined to go down.

The descent was four hundred and seventy-nine yards in a straight line, and opened in a view of meadows, scattered trees, and streams, that were enchantingly fine. There appeared to be about four and twenty acres of fine land, quite surrounded with the most frightful precipices in the world, and in the centre of it a neat and pretty little country house, on an easy rising ground. I could discover with my long glass a young and handsome woman sitting at the door, engaged in needle-work of some kind; and on the margin of a brook hard by, another charmer stood, angling for fish of some sort: a garden appeared near the mansion that was well improved; and in the fields were sheep and goats, horses and cows; cocks and hens, ducks and geese, were walking about the ground; and I could perceive a college of bees. The whole formed a charming scene.

Pleased with the view, and impatient to know who the two charmers were, I quite forgot the poor situation in which I left TIM, holding the horses at the mouth of the cavern, on the dangerous side of so high a hill, and proceeded immediately to the house, as soon as I had recovered myself from a fall. My foot slip'd in the passage, about six yards from the day, and I came rolling out of the mountain in a violent and surprising manner. It was just mid-day when I came up to the ladies, and as they did not see me till they chanced to turn round, they were so amazed at my appearing, they changed colour, and one of them shrieked aloud; but this fright was soon over, on my assuring them that I was their most humble servant, and had against my will tumbled out of the hole that was at the bottom of that vast mountain before them. This I explained, and protested that I had not thought of paying them a visit, when curiosity led me into an opening near the top of the hill, as I was travelling on; but that when I did get through so wonderful a passage, and saw what was still more strange, when I arrived in the vale, to wit, two ladies, in so wild and silent a place, I judged it my duty to pay my respects, and ask if you had any commands that I could execute in the world? This was polite, they said, and gave me thanks; but told me, they had no other favour to ask than that I would dine with them, and inform them how it happened that I was obliged to travel over these scarce passable mountains, where there was no society nor support to be had. Beside if in riding here you should receive a mischief, there was not a possibility of getting any relief. There must be something very extraordinary surely, that could cause you to journey over such frightful hills, and through the deep bottoms at the foot of them.

'Ladies,' I replied, 'necessity and curiosity united are the spring that move me over these mountains, and enable me to bear the hardships I meet with in these ways. Forced from home by the cruelties of a step-mother, and forsaken by my father on her account, I am wandering about the precipices of Richmondshire in search of a gentleman, my friend; to whose hospitable house and generous breast I should be welcome, if I could find out where he lives in some part of this remote and desolate region: and as my curiosity is more than ordinary, and I love to contemplate the works of nature, which are very grand and astonishing in this part of the world, I have gone many a mile out of my way while I have been looking for several days past for my friend, and have ventured into places where very few I believe would go. It was this taste for natural knowledge that travelled me down the inside of the mountain I am just come out of. If I had not had it, I should never have known there was so delightful a little country here as what I now see: nor should I have had the honour and happiness of being known to you.'

'But tell me, Sir,' one of these beauties said, 'how have you lived for several days among these rocks and desert places, as there are no inns in this country, nor a house, except this, here, that we know? are you the favorite of the fairies and genies, or does the wise man of the hills, bring you every night in a cloud to his home?'

'It looks something like it, Madam,' I answered, 'and the thing to be sure must appear very strange, but it is like other strange things, when the nature of them is known, they appear easy and plain. This country I find consists, for the most part, of ranges and groups of mountains horrible to behold, and of bogs, deep swampy narrow bottoms, and waters that fall and run innumerable ways, but this is not always the case, like the charming plain I am now on, there are many flowery and delicious extensive pieces of ground, enclosed by vast surrounding hills; the finest intervals betwixt the mountains: the sweetest interchange between hill and valley, I believe in all the world, is to be found in Richmondshire, and in several of those delightful vales I discovered inhabitants as in this place, but the houses are so separated by fells scarcely passable, and torrents of water, that those who live in the centre of one group of mountains, know nothing of many agreeable inhabitants that may dwell on the other side of the hills in an adjacent vale. If there had been a fine spot at the bottom of the precipice I found the opening in, and people living there, as might have been the case, you ladies who live here, could have no notion of them, as you knew nothing of a passage from the foot to the summit of yonder mountain, within side of the vast hill, and if you did, would never venture to visit that way: and as there is not a pass in this chain of hills, to ride or walk through, to the other side of them: but the way out of this valley we are now in, as I judge from the trembling of the mountains all round us, must be an opening into some part of Cumberland. For this reason Stanemore hills may have several families among them, though you have never heard of them, and I will now give you an account of some, who behaved in the most kind and generous manner to me. Here I began to relate some particulars concerning my friend PRICE and his excellent wife; the admirable Mrs. BURCOT and Mrs. FLETCHER; the philosophers who lived at Ulubræ, to whom I was returning; and the generous Mr. HARCOURT, and his excellent daughter, whom I left in the morning; and at whose house I arrived by travelling up the dark bowels of a tremendous mountain; as, on the contrary, I arrived at theirs by a descent through yonder frightful hill, till I came rolling out from within, in a very surprising and comical way; a way that would have made you laugh, ladies; or, in a fright, cry out, if you had happened to be walking near the hole or opening in the bottom of that hill, when, by a slip of my foot, in descending, a few yards from the day, I tumbled over and over, not only down what remained of the dark steep within, but the high sloping bank that reaches from the outside of the opening to the first flat part of the vale. There is nothing wonderful then in my living in this lone country for so many days. The only strange thing is, considering the waters and swamps, that I was not drowned; or, on account of the precipices and descents I have been engaged on, that I did not break my neck, or my bones; but so long we are to live as Providence hath appointed for the accomplishment of the grand divine scheme. Till the part allotted us is acted, we are secure. When it is done, we must go, and leave the stage for other players to come on.'

The ladies seemed greatly entertained with my histories, and especially with my tumbling out of the mountain into their vale. They laughed very heartily; but told me, if they had happened to be sitting near the hole, in the bottom of that tremendous rocky mountain, as they sometimes did, and often wondered where the opening went to, and that I had come rolling down upon them, they would have been frightened out of their senses, for they must have thought it a very strange appearance; without hearing the history of it, they must think it a prodigious occurrence, or exception, from the constant affairs of nature....

Here a footman came up to us, to let his mistress know that dinner was on the table, and we immediately went in to an excellent one. The ladies were very civil to me, and exerted a good humour to shew me, I suppose, that my arrival was not disagreeable to them, though I tumbled upon their habitation, like the genie of the caverns, from the hollows of the mountains. They talked in an easy, rational manner, and asked me many questions that shewed they were no strangers to books and men and things: but at last it came to pass, that the eldest of those ladies, who acted as mistress of the house and seemed to be about one or two and twenty, desired to know the name of the gentleman I was looking for among these hills, and called my friend. 'My reason, Sir, for asking is, that you answer so exactly in face and person to a description of a gentleman I heard not very long ago, that I imagine it may be in my power to direct you right.'

'Madam,' I replied, 'the gentleman I am in search of is CHARLES TURNER, who was my schoolfellow, and my senior by a year in the university, which he left two years before I did, and went from Dublin to the north of England, to inherit a paternal estate on the decease of his father. There was an uncommon friendship between this excellent young man and me, and he made me promise him, in a solemn manner, to call upon him as soon as it was in my power; assuring me at the same time, that if by any changes and chances in this lower hemisphere, I was ever brought into any perplexities, and he alive, I should be welcome to him and what he had, and share in his happiness in this world, while I pleased. This is the man I want, a man, for his years, one of the wisest and best of the race. His honest heart had no design in words. He ever spoke what he meant, and therefore, I am sure he is my friend.'

To this the lady answered, 'Sir, since CHARLES TURNER is the man you want, your enquiry is at an end, for you are now at his house; and I, who am his sister, bid you welcome to Skelsmore-Vale in his name. He has been for a year and a half last past in Italy, and a little before he went, gave me such a description of you as enabled me to guess who you were after I had looked a while at you, and he added to his description a request to me, that if you should happen to call here, while I happened to be in the country, that I would receive you, as if you were himself; and when I removed, if I could not, or did not choose to stay longer in the country that I would make you an offer of the house, and give you up all the keys of it, to make use of it and his servants, and the best things the place affords, till his return; which is to be, he says, in less than a year. Now, Sir, in regard to my brother and his friend, I not only offer you what he desired I should, but I will stay a month here longer than I intended; for this lady, my cousin, MARTHA JACQUELOT, and I, had determined to go to Scarborough next week, and from thence to London: nor is this all, as I know I shall the more oblige my brother the civiller I am to you, I will, when the Scarborough season is over, if you choose to spend the winter here, come back to Skelsmore-Vale, and stay till Mr. TURNER returns.'

This discourse astonished me to the last degree, to hear that I was at my friend TURNER's house, he abroad, and to be so for another year; the possession of his seat offered me; and his charming sister so very civil and good, as to assure me she would return from the Spa, and stay with me till her brother came home: were things so unexpected and extraordinary, that I was for some time silent, and at a loss what to say. I paused for some minutes, with my eyes fastened on this beauty, and then said 'Miss TURNER, the account you have given of your brother, and the information that I am now at his house, his friendly offers to me by you, and your prodigious civility, in resolving to return from Scarborough, to stay with me here till your brother arrives, are things so strange so uncommon, and exceedingly generous and kind, that I am quite amazed at what I hear, and want words to express my obligations, and the grateful sense I have of such favours. Accept my thanks, and be assured, that while I live, I shall properly remember the civility and benevolence of this day; and be ever ready if occasion offered, and the fates should put in my power, to make a due return. Your offer, Madam, in particular, is so high an honour done me, and shews a spirit so humane, as I told you I was an unfortunate one, that I shall ever think of it with pleasure, and mention it as a rare instance of female worth; but as to accepting these most kind offers I cannot do it. Since Mr. TURNER is from home, I will go and visit another friend I have in this country, to whom I shall be welcome, I believe, till your brother returns. To live by myself here at my friend's expence, would not be right, nor agreeable to me: and as to confining you, Madam, in staying with me, I would not do it for the world.' 'Sir,' Miss TURNER replied, 'in respect of my staying here, it will be no confinement to me, I assure you. My heart is not set upon going to London. It was only want of company made Miss JACQUELOT and me think of it, and if you will stay with us, we will not even go to Scarborough this season.' This was goodness indeed, but against staying longer than two or three days, I had many good reasons that made it necessary for me to depart: beside the unreasonableness of my being an expence to Mr. TURNER in his absence, or confining his sister to the country; there was Orton-Lodge, where I had left O'FIN, my lad, at work, to which I could not avoid going again: and there was Miss MELMOTH, on whom I had promised to wait, and did intend to ask her if she would give me her hand, as I liked her and her circumstances, and fancied she would live with me in any retreat I pleased to name; which was a thing that would be most pleasing to my mind. It is true, if CHARLES TURNER had come home, while I stayed at his house, it was possible I might have got his sister, who was a very great fortune: but this was an uncertainty however, and in his absence, I could not in honour make my addresses to her: if it should be against his mind, it would be acting a false part, while I was eating his bread. Miss TURNER to be sure had fifty thousand pounds at her own disposal, and so far as I could judge of her mind, during the three days that I stayed with her at Skelsmore-Vale, I had some reason to imagine her heart might be gained: but for a man worth nothing to do this, in her brother's house, without his leave, was a part I could not act, though by missing her I had been brought to beg my bread. Three days then only I could be prevailed on to stay, and the time indeed was happily spent....

This man [a publican] informed me, that about a mile from his habitation, in the middle of the wood, there dwelt an old physician, one DR. FITZGIBBONS, an Irish gentleman, who had one very pretty daughter, a sensible woman, to whom he was able to give a good fortune, if a man to both their liking appeared; but as no such one had as yet come in their way, my landlord advised me to try the adventure, and he would furnish me with an excuse for going to the doctor's house. This set me a thinking. Dr. FITZGIBBONS, an Irish gentleman, said I, I know the man. I saved his son's life in Ireland, when he was upon the brink of destruction, and the old gentleman was not only then as thankful as it was possible for a man to be, in return for the good I had done him, at the hazard of my own life, but assured me, a thousand times over, that if ever it was in his power to return my kindness, he would be my friend to the utmost of his ability. He must ever remember, with the greatest gratitude, the benefit I had so generously conferred on him and his. All this came full into my mind, and I determined to visit the old gentleman in the morning.

Next day, as I had resolved, I went to pay my respects to Dr.

FITZGIBBONS, who remembered me perfectly well, was most heartily glad to see me, and received me in the most affectionate manner. He immediately began to repeat his obligations to me, for the deliverance I had given his son, and that if it was in his power to be of service to me in England, he would leave nothing undone that was possible for him to do, to befriend me. He told me, that darling son of his, whose life I had saved, was an eminent physician at the court of Russia, where he lived in the greatest opulence and reputation, and as he owed his existence as such to me, his father could never be grateful enough in return. 'Can I any way serve you, Sir? Have you been fortunate or unfortunate, since your living in England? Are you married or unmarried? I have a daughter by a second wife, and if you are not yet engaged, will give her to you, with a good fortune, and in two years time, if you will study physic here, under my direction, will enable you to begin to practice, and get money as I have done in this country. I have so true a sense of that generous act you did to save my son, that I will with pleasure do any thing in my power that can contribute to your happiness.'

To this I replied, by thanking the doctor for his friendly offers, and letting him know, that since my coming to England several years ago, which was occasioned by a difference between my father and me, I had met with several turns of fortune, good and bad, and was at present but in a very middling way, having only a little spot among the mountains of Richmondshire, with a cottage and garden on it, and three or four beasts, which I found by accident without an owner, as I travelled through that uninhabited land; and a small farm of fifty acres with some stock, on the borders of Cumberland, which I got by a deceased wife. This, with about fifty guineas in my purse, was my all at present; and I was going up to London, to try if I could meet with any thing fortunate in that place; but that, since he was pleased to make me such generous offers, I would stop, study physic as he proposed, and accept the great honour he did me in offering me his daughter for a wife. I told him likewise very fairly and honestly, that I had been rich by three or four marriages since my being in this country; but that I was unfortunately taken in at a gaming-table, by the means of two Irish gentlemen he knew very well, and there lost all; which vexed me the more, as I really do not love play; that as to my father, I had little to expect from him, though he had a great estate, as our difference was about religion; which kind of disputes have always the most cruel tendency; and the wife he had, a low cunning woman, did all she could to maintain the variance, and keep up his

anger to me, that her nephew might do the better on my ruin. That I
had not written to him since my being in England; nor had I met with
any one who could give me any account of the family....

The doctor wondered not a little at the account I had given him,
as my father was reckoned a man of great abilities, and taking me by
the hand, said, I had acted most gloriously; that what lost me my
father's affection, was the very thing that ought to have induced him
to erect a statue to my honour in his garden – that since I was pleased
to accept of his offer, his friendship I might depend on – that if I
would, I should begin the next day the study of physic under his
direction, and at the end of two years, he would give me his daughter, who was not yet quite twenty.

Just as he had said this, Miss FITZGIBBONS entered the room, and
her father introduced me to her. The sight of her astonished me,
though I had before seen so many fine women, I could not help looking with wonder at her. She appeared one of those finished creatures,
whom we cannot enough admire, and upon acquaintance with her,
became much more glorious.

What a vast variety of beauty do we see in the infinity of nature.
Among the sex, we may find a thousand and a thousand perfect images
and characters ; all equally striking, and yet as different as the pictures
of the greatest masters in Italy. What amazing charms and perfections
have I beheld in women as I have journeyed through life. When I have
parted from one; well I said, I shall never meet another like this inimitable maid; and yet after all, JULIA appeared divinely fair, and happy in
every excellence that can adorn the female mind. Without that exact reg-
ularity of beauty, and elegant softness of propriety, which rendered Miss
DUNK, whom I have described in these *Memoirs*, a very divinity, JULIA
charmed with a graceful negligence, and enchanted with a face that
glowed with youthful wonders, beauties that art could not adorn but
always diminished. The choice of dress was no part of JULIA's care, but
by the neglect of it she became irresistible. In her countenance there ever
appeared a bewitching mixture of sensibility and gaiety, and in her soul,
by converse was discovered that generosity and tenderness were the first
principles of her mind. To truth and virtue she was inwardly devoted,
and at the bottom of her heart, though hard to discover it, her main business to serve God, and fit herself for eternity. In sum, she was one of the
finest originals that ever appeared among womankind, peculiar in perfections which cannot be described; and so inexpressibly charming in an
attractive sweetness, a natural gaiety, and a striking negligence, a fine
understanding, and the most humane heart; that I found it impossible to

know her without being in love with her: her power to please was extensive indeed. In her, one had the loveliest idea of woman.

To this fine creature I was married at the end of two years from my first acquaintance with her; that is, after I had studied physic so long, under the care and instruction of her excellent father, who died a few weeks after the wedding, which was in the beginning of the year 1734, and the 29th of my age. Dying, he left me a handsome fortune, his library, and house; and I imagined I should have lived many happy years with his admirable daughter, who obliged me by every endearing means, to be excessively fond of her. I began to practise upon the old gentleman's death, and had learned so much in the two years I had studied under him, from his lecturing and my own hard reading, that I was able to get some money among the opulent round me; not by art and collusion, the case of too many doctors in town and country, but by practicing upon consistent principles.

[The Doctor was instructing me]... He had told me that 'the active salts of the fly penetrate the whole animal machine, become a glandular lymphatic purge, and perform the same thing in all the small straining conveying pipes, that common purgatives effect in the intestines: and as by this means, all the sluices and outlets of the glandular secretions are opened, the cantharides must be cooling, diluting, and refrigerating in their effects to the greatest degree, though so very hot, caustic, and pungent in themselves. So wonderfully has the great Creator provided for his creature, man; in giving him not only a variety of the most pleasing food, but so fine a medicine, among a thousand others, as the Spanish fly, to save him from the destroying fever, and restore him to health again. It is not by a discharge of serum, as too many doctors imagine that a blister relieves, for five times the quantity may be brought off by bleeding, vomitting, or purging; but the benefit is entirely owing to that heating, attenuating, and pungent salt of this fly, and this fly only, which the divine power and goodness has made a lymphatic purgative, or glandular cathartic for the relief of man, in this fatal and tormenting malady. Vast is our obligation to God for all his providential blessings. Great are the wonders that he doth for the children of men.'

Here the Doctor dropt off his chair, just as he had pronounced the word men, and in a moment became a lifeless sordid body. His death was occasioned by the blowing up of his stomach, as I found upon opening his body, at the request of his lady. When the blood which is confined within the vessels of the human body, is agitated with a due motion, it maintains life; but if there be a stagnation of it in an artery, it makes an aneurism; in a vein, a varix; under the skin, a bruise; in the nose, it may excite an haemorrhage; in the vessels of the brain, an apoplexy; in the lungs, an hæmoptoe; in the cavity of the thorax, an empyema; and when it perfectly stagnates there, immediate death.

An animal, observe me, Reader, must live so long as this fluid circulates through the conical pipes in his body, from the lesser base in the centre, the heart, to the greater in the extreme parts; and from the capillary evanescent arteries, by the nascent returning veins to the heart again; but when this fluid ceases to flow through the incurved canals, and the velocities are no longer in the inverse duplicate ratio of the inflated pipes, then it dies. The animal has done for ever with food and sex; the two great principles which move this world, and produce not only so much honest industry, but so many wars and fightings, such cruel oppressions, and that variety of woes we read of in the tragical history of the world. Even one of them does wonders. Cunnus teterrima belli causa.[1] And when united, the force is irresistible.

But as I was saying, when this fluid ceases to flow, the man has done with lust and hunger. The pope, the warrior, and the maid, are still. The machine is at absolute rest, that is, in perfect insensibility; and the soul of it is removed to the vestibulum or porch of the highest holy place; in a vehicle, says Wollaston, and Burnet of the Charterhouse, as needful to our contact with the material system, as it must exist with a spiritual body, says the Rev. Caleb Fleming, in his *Survey of the Search after Souls*, because of its being present with its Saviour, beholding his glory, who is in human form and figure, which requires some similitude in the vehicle, in order to the more easy and familiar society and enjoyment. Or, as the learned Master of Peter-house, Dr. Edmund Law, and Dr. Sherlock, bishop of London inform us, it remains insensible for ages, till the consummation of all things; from the dissolution of the body, is stupid, senseless, and dead asleep till the resurrection.

Such was the case of my friend Dr. STANVIL; he dropt down dead at once. A rarefaction in his stomach, by the heat and fermentation of what he had taken the night before at supper, destroyed him. That concave viscus, or bowel, which is seated in the abdomen below the diaphragm, I mean the stomach, was inflamed, and as the descending trunk of the aorta passes down between it and the spine, that is, between the stomach and back part of the ribs, the inflation and distention of the bowel compressed and constringed the transverse section of the artery aorta, in

---

1 *Cunnus ... causa*: 'Nam fuit ante Helenam Cunnus teterrina belli Causa' (Horace, Satires, I. 3, 107–108): 'Because already before Helen the unchaste was the most loathsome cause of war'.

its descending branch, and by lessening it, impeded the descent of the blood from the heart, and obliged it to ascend in a greater quantity than usual to the head. By this means, the parts of the head were distended and stretched with blood, which brought on an apoplexy, and the operation upward being violent, the equilibrium was entirely broken, and the vital tide could flow no more. This I found on opening the body. I likewise observed that, exclusive of the compressure of the descending trunk of the artery aorta, the muscular coats of the stomach were stretched, inflated, and distended; and of consequence, the blood-vessels which enter into the constitution of these muscles, were stretched, dilated, and turgid with blood, and therefore the blood could not be driven forward in the course of its circulation with its natural and due velocity, but must prove an obstacle to the descent of the blood from the heart, and oblige almost the whole tide to move upwards. This, and the constringing the aorta, at its orifice or transverse section, between the costæ and the bowel called the stomach, is enough, I assure you. Reader, to knock up the head of a giant, and put a stop to all the operations of nature. Thus fell this gentleman in the thirty-second year of his age....

... When I consider how happy I have been in the married state, and in a succession of seven wives, never had one uneasy hour; that even a Paradise, without an Eve, would have been a wilderness to me; that the woods, the groves, the walks, the prospects, the flowers, the fruits, the day, the night, all would have wanted a relish, without that dear, delightful companion, a wife; it amazes me to hear many sensible people speak with abhorrence of matrimony, and insist upon it, that wedlock produces so many troubles, even where the pair have affection, and sorrows so very great, when they have no love for each other, or begin to fail in the kind and obliging offices, that it is contrary to reason to contract, if we have a just regard to peace and satisfaction of mind, and would avoid, as much as possible, the woes and bewailings of this turbid period. If you have acquired the divine habits, marriage may unhinge them. It often forces even the pious into immoralities. True, unhappy are many a wedded pair: years of calamity this engagement has produced to thousand of mortals; it has made the most pious divines become very cruel, as I could relate: it has caused the most generous, sensible men, to murder the women they adored before they were their wives....

June 8th.—Having thus lost my charming companion, I travelled into a vast valley, enclosed by mountains whose tops were above the clouds, and soon came into a country that is wilder than the campagna of Rome, or the uncultivated vales of the Alps and Appenines.

Warm with a classical enthusiasm, I journey'd on, and with fancy's eye beheld the rural divinities, in those sacred woods and groves, which shade the sides of many of the vast surrounding fells, and the shores and promontories of many lovely lakes and bright running streams. For several hours I travelled over mountains tremendous to behold, and through vales the most enchanting in the world. Not a man or house could I see in eight hours time, but towards five in the afternoon, there appeared at the foot of a hill a sweetly situated cottage, that was half covered with trees, and stood by the side of a large falling stream: a vale extended to the south from the door, that was terminated with rocks and precipices on precipices, in an amazing point of view, and through the flowery ground, the water was beautifully seen, as it winded to a deeper flood at the bottom of the vale. Half a dozen cows were grazing in view: and a few flocks of feeding sheep added to the beauties of the scene.

To this house I sent my boy, to enquire who lived there, and to know, if for the night I could be entertained, as I knew not where else to go. O'FIN very quickly returned, and informed me, that one farmer PRICE was the owner of the place, but had gone in the morning to the next town, and that his wife said I was welcome to what her house afforded. In then I went, and was most civilly received by an exceedingly pretty woman, who told me her husband would soon be at home, and be glad she was sure to see me at their lonely place; for he was no stranger to gentlemen and the world, though at present he rarely conversed with any one. She told me, their own supper would be ready in an hour hence, and in the mean time would have me take a can of fine ale and a bit of bread. She brought me a cup of extraordinary malt-drink and a crust, and while I was eating my bread, in came Mr. PRICE.

The man seemed very greatly astonished at entering the room, and after he had looked with great earnestness at me for a little while, he cried out, 'Good heaven! What do I see! FALSTAFF, my class-fellow, and my second self. My dear friend you are welcome, thrice welcome to this part of the world.' All this surprised me not a little, for I could not recollect at once a face that had been greatly altered by the small-pox: and it was not till I reflected on the name PRICE, that I knew I was then in the house of one of my school-fellows, with whom I had been most intimate, and had played the part of Plump Jack in *Henry the Fourth*, when he did Prince Henry. This was an unexpected meeting indeed: and considering the place, and all the circumstances belonging to the scene, a thing more strange and affecting never came in my way. Our pleasure at this meeting was very great, and when the most affectionate salutations were over, my friend PRICE proceeded in the following manner.

'Often have I remember'd you since we parted, and exclusive of the Greek and English plays we have acted together at Sheridan's school,[1] in which you acquired no small applause, I have frequently thought of our frolicsome rambles in vacation time, and the merry dancings we had at Mother RedCap's in Back-Lane; the hurling matches we have play'd at Dolphin's-barn, and the cakes and ale we used to have at the Organ-house on Arbor-Hill. These things have often occurred to my mind: but little did I think we should ever meet again on Stainmore-hills. What strange things does time produce! It has taken me from a town life to live on the most solitary part of the globe:—and it has brought you to journey where never man I believe ever thought of travelling before.' 'So it is,' I replied, 'and stranger things, dear JACK, may happen yet before our eyes are closed: why I journey this untravelled way, I will inform you by and by; when you have told me by what strange means you came to dwell in this remote and silent vale.' 'That you shall know,' said he, 'very soon, as soon as we have eaten a morsel of something or other which my dear MARTHA has prepared against my return. Here it comes, a fowl, bacon and greens, and as fine I will answer as London market could yield. Let us sit down, my friend, and God bless us and our meat.'

Down then we sat immediately to our dish, and most excellent every thing was. The social goodness of this fond couple added greatly to the pleasure of the meal, and with mirth and friendship we eat up our capon, our bacon, and our greens. When we had done, PRICE brought in pipes and tobacco, and a fresh tankard of his admirable ale. 'Listen now,' said he, 'to my story, and then I will hearken to yours.

'When I left you at Sheridan's school, my remove was from Ireland to Barbadoes, to become a rich uncle's heir, and I got by my Indian airing a hundred thousand pounds. There I left the bones of my mother's brother, after I had lived two years in that burning place, and from thence proceeded to London, to spend what an honest, laborious man had long toiled to save. But I had not been above three months in the capital of England, when it came into my head to pass sometime in France, and with a girl I kept made haste to the French metropolis. There I lived at a grand rate, and took from the French

---

1 *Sheridan's school*: The School-house of the famous Dr. Sheridan, in Capel Street, Dublin, where many of the younger branches of most distinguished families in Ireland, at that period, received the first rudiments of their education; was formerly King James II's Mint-house. The only view of it extant, is a vignette in Samuel Whyte's *Poems*, printed by subscription at Dublin, in 1793. 8vo. p. 44. [*Amory's note.*]

Opera-house another whore. The Gaul and the Briton were both extreme fine girls, and agreed so well together, that I kept them both in one house. I thought myself superlatively happy in having such a brace of females, and spared no cost in procuring them all the finery and pleasures that Paris and London could yield. I had a furnished house in both these cities, and with an expensive equipage went backwards and forwards. In four years time I spent a great deal of money, and as I had lost large sums at play, and these two whores agreed in the end to rob me, and retire with the money, where I should never discover them, I found myself in very middling circumstances, and had not six hundred pounds left in the fourth year from my uncle's death. How to dispose of this and myself was now the question. What I should do, was my deliberation, to secure bread and quiet? Many a thoughtful hour this gave me, and at length I determined to purchase a little annuity. But before this could be effected. I went down to Westmoreland, on an information I had received, that my two ladies were at Appleby with other names, and on my money appeared as women of fortune. But this journey was to no purpose, and I was preparing to return to London, when my wife you saw at the head of the table a while ago, came by chance in my way, and pleased me so well with her good understanding, face and person, that I resolved to marry her, if she would have me, and give her the management of my five hundred pounds on a farm, as she was a farmer's daughter, and could manage one to good advantage. Her father was lately dead, and this little mountain farm she continued to occupy: therefore nothing could be more to my purpose, if I could prevail on her to make me her husband, and with some difficulty she did, to my unspeakable felicity. She had no money worth mentioning: but her house was pretty and comfortable, and her land had grain and cattle; and as I threw into her lap my five hundred pounds, a little before we were married, to be by her disposed of and managed, according to her pleasure, she soon made some good improvements and additions, and by her fine understanding, sweet temper, and every Christian virtue, continues to render my life so completely happy; so joyous and delightful; that I would not change my partner and condition, for one of the first quality and greatest fortune. In her I have every thing I could wish for in a wife and a woman, and she makes it the sole study and pleasure of her life to crown my every day with the highest satisfactions and comforts. Two years have I lived with her on these wild mountains, and in that time I have not had one dull or painful minute, but in thinking that I may lose her, and be the wretched survivor. That thought does

sometimes wound me. In sum, my friend, we are the happiest of wedded mortals, and on this small remote farm, live in a state of bliss to
be envied. This proves that happiness does not flow from riches only:
but, that where pure, and perfect love, strict virtue, and unceasing
industry, are united in the conjugal state, they can make the Stainmore
mountains a Paradise to mortals in peace and little.

   'But it is not only happiness in this world that I have acquired by
this admirable woman, but life eternal. You remember, my friend,
what a wild and wicked one I was when a school-boy, and as
Barbadoes of all parts of the globe is no place to improve a man's
morals in, I returned from thence to Europe as debauched a scelerate
as ever offended Heaven by blasphemy and illiberal gratifications.
Even my losses and approaching poverty were not capable of making
any great change in me. When I was courting my wife, she soon dis-
cerned my impiety, and perceived that I had very little notion of hell
and heaven, death and judgment. This she made a principal objection
against being concerned with me, and told me, she could not venture
into a married connexion with a man, who had no regard to the
divine laws, and therefore, if she could not make me a Christian, in
the true sense of the word, she would never be Mrs. PRICE.

   'This from a plain country girl, surprised me not a little, and my
astonishment arose very high, when I heard her talk of religion, and the
great end of both, a blessed life after this. She soon convinced me that
religion was the only means by which we can arrive at true happiness.'…

CHARLES MACKLIN (?1697-1797)

Actor and playwright, born in Co. Donegal, Macklin went to a boarding school in
Dublin after his father's death. He ran away to London to become an actor, was
brought back to Dublin where he worked in Trinity College as a servant until he was
twenty-one, then became a waiter in London. After returning to Ireland he was back
in London again by 1725, acting with the Lincoln's Inn Fields company. Convicted
of manslaughter after killing a fellow actor in a green-room quarrel he was 'punished'
by being branded with a cold iron. His most successful interpretation of Shylock in
1741 marked his avoidance of the current declamatory style of acting in favour of a
realistic delivery. He opened the Haymarket Theatre in 1744 and subsequently acted
alternately in London and Dublin (performing in the Smock Alley Theatre and later
in the Crow Street and Capel Street theatres), giving up his acting career at the age
of eighty on account of losing his memory.

   Macklin's plays included *Love à la Mode* (1784; produced in 1759), which con-

tains Sir Callaghan O'Brallagan, a genial stage Irishman. *The Man of the World*
(1781), however, was enlivened by an over-ambitious Scot, Sir Pertinax
MacSycophant. Macklin's best play was probably *The True-Born Irishman: or the Irish
Fine Lady* (1762). In it he uses a fairly orthodox subject: the reform of a wife (who
is Irish) tempted by a treacherous nature. The realism of the farce centres on her
infatuation with English modes of life, which makes her very affected, as her Irish
husband and her brother, Counsellor Hamilton, point out. In the second act, included here, she is advised by her husband to be true to her origins and be proud of them.
Something of this attitude emerges in Macklin's stern advice given in the letters he
wrote to his son John, who found the life of a merchant in India unattractive and
eventually returned to become a successful soldier.

From *The True-Born Irishman; or The Irish Fine Lady*

(1762)

ACT II

[*Mrs O'Dogherty is no longer 'the plain, modest, good-natured, domestic obedient Irish Mrs O'Dogherty': she calls herself Mrs Diggerty, ashamed of being
thought Irish. Her affected way of speaking appears in the first act; in the second she has seen the error of her ways, persuaded by her brother Counsellor
Hamilton.*]

KATTY *and* O'DOGHERTY *without*

O'DOGHERTY:	I shall be in here with the counsellor, Katty, and the moment he comes, bring me word.
KATTY:	I shall, sir.
COUNSELLOR HAMILTON:	Here your husband comes.
MRS DIGGERTY:	I am ashamed to see him.

Enter O'DOGHERTY

O'DOGHERTY:	Well, brother, have you spoke to her?
COUNSELLOR HAMILTON:	There she is, sir – and as she should be – bathed in the tears of humility and repentance.
O'DOGHERTY:	Ogh! I am sorry to see this indeed – I am afraid you have gone too far. If I had been by, I assure you, brother, you should not have made her cry. – Yerrow, Nancy, child, turn about, and don't be crying there.

MRS DIGGERTY:	Sir, I am asham'd to see your face –my errors I acknowledge – and for the future –
O'DOGHERTY:	Pooh, pooh – I will have no submissions nor acknowledgments; if you have settled every thing with your brother, that is sufficient.
MRS DIGGERTY:	I hope he is satisfied – and it shall be the business of my life –
O'DOGHERTY:	Pooh, pooh! say no more I tell you, but come, give me a kiss, and let us be friends at once – there – so, in that kiss, now, let all tears and uneasiness subside with you, as all fears and resentment shall die with me.
COUNSELLOR HAMILTON:	Come, sister, give me your hand, for I must have my kiss of peace too. I own I have been a little severe with you, but your disease required sharp medicines.
O'DOGHERTY:	Now we are friends, Nancy, I have a favour or two to beg of you.
MRS DIGGERTY:	Pray, command them.
O'DOGHERTY:	Why, then, the first thing that I ask, is, that you will send away that French rascal the cook, with his compots and combobs, his alamodes and aladobes, his crapandoes and frigandoes, and a thousand outlandish kickshaws,[1] that I am sure were never designed for Christian food; and let the good rough rumps of beef, the jolly surloins, the geese and turkies, cram fowls, bacon and greens; and the pies, puddings and pasties, that used to be perfectly shoving one another off of the table, so that there was not room for the people's plates; with a fine large cod too, as big as a young alderman – I say, let all those French kickshaws be banished from my table, and these good old Irish dishes be put in their places; and then the poor every day will have something to eat.
MRS DIGGERTY:	They shall, sir.
O'DOGHERTY:	And as to yourself, my dear Nancy, I hope I shall never have any more of your London

---

1 *kickshaws*: a small elaborate or exotic delicacy.

English; none of your this here's, your that there's, your winegars, your weals, your vindors, your toastesses, and your stone postesses; but let me have our own good plain, old Irish English, which I insist upon is better than all the English English that ever coquets and coxcombs brought into the land.

MRS DIGGERTY: I will get rid of these as fast as possible.

O'DOGHERTY: And pray, above all things, never call me Mr Diggerty – my name is Murrogh O'Dogherty, and I am not ashamed of it; but that damn'd name Diggerty always vexes me whenever I hear it.

MRS DIGGERTY: Then, upon my honour, Mr O'Dogherty, it shall never vex you again.

O'DOGHERTY: Ogh, that's right, Nancy – O'Dogherty for ever – O'Dogherty!—there's a sound for you – why they have not such a name in England as O'Dogherty – nor as any of our fine sounding Milesian[1] names—what are your Jones and your Stones, your Rice and your Price, your Heads and your Foots, and Hands and your Wills, and Hills and Mills, and Sands, and a parcel of little pimping names that a man would not pick out of the street, compared to the O'Donovans, O'Callaghans, O'Sullivans, O'Brallaghans, O'Shagnesses, O'Flahertys, O'Gallaghers, and O'Doghertys, – Ogh, they have courage in the very sound of them, for they come out of the mouth like a storm; and are as old and as stout as the oak at the bottom of the bog of Allen, which was there before the flood – and though they have been dispossessed by upstarts and foreigners, buddoughs and sassanoughs,[2] yet I hope they will flourish in the Island of Saints, while grass grows or water runs.

---

1 *Milesian*: the Milesians were early invaders of Ireland.
2 *buddoughs and sassanoughs*: Irish, 'churls and Englishmen'.

Letter to his Son

London, June 23rd, 1770.

Dear John,

Your letter, dated 16th of September, 1769, from Fort St. George, came to my hands on the 18th of April 1770, and this will be conveyed to the East Indies by the Dolphin man of war, the business or purport of whose voyage, at present, I am a stranger to; but, before I seal this letter, I shall enquire about it, and shall insert my intelligence. You must imagine that the receipt of a letter from you, that gave an account of your safe arrival at Fort St. George, and of your health and good spirits afforded your mother and me great joy; for while you have health, spirits, and a fair character, which is better than both, we shall think you and ourselves happy, let other circumstances of life be as they may; but besides health, spirits, and a fair character, I should also wish you to have a meritorious character, that is, a character as a man who knows his business. To be a good servant to the Company should be your constant endeavour. My reason for being so particular on this subject, at present, arises from your unsatisfactory, imperfect letter, from Fort St. George, which is written so unlike that of a gentleman, a scholar, or a man of business. Pray attend to the following instance of your want of precision: – you tell me, 'that you are at length arrived, after a very tedious passage, and in every shape a disagreeable voyage.'

I begged it, as a favor, that you would keep a journal of your voyage: – I made you a book for that purpose; but you did not think it worth your while to oblige me in that point, or you have not thought proper to convey me a single passage of it. By your not mentioning Mr. Hastings's name in your letter, I must conclude that you had some very cogent reason for it. I must suppose that you had offended or disgusted him, and so were ashamed to mention him, as you could not do it with any honor or grace to yourself. Some such circumstance I must imagine, in consequence of your silence, on so respectable a part of your company, so amiable a character, and one on whom you had some dependance. Do you not think, that it would have been some satisfaction to me, if you had pointed out how, or from what your disappointments arose. You say, that your living is expensive, and without a prospect of getting any money. What! did you expect to find money in the streets? or to be put into a post or office of getting money immediately on your arrival? Before you know your business, before you can even write a letter to your parents, without being blotted and scratched, with words omitted, sense imperfect, and so deficient in matter, and incorrect in every respect, that they are ashamed to shew it to any of your friends. Before you expect to get money in your employer's service, you must first qualify yourself to deserve it, by learning to write a letter like a man of business, and to know your business in your station. Study it – apply to nothing else – do not spend your time in reading books for your amusement, but in studying to qualify yourself for your situation. Do this, Sir, and prospects of getting money will arise of course; without it they never will arise. You write me a letter, and never tell me by what ship you send it, what the captain's name is, whence the ship sailed, when she was to sail from Fort St. George, or when you expected that she would arrive in England. All these points are necessary, and shew a man of business, – never omit such circumstances again, and always take notice to your correspondent of the time, the ship, the captain, through whose hands you receive your correspondent's letter. – Have you no book of letters upon business that you can form yourself upon? – Certainly you have. You request me to send you a little money, to keep you from borrowing. Surely you cannot want money more than Mr. Corbet, or any other young man. Mr. Corbet tells his father, that the allowance from the Company is small; but that he will make it do. Cannot you do so too? You talk of buying a share in a country ship; which is the only way of making money in your situation, you say. Pray who is to freight that ship? To lay out money, in the purchase of a ship, is easily said; but it seems to me to be a very absurd, or, at least, a very precarious scheme for a young man to engage in an undertaking of that nature, before he has any knowledge of markets, commodities, or of any of the conditions or circumstances of commerce, or the persons concerned in it; and it appears to me, at this distance, that this must be your case in every respect. Is Mr. Corbet's son engaged in *such an adventure*? John, do not be impatient; be sure that you *know*, always, before you *judge, speak*, or *adventure*. But why did you not send me an account of the nature of your country ship, its commerce, and of all the circumstances of the undertaking? as well as to send to me for money for such a business. You had a letter from Lord Clive to the late Governor, and one from Mr. Nuthall to Mr. Chaneau. Pray do you not think that it would have been, in some degree, proper, that you should have given me some account of the particulars how you were received in consequence of these letters, that I might know how to address, or to thank Lord

Clive, or Mr. Nuthall, on that business. O fie! fie! never be guilty of such shameful omissions again! You desire me to procure you some letters of recommendation:—how can you expect me to ask for any letters, after such a shameful neglect in you? I charged you to keep a journal, or book of memorandums, of ordinary as well as extraordinary occurrences. – Have you done so? I am sure you have not. From such a book, had you kept one, you might, at any time, when you were to write to me, or to any person, take extracts, or heads of intelligence, and commit them to your letter, according to order. Remember, Sir, as an invariable rule, that a merchant, or a man in any kind of business, is to trust nothing to memory; every thing is to be committed to paper. Again I charge you to practise it. I can tell by your letter, at first sight, whether or no you do it: so do not deceive yourself, by thinking that you can deceive me, by telling me that you do it. Remember that business has but one profitable rule – I mean a governing rule – and that is METHOD; without which, no man in business can be sure of ease, peace, character, or profit. Pray oblige me, and practise this journalising; ten minutes a day will be sufficient for that business; and I request that you will read Dr. Lowth's Grammar critically, and commit his observations to your memory. Get the instances that he gives, of the mistakes and errors of other writers, by heart; and, particularly, read his account of punctuation – for you are deficient in it. Send me the names of the Council at Madras, and, if you can, of their friends and connections in England; that I may apply properly for letters of recommendation for you. Your list of things shall be duly answered. If you can send some presents to Lady Mexborough, Lady Stanhope, and Miss Fanny, cost what they will, I will be at the expence of them; and could you send a gown, or a trifle, to Neddy Delaval, for Miss Sally, it would be proper, and well taken. The Dolphin man of war, that conveys this letter, carries out a gentleman of the name of *Brereton*, to view the works of some fortification, belonging to the French in India, which our people have obliged them to demolish, of which the French have complained to our Court, and this Mr. Brereton is to report the state of the works, and the conduct of the French and English, respecting this dispute, to our Court, in order that they may be able to give a proper answer to the remonstrance of the Court of France, on that subject. I shall write to you at large by the annual ships, and shall send you a chest of wine, and other things. Mr. Peter Corbet has shewn me a letter from his son, per Cingingo. Pray, why did not you write by the same ship? He tells me, too, that his son had the honor of copying the general letter, which was sent by the President and Council to the Directors. I hope that, some time or other, you will write a hand good enough, and arrive at merit sufficient, to be entrusted with that service. Do you recollect in what manner you sealed your letter to me of the 16th of September, 1769, from Fort St. George? I do not think you do. The case in which it was enclosed to Mr. Corbet, was sealed directly on the seal of my letter; so that the wax of the case melted the wax of my letter, and so mixed with it, thro' the case, that there was no opening the case, without opening my letter at the same time. Be more attentive to this in future; and pray, Sir, in good manners, ought you not to have said something in your case, directed to Mr. Corbet, about the health of his son, or of your own obligations to him for his trouble of forwarding my letters to me? Such omissions are great indecorums, and will always make enemies in society; whereas, the contrary behaviour, will always make friends. You should never omit acknowledging the most trifling civility, from any person; such conduct marks attention and gratitude. It is by such qualities, and integrity, and industry, that you must hope to rise in your station. My best respects wait on Mr. Hastings. I had the pleasure of seeing his brother, and sister, and nephew, some time since; they were then very well. Pray remember me to Mr. Thomas Corbet, and Mr. Garrow. Mr. Corbet and I drank all your healths the other day very sincerely. I am, my dear Child, with the warmest affection, your most anxious Father,

Charles Macklin.

GEORGE FAULKNER (?1699-1775)

After serving a printer's apprenticeship, Faulkner formed a bookselling partnership with James Hoey in 1726. He began *Faulkner's Dublin Journal* in 1728 and set up independently after that, printing the first Edition of Swift's works in 1735. Swift praised him as 'the Prince of Dublin Printers', and he was offered a peerage by the viceroy, Lord Chesterfield, which he refused. His major achievements included a seven volume *Ancient Universal History* and the twenty volume edition of Swift's *Works* (1772), which he annotated. He was criticized for publishing Lord Orrery's digressive *Remarks on the Life and Writings of Dr Jonathan Swift...* (1752). Both Patrick Delany and Deane Swift wrote in refutation of these remarks of a somewhat sycophantic friend of Swift. The passage included here is the Advertisement to volume II of the four volume 1735 edition of Swift's *Works*. Swift did not wish any critical or prefatory comment to be included in the edition.

[*On Swift's Poetry*]

The following poems chiefly consist either of Humour or Satyr, and very often of both together. What Merit they may have, we confess ourselves to be no Judges of in the least; but out of due Regard to a Writer, from whose Works we hope to receive some Benefit, we cannot conceal what we have heard from several Persons of great Judgment; that the Author never was known either in Verse or Prose to borrow any Thought, Simile, Epithet, or particular Manner of Style; but whatever he writ, whether good, bad, or indifferent, is an Original in itself.

Although we are very sensible that, in some of the following Poems, the Ladies may resent certain satyrical Touches against the mistaken Conduct in some of the fair Sex: And that, some warm Persons on the prevailing Side may censure this Author, whoever he be, for not thinking in publick Matters exactly like themselves: Yet we have been assured by several judicious and learned Gentlemen, that what the Author hath here writ, on either of those two Subjects, had no other Aim than to reform the Errors of both Sexes.

LAURENCE WHYTE (?1700-1755)

Born in Co. Westmeath, he taught mathematics in Dublin and was a friend of John Neal and his son William, the Dublin musical publishers of the time, who included some of Whyte's poems in their *Collections of the Most Celebrated Tunes for Violin, German Flute or Hautboy* (1724). His *Poems on Various Subjects* (1740) was followed by his *Original Poems* (1742). His 156-line poem 'A Dissertation on Italian and Irish Musick, with some Panegyrick on Carrallan[1] our late Irish Orpheus', included in his 1740 collection, gives a good picture, mildly satiric, of the state of music in Dublin in the first half of the eighteenth century, which is complemented by Matthew Pilkington's* 'The Progress of Music in Ireland. To Mira' (1725).

The Hue and Cry after the Clieve-Boy[2]
Dublin Feb. 22d. 1725

> Last *Saturday* a *French* Ale-Drapier,
> To Market gave a nimble Caper,
> To buy provisions for they say,
> That *Sunday* is his Kettle Day[3];

---

1 *Carallan*: Turlough Carolan (1670-1738), the last of the Irish bards.
2 *Clieve-Boy*: a servant who cleaved the meat.
3 *Kettle Day*: the day on which it was the host's turn to entertain his guests.

And once a Week did treat his Guest,
With boiled and roasted of the best,
His Pockets were well lin'd with Gold,
But *Meat* was dear that Day I'm told,
This with the Scarcity of Bread,
Made frugal *Peter* scratch his Head.
Quoth he I'm loth to give offence –
But Ale won't Ballance this Expence,
I must contrive some cunning Scheme,
To save my Money and my Fame,
Then I must draw a Bill of Fare,
To make this Project look more clear.

    First then a Turky, Sprouts and Bacon,
Next comes a Sallad and fat Capon,
And then a stately leg of Mutton,
Enough for twelve at least to glut on,
For sure the Thoughts of such a Treat,
May serve for once instead of Meat.

    Next night his Friends together met,
And each Man in his Post being set,
To chat and drink had equal right,
Which was the bus'ness of that Night;
Pipes and Tobacco on the Table,
To smoak and drink while they were able;
At Eight a Clock, by Watch and Chimes,
The Cup went round just twenty times,
And just so many Chalks were scor'd
In parallels upon the Board.

    The Parish Clerk took up his Place,
And, came, as usual, to say Grace,
The Hour was past, and all did wait,
But lo! there was no smell of Meat,
No sign of *Catty's* lay'ng the Cloth,
To bring us either Meat or Broth,
No noise of Plates or Knives cou'd hear,
As true forerunners of good Chear.

    Then *Peter* comes, and to be brief,
Tells how his Cleave-boy had turn'd Thief
Took leg and ran away with all
That he bought for the Carnival,
The Capon and the Turkey too,

175

Took Wings, and both together flew,
The very Sallad, Sprouts and Bacon,
Cou'd never more be overtaken.
In vain let *Peter* for them seek.
Soop Meager be his Food this Week,
Let him do Penance and repent,
Then fast the forty days of *Lent*,
Lest Vengeance fall upon his Head
Who sent us supperless to Bed.

LORD ORRERY (1701-1762)

John Boyle, fifth Earl of Orrery, was a son of the Charles Boyle who edited the *Letters of Phalaris* (1695). These caused the quarrel between Sir William Temple, who had praised them, and Richard Bentley, who proved them spurious; the controversy was echoed in Swift's *The Battle of the Books*. Orrery, a somewhat sycophantic friend in Swift's later years in Dublin, published his *Remarks on the Life and Writings of Dr Jonathan Swift, Dean of St Patrick's, Dublin In a Series of Letters from John, Earl of Orrery to his Son, the Honourable Hamilton Boyle* (1751). These *Remarks* were inaccurate and spiteful; they were refuted by Patrick Delany and Deane Swift.

From Remarks on the Life and Writings of Dr Jonathan Swift (1752)

... Dr. SWIFT ... appears like a masterly gladiator. He wields the sword of party with ease, justness and dexterity: and while he entertains the ignorant and the vulgar, he draws an equal attention from the learned and the great. When he is serious, his gravity becomes him. When he laughs, his readers must laugh with him. But, what shall be said for his love of trifles, and his want of delicacy and decorum? Errors, that if he did not contract, at least he encreased in *Ireland*. They are without a parallel. I hope they will ever remain so. The first of them, arose merely from his love of flattery, with which he was daily fed in that kingdom: the second, proceeded from the misanthropy of his disposition, which induced him peevishly to debase mankind, and even to ridicule human nature itself. Politics were his favourite topic, as they gave him an opportunity of gratifying his ambition, and thirst of power: yet even in this road, he has seldom continued long in one particular path. He has written miscellaneously, and has chosen rather to appear a wandering comet, than a fixed star. Had he applied the faculties of his mind to one great, and useful work, he must have shined more gloriously, and might have enlightened a whole planetary system in the political world.

The poetical performances of Dr. SWIFT ought to be considered as occasional poems written either to please, or vex some particular persons. We must not suppose them designed for posterity: if he had cultivated his genius in that way, he must certainly have excelled, especially in satyr. We see fine sketches, in several of his pieces: but he seems more desirous to inform, and strengthen his mind, than to indulge the luxuriancy of his imagination. He chooses to discover, and correct errors in the works of others, rather than to illustrate, and add beauties to his own. Like a skilful artist, he is fond of probing wounds to their depth, and of enlarging them to open view. He prefers caustics, which erode proud flesh, to softer balsamics, which give more immediate ease. He aims to be severely useful, rather than politely engaging: and as he was either not formed, or would not take pains to excel in poetry, he became, in some measure, superior to it; and assumed more the air and manners of a critic, than of a poet. Had he lived in the same age with HORACE, he would have approached nearer to him, than any other poet: and if we may make an allowance for the different course of study, and different form of government, to which each of these great men were subject, we may observe, in several instances, a strong resemblance between them. Both poets are equally distinguished for wit and humour. Each displays a peculiar felicity in diction: but, of the two, HORACE is the more elegant and delicate: while he condemns, he pleases. SWIFT takes pleasure in giving pain: The dissimilitude of their tempers might be owing to the different turns in their fortune. SWIFT early formed large views of ambition, and was disappointed. HORACE, from an exiled low state, rose into affluence, and enjoyed the favour and friendship of AUGUSTUS. Each poet was the delight of the principal persons of his age. *Cum magnis vixisse*[1] was not more applicable to HORACE, than to SWIFT. They both were temperate: both were frugal; and both were of the same Epicurean taste. HORACE had his LYDIA, SWIFT had his VANESSA. HORACE had his MECÆNAS, and his AGRIPPA. SWIFT had his OXFORD and his BOLINGBROKE. HORACE had his VIRGIL. SWIFT had his POPE.

You seem not only desirous, but impatient, that I should pass critically through all the works of my friend SWIFT. Your request is unreasonable

---

1 *Cum magnis vixisse*: 'To have lived among great men' (Horace, *Satires* II. 1.76).

if you imagine, that I must say something upon every individual performance. There are some pieces that I despise, others that I loath, but
many more that delight and improve me: and these last shall be dis-
cussed particularly. The former are not worthy of your notice. They
are of no further use than to shew us, in general, the errors of human
nature; and to convince us, that neither the height of wit, nor genius,
can bring a man to such a degree of perfection, as vanity would often
prompt him to believe.

MATTHEW PILKINGTON (?1701-1774)

Born in Ballyboy, Co. Offaly, the son of a clockmaker there, he was educated at
Trinity College, Dublin, and became a Church of Ireland clergyman, rector of
Donabate and Portrane in north Co. Dublin from about 1724 to his death. In 1732
he married Laetitia van Lewen*; they were subsequently divorced. Initially close
friends of Swift (whose life is described vividly in her *Memoirs*) they were subsequently characterised when he became disillusioned with them as 'the falsest rogue
and the most profligate whore in either kingdom'. Pilkington, a good classical scholar and musician, published in 1725 'The Progress of Music in Ireland. To Mira', a
neo-classical poem in which, like Laurence Whyte, he praised Carolan*, the famous
itinerant harper. The Dublin edition of his *Poems on Several Occasions* (1730) was
followed the next year by an expanded London edition.

The Gift

Oppress'd *Hibernia*, in Despair,
Complains to *Jove* in fervent Pray'r
How fast her Liberties decay,
How fast her Honours fade away;
Her *Sons* to no Preferment rise
Tho' Earth can boast of few so Wise;
How Poor, how Desolate she grows,
And begs Redress of all her Woes.

Then *Jove*: '*Hibernia* sues too late,
Her Sorrows are decreed by Fate;
But Heav'n those Sorrows shall Repay
With Blessings in a nobler Way.
Let Haughty *Britain* boast no more,
With scornful Pride, her golden Store,

That distant Worlds her Name revere,
That Arts and Learning flourish there;
To raise thy glory, we design
To bless thee with a *Gift* Divine,
A *Gift* by which thy injur'd Name
Shall fill th'immortal voice of Fame,
That *Albion* may with Envy see
Her Glories far surpass'd by thee.'

Hibernia thanks him for the Gift,
And owns, She's overpaid in *Swift*.

HENRY BROOKE (?1703-1783)

Born in Co. Cavan, the son of a Church of Ireland clergyman, he was educated at Trinity College, Dublin and the Temple in London. First known for his poem *Universal Beauty* (1735) and his translation of part of Tasso's *Gerusalemme Liberata* (1738), he wrote *Gustavus Vasa: the Deliverer of his Country*, a play banned because Walpole, the prime minister, took it as a personal attack on himself; it was, however, successfully produced in Dublin as *The Patriot* (1744). He followed it with other plays; one of them, *Jack the Giant Queller*, was only staged once in Dublin before being prohibited as a satire on government and the corporation. He attempted various historical projects, wrote books on Irish politics, at first warning Protestants about Catholic dangers in the Jacobite Rebellion then arguing the case for freeing Catholics from the effects of the Penal Laws. He is remembered mainly for his eclectic novel *The Fool of Quality* (5 vols, 1765–1770). Influenced by Rousseau's *Émile*, he describes at length the education of Henry, Earl of Moreland. The sentimentalism of this novel was followed by *Juliet Grenville* (1774), both novels stressing the role of feeling in creating a spirit of benevolence, but exhibiting some critical irony in treating sentimentality. Brooke lived on his small estate in Cavan before having to mortgage it; he then retired to Kildare where Charlotte*, his only surviving child, whom he had encouraged in her study of Irish and Gaelic antiquity, cared for him until his death.

From *The Fool of Quality; or, the History of Henry Earl of Moreland* (1765–1770)

[*On his way back to his foster-home, Harry, the young protagonist, meets a stranger*]

The old gentleman turned and gazed at the child, as on some sudden apparition. His tears stopped. He returned the picture, which he held, into his bosom. And, lifting up his eyes, 'Great Power,' he cried, 'is this the one, of all the world, who has any feelings for me? Is it this babe, this suckling, whom thou hast sent, to be a partaker in my griefs, and the sharer of my afflictions? Welcome, then, my little friend,' said he, tenderly turning and caressing the child, 'I will live the longer for thy sake, and endeavour to repay the tears thou hast shed in my behalf.'

The language of true love is understood by all creatures, and was that of which *Harry* had, almost the only perception. He returned his friend's caresses with unaffected ardour, and no two could be more highly gratified in the endearments of each other.

'What is your name, my dear?' said the old gentleman. '*Harry Clinton*, Sir.' '*Harry Clinton!*' repeated the old man, and started. 'And pray who is your father?' The child, then looking tenderly at him, replied; 'I'll have you for a father, if you please, Sir.' The stranger, then caught him up in his arms, and passionately exclaim'd, 'You shall, you shall, my darling, for the tenderest of fathers, never to be torn asunder, till death shall part us.'

Then asking him where he lived, and *Harry* pointing to the town before them, they both got up and went towards it. Our hero was now again all glee, all action; he sprung from and to his friend, and play'd and gambol'd about him, like a young spaniel in a morning, just loos'd from his chain, and admitted to accompany his master to the field. As his two dogs frisked about him, he would now mount upon one, then bound upon t'other, and each pranced and paraded under him as delighted with the burden. The old gentleman beheld all with a pleasure that had long been a stranger to his breast, and shared in the joys of his young associate.

Being arrived near the farm house, Nurse, who stood at the door, saw them approaching, and cried out, '*Gaffer, Gaffer*, here comes our *Harry* with the dumb gentleman.' When they were come up, 'Good people,' says the stranger, 'is this your child!' 'No, no, Sir,' answered the nurse, 'we are but his fosterers.' 'And, pray, who is his father?' 'He is second son, Sir, to the Earl of *Moreland*.' 'The Earl of *Moreland*! you amaze me greatly, is this all the notice and care they take of such a treasure?' 'Sir,' replied the nurse, 'they never sent for him but once; they don't mind him, they take him for a fool.' 'For a fool?' cried he, and shook his head in token of dissent. 'I am sure he has the wisest of all human hearts.' 'I wish it may be so, Sir,' said the nurse, 'but he behaved very sadly, some time ago, at the great house.' She then made a recital of all our young hero's adventures in the mansion-parlour; whereat the old gentleman inwardly chuckled, and, for the first time, of some years, permitted his features to relax into a smile of chearfulness.

'Nurse,' said he, 'every thing that I hear and see of this child serves the more to endear and bind me to him. Pray, be so good as to accompany us to my house, we will try to equip him better both as to person and understanding.'

As this stranger's seat made part of the village, they were soon there. He first whispered his old domestic, who, then, looked upon the child with surprise and pleasure. The footman was next sent to bring the taylor, and some light stuffs from the town shop. Matters being thus dispatched, with respect to our hero's first coat and britches, Nurse was kept to dinner; and after this gentleman had entertained his young guest with a variety of little tricks, childish plays, and other fooleries, toward evening, he dismissed him and his nurse, with a request that she would send him every day, and a promise that he should be returned every night if she desired it.

Harry, being thus furnished with the external tokens of a man child, having been born into the world, became an inseparable friend and playfellow to his patron. At times of relaxation, the old gentleman, with the most winning and insinuating address, endeavoured to open his mind and cultivate his morals, by a thousand little fables, such as of bold sparrows, and naughty kids, that were carried away by the hawk, or devoured by the wolf, and of good robbins, and innocent lambs, that the very hawks and wolves themselves were fond of. For he never proposed any encouragement or reward to the heart of our hero, save that of the love and approbation of others. At the times of such instruction, *Harry*, who knew no other dependance, and beheld his patron as his father and as his God, would hang upon his knee, look up to his face, delighted, and greedily imbibe the sweetness of those lessons whose impressions neither age, nor any occurrence, could ever after erase: so prevalent are the dictates of lips that are beloved.

At other times, the stranger would enter, with our hero, into all his little frolicks and childish vagaries, would run and wrestle with him, ride the rods, roll down the slope, and never felt such sweet sensations and inward delight, as when he was engaged in such recreations.

There was a cock at *Harry's* nurse, the Lord of the Dunghill, between whom and our hero a very particular intimacy and friendship had been contracted. *Harry's* hand was his daily caterer; and *Dick*, for the cock was so called, would hop into the child's lap and pick his cloaths, and rub his feathers against him, and court *Harry* to tickle and stroak and play with him.

Upon a *Shrove-Tuesday*, while *Harry* was on his road, from his patron's, intending a short visit to his nurse and foster father, a lad came to their door and offer'd *Gaffer* a double price for *Dick*; the bargain was quickly made, the lad bore off his prize in triumph, and *Gaffer* withdrew to the manuring of a back field. Just at that crisis *Harry* came up, and enquired of the maid for his daddy and mammy, but was answered that neither of them was within. He then asked after his favourite cock, but was told that his daddy had, that minute, sold him to yonder man who was almost out of sight.

Away sprung our hero, like an arrow from a bow, and held the man in view till he saw him enter a great crowd, at the upper end of the street. Up he comes, at last, quite out of breath, and making way through the assembly, perceived his cock, at some distance, tied to a short stake, and a lad preparing to throw him with a stick. Forward he rushed, again, and stopped resolutely before his bird, to ward the blow with his own person, at the instant that the stick had taken its flight, and that all the people cried out, hold! hold! One end of the stick took *Harry* in the left shoulder, and bruised him sorely, but, not regarding that, he instantly stooped, delivered his captive favourite, whipt him under his arm, caught up the stick, flourish'd it, as in defiance of all opponents, made homeward thro' the crowd, and was followed by acclamations of the whole assembly.

The old gentleman was standing before his court door when his favourite arrived, all in a sweat; 'what's the matter, my dear,' says he, 'what made you put yourself into such a heat? what cock is that you have under your arm?' In answer to these several questions *Harry* ingenuously confessed the whole affair. And, when his patron with some warmth, cried, 'why, my love, did you venture your life for a silly cock?' 'why did I?' repeated the child, 'why, Sir, because he loved me.' The stranger, then, stepping back and gazing upon him with eyes of tender admiration; 'may Heaven for ever bless thee, my little angel,' he exclaimed, 'and continue to utter from my lips the sentiments that it inspires.' Then, catching him up in his arms, he bathed him with his tears, and almost stifled him with his caresses.

In a few days, our hero was again restored, by frequent fomentations, to the use of his arm; and his dada, as he called him, and he returned to their old recreations.

As *Harry's* ideas began to open and expand, he grew ambitious of greater power and knowledge. He wished for the strength of that bull, and for the swiftness of yonder horse. And, on the close of a solemn and serene summer's evening, while he and his patron walked in the garden, he wished for wings that he might fly up and see what the sky and the stars, and the rising moon were made of.

In order to reform this inordinancy of his desires, his patron addressed him in the following manner.

'I will tell you a story, my Harry. On the other side of yonder hill there runs a mighty clear river, and in that river, on a time, there lived three silver trouts, the prettiest little fishes that any one ever saw. Now God took a great liking and love to these pretty silver trouts, and he let them want for nothing that such little fishes could have occasion for. But two of them grew sad and discontented; and the one wished for this thing, and the other wished for that thing, and neither of them could take pleasure in any thing that they had, because they were always longing for something that they had not.

'Now, *Harry*, you must know that all this was very naughty in those two little trouts; for God had been exceedingly kind to them; he had given them every thing that was fittest for them; and he never grudged them any thing that was for their good; but instead of thanking him for all his care and his kindness, they blamed him, in their own minds, for refusing them any thing that their silly fancies were set upon. In short there was no end of their wishing, and longing, and quarrelling, in their hearts, for this thing and t'other.

'At last, God was so provoked, that he resolved to punish their naughtiness by granting their desires, and to make the folly of those two little stubborn trouts an example to all the foolish fish in the whole world.

'For this purpose, he called out to the three little silver trouts, and told them they should have whatever they wished for.

'Now, the eldest of these trouts was a very proud little fish, and wanted, forsooth, to be set up above all other little fishes. "May it please your greatness," says he, "I must be free to tell you that I do not, at all, like the way in which you have placed me. Here you have put me into a poor, narrow, and troublesome river, where I am straitened on the right side, and straitened on the left side, and can neither get down into the ground, nor up into the air, nor go where, nor do any one thing I have a mind to. I am not so blind, for all, but that I can see, well enough, how mighty kind and bountiful you can be to others. There are your favourite little birds, who fly this way and that way, and mount up to the very heavens; and do whatever they please, and have every thing at command, because you have given them wings. Give me such wings, also, as you have given to them, and then I will have something for which I ought to thank you."

'No sooner ask than have. He felt the wings he wished for growing from either side, and, in a minute, he spread them abroad, and rose out of the water. At first he felt a wonderful pleasure in finding himself able to fly. He mounted high into the air, above the very clouds, and he looked down with scorn on all the fishes in the world.

'He now resolved to travel, and to take his diversion far and wide. He flew over rivers, and meadows, and woods, and mountains; till, growing faint with hunger and thirst, his wings began to fail him, and he thought it best to come down to get some refreshment.

'The little fool did not consider that he was now in a strange country, and many a mile from the sweet river, where he was born and bred, and had received all his nourishment. So, when he came down, he happened to alight among dry sands and rocks, where there was not a bit to eat nor a drop of water to drink; and so there he lay faint and tired, and unable to rise, gasping and fluttering, and beating himself against the stones, till at length he died in great pain and misery.

'Now, the second silver trout, though he was not so high minded as the first little proud trout; yet he did not want for conceit enough, and he was moreover a narrow hearted and very selfish little trout, and, provided he himself was snug and safe, he did not care what became of all the fishes in the world. So he says to God:

'"May it please your honour. I don't wish, not I, for wings to fly out of the water, and to ramble into strange places, where I don't know what may become of me. I lived contented and happy enough till the other day, when, as I got under a cool bank from the heat of the sun, I saw a great rope coming down into the water, and it fastened itself, I don't know how, about the gills of a little fish that was basking beside me, and he was lifted out of the water, struggling and working in great pain, till he was carried, I know not where, quite out of my sight. So I thought in my own mind, that this evil, some time or other, may happen to myself, and my heart trembled within me, and I have been very sad and discontented ever since. Now, all I desire of you, is, that you would tell me the meaning of this, and of all the other dangers to which you have subjected us poor little mortal fishes; for then I shall have sense enough to take care of my own safety, and I am very well able to provide for my own living, I warrant you."

'No sooner said than done. God immediately opened his understanding; and he knew the nature and meaning of snares, nets, hooks, and lines, and of all the dangers to which such little trouts could be liable.

'At first he greatly rejoiced in this his knowledge; and he said to himself, "now surely I shall be the happiest of all fishes; for, as I understand and am forewarned of every mischief that can come near me, I'm sure I love myself too well not to keep out of harm's way."

'From this time forward, he took care not to go into any deep holes, for fear that a pike, or some other huge fish might be there, who would make nothing of swallowing him up at one gulp. He also kept away from the shallow places, especially in hot weather, lest the sun should dry them up and not leave him water enough to swim in. When he saw the shadow of a cloud coming and moving upon the river, "A ha!" said he to himself, "here are the fishermen with their nets," and immediately he got on one side and skulked under the banks, where he kept trembling in his skin, till the cloud was past. Again when he saw a fly skimming on the water, or a worm coming down the stream, he did not dare to bite, however hungry he might be; "no no," said he to them, "my honest friends, I am not such a fool as that comes to neither; go your ways and tempt those who know no better, who are not aware that you may serve as baits to some treacherous hook, that lies hid for the destruction of those ignorant and silly trouts that are not on their guard."

'Thus, this over careful trout kept himself in continual frights and alarms, and could neither eat, nor drink, nor sleep in peace, lest some mischief should be at hand, or that he might be taken napping. He daily grew poorer and poorer, and sadder and sadder, for he pined away with hunger, and sigh'd himself to skin and bone; till, wasted almost to nothing with care and melancholy, he at last died, for fear of dying, the most miserable of all deaths.

'Now, when God came to the youngest silver trout, and asked him what he wished for. "Alas" (said this darling little trout) "you know, may it please your Worship, that I am but a very foolish and good for nothing little fish; and I don't know, not I, what is good for me or what is bad for me; and I wonder how I came to be worth bringing into the world, or what you could see in me to take any thought about me. But, if I must wish for something, it is that you would do with me whatsoever you think best; and that I should be pleased to live, or die, even just as you would have me."

'Now, as soon as this precious trout made this prayer in his good and his humble little heart, God took such a liking and a love to him, as the like was never known. And God found it in his own heart, that he could not but take great care of this sweet little trout, who had trusted himself so wholly to his love and good pleasure, and God went wheresoever he went, and was always with him and about him, and was to him as a father and a friend and companion; and he put contentment into his mind and joy into his heart; and so this little trout slept always in peace, and wakened in gladness; and whether he was full or hungry, or whatever happened to him, he was still pleased and thankful; and he was the happiest of all fishes that ever swam in any water.'

Harry at the close of this fable, looked down and grew thoughtful, and his patron left him to himself to ruminate on what he had heard. Now, *Harry* had often heard talk of God, and had some general though confused notions of his power.

The next day, he requested his patron to repeat the story of the three little silver trouts. When he had ended, 'Dada,' says *Harry*, 'I believe I begin to guess a little at what you mean. You wou'dn't have me wish for any thing, but leave every thing to God; and, if I thought that God loved me half as well as you love me, I would leave every thing to himself, like the good little trout.' 'He does, my Harry, he loves you a thousand times better than I love you, nay a thousand times better than you love yourself. God is all love; it is he who made every thing, and he loves every thing that he has made.' 'Ay, but Dada, I can't, for the heart of me, help pitying the poor little naughty trouts. If God loves every thing, why did he make any thing to dye?' 'You begin to think too deeply, *Harry*; we will speak more of these matters another time. For the present, let it suffice to know that, as he can kill, he can also make alive, again, at his own pleasure.'

Harry had now remained about twelve months with his patron, when it was intimated to the Earl and his Lady that the dumb man had taken a fancy to their child, and that he was almost constantly resident at his house. Alarmed at this news, and apprehending that this man might be some imposter· or kidnapper, they, once more, sent orders to the nurse to bring the boy home.

Nurse ran in a hurry to the stranger's, and, having informed him of the necessity she was under to take away the child, many mutual tears were shed at parting, but *Harry* was the sooner pacified when Nurse told him that it was but for a short visit, as before.

When they came to the castle, there was no company in the parlour, but the Earl and his Lady, with Lord *Richard* and some other masters of quality, about his age and size. *Harry*, however, looked about with a brow of disgust; and, when my Lady desired him to come and kiss her, 'maybe you'll whip me,' he answer'd sullenly; 'No,' she replied, 'if you don't strike your Brother *Dicky* any more.' 'I won't beat him,' says *Harry*, 'if he won't beat Mammy.' 'Come then and kiss me, my Dear,' said my Lady, 'whereon *Harry* advanced with a slow caution, and held up his little mouth to receive her salute. He was then kiss'd by his father, his brother, and the little masters, and all things promised future reconcilement and amity.

A number of glittering toys were then presented to *Harry* on all sides; he received them, indeed, in good part, but laid them all aside again as things of whose use he yet was not wise enough to be apprehensive....

CONSTANTIA GRIERSON (1703/1705-1732)

Constantia Phillips was born at Graigvenamanagh, Co. Kilkenny and was apprenticed in her teens to the Dublin physician Dr Van Lewen (father of Laetitia, who married Matthew Pilkington*) to train as a midwife. She became learned in Hebrew, Greek and Latin. A member, with Mary Barber, Mary Delany and Laetitia Pilkington, of Swift's female 'senate', she married George Grierson, the King's printer in Ireland, with whom she worked on his editions of Terence (1727) and Tacitus (1730), being not only a scholar but an editor and proofreader, working on an edition of Sallust when she died in Dublin. Thirteen of her poems survive, in *Poems by Eminent Ladies* (1755) and in Mary Barber's *Poems on Several Occasions* (1734) and Laetitia Pilkington's *Memoirs* (1748–54).

To Miss Laetitia van Lewen in a Country-Town at the Time of the Assizes

The fleeting birds may soon in ocean swim,
And northern whales thro' liquid azure skim.
The Dublin ladies their intrigues forsake,
To dress and scandal an aversion take;
When you can in the lonely forest walk,
And with some serious matron gravely talk
Of possets, poultices, and waters still'd,
And monstrous casks with mead and cider fill'd;
How many hives of bees she has in store,
And how much fruit her trees this Summer bore;
Or home returning in the yard can stand,
And feed the chickens from your bounteous hand:
Of each one's top-knot tell, and hatching pry,
Like *Tully*[1] waiting for an augury.

---

1 *Tully*: Marus Tullius Cicero (106-43BC). He became consul in 63. In the civil war between Caesar and Pompey he supported the latter but was pardoned by Caesar after the battle of Pharsalia. He attacked Mark Antony after Caesar's assassination. After the triumvirate was formed he was proscribed and put to death. He wrote on rhetoric, politics and moral philosophy and theology. A large number of his orations survive.

When night approaches, down to table sit,
With a great crowd, choice meat, and little wit;
What horse won the last race, how mighty *Tray*,
At the last famous hunting, caught the prey;
Surely, you can't, but such discourse despise,
Methinks, I see displeasure in your eyes:
O my *Laetitia*, stay no longer there,
You'll soon forget, that you yourself are fair;
Why will you keep from us, from all that's gay,
There in a lonely solitude to stay?
Where not a mortal thro' the year you view,
But bob-wigg'd hunters, who their game pursue
With so much ardor, they'd a cock or hare,
To thee, in all thy blooming charms, prefer.

    You write of belles and beaux that there appear,
And gilded coaches, such as glitter here;
For gilded coaches, each estated clown
That gravely slumbers on the bench has one;
But Beaux! they're young attorneys! sure you mean!
Who thus appear to your romantik brain.
Alas! no mortal there can talk to you,
That love, or wit, or softness ever knew:
All they can speak of's *Capias*'s[1] and Law,
And writs to keep the country fools in awe.
And, if to wit, or courtship they pretend,
'Tis the same way that they a cause defend;
In which they give of lungs a vast expence,
But little passion, thought or eloquence:
Bad as they are, they'll soon abandon you,
And gain, and clamour, in the town pursue.
So haste to town, if ev'n such fools you prize;
O haste to town! and bless the longing eyes
    Of *your* Constantia.

---

1 *Capias's*: writs for an arrest ('you may take').

ANNE BERKELEY (1706-1786)

Born Anne Forster, the eldest daughter of John Forster, who had been recorder of Dublin, Speaker of the Irish House Commons (1707-1709) and Chief Justice, she married George Berkeley in 1728 before they sailed to America. He praised her 'for the qualities of her mind and her unaffected inclination to books'. A pious mystic, follower of Fénelon and Madame de Guyon, she had been educated in France and spoke and wrote French. In addition to being very well-read and a writer of lively letters, she was most practical; when Berkeley became Bishop of Cloyne she managed relief works employing a hundred men, supervising the work in person and, having farmed nearly a hundred acres at Whitehall, their home when they were living on Rhode Island, she also farmed the glebe at Cloyne, a much larger area of land. She retained her powers of mind to the end of her life, being described as 'the finest old lady ... sensible, lively, facetious and benevolent'. The letter to her son George seems to have been prompted by his asking why Berkeley had not left his family better off. George became a canon of Canterbury Cathedral.

Letter to her son George

...The slight reflection you made on your dear father and my dear husband carried me back many years.... How carefully was your infancy protected by your dear father's skill and mother's care. You were not, for our ease, trusted to mercenary hands; in childhood you were instructed by your father—he though old and sickly, performed the constant tedious task himself, and would not trust it to another's care. You were his business and his pleasure.... He never raised your vanity, or your love for vanity, by prizing or mentioning the vanities of life (unless with the derision they deserve)—which we have all renounced in baptism—before you, such are titles, finery, fashion, money, fame. His own temperance in regard to wine was a better lesson to you than forbidding it would have been. He made home pleasant by a variety of employments, conversation, and company; his instructive conversation was delicate, and when he spoke directly of religion (which was seldom) he did it in so masterly a manner, that it made a deep and lasting impression. You never heard him give his tongue the liberty of speaking evil. Never did he reveal the fault or secret of a friend. Most people are tempted to detraction by envy, barrenness of conversation, spite and ill-will. But as he saw no one his superior, or perhaps his equal, how could he envy any one? Besides, an universal knowledge of men, things, and books prevented the greatest wit of his age from being at a loss for subjects of conversation; but had he kept as dull as he was bright, his conscience and good nature would have kept close the door of his lips rather than to have opened them to vilify or lessen his brother. He was also pure in heart and speech; no wit could season any kind of dirt to him, not even Swift's. Now he was not born to all this, no more than others are, but in his own words, his industry was greater; he struck a light at twelve to rise and study and pray, for he was very pious, and his studies were no barren speculations, for he loved God and man, silenced and confuted atheists, disguised as mathematicians and fine gentlemen.... Humility, tenderness, patience, generosity, charity to men's souls and bodies, was the sole end of all his projects, and the business of his life. In particular I never saw so tender and amiable a father, or so patient and industrious a one.... Exactness and care (in which consists economy) was the treasury on which he drew for charity, generosity, munificence....

WILLIAM DUNKIN (?1709-1765)

Born in Dublin, educated at Trinity College, Dublin and ordained in 1735, Dunkin taught at St Michael-le-Pole School in Dublin before being appointed Headmaster at Portora Royal School at Enniskillen in 1746. A friend of Swift, he was reputed to have written the best Latin verse in Ireland in his time and his own poetry, in his Dublin edition, *Selected Poetical Works* (2 vols, 1769–1770) and in the London edition of *The Poetical Works of William Dunkin* (2 vols, 1774), is often sharply witty as in his comic views of country life in 'The Parson's Revels'. He wrote some good poems of place as in 'Carbery Rocks in the County of Cork' and 'On the New Bridge Built on the Eastern Side of Dublin'. His mock-heroic *The Art of Gate-Passing: or, The Murphæid* (1728) treats the pretensions of a Trinity College under-porter who claims he is descended from the ancient Kings of Ireland.

The Modish School-Master

'Well!' said Hopkins, on the lurch,
When a coffin passed his church:
'Turn, good people, turn the bier,
You had better bury here;
For you cannot find around
Finer mould on Christian ground.'
So, when Bubo,[1] lucky man,
Opened school, he thus began:

---

1 *Bubo*: Latin for 'owl'.

William Dunkin

Gentlemen, and ladies fair,
—— is a special air,
Most commodious for your boys,
Free from all the daily noise,
And the vices of the town;
Prithee sent them hither down.
Dublin, barring all disasters,
Has too many idle masters:
I may say, without aspersions,
They mind only their diversions.

    As for me, you need not fear,
I'm not absent thrice a year.
Then I have a short, unknown,
Charming method of my own.

    I DESPISE the musty rules,
Practised in your city-schools.
Others dig, to lay foundations
For their future habitations;
But, indignant of a prop,
I begin my house a-top.

    GRAMMAR is but fit for slaves,
Laws were only made for knaves.
Link your asses with your collars,
I shall never yoke my scholars:
They shall want no other model,
Than what issues from this noddle.
Garrans[1] on the common roads
Jog along with heavy loads:
But the steed, which travels faster,
Bears no burthen, save – his master.
Thus he said, and men of sense
Even favoured his pretence.
So the queen of wisdom bright
Fain would shew her love for night,
And from all the flocks of fowl
Gravely chose the boding owl.

---

1 *Garrans*: small horses, used in Ireland and Scotland.

Laetitia Pilkington (?1707/1712–1750)

Autobiographer and dramatist, she was born in Dublin, the daughter of Dr van Lewen, an obstetrician of Dutch lineage. She was, like Mary Barber, Mary Delany and Constantia Grierson, one of Swift's friends and her *Memoirs* (1748-54) tell us about his later years in Dublin. Virginia Woolf called her a 'cross between Moll Flanders and Lady Ritchie'. She married the Rev. Matthew Pilkington* in 1732 ('my mother's capricious temper made her reject every advantageous proposal offered, and at last condemn me to the arms of one of the greatest villains, with reverence to the priesthood be it spoken, that ever was wrapped up in crape'). The marriage ended in divorce. In London she attempted suicide, was sentenced for debt, and opened a bookshop. Her burlesque *The Turkish Court* (1748) was staged but not printed, and she wrote a tragedy, *The Roman Father*. Her son may have compiled *The Celebrated Mrs Pilkington's Jests* (1755; 1764).

Song

Strephon,[1] your breach of faith and trust
  Affords me no surprise;
A man who grateful was, or just,
  Might make my wonder rise.

That heart to you so fondly tied,
  With pleasure wore its chain,
But from your cold neglectful pride,
  Found liberty again.

For this no wrath inflames my mind,
  My thanks are due to thee;
Such thanks as gen'rous victors find,
  Who set their captives free.

From The Memoirs
(1748)

[*Seventeen years old, recently married to Matthew Pilkington, a poor but poetic clergyman, Laetitia wanted to meet Dean Swift, and sent him a poem she had written on his birthday through their common his friend the Rev. Patrick Delany, Dean of Down.*]

To the Rev. Dr Swift, on his Birthday

While I the God-like men of old
In admiration wrapt behold!

---

1 *Strephon*: stock name for a rustic lover.

Rever'd antiquity explore,
And turn the long-liv'd volumes o'er,
Where Cato, Plutarch, Flaccus shine
In every excellence divine;
I grieve that our degen'rate days
Produce no mighty souls like these;
Patriot, philosopher, and bard
Are names unknown and seldom heard.
Spare your reflection, Phoebus cries,
'Tis as ungrateful as unwise;
Can you complain this sacred day
That virtues or that arts decay?
Behold in SWIFT reviv'd appears
The virtues of unnumber'd years;
Behold in him with new delight,
The patriot, bard, and sage unite;
And know, Ierne[1] in that name
Shall rival Greece and Rome in fame.

[First Meeting]

[*Swift told Delany, with whom he was dining at Delany's Dublin home, Delville, that he would like to meet the Pilkingtons. The party met on a terrace, Laetitia presented to the Dean by a lady, who told him she was Mrs Pilkington when he asked if she was her daughter. Laetitia's account gives us some idea of Swift's jesting manner.*]

… 'What', says he, 'this poor little child married! God help her, she is early engaged in trouble.' We passed the day in a most elegant and delightful manner; and the Dean, engaging Mr Pilkington to preach for him at the Cathedral the Sunday following, gave me also, with the rest of the company, an invitation to dinner. As the Communion is administered every Sunday in this antique Church, dedicated to St Patrick, the first prelate who taught the Gospel in Ireland, I was charmed to see with what a becoming piety the Dean performed that solemn service; which he had so much at heart that he wanted not the assistance of the Liturgy, but went quite through it without ever look-ing in the Prayer Book. Indeed, another part of his behaviour on this occasion was censured by some, as favouring of Popery; which was that he bowed to the Holy Table. However, this circumstance may vin-dicate him from the wicked aspersion of being deemed an unbeliever,

---

1 *Ierne*: Ireland.

since 'tis plain he had the utmost reverence for the Eucharist. Service being over, we met the Dean at the Church door, surrounded by a crowd of poor, to all of whom he gave charity, excepting one old woman, who held out a very dirty hand to him: he told her very gravely: 'That though she was a beggar, water was not so scarce but she might have washed her hands.' And so we marched with the silver verge[1] before us to the Dean's House. When we came into the parlour, the Dean kindly saluted me, and, without allowing me time to sit down, bade me come and see his study; Mr Pilkington was for following us, but the Dean told him merrily: 'He did not desire his company'; and so he ventured to trust me with him into the library. 'Well,' says he, 'I have brought you here to show you all the money I got when I was in the Ministry but do not steal any of it.' 'I will not indeed, Sir,' says I; so he opened a cabinet, and showed me a whole parcel of empty drawers. 'Bless me,' says he, 'the money is flown!' He then opened his bureau, wherein he had a great number of curious trinkets of various kinds, some of which he told me: 'Were presented to him by the Earl and Countess of Oxford; some by Lady Masham, and some by Lady Betty Germain,'[2] at last, coming to a drawer, filled with medals, he bade me choose two for myself, but he could not help smiling when I began to poise them in my hands, choosing them by weight rather than antiquity, of which indeed I was not then a judge.

The Dean amused me in this manner till we were summoned to dinner, where his behaviour was so humorous that I cannot avoid relating some part of it. He placed himself at the head of the table, opposite to a great pier-glass under which was a marble sideboard, so that he could see in the glass whatever the servants did at it. He was served entirely in plate [silver], and with great elegance; but, the beef being over-roasted, put us all in confusion: the Dean called for the cook-maid, and ordered her to take it downstairs, and do it less; the maid answered very innocently: 'That she could not.' 'Why, what sort of a creature are you,' says he, 'to commit a fault which cannot be amended?' And, turning to me, he said very gravely: 'That he hoped, as the cook was a woman of genius, he should, by this manner of arguing, be able in about a year's time to convince her she had better send up the meat too little than too much done'; charging the menservants: 'Whenever they imagined the meat was ready, they should take it, spit and all, and bring it up by force,' promising to aid them

---

1 *silver verge*: a rod of office carried before a Dean.
2 the ... Lady Betty Germain: these were some of his well-connected friends in London when Swift was there in an influential role from 1710 to 1714.

in case the cook resisted. The Dean then turning his eye on the look-ing-glass espied the butler opening a bottle of ale, helping himself to the first glass and very kindly jumbling the rest together, that his mas-ter and guests might all fare alike. 'Ha! friend,' says the Dean, 'Sharp's the word, I find; you drank my ale, for which I stop two shillings of your board-wages this week, for I scorn to be outdone in any thing, even in cheating.' Dinner at last was over, to my great joy; for now I had hope of a more agreeable entertainment than what the squabbling with the servants had afforded us.

The Dean thanked Mr Pilkington for his sermon: 'I never,' says he, 'preached but twice in my life, and then they were not sermons, but pamphlets.' I asked him: 'What might be the subject of them:' he told me: 'They were against Wood's half-pence.' 'Pray, Madam,' says he, 'do you smoke?' 'No, indeed, Sir,' says I. 'Nor your husband?' 'Neither, Sir.' 'It is a sign,' said he, 'you were neither of you bred in Oxford; for drinking and smoking are the first rudiments of learning taught there; and in those two arts no University in Europe can out-do them. Pray Mrs Pilkington tell me your faults.' 'Indeed, Sir, I must beg to be excused, for, if I can help it, you shall never find them out.' 'No,' says he, 'then Mr Pilkington shall tell me.' 'I will, Sir,' says he, 'when I have discovered them.' 'Pray Mr Dean,' says Dr Delany, 'why will you be so impolite as to suppose Mrs Pilkington had any faults?' 'Why, I will tell you,' replied the Dean; 'whenever I see a number of agreeable qualities in any person, I am always sure they have had ones sufficient to poise the scale.' I bowed, and told the Dean: 'He did me great honour.' And in this I copied Bishop Berkeley,[1] whom I have fre-quently heard declare: 'That when any speech was made to him which might be construed either into a compliment or an affront, or that (to make use of his own word) had two handles, he was so meek and so mild that he always took hold of the best.'

The Dean then asked me: 'If I was a Queen, what I should choose to have after dinner?' I answered: 'His conversation.' 'Pooh!' says he, 'I mean what regale?' 'A dish of coffee, Sir.' 'Why then I will so far make you as happy as a Queen – you shall have some in perfection; for when I was Chaplain to the Earl of Berkeley',[2] who was in the Government here, I was so poor I was obliged to keep a coffee-house, and all the nobility resorted to it to talk treason.' I could not help smiling at this oddity, but I really had such an awe on me that I could

---

1 *Bishop Berkeley*: George Berkeley, the philosopher and Bishop of Cloyne [q.v.].
2 *Chaplain ... Berkeley*: Swift had been Chaplain to the 2nd Earl of Berkeley (1649– 1710) when he was Lord Justice of Ireland.

not venture to ask him, as I longed to do, what it meant. The bottle
and glasses being taken away, the Dean set about making the coffee;
but, the fire scorching his hand, he called me to reach him his glove,
and changing the coffee-pot to his left hand, held out his right one,
ordered me to put his glove on it, which accordingly I did; when, taking up part of his gown to fan himself with, and acting in character of
a prudish lady, he said: 'Well, I do not know what to think. Women
may be honest that do such things, but, for my part, I never could bear
to touch any man's flesh except my husband's, whom perhaps,' says
he, 'she wished at the Devil.'

'Mr Pilkington,' says he, 'you would not tell me your wife's faults.
But I have found her out to be a d—ned, insolent, proud, unmannerly
slut.' I now looked confounded, not knowing what offence I had committed. – Says Mr Pilkington, 'Ay, Sir, I must confess she is a little saucy
to me sometimes, but – what has she done now?' 'Done! why nothing
but sat there quietly, and never once offered to interrupt me in making
the coffee; whereas, had I had a lady of modern good breeding here,
she would have struggled with me for the coffee-pot till she had made
me scald myself and her, and throw the coffee in the fire – or perhaps
at her head, rather than permit me to take so much trouble for her.'

This raised my spirits, and, as I found the Dean always prefaced a
compliment with an affront, I never afterwards was startled at the latter (as too many have been, not entering into his peculiarly ironical
strain), but was modestly contented with the former, which was more
than I deserved, and which the surprise rendered doubly pleasing.

By this time the bell rang for Church; and Dr Delany and Mr
Pilkington, who with myself were now all the company (for the rest
departed before the coffee was out), were obliged to attend the summons. But, as there is no service in the Cathedral but Evening Prayer
at six o'clock, I chose rather to attend the Dean there than go to hear
another sermon: by this means I had him all to myself for near three
hours, during which time he made me read to him the annals of the
four last years of the Reign of Queen Anne, written by himself; the
intention of which seemed to be a vindication of the then Ministry
and himself from having any design of placing the Pretender[1] on the
throne of Great Britain. It began with a solemn adjuration that all the
facts therein contained were truth, and then proceeded, in the manner of Lord Clarendon,[2] with giving the particular characters of every

1 *the Pretender*: James Francis Edward Stuart (1688–1766), a son of James II, claimant to the
throne of England, Scotland and Ireland, known as the Old Pretender.
2 *Lord Clarendon*: Henry Hyde (1638–1709), the second earl, a noted historian.

person whom he should have occasion to mention; amongst whom, I remember, he compared Lord Bolingbroke[1] to Petronius,[2] as one who agreeably mixed business with pleasure, At the conclusion of every period, he demanded of me whether I understood it. 'For I would,' says he, 'have it intelligent to the meanest capacity, and, if you comprehend it, 'tis possible everybody may.' I bowed, and assured him I did. And, indeed, it was written with such perspicuity and elegance of style that I must have had no capacity at all if I did not taste what was so exquisitely beautiful....

LAURENCE STERNE (1713-1768)

Born in Clonmel, Co. Tipperary, Sterne spent much of his early childhood with Irish relatives (he fell into a mill-race at Annamoe, Co. Wicklow and emerged unharmed) before going to school in Halifax in Yorkshire at the age of ten; he entered Jesus College, Cambridge in 1733. He was influenced by Locke's theory of perception, and by Cervantes, Rabelais, Sir Thomas Browne and Robert Burton. He became a clergyman, with a living at Sutton-on-the-Forest, and one at Stillington in Yorkshire. He married in 1741; the marriage was unhappy, though he was devoted to his daughter, an only child. In 1760 he acquired a third living at Coxwold in Yorkshire and settled there in the house he called Shandy Hall.

In 1759 the first two volumes of *The Life and Opinions of Tristram Shandy* appeared, followed by the other volumes at intervals up to 1767. It was immediately popular and Sterne followed *Tristram Shandy* with *The Sermons of Mr Yorick* (1760-69), which was also extremely successful. He travelled to France (1762-64) and to France and Italy (1765-66). He was suffering from tuberculosis.

In London in 1767 he fell in love with the wife of an East Indian Company official, Elizabeth Draper. His despair when she went to India to join her husband is recorded in *The Journal to Eliza* (published in 1904). In 1768 *A Sentimental Journey* gave his reactions to his continental travels. He died of pleurisy in London. Sterne was an innovative novelist, an early experimenter with the stream of consciousness technique; he used diagrams and squiggles, dots, blanks and marbled pages as well as digressions, all effectively questioning, reversing, mocking, employing absurdity in relating current sensational experience, and achieving a fine sense of comedy.

---

1 *Lord Bolingbroke*: Henry St John (1678–1751) Viscount Bolingbroke, who shared the leadership of the Tory party with Robert Harley, 1st Earl of Oxford. He negotiated the Treaty of Utrecht in 1713 and was plotting a Jacobite rebellion when Queen Anne died; this led to his dismissal and subsequent exile in France.
2 *Petronius*: Petronius Arbiter, one of Nero's chosen companionns, notorious for his excesses, and the reputed author of the *Satiricon*.

From *The Life and Opions of Tristram Shandy, Gentleman* (1759–1767)

VOLUME IV. CHAPTER XII

– And how does your mistress? cried my father, taking the same step over again from the landing, and calling to *Susannah*, whom he saw passing by the foot of the stairs with a huge pin-cushion in her hand – how does your mistress? As well, said *Susannah*, tripping by, but without looking up, as can be expected – What a fool am I, said my father! drawing his leg back again – let things be as they will, brother *Toby*, 'tis ever the precise answer – And how is the child, pray? – No answer. And where is doctor *Slop*? added my father, raising his voice aloud, and looking over the ballusters – *Susannah* was out of hearing.

Of all the riddles of a married life, said my father, crossing the landing, in order to set his back against the wall, whilst he propounded it to my uncle *Toby* – of all the puzzling riddles, said he, in a marriage state, – of which you may trust me, brother *Toby*, there are more asses loads than all *Job*'s stock of asses could have carried – there is not one that has more intricacies in it than this – that from the very moment the mistress of the house is brought to bed, every female in it, from the lady's gentlewoman down to the cinder-wench, becomes an inch taller for it; and give themselves more airs upon that single inch, than all their other inches put together.

I think rather, replied my uncle *Toby*, that 'tis we who sink an inch lower. – If I meet but a woman with child – I do it – 'Tis a heavy tax upon that half of our fellow-creatures, brother *Shandy*, said my uncle *Toby* – 'tis a piteous burden upon 'em, continued he, shaking his head. – Yes, yes, 'tis a painful thing – said my father, shaking his head too – but certainly since shaking of heads came into fashion, never did two heads shake together, in concert, from two such different springs.

God bless } 'em all – said my uncle
Deuce take } *Toby* and my father, each to himself.

CHAPTER XIII

Holla! – you chairman! – here's sixpence—do step into that bookseller's shop, and call me a *Day-ball* critick. I am very willing to give any one of 'em a crown to help me with his tackling, to get my father and my uncle *Toby* off the stairs, and to put them to bed. –

– 'Tis even high time; for except a short nap, which they both got whilst *Trim* was boring the jack-boots – and which, by the bye, did my father no sort of good upon the score of the bad hinge – they have not else shut their eyes, since nine hours before the time that doctor *Slop* was led into the back parlour in that dirty pickle by *Obadiah*.

Was every day of my life to be as busy a day as this, – and to take up, – truce –

I will not finish that sentence till I have made an observation upon the strange state of affairs between the reader and myself, just as things stand at present – an observation never applicable before to any one biographical writer since the creation of the world, but to myself – and I believe will never hold good to any other, until its final destruction – – and therefore, for the very novelty of it alone, it must be worth your worships attending to.

I am this month one whole year older than I was this time twelve-month; and having got, as you perceive, almost into the middle of my fourth volume – and no farther than to my first day's life – 'tis demonstrative that I have three hundred and sixty-four days more life to write just now, than when I first set out; so that instead of advancing, as a common writer, in my work with what I have been doing at it – on the contrary, I am just thrown so many volumes back – was every day of my life to be as busy a day as this – And why not? – and the transactions and opinions of it to take up as much description – And for what reason should they be cut short? as at this rate I should just live 364 times faster than I should write – It must follow, an' please your worships, that the more I write, the more I shall have to write – and consequently, the more your worships read, the more your worships will have to read.

Will this be good for your worships eyes?

It will do well for mine; and, was it not that my OPINIONS will be the death of me, I perceive I shall lead a fine life of it out of this self-same life of mine; or, in other words, shall lead a couple of fine lives together.

As for the proposal of twelve volumes a year, or a volume a month, it no way alters my prospect – write as I will, and rush as I may into the middle of things[1], as *Horace* advises, – I shall never overtake myself – whipp'd and driven to the last pinch, at the worst I shall have one day the start of my pen – and one day is enough for two volumes – and two volumes will be enough for one year. –

Heaven prosper the manufacturers of paper under this propitious

---

1 *into the middle of things*: 'in medias res', Horace, *Ars Poetica*, 148.

reign, which is now open'd to us, – as I trust its providence will prosper every thing else in it that is taken in hand.

As for the propagation of Geese – I give myself no concern – Nature
is all bountiful – I shall never want tools to work with.

– So then, friend! you have got my father and my uncle *Toby* off
the stairs, and seen them to bed ? – And how did you manage it? –
You dropp'd a curtain at the stairs foot – I thought you had no other
way for it – Here's a crown for your trouble.

CHAPTER XIV

– Then reach me my breeches off the chair, said my father to
Susannah – There is not a moment's time to dress you, Sir, cried
Susannah – the child is as black in the face as my – As your what? said
my father, for like all orators, he was a dear searcher into comparisons
– Bless me, Sir, said *Susannah*, the child's in a fit – And where's Mr.
Yorick – Never where he should be, said *Susannah*, but his curate's in
the dressing-room, with the child upon his arm, waiting for the name
– and my mistress bid me run as fast as I could to know, as captain
Shandy is the godfather, whether it should not be called after him.

Were one sure, said my father to himself, scratching his eye-brow,
that the child was expiring, one might as well compliment my brother *Toby* as not – and 'twould be a pity, in such a case, to throw away
so great a name as *Trismegistus* upon him – But he may recover.

No, no, – said my father to *Susannah*, I'll get up — There is no
time, cried *Susannah*, the child's as black as my shoe. *Trismegistus*,
said my father – But stay – thou art a leaky vessel, *Susannah*, added
my father; canst thou carry *Trismegistus* in thy head, the length of the
gallery without scattering – Can I? cried *Susannah*, shutting the door
in a huff – If she can, I'll be shot, said my father, bouncing out of bed
in the dark, and groping for his breeches.

Susannah ran with all speed along the gallery.

My father made all possible speed to find his breeches.

Susannah got the start, and kept it – 'Tis *Tris* – something, cried
Susannah – There is no christian name in the world, said the curate,
beginning with *Tris* – but *Tristram*. Then 'tis *Tristram-gistus*, quoth
Susannah.

– There is no *gistus* to it, noodle! – 'tis my own name, replied the
curate, dipping his hand as he spoke into the bason – *Tristram!* said
he, &c. &c. &c. &c. so *Tristram* was I called, and *Tristram* shall I be
to the day of my death.

My father followed *Susannah* with his night-gown across his arm, with nothing more than his breeches on, fastened through haste with but a single button, and that button through haste thrust only half into the button-hole.

– She has not forgot the name, cried my father, half opening the door – No, no, said the curate, with a tone of intelligence – And the child is better, cried *Susannah* – And how does your mistress? As well, said *Susannah*, as can be expected – Pish! said my father, the button of his breeches slipping out of the button hole – So that whether the interjection was levelled at *Susannah*, or the button-hole, – whether pish was an interjection of contempt or an interjection of modesty, is a doubt, and must be a doubt till I shall have time to write the three following favorite chapters, that is, my chapter of *chamber-maids* – my chapter of *pishes*, and my chapter of *button-holes*.

All the light I am able to give the reader at present is this, that the moment my father cried Pish! he whisk'd himself about – and with his breeches held up by one hand, and his night-gown thrown across the arm of the other, he returned along the gallery to bed, something slower than he came.

VOLUME IX.
CHAPTER IV.

She cannot, quoth my uncle Toby, halting, when they had march'd up to within twenty paces of Mrs. Wadman's door – she cannot, Corporal, take it amiss. –

– She will take it, an' please your honour, said the Corporal, just as the Jew's widow at Lisbon took it of my brother Tom. –

– And how was that? quoth my uncle Toby, facing quite about to the Corporal.

Your honour, replied the Corporal, knows of Tom's misfortunes; but this affair has nothing to do with them any further than this, That if Tom had not married the widow – or had it pleased God after their marriage, that they had but put pork into their sausages, the honest soul had never been taken out of his warm bed, and dragg'd to the inquisition – 'Tis a cursed place – added the Corporal, shaking his head, – when once a poor creature is in, he is in, an' please your honour, for ever.

'Tis very true; said my uncle Toby, looking gravely at Mrs Wadman's house, as he spoke.

Nothing, continued the Corporal, can be so sad as confinement for life – or so sweet, an' please your honour, as liberty.

Nothing, Trim – said my uncle Toby, musing –

Whilst a man is free, – cried the Corporal, giving a flourish with his stick thus –

A thousand of my father's most subtle syllogisms could not have said more for celibacy.

My uncle Toby look'd earnestly towards his cottage and his bowling-green.

The Corporal had unwarily conjured up the Spirit of calculation with his wand; and he had nothing to do, but to conjure him down again with his story, and in this form of Exorcism, most un-ecclesiastically did the Corporal do it.

From *A Sentimental Journey Through France and Italy* (1768)

THE CASE OF DELICACY

When you have gain'd the top of Mount Taurira, you run presently down to Lyons; adieu, then, to all rapid movements! – 'tis a journey of caution; and it fares better with sentiments, not to be in a hurry with them; so I contracted with a *voiturin* to take his time with a couple of mules, and convey me in my own chaise safe to Turin, through Savoy.

Poor, patient, quiet, honest people! fear not; your poverty, the treasury of your simple virtues, will not be envied you by the world, nor will your valleys be invaded by it. – Nature! in the midst of thy disorders, thou art still friendly to the scantiness thou hast created:

with all thy great works about thee, little hast thou left to give, either to the scythe or to the sickle; – but to that little thou grantest safety and protection; and sweet are the dwellings which stand so shelter'd.

Let the wayworn traveller vent his complaints upon the sudden turns and dangers of your roads, your rocks, your precipices; the difficulties of getting up, the horrors of getting down, mountains impracticable, – and cataracts, which roll down great stones from their summits, and block up his road! The peasants had been all day at work in removing a fragment of this kind between St. Michael and Madame; and, by the time my *voiturin* got to the place, it wanted full two hours of completing, before a passage could any how be gain'd. There was nothing but to wait with patience; – 'twas a wet and tempestuous night; so that, by the delay, and that together, the *voiturin* found himself obliged to put up five miles short of his stage at a little decent kind of an inn by the roadside.

I forthwith took possession of my bedchamber, got a good fire, order'd supper; and was thanking Heaven it was no worse, – when a *voiturin* arrived with a lady in it and her servant-maid.

As there was no other bedchamber in the house, the hostess, without much nicety, led them into mine, telling them, as she usher'd them in, that there was nobody in it but an English gentleman; – that there were two good beds in it, and a closet within the room which held another. The accent in which she spoke of this third bed, did not say much for it; – however, she said there were three beds, and but three people, – and she durst say the gentleman would do anything to accommodate matters. – I left not the lady a moment to make a conjecture about it, so instantly made a declaration that I would do anything in my power.

As this did not amount to an absolute surrender of my bedchamber, I still felt myself so much the proprietor, as to have a right to do the honours of it; – so I desired the lady to sit down, pressed her into the warmest seat, call'd for more wood, desired the hostess to enlarge the plan of the supper, and to favour us with the very best wine.

The lady had scarce warmed herself five minutes at the fire, before she began to turn her head back, and give a look at the beds; and the oftener she cast her eyes that way, the more they return'd perplexd. – I felt for her – and for myself; for in a few minutes, what by her looks, and the case itself, I found myself as much embarrassed as it was possible the lady could be herself.

That the beds we were to lie in were in one and the same room, was enough simply by itself to have excited all this; – but the position of them (for they stood parallel, and so very close to each other as only to allow space for a small wicker chair betwixt them) rendered the affair still more oppressive to us; – they were fixed up, moreover, near the fire; and the projection of the chimney on one side, and a large beam which cross'd the room on the other, form'd a kind of recess for them that was no way favourable to the nicety of our sensations: – if anything could have added to it, it was that the two beds were both of them so very small, as to cut us off from every idea of the lady and the maid lying together; which in either of them, could it have been feasible, my lying beside them, though a thing not to be wish'd, yet there was nothing in it so terrible which the imagination might not have pass'd over without torment.

As for the little room within, it offer'd little or no consolation to us: 'twas a damp, cold closet, with a half dismantled window-shutter, and with a window which had neither glass nor oil-paper in it to keep out the tempest of the night. I did not endeavour to stifle my cough when the lady gave a peep into it: so it reduced the case in course to this alternative, – That the lady should sacrifice her health to her feelings, and take up with the closet herself, and abandon the bed next mine to her maid, – or that the girl should take the closet, &c.

The lady was a Piedmontese of about thirty, with a glow of health in her cheeks. The maid was a Lyonoise of twenty, and as brisk and lively a French girl as ever moved. There were difficulties every way, – and the obstacle of the stone in the road, which brought us into the distress, great as it appeared whilst the peasants were removing it, was but a pebble to what lay in our ways now. – I have only to add, that it did not lessen the weight which hung upon our spirits, that we were both too delicate to communicate what we felt to each other upon the occasion.

We sat down to supper; and had we not had more generous wine to it than a little inn in Savoy could have furnish'd, our tongues had been tied up till Necessity herself had set them at liberty; – but the lady, having a few bottles of Burgundy in her *voiture*, sent down her *fille de chambre* for a couple of them; so that by the time supper was over, and we were left alone, we felt ourselves inspired with a strength of mind sufficient to talk, at least, without reserve upon our situation. We turn'd it every way and debated and considered it in all kinds of lights in the course of a two-hours' negotiation; at the end of which the articles were settled finally betwixt us, and stipulated for in form and manner of a treaty of peace, – and, I believe, with as much religion and good faith on both sides, as in any treaty which has yet had the honour of being handed down to posterity.

They were as follow: –

First, as the right of the bed-chamber is in Monsieur, – and he thinking the bed next to the fire to be the warmest, he insists upon the concession on the lady's side of taking up with it.

Granted, on the part of Madame; with a proviso, That as the curtains of that bed are of a flimsy transparent cotton, and appear likewise too scanty to draw close, that the *fille de chambre* shall fasten up the opening, either by corking-pins, or needle and thread, in such manner as shall be deem'd a sufficient barrier on the side of Monsieur.

2dly. It is required on the part of Madame, that Monsieur shall lie the whole night through in his *robe de chambre*.

Rejected: inasmuch as Monsieur is not worth a *robe de chambre*; he having nothing in his portmanteau but six shirts and a black silk pair of breeches.

The mentioning the silk pair of breeches made an entire change of the article, – for the breeches were accepted as an equivalent for the *robe de chambre*; and so it was stipulated and agreed upon, that I should lie in my black silk breeches all night.

3dly. It was insisted upon, and stipulated for by the lady, that after Monsieur was got to bed, and the candle and fire extinguished, that Monsieur should not speak one single word the whole night.

Granted, provided Monsieur's saying his prayers might not be deem'd an infraction of the treaty.

There was but one point forgot in this treaty, and that was the manner in which the lady and myself should be obliged to undress and get to bed; – there was but one way of doing it, and that I leave to the reader to devise, protesting as I do it, that if it is not the most delicate in nature, – 'tis the fault of his own imagination, – against which this is not my first complaint.

Now, when we were got to bed, whether it was the novelty of the situation, or what it was, I know not, but so it was, I could not shut my eyes: I tried this side and that, and turn'd and turn'd again, till a full hour after midnight, when Nature and Patience both wearing out, – O, my God! said I.

– You have broke the treaty, Monsieur, said the lady, who had no more slept than myself. – I begg'd a thousand pardons; but insisted it was no more than an ejaculation. – She maintained 'twas an entire infraction of the treaty. – I maintain'd it was provided for in the clause of the third article.

The lady would by no means give up her point, though she weakened her barrier by it; for, in the warmth of the dispute, I could hear two or three corking-pins fall out of the curtain to the ground.

– Upon my word and honour, Madame, said I, stretching my arm out of bed by way of asseveration, –

(I was going to have added, that I would not have trespass'd against the remotest idea of decorum for the world); –

– But the *fille de chambre* hearing there were words between us, and fearing that hostilities would ensue in course, had crept silently out of her closet; and it being totally dark, had stolen so close to our beds, that she had got herself into the narrow passage which separated them, and had advanced so far up as to be in a line betwixt her mistress and me; –

So that, when I stretch'd out my hand, I caught hold of the *fille de chambre's* –

JAMES EYRE WEEKES (?1719-1754)

He was probably the son of Thomas Eyre Weekes of Cork. (He is not to be confused with another James Eyre Weekes, also of Cork and about the same age, whose father was James Eyre Weekes. This second James Eyre Weekes was at Trinity College, Dublin from 1735 to 1739 and became a clergyman, a curate in Holy Trinity Church, Cork, and later Rector of Ballinadee, Co. Cork. He wrote several books under the name James Eyre Weeks, the earliest appearing in 1745. He died in 1775). James Eyre Weekes was the author of *Poems on Several Occasions* (Cork, 1743) a volume he dedicated to Prince Nobody, the Preface excusing the few liberties he took by his age ('when the judgement is weak and the imagination luxuriant and unbounded'). It seems likely that he was the James Eyre Weekes whose throat was slit before his body was thrown in the Liffey for failing to drink a toast to the Court party.

Poem Left in a Lady's Toilet

Oh that I was my Sylvia's stays!
to clasp her lovely waist,
to press those breasts, where rapture plays,
where love and pleasure feast.

That I was but her smock so white,
to feel her velvet skin,
to bless my touch with soft delight
and kiss it without sin.

Or that I was her stocking neat,
gartered above her knee,

that I, so near the happy seat,
the happy seat might see.

Why am I not her lace, her ring,
her dicky or her fan,
her dog, her monkey, anything
but what I am – a man.

Answer by the Lady's Maid

Ah simple poet, ill-judged prayer!
how like an owl you sing,
better for thee the ring to wear
than be thyself the ring.

Where is thy feeling, senseless stock?
thou injudicious Elf –
better for thee to lift the smock
than be the smock itself.

Would you, fond simpleton, desire
to be your lady's fan,
If you would nightly cool her fire
Wish still to be a man.

To a Lady with a Fan

Go, cooling fan, and let my Anna see
how near thy form her eyes have rendered me,
a mere anatomy! Thy ribs like mine
with nothing on them but a painted skin.

Go, cooling fan, import thy cooling breeze
to those white regions which already freeze,
those icy breasts, where snow eternal lies,
nor melts, though near the sunshine of her eyes.

Go, cooling fan, and in thy folds enclose
those sultry sighs with which my body glows,
go tell the fair one that the love-sick boy
is like the messenger he sends, her toy,

flirted and twirled and furled and twirled again,
like sails obedient to the winds and rain.

Say that her presence, as the sun the rose,
spreads all my hopes and all my blushes shows,
say, when she's gone, my folding hopes decay,
are furled like thee and wait her hand to play.

THOMAS SHERIDAN (1719-1788)

Born in Dublin or at Quilca, the third son of Thomas Sheridan* and godson of Swift*, Sheridan was educated at his father's school in Capel Street, Dublin, at Westminster College, London, and at Trinity College, Dublin, taking his B.A. degree in 1739 and his M.A. in 1743. He starred in Smock Alley in 1743 as Richard III, and in the same year he produced his farce, *Captain O'Blunder* (retitled *The Brave Irishman*); its popular hero is an outstanding stage Irishman. Sheridan became embroiled with a fellow actor in the *Cato* affair – the actor, Theophilus Cibber, had taken his costume in that play. It led to a storm of pamphlets, among them a defence of Sheridan in verse by Frances Chamberlaine*, whom he married in 1747. He acted in Drury Lane and Covent Garden before managing the Theatre Royal in Dublin. He brought David Garrick to Ireland for a very successful season (1745-46). Sheridan dominated the Dublin theatre world until the Crow Street Theatre was reopened, and he retired to London, where he continued to appear on stage up to 1776. In 1763 he had returned to Dublin, where he devoted much time to propagating educational reform and teaching elocution, and to the foundation of an Irish Academy. He compiled *A General Dictionary of the English Language* (2 vols, 1780) and *A Complete Dictionary of the English Language* (1789). He also wrote a life of Swift.

From Lectures on the Art of Reading

(1775)

... For a long time after letters had been introduced into Britain, the art of reading was known only to a few. Those were days of ignorance and rudeness; and to be able to read at all was thought little less than miraculous. Such times were not proper for cultivating that art, or bringing it to perfection. After the revival of the dead languages amongst us, which suddenly enlightened the minds of men, and diffused general knowledge, one would imagine that great attention would have been paid to an art, which was cultivated with so much care by those ancients, to whom we were indebted for all our lights; and that it would have made an equal progress amongst us, with the rest which we had borrowed from them. But it was this very circumstance, the revival of the dead languages, which put a stop to all improvement in the art of Reading; and which has continued it in the same low state from that time to this. From that period, the minds of men took a wrong bias. Their whole attention was employed in the cultivation of the artificial, to the neglect of the natural language. Letters, not sounds; writing, not speech, became the general care. To make boys understand what they read; to explain the meaning of the Greek and Roman authors; and to write their exercises according to the laws of grammar or prosody in a dead language, were the chief objects of instruction. Whilst that of delivery, was so wholly neglected, that the best scholars often could not make themselves understood in repeating their own exercises; or disgraced beautiful composition by an ungracious delivery. Those who taught the first rudiments of reading, thought their task finished when their pupils could read fluently, and observe their stops. This employment, requiring no great talents, usually fell to the lot of old women, or men of mean capacities; who could teach no other mode of utterance than what they possessed themselves; and consequently were not likely to communicate any thing of propriety or grace to their scholars. If they brought with them any bad habits, such as stuttering, stammering, mumbling, an indistinct articulation, a constrained unnatural tone of voice, brought on from imitation of some other; or if they were unable to pronounce certain letters, these poor creatures, utterly unskilled in the causes of these defects, sheltered their ignorance under the general charge of their being natural impediments, and sent them to the Latin school, with all their imperfections on their heads. The master of that school, as little skilled in these matters as the other, neither knew how, nor thought it part of his province to attempt a cure; and thus the disorder generally passed irremediable through life. Such was the state of this art on the first propagation of literature, and such it notoriously remains to this day.

When we reflect on the general benefit that would accrue from bringing this art to perfection; that it would be useful to many professions; necessary to the most numerous and respectable order established amongst us; ornamental to all individuals, whether male or female; and that the state of public elocution must in a great measure be affected by it, it would be apt to astonish one to think that there has been so little progress made in it.

When we consider too that the world has always been clamorous in their complaints upon this head, having too generally occasion to regret the low state of this art, in their attendance on the most important duty, that of public worship; and that there are multitudes whose interest and inclination it would be to improve themselves in it, had they the means in their power, and could they obtain regular instruction; it would surprise one at first that no one has as yet struck out such a method, which would certainly be attended with great emoluments to him. And indeed the prospect was so inviting, that many have been the attempts which have been made in that way from time to time; but they all failed from the same cause; which was, that they who attempted it were men skilled in letters, but not in sounds; and they were blind enough to imagine that the knowledge of the one necessarily included that of the other. Whereas the very reverse is true; as it would be impossible to treat justly of sounds, until the man of letters shall have first diverted himself of all the prejudices and errors which he had imbibed with regard to that article, from the time of his first learning the alphabet; for in that lies the source of all our mistakes. They took the alphabet as they found it, and thought it perfect; whereas this alphabet, on the revival of the learned languages, was borrowed from the Roman, though it by no means squared with our tongue. As a proof of which it is certain that we have 28 simple sounds in our tongue, and have in reality but 20 characters to mark them, though more letters appear in the alphabet, as will presently be shewn. This reduced men in the beginning to a thousand clumsy contrivances, in those unenlightened days, to make such an alphabet answer the end at all; but it was done at such an expense as to make the learning to read and spell properly a tedious and difficult task, which required the labour of many years to accomplish. These contrivances of theirs in spelling, to make a defective alphabet answer the end of representing words, have so confounded our ideas with regard to the powers of several letters, applied to a variety of different uses, that all the systems hitherto produced upon that point have been a perfect chaos. Nothing can be a stronger proof of the gross errours into which literary men fell, in their several grammars and treatises upon this subject, than that the best of them have mistaken diphthongs for simple sounds, and simple sounds for diphthongs; compound consonants for single, and single for compound. Nay, what it still more extraordinary, that they have even mistaken vowels for consonants, all which I shall presently make appear. What superstructure built on such fundamental errors could stand?

From Sheridan's & Henderson's *Practical Method of Reading and Reciting English Poetry*

(1796)

THE HERMIT.

By Dr. Goldsmith

Begin this poem in a *plaintive, affecting* tone of voice.

> Turn, gentle hermit of the dale,
>   And guide my lonely way,
> To where yon taper cheers the vale,
>   With hospitable ray.

If you point with your finger when you repeat the third line, as if observing the light, alluded to by the poet, the effect will be pleasing. We shall mention several things during our progress, that, although trifling, apparently, still, when properly put into practice, frequently add, in the delivery, the greatest beauty to the meaning of an author.

> For here forlorn and lost, I tread
>   With fainting steps and slow;
> Where wilds *immeasurably* spread,
>   Seem *length'ning* as I go.

The words marked, in a *heavy, lengh'ning kind of tone.* – Alter your voice in the next verse.

> 'Forbear, my son,' the hermit cries,
>   'To tempt the dang'rous gloom;
> For yonder faithless phantom flies,
>   To lure thee to thy doom.

> 'Here to the houseless child of want,
>   My door is open still,
> And tho' my portion is but scant,
>   I give it with good will.

> 'Then turn to night, and freely share
>   Whate'er my cell bestows;

My rushy couch, and frugal fare,
  My blessing and repose.

The last line more *solemn* than the others.

'No flocks that range the valley free,
  To laughter I condemn:
Taught by that Pow'r that pities me,
  I learn to pity them.'

'Then, Pilgrim, turn, thy cares forego;
    All earth-born cares are wrong:
Man wants but little here below,
    Nor wants that little long.

Alter your voice as you now come to the descriptive part.

Soft as the dew from heav'n descends,
  His gentle accents fell;
The modest stranger lowly bends,
  And follows to the cell.

Far in a wilderness obscure,
  The lonely mansion lay;
A refuge to the neighbouring poor,
  And strangers led astray.

No stores beneath its humble thatch
  Requir'd a master's care;
The wicket opening with a latch,
  Receiv'd the harmless pair.

And now when busy crowds retire
  To revel or to rest,
The hermit trimm'd his little fire,
  And cheer'd his pensive guest:

And spread his vegetable store,
  And gaily press'd and smil'd;
And, skill'd in legendary lore,
  The ling'ring hours beguil'd.

> Around in sympathetic mirth
> Its tricks the kitten tries;
> The cricket chirrups in the hearth;
> The crackling faggot flies.

Although we recommend in the foregoing verses an *impressive* descriptive manner of delivery, still the whole must go off *trippingly* from the tongue, and not hurt the ear with the least *heaviness*, except in those parts which we shall point out. – In the next verse assume something more of the melancholy, so as the prepare the reader for what is to follow.

> But nothing could a charm impart
> To sooth the stranger's woe;
> For grief lay heavy at his heart,
> And tears began to flow.

'*Heavy*' in the third line with a tone *long*, and, as it were, *dragging*.

> His rising cares, the hermit spy'd,
> With answering care opprest;
> 'And whence unhappy youth!' he cry'd,
> 'The sorrows of thy breast?

From the beginning of the third line you alter your voice, as if the hermit was in the act of speaking.

> 'From better habitations spurn'd,
> Reluctant dost thou rove;
> Or grieve for friendship unreturn'd,
> Or unregarded love?

You ought to deliver the last line with a *sigh*, and peculiarly *affecting*, as it comes home so nearly to his own situation.

> 'Alas! the joys that fortune brings,
> Are trifling, and decay;
> And those who prize the paltry things,
> More trifling still than they.

> And what is friendship but a name?

A charm that lulls to sleep;
A shade that follows wealth or fame,
And leaves the wretch to weep?

'And love is still an emptier sound,

Pause a little after the word '*love*' with the voice up.

The modern fair-one's jest:
On earth unseen, or only found,
To warm the turtle's nest.

'For shame! fond youth, thy sorrows hush,
And spurn the sex,' he said;
But, while he spoke, a rising blush
The bashful guest betray'd.

Change your voice from the third line as you resume the descriptive part, but at the same time take care to keep up the interest of the scene by your *tone*, *look*, and *manner*.

Surpris'd he sees new beauties rise,
Swift mantling to the view;
Like colours o'er the morning skies,
As bright, as transient too.

Your whole manner must express surprise to accord with the meaning of the verse. In the third line cast a look upwards as you read it.

Her bashful look, her rising breast,
Alternate spread alarms:
The lovely stranger stands confest
A maid in all her charms.

Speak the last line with a *glow of expression*, as you thereby properly mark to the hearer the discovery made. The stranger's account of herself you must read in an *affecting modest* manner.

'And ah! forgive a stranger rude,
A wretch forlorn' she cry'd;
Whose feet unhallow'd thus intrude,

Where heav'n, and you reside.

'But let a maid thy pity share,
 Whom love has taught to stray;
Who seeks for rest, but finds despair
 Companion of her way.

'My father liv'd beside the Tyne,
 A wealthy lord was he;
And all his wealth was mark'd as mine,
 He had but only me.

'To win me from his tender arms,
 Unnumber'd suitors came;
Who prais'd me for imputed charms,
 Or felt, or feign'd a flame.

'Each morn, the mercenary crowd
 With richest proffers strove:
Among the rest young Edwin bow'd,
 But never talk'd of love.

'In humblest, simplest habit clad,
 No wealth nor pow'r had he;
Wisdom and worth were all he had,
 But these were all to me.

'The blossom op'ning to the day,
 The dews of heav'n refin'd,
'Could naught of purity display,
 To emulate his mind.

'The dews, the blossom of the tree,
 With charms inconstant shine;
Their charms were his, but woe to me:
 Their constancy was mine.

'For still I try'd each fickle art,
 Importunate and vain;
And while his passion touch'd my heart,
 I triumph'd in his pain.

'Till quite dejected with my scorn,
    He left me to my pride;
And sought a solitude forlorn,
    In secret, where he died.

'But mine the sorrow, mine the fault,
    And well my life shall pay;
I'll seek the solitude he sought,
    And stretch me where he lay.

'And there forlorn, despairing, hid,
    I'll lay me down and die:
'Twas so for me that Edwin did,
    And so for him will I.'

Through the whole of the foregoing, you ought to be *simply affecting* in your utterance, and in the concluding verses you may use the *pathetic* with great advantage.

'Forbid it heav'n!' the hermit cry'd,
    And clasp'd her to his breast:
The wond'ring fair-one turn'd to chide,
    'Twas Edwin's self that press'd.

Let your voice in the last line break out into a tone of *happy exultation*. All the rest must be delivered with great *warmth of expression*.

'Turn, Angelina, ever dear,
    My charmer, turn to see
Thy own, thy long-lost Edwin here,
    Restor'd to love and thee.

'Thus let me hold thee to my heart,
    And ev'ry care resign:
And shall we never, never part,
    My life, my all that's mine!

'No never from this hour to part,
    We'll live and love so true;
The sigh that rends thy constant heart,
    Shall break thy Edwin's too.'

Here closes this charming ballad. It is remarkable for its peculiar simplicity of expression, so that your mode of reading it must be entirely unaffected; and, in many places, which we have not pointed out, and which the reader's taste and judgment must select, there are fine opportunities where the *tender* and *pathetic* may be used with great effect.

FRANCES SHERIDAN (1724-1760)

Born in Dublin, the daughter of Dr Philip Chamberlaine, a Church of Ireland cler-gyman who was so opposed to the education of women that she was secretly taught to write by her older brother Walter. She wrote her first novel, *Eugenia and Adelaide* (posthumously published) at the age of fifteen. She wrote a poem 'The Owls' to support Thomas Sheridan the Younger when the actor and theatre manager was involved in the *Cato* riot in 1745: they married in 1747; their five children included Richard Brinsley Sheridan and Alicia, who completed a memoir of her mother.

Frances Sheridan followed her most successful novel *Memoirs of Miss Sidney Bidulph* (2 vols, 1761-67) with two social comedies, *The Discovery* (1762) and the less successful *The Dupe* (1762). *A Journey to Bath* was not staged but its character Mrs Tryfort is seen as a model for Mrs Malaprop in her son's *The Rivals*. She died at Blois where the family were sheltering from creditors.

From Memoirs of Miss Sidney Bidulph
(1761)

[*The heroine's journal, prefaced by an Editor's Introduction, recounts her unfortunate love affair with Orlando Faulkland. Her mother disapproves of him as he has had an affair which her brother dismisses as a trifling intrigue despite the fact that the young lady involved is about to have his child. Her mother influences her refusal of Faulkland.*]

July 27 [1705].———…What a strange alteration have a few days pro-duced! our domestic peace broke in upon by the unlucky difference between my mother and my brother. My near prospect of——of—— oh! let me be ingenuous, and say Happiness, vanished – Poor Mr. Faulkland! *Poor* do I call him? for shame, Sidney – but let the word go; I will not blot it. Mr. Faulkland forbid the house, myself harrassed by a cruel disorder, and hardly able to crawl out of bed. All this has fallen on me within these last fourteen black days. Then I dread the going abroad, or seeing company, I shall look so silly; for the intend-ed wedding began to be talked of; – and the curiosity of people to know the cause of it's being broke off – What wild guesses will be made by some, and what lies invented by others! Then the ill-natured mirth of one half of the girls of my acquaintance, and the *as* provok-ing condolements of the other half – I am fretted at the thoughts of it – but it cannot be helped; I must bear it all – I wish I were well enough to get into the country, to be out of the reach of such impertinence.

I long to know who this ill-fated girl is, that has been the cause of all this. *A gentlewoman, and very pretty; one that loves Mr. Faulkland, and will shortly make him a parent.* Thus my mother described her to Mr. Faulkland, and he assented to it. Oh! fie, fie, Mr. Faulkland, how could you be so cruel to *her*? How could you use *me* so ill? and Sir George knew of all this, and makes light of it! it is a strange story! My mother is severe in her virtue, but she is in the right – My brother would sacrifice every consideration to aggrandize his family – To make a purchase of the unhappy creature, and that without her knowledge too, it is horrid! Away, away from my thoughts, thou vile intruder – Return to your Bath mistress, she has a better right to you than I have; she implores your pity; she has no refuge but you; and she may be every way preferable to me – I wish I knew her name, but what is it to me; *mine* will never be Faulkland, *hers* ought. Perhaps Mr. Faulkland may be induced to marry her, when he sees her in her present interesting situation. He says he will provide a retreat for her; to be sure he will have the compassion to visit her: and then who knows what may happen? If I know my own heart, I think I do most sincerely wish he may make her his wife; but then I would not chuse to have it known suddenly; that might look as if he forsook me for her. *That*, I own, would a little hurt my pride. I wish not the truth to be known, for Mr. Faulkland's sake; but then I should not like to have a slur thrown on me.

I will add no more to this, but send the packet off at all events; I think it will find you at Paris....

August 12 [1705].——I never was so disconcerted as I have been this day: you will be surprized when I tell you, it was by my good lady V——. She came to pass the day with me, Mr. Arnold being engaged abroad.

We were both sitting at work in the parlour: lady V——had con-tinued silent for a good while; at last looking at me with a most benign smile, for I had at the same instant cast my eyes at her; I was just then thinking, my dear Mrs. Arnold, said she, that I once (though perhaps you did not know it) flattered myself with the hopes of being related to you. Her words threw me into confusion, though I did not know their meaning. It would have been both an honour and a happiness to me, madam, I replied, though I don't know by what means I was ever likely to possess it. She continued smiling, but seemed in suspence whether she should proceed. You will pardon my curiosity, my dear, said she, but give me leave to ask, whether Mr. Arnold was not once near losing the happiness he now enjoys? I felt my face glow as she spoke. There was once a treaty of marriage on foot, madam, I answered, between me and another gentleman. I am sorry I mentioned it, said my lady, observing my confusion; but as I was no stranger to the affair while it was transacting, and Mr. Faulkland is a kinsman of mine, I hope you will forgive my inquisitiveness; for I own I have a curiosity, which I believe nobody but yourself can gratify; and if I did not think you the most candid, as well as the best tempered creature living, I durst not push my inquiry. My lord, you are to know, was in London at the time Mr. Faulkland was first introduced to you; and as they are extremely fond of each other, Mr. Faulkland did not scruple to disclose his passion to him, nor the success it then appeared likely to be crowned with, giving him at the same time such a character of you, as I have since found you deserve.

When my lord returned to V——hall, which he was obliged to do very soon after Mr. Faulkland had made this discovery to him, he informed me of the alliance my cousin Faulkland was going to make; and we were pleasing ourselves with the thoughts of congratulating him on his happiness, when we received a letter from him that put an end to all our expectations; this letter contained but four distracted lines: he told my lord, in broken sentences, that he had lost all hopes of Miss Bidulph; that an act of indiscretion had been construed into a capital crime; and that being banished from the presence of the woman he adored, he was immediately about to bid adieu to England, perhaps for ever.

This was the substance of what he wrote to us: we have heard from him since a few times, but he never cleared up the matter to us, nor ever so much as mentioned it. I have not been in London since; my lord has; but he never could get any light into the mystery: he heard from some of our friends, who knew of the intended match, that it was broke off nobody knew why. There were, however, several idle surmises thrown out; some laid the blame on Mr. Faulkland, and some on you; but the truth I believe remains still a secret. Now, my dear, if my curiosity is improper, or if there was any particular motive to this disappointment of my kinsman's hopes, which you don't choose to reveal, forgive my inquiry, and think no more of it; but take up that book, and read to me while I work.

Though my lady gave me this kind opportunity of evading her question, I did not lay hold of it: I did not indeed choose to reveal the whole of this affair, because I did not think myself at liberty to divulge Miss Burchell's secret, however I might discover my own. I told my lady in general terms, that though Mr. Faulkland might pretend to a lady every way my superior, yet there was an objection to him of no small weight with us; that my mother had been informed of a very recent piece of gallantry he had had with a person of some condition, and that it had disgusted her so much, she could not think of uniting me with a man whose passions were not a little more staid; and that this was the sole reason of her dislike to a gentleman, who was in every other respect unexceptionable. I am glad it was no worse, said lady V——, smiling; I am sure Mr. Faulkland is not capable of a base action; youthful follies he may have had, though I believe as few even of those to answer for as most men of his years. I make not the least doubt, however, that Lady Bidulph was guided by prudence in what she did. She certainly could not be too cautious in the disposal of such a child as you; and whatever Mr. Faulkland's disapointment may be, you I hope are happy. Lady V——looked at me as she pronounced these words, with an inquisitive, though tender regard. I was glad of an opportunity of enlarging on the merits of Mr. Arnold, and told her, I was as happy as my heart could wish, or the worthiest of men could make me. I am glad of it, said she, with a quickness in her voice; but don't imagine, my dear Mrs. Arnold (and she took me by the hand) that I introduced this conversation merely to gratify a curiosity which I fear you must condemn in your private thoughts, though you have been so good as to satisfy it: I had another reason, a much stronger one. What is it, dear madam? almost starting with apprehensions of I did not know what. Don't be alarmed, said she, smiling, it is only this; a great aunt of Mr. Faulkland's is lately dead, who has left him a considerable personal estate, and he is coming over to take possession of it; otherwise I don't know when we should have seen him in England. My lord had a letter very lately from him; he was then at Turin, where he had met with our eldest son, who is now on his travels: he told us he had letters and some tokens of love to deliver us from him; and that he should immediately on his arrival in England come to V—— hall, where he would pass a month with us. Now as we expect him daily, I had a mind to apprize you of his intended visit, that you might not be surprized, by perhaps unexpectedly meeting him at my house. I thanked her ladyship for her obliging caution, though I thought it had something in it that mortified me. I told her, that though I should not seek to renew my acquaintance with Mr. Faulkland, I had yet no reason to avoid him. Lady V——, who is extremely quick of apprehension, replied, Without doubt, madam, you have not; but you might be surprized at seeing him notwithstanding.

She presently turned the discourse: but made me happy the whole day, by that inexhaustible fund of good sense and improving knowledge of which she is mistress.

Mr. Arnold came not home till very late; he complains that he is got into a know of acquaintance that like the bottle too well; but I am sure his natural sobriety is such, that it will not be in the power of example to lead him into intemperance; though I am vexed he has fallen into such acquaintance, because I know drinking is disagreeable to him: yet a country gentleman must sometimes give a little into it, to avoid the character of being singular.

[*The heroine had married Mr Arnold, who is not only dull but unfaithful, and she realises the enormity of what has happened. She finds the fatal letter Faulkland had written to her brother which her mother had read.*]

October 29 [1706].——Ah, my Cecilia, what an aggravation is here to the already too deep regret I began to feel on Mr. Faulkland's account! His triumph over me is now complete!

In sorting my mother's papers (as I am to leave these lodgings to-morrow) I found that letter which Mr. Faulkland wrote to my brother from Bath. You may remember I told you my mother had, in her resentment, flung it to Sir George, and that, as it happened to fall on the ground, he had quitted the room in a passion without taking it up. My mother, I suppose, when she cooled, laid it by, though I dare say she never looked into it afterwards. Read it, and see by what a fatality we have been governed. Mr. Faulkland's letter to Sir George Bidulph.

Bath, May 9, 1703.

How you mortify me, my dear Bidulph, when you tell me of the happiness I lose by staying so long at Bath! *The ladies are impatient to see me,* say you? Ah! Sir George, thou hast spoke better of me than I deserve, I fear.

I am sadly out of humour with myself at present. I have got into a very foolish sort of a scrape here. My wrist is quite well, and I should have thrown myself at Miss Bidulph's feet before now, but to tell you a secret, my virtue not being proof against temptation, I have been intercepted.

'Tis but a slight lapse, however, a flying affair; neither my honour, nor my heart in the question. A little vagrant Cupid has contented himself with picking my pocket, just lightly fluttering through my breast, and away.

Are you fallen so low as that, Faulkland, say you? to *buy* the favour of the fair? No, George, no; not quite so contemptible as that neither: and yet, faith, I did *buy* it too, for it cost me three hundred pounds; but the lady to whom I am obliged knows nothing of this part of her own history; at least, I hope so, for my credit sake. The case in short is this: an old gouty officer, and his wife (a very notable dame; a fine woman too) happened to lodge in the same house with me. The man came hither to get rid of his aches; the lady of her money, and her virtue, if she has any, for she is eternally at the card tables.

Under the conduct of this hopeful guide, came a niece of the husband's; an extremely fine girl, innocent too, I believe, and the best dancer I ever saw. I don't know how it happened, but she took a fancy to me, which, upon my word, and I am sure you have no doubts of me, I was far from wishing to improve. You know I always despised the mean triumph of gaining a heart, for which I could not give another in return. I saw with pain her growing inclination for me; but as we lived in the same house, and met every day in the rooms, it was impossible for me to avoid her as much as I wished to do. The aunt I found, had her eyes upon me, and took some pains to promote a liking on my side. I saw her design, and was so much upon my guard, that she, who I soon found was an adept in love-matters, almost despaired of gaining her ends. The young lady's inclination however seemed to increase; a pair of fine blue eyes told me so every day; and I was upon the point of flying to avoid the soft contagion, when an accident happened that totally overthrew all my good resolutions.

I had not seen the young lady for two or three days; I enquired for her, and her aunt answered, with a mysterious smile. She is ill, poor thing, why don't you look in upon her, and ask her how she does? I replied, if the lady will permit me, I will do myself that honour, and intended literally to have kept my word, by just asking her at her chamber door how she did.

You are very cruel, said the aunt; would you persuade me that you don't know the girl is in love with you? Oh, your Servant, Madam; if you think me vain, I thank you for the reprimand. Come, come, said she, this is all affectation, we'll drink tea with her this evening. Upon my word, said I, if I am to believe what you say, I think you ought not to desire me. I am not blind to the young lady's merit, but am so unfortunate as not to have it in my power to make such returns as she deserves. I found the occasion required my being serious.

If you have not love, said she, you may at least have a little complaisance. Was there ever such a barbarian, not to go and see a woman that is dying for him? I promised to bring you, and she expects you. What is the pretty creature afraid of (patting my cheek). I'll stay by it all the while. There was no withstanding this; I promised to wait on her.

She knocked at my door about six o'clock, and looking in, asked if the coy Narcissus[1] was ready? I went with her, and she led me directly to her niece's chamber. The young lady looked pale and languishing, but very pretty. I was really grieved to see her, and enquired with an unaffected concern after her health. The tea-things were set, and I tried to force something like conversation, but I believe I was rather formal.

When we had done tea, the aunt looked at her watch, started off her chair, said she had outstaid her appointment with the party she was to meet at cards, and turning to me, I hope, Sir, you will have the *Charity* to stay with my niece; and then hurried out of the room. I begged leave to hand her to her chair, intending to take that opportunity of slipping away, and resolved to quit the house the next morning. But the determined gipsey was prepared for this motion, and insisting that I should not stir, thrust me back from the door, which she shut, and flew down stairs.

What was to become of me now, George? My situation was dangerous, and really critical. To be short, I forgot my prudence, and found the young lady's heart too, too tender.

I never felt remorse before. I never had cause. I accuse myself of indiscretion, but I have not the aggravating addition to my

---

1 *Narcissus*: in Greek mythology Narcissus was a beautiful youth who fell in love with his reflection in a pool; he pined away, becoming the flower that bears his name.

fault of oaths and promises to fly in my face. I made none – love, foolish love did all, and led a willing victim to his altar, who asked nothing in return for the sacrifice she offered; and received nothing but unavailing repentance on my side. I know not any thing now that would give me so much pleasure as to find that the girl hated me heartily, though I have given her no cause.

A just reparation I cannot make her. Every thing forbids that thought. I do not consider myself as free; but if I were so, I am not a seducer, and therefore do not think myself bound to carry my penitence to such lengths. The damned aunt has been the serpent. And here let me explain to you what I call buying the lady's favour. You must know, the aunt one night (the greatest part of which she had spent at hazard) lost two hundred pounds; at least she told me so the next morning, and with tears in her eyes besought me, in the most earnest manner, to lend her that sum. She said, she should be undone if her husband were to know it, and that she would pay me in a very few days, as she had as much due to her from different people who had lost to her at play. Though our short acquaintance could hardly warrant her making such a request, I nevertheless did not hesitate, but gave her the money directly. She meant indeed to pay me, but it was in a different coin, and this I suppose was the price she set on the unhappy girl's honour.

My reflections on this unlucky affair make me very grave. I have explained my situation to the young lady, and expressed my concern at not having it in my power to be any other than a friend to her. She blames her own weakness, and her aunt's conduct, but does not reproach me. She cannot with justice, yet I wish she would, for then I should reproach myself less.

'Tis a foolish business, and I must get off as handsomely as I can. Prithee, Bidulph, say something to encourage me, and put me into more favour with myself. You have often been my confessor, but I never wanted absolution so much as now; nor ever was so well entitled to it, for I am really full of penitence, and look *so* mortified, you would pity me. I am ashamed of having been surprised into a folly; I who *ought* to have been upon my guard, knowing the natural impetuosity of my own temper.

I must not conclude without telling you, that this very morning, the precious aunt, instead of paying me the two hundred pounds she had of me before, very modestly requested I would oblige her with another hundred, to redeem a pair of diamond earrings which she had been obliged to part with for the supply of some other necessary demands; and with abundance of smooth speeches, she assured me, in a fortnight she would pay me all together, having notes to that value which would then become due to her. I was such a booby as to give it to her. – Why, fare it well! I never expect to see a shilling of it. She thinks, perhaps, there is value received for it. Vile woman! The affair fortunately for us all, has not taken wind; and for me, the names of both aunt and niece, may ever stand enrolled amongst those of chaste matrons and virgins. The family quits this place soon, as the old gentleman is better.

I thank you for your care, in relation to my house. I hope to take possession of it in a week or ten days; you are very good in fixing me so near yourself. Adieu.

I am, &c.

What do you think of this letter, my Cecilia, written in confidence to my brother? Mr. Faulkland could not conceive it probable that any body but Sir George should ever see it; he had no reason therefore to gloss over any of the circumstances. *Had* I seen it but in time – Oh what anguish of heart might we all have been spared! Miss Burchell singly, as she *ought*, would have borne the punishment of her folly.

My mother had not the patience to read this letter through; nice and punctilious as her virtue was, she passed a censure on the crime in gross, without admitting any palliating circumstance. But I blame her not; the excellence of her own morals, made her scrupulous in weighing those of others; she read the letter in a cursory way, and it is plain but half of it; prepossessed as she was before, by knowing the material point.

The account was given with levity at the *first* mention of the young lady. Then she understood he had *bought* her of her aunt; there is a paragraph which *looks* like it, and to be sure she attended not to the explanation. Fatal oversight! she read not far enough to have this matter cleared up. She took nothing but the bare facts into her account. A young lady dishonoured, her disgrace likely to be public, then her tenderness for the man who had undone her, and that man rejecting her, and on the point of marrying another. These were the only points of view in which my mother beheld the story. Her justice, her humanity, and her religion prompted her to act as she did; and her conduct stands fully acquitted to my judgment, though my heart must, upon this full conviction of Mr. Faulkland's honour, sigh at recollecting the past.

I know that the memory of my mother's own first disastrous love wrought strongly on her mind. She was warm in her passions, liable to deep impressions, and always adhered strictly to those opinions she first imbibed. Her education had been severe and recluse; and she had drawn all her ideas of mankind from her own father and mine, who, I have been told, were both men of exemplary lives. From all these considerations, I must again say, that I entirely acquit my dear mother, in regard to her whole conduct, however I have suffered by it. *October 30.* —— I am now fixed in a very humble habitation. Shall I own it to you, my Cecilia? I was shocked at the change. A room two pair of stairs high, with a closet, and a small indifferent parlour, compose the whole of my apartment. Hither did my faithful Patty, my two children, and myself, remove this day. It put us not to much trouble, having nothing to take with us but our wearing apparel, which is all the worldly goods of which I am now possessed....

From a letter dated 29 November 1762 about her comedy *The Discovery* (1763)

[*Honest Exultation at Success*]

It was not in *revenge* that I did not answer your's of October sooner. The truth is, since my return to town from Windsor, I have been much employed, though often interrupted by intervals of bad health, which of late have frequently returned on me. I have, however, mustered up spirits enough to write – what do you think? Why a Comedy! which is now in rehearsal at Drury Lane.

Mr. Garrick[1] was pressing to see it, and accordingly I read it to him myself. *What his opinion of it is you may judge* by his immediately requesting it to be put into his hands, and undertaking to play the *second* character, a comic and very original one.

My first theatrical essay has so far met with an almost unprecedented success. Most of *us* poor authors find a difficulty in getting our pieces on the stage, and perhaps are obliged to dangle after managers a season or two: *I*, on the contrary, was *solicited* to give *mine*, as soon as it was seen.

---

1 *Mr Garrick*: David Garrick (1717–1779), the famous actor who shared the management of Drury Lane with Lacy, selling a moiety of his patent to Sheridan and others in 1776. He also wrote various farces and was a member of Dr Johnson's Literary Club.

ANONYMOUS
(Between 1725 and ?1728)

This poem offers a contemporary comment on the Rev. George Berkeley's*
prospect of founding St Paul's College in Bermuda, in pursuit of which plan he
went to Rhode Island in 1729 (having married in 1728) subsequently establishing
himself at Newport until he realised in 1731 that the promised governmental funding would not be released by Walpole, the Prime Minister.

The Humble Petition of a Beautiful Young Lady
To the Reverend Doctor B-rK——y

Dear Doctor, here comes a young virgin untainted
To your Shrine at Bermuda to be married and sainted;
I am young, I am soft, I am blooming and tender,
Of all that I have I make you a surrender;
My innocence led by the voice of your fame
To your person and virtue must put in its claim:
And now I behold you, I truly believe
That you're as like Adam, as I am like Eve:
Before the dire serpent their virtue betrayed,
And taught them to fly from the sun to the shade;
But you, as in you a new race has begun,
Are teaching to fly from the shade to the sun;
For you, in great goodness, your friends are persuading
To go, and to live, and be wise in your Eden.
Oh! let me go with you, oh! pity my youth,
Oh! take me from hence, let me not lose my truth;
Sure you that have virtue so much on your mind
Can't think to leave me, who am virtue, behind;
If you make me your wife, Sir, in time you may fill a
Whole town with your children, and likewise your villa;
I famous for breeding, you famous for knowledge,
I'll found a whole nation, you'll found a whole college.
When many long ages in joys we have spent,
Our souls we'll resign with utmost content;
And gently we'll sink beneath cypress and yew,
You lying by me, and I lying by you.

ANONYMOUS

The Coughing Old Man

Each female so pretty in country and city,
I pray you will pity a languishing maid,
That is daily vexed and nightly perplexed,
All by my old husband – I wish he were dead.
He's cross grained and crooked and doating stupid,
And has no more sense than a young sucking calf,
Although he lies by me he ne'er can enjoy me,
For still when he is noodling he is killed with the cough.

The very first night that he came to bed to me,
I longed for a trial at Venus's game,
But to my sad vexation and consternation,
His hautboy was feeble and weak in the main.
For instead of pleasing he only kept teasing;
To him then I turned my back in a huff,
But still he did cry, 'twill do by-and-by,
A *chusla se sthere!*[1] I am killed with the cough.

This doating old creature a remnant of nature,
His shins are so sharp as the edge of a knife,
His knees they are colder than snow on a mountain,
He stands more in need of a nurse than a wife;
I by him sit weeping whilst he lies a-sleeping,
Like hog in a sty he does grunt and puff,
A wheezing and harking both sneezing and farting,
And worse than all that he's killed with the cough.

His breath it does stink like asafoetadu,[2]
His blobbring and slobbring I can't bear,
For each night when I lie beside him,
He must have a spitting cup placed on his chair;
His nose and his chin are joined together,
His tawny old skin is yellow and tough,
Both trembling and shaking like one in the ague,
Still smothering and spitting and killed with the cough.
For sake of cursed money my father has undone me,

---

1 A *chusla se sthere*: *a cushla* is *a stór* 'my darling, my dear'.
2 *asafoetadu*: asafoetida – an ill-smelling medicinal gum-resin.

By making me wed this doating old man,
Although some might shame me what Maid can blame me,
To crown him with horns as soon as I can;
What signifies treasure without any pleasure,
I'm young and would have enjoyed enough,
And not to be tied to a gouty old fellow,
That's withered and worn and killed with the cough.

Since fortune to me has proved so cruel,
In brief my intention to you I'll relate
If he does not alter and fare the better,
No longer on him I mean to wait.
I'll have a look out for some rousing young fellow,
That's able to give me some reason to laugh;
If such I can find then I'll swap my old cuckold,
And pitch to the vengeance himself and his cough.

ANONYMOUS

The Colleen Rue

As I roved out one summer's morning, speculating most curiously,
To my surprise, I soon espied a charming fair one approaching me;
I stood awhile in deep meditation, contemplating what I should do,
But recruiting all my sensations, I thus accosted the Colleen Rue:

'Are you Aurora, or the beauteous Flora, Euterpasia, or Venus bright?
Or Helen fair, beyond compare, that Paris stole from her Grecian's sight?
Thou fairest creature, you have enslaved me, I am intoxicated by Cupid's clue,
Whose golden notes and infatuations deranged my ideas for you, Colleen Rue.'

'Kind sir, be easy, and do not tease me, with your false praise so jestingly,
Your dissimulations and invitations, your fantastic praises, seducing me.
I am not Aurora, or the beauteous Flora, but a rural maiden to all men's view,
That's here condoling my situation, and my appellation is the Colleen Rue

'Was I Hector, that noble victor, who died a victim of Grecian skill,
Or was I Paris, whose deeds were various, as an arbitrator on Ida's Hill,[1]

---

1 *Ida's Hill*: Paris, a son of Priam, King of Troy, was appointed by the gods to choose which of
the three goddesses, Hera, Athena or Aphrodite, should be awarded the prize of beauty.
Aphrodite promised him the fairest woman in the world; his subsequent persuasion of Helen,
wife of Menelaus, to elope with him to Troy was the cause of the Trojan War

I would roam through Asia, likewise Arabia, through Pennsylvania seeking you,
The burning regions, like famed Vesuvius, for one embrace of the Colleen Rue.'

'Sir, I am surprised and dissatisfied at your tantalising insolence,
I am not so stupid, or enslaved by Cupid, as to be duped by your eloquence,
Therefore desist from your solicitations, I am engaged, it's true,
To a lad I love beyond all earthly treasures, and he'll soon embrace his Colleen
   Rue.'

ANONYMOUS

On Deborah Perkins of the County of Wicklow

Some sing ye of Venus the goddess
Some chant ye of rills, and of fountains;
    But the theme of such praise,
    As my fancy can raise,
Is a wench of the Wicklow mountains.

Mount Ida they surely surpass,
Which the Wood-nymphs recess, and their lurkings;
    O! 'tis there that I play
    And wanton all day,
With little black Deborah Perkins.

King Solomon, he had nine hundred, at least,
To humour his taste, with their smirkings;
    But none of 'em all,
    When she led up a ball,
Could foot it like Deborah Perkins.

The fair Cleopatra, Anthony loved,
But, by heaven, I'd give him her jerkings;
    If that he was here,
    And shou'd think to compare
That trollop, with Deborah Perkins.

Bacchus he prized Ariadne the sweet,
But I wish we were now at the firkins;
    I'd make him reel off,
    In contemptible scoff,
While I toasted plump Deborah Perkins.

Might I have all the girls at command,
That boast of Dresden, or markings;
I'd rather feed goats,
And play with the coats
Of cherry-cheeked Deborah Perkins.

A fig for the eclogues of Maro,[1]
Or Ovid's fantastical workings;
If I haven't their letters,
I sing of their betters,
When I touch up young Deborah Perkins.

EDMUND BURKE (1729-1797)

Born in Dublin, he attended a hedge school in Cork, then the Quaker School at Ballitore before studying law at Trinity College, Dublin (where he founded the College Historical Society, 'Mr Burke's Debating Club', the oldest debating society in existence) and at the Middle Temple in London.

His influential treatise on aesthetics, *A Philosophical Enquiry into the Origin and Ideas of the Sublime and Beautiful*, appeared in 1757. It had an effect on such poems as Gray's *Odes*, and on the Gothic novel. The next year he married Jane Nugent. He became editor of the *Annual Register* from 1758 to 1764. In the latter year he returned from being secretary to the Irish Chief Secretary in Dublin to London where he was one of the original members of the Literary Club founded by Dr Johnson. He was elected an MP in 1766, and achieved great praise for his oratory. Having become secretary to Lord Rockingham, who was briefly Prime Minister, and then acting as a spokesman for the Whigs, his *Thoughts on the Cause of the Present Discontents* (1770) expressed his own conservatism and the Whigs' constitutionalism.

On his extended visit to France in 1773 he saw and admired the French Queen, but he distrusted the French *philosophes*. Then, having become MP for Bristol in 1774, he voiced his opposition to the government's policy in his *Speech on American Taxation*, the next year arguing strongly in his *Speech on Conciliation with America* for a sensible attitude, to preserve the colonial relationship, to take a large view of how an empire should be run,

He began to interest himself in Indian affairs, attacking the regime of Warren Hastings as Governor of Bengal, his impeachment occupying Burke from 1786 to 1795. His last campaign was sparked off by the French Revolution, his fear of its effects well put in his *Reflections on the Revolution in France* (1790); his awareness of the danger

---

1 *Maro*: Publius Vergilius Maro (70–19BC), the great Roman poet, author of the *Eclogues*, the *Georgics* and the *Aeneid*.

of its likely influence on Ireland found expression in his *Letter to Sir Hercules Langrishe* (1792) where he argued the need for Catholics in Ireland to be given representation. His *Letters on a Regicide Peace* (1795) urged the defence of order in Europe while his despair about the general political situation was deepened by the death of his son Richard in 1794. His *Letter to a Noble Lord* (1796) is a dignified rebuttal of an attack on the pension he was given in 1794 and an apologia for his defence of constitutional freedom, which in effect shaped British conservative thought through his belief that freedom should be attained by gradualism, through tradition rather than revolution.

From *A Philosophical Enquiry into the Origin of Our Ideas of the Sublime and Beautiful*

FROM PART I
SECTION VII. – Of the SUBLIME
(1756)

Whatever is fitted in any sort to excite the ideas of pain and danger, that is to say, whatever is in any sort terrible, or is conversant about terrible objects, or operates in a manner analogous to terror, is a source of the *sublime;* that is, it is productive of the strongest emotion which the mind is capable of feeling. I say the strongest emotion, because I am satisfied the ideas of pain are much more powerful than those which enter on the part of pleasure. Without all doubt, the torments which we may be made to suffer are much greater in their effect on the body and mind, than any pleasure which the most learned voluptuary could suggest, or than the liveliest imagination, and the most sound and exquisitely sensible body, could enjoy. Nay, I am in great doubt whether any man could be found, who would earn a life of the most perfect satisfaction, at the price of ending it in the torments, which justice inflicted in a few hours on the late unfortunate regicide in France.[1] But as pain is stronger in its operation than pleasure, so death is in general a much more affecting idea than pain; because there are very few pains, however exquisite, which are not preferred to death: nay, what generally makes pain itself, if I may say so, more painful, is, that it is considered as an emissary of this king of terrors. When danger or pain press too nearly, they are incapable of giving any delight, and are simply terrible; but at certain distances, and with certain modifications, they may be, and they are, delightful, as we every day experience. The cause of this I shall endeavour to investigate hereafter.

1 *the late unfortunate regicide in France*: Robert Damiens (1714–1757) attempted to assassinate Louis XV, and was tortured to death.

Edmund Burke

FROM PART II
SECTION I. – Of the passion caused by the SUBLIME

The passion caused by the great and sublime in *nature*, when those causes operate most powerfully, is Astonishment; and astonishment is that state of the soul, in which all its motions are suspended, with some degree of horror. In this case the mind is so entirely filled with its object, that it cannot entertain any other, nor by consequence reason on that object which employs it. Hence arises the great power of the sublime, that far from being produced by them, it anticipates our reasonings, and hurries us on by an irresistible force. Astonishment, as I have said, is the effect of the sublime in its highest degree; the inferior effects are admiration, reverence, and respect.

SECTION II. – TERROR

No passion so effectually robs the mind of all its powers of acting and reasoning as fear. For fear being an apprehension of pain or death, it operates in a manner that resembles actual pain. Whatever therefore is terrible, with regard to sight, is sublime too, whether this cause of terror be endued with greatness of dimensions or not; for it is impossible to look on any thing as trifling, or contemptible, that may be dangerous. There are many animals, who though far from being large, are yet capable of raising ideas of the sublime, because they are considered as objects of terror. As serpents and poisonous animals of almost all kinds. And to things of great dimensions, if we annex an adventitious idea of terror, they become without comparison greater. A level plain of a vast extent on land, is certainly no mean idea; the prospect of such a plain may be as extensive as a prospect of the ocean: but can it ever fill the mind with anything so great as the ocean itself? This is owing to several causes; but it is owing to none more than this, that the ocean is an object of no small terror. Indeed, terror is in all cases whatsoever, either more openly or latently, the ruling principle of the sublime. Several languages bear a strong testimony to the affinity of these ideas. They frequently use the same word, to signify indifferently the modes of astonishment or admiration, and those of terror....

SECTION III. – OBSCURITY

To make any thing very terrible, obscurity seems in general to be necessary. When we know the full extent of any danger, when we can

233

accustom our eyes to it, a great deal of the apprehension vanishes. Every one will be sensible of this, who considers how greatly night adds to our dread, in all cases of danger, and how much the notions of ghosts and goblins, of which none can form clear ideas, affect minds, which give credit to the popular tales concerning such sorts of beings. Those despotic governments, which are founded on the passions of men, and principally upon the passion of fear, keep their chief as much as may be from the public eye. The policy has been the same in many cases of religion. Almost all the heathen temples were dark. Even in the barbarous temples of the Americans at this day, they keep their idol in a dark part of the hut, which is consecrated to his worship. For this purpose too the druids performed all their ceremonies in the bosom of the darkest woods, and in the shade of the oldest and most spreading oaks. No person seems better to have understood the secret of heightening, or of setting terrible things, if I may use the expression, in their strongest light by the force of a judicious obscurity, than Milton. His description of Death in the second book is admirably studied; it is astonishing with what a gloomy pomp, with what a significant and expressive uncertainty of strokes and colouring, he has finished the portrait of the king of terrors.

> The other shape,
> If shape it might be called that shape had none
> Distinguishable, in member, joint, or limb;
> Or substance might be called that shadow seemed,
> For each seemed either; black he stood as night;
> Fierce as ten furies; terrible as hell;
> And shook a deadly dart. What seemed his head
> The likeness of a kingly crown had on.
> [*Paradise Lost* II. 666-673]

In this description all is dark, uncertain, confused, terrible, and sublime to the last degree.

SECTION VI. – POWER

Besides those things which *directly* suggest the idea of danger, and those which produce a similar effect from a mechanical cause, I know of nothing sublime, which is not some modification of power. And this branch rises as naturally as the other two branches, from terror, the common stock of every thing that is sublime. The idea of power at first view seems of the class of these indifferent ones, which may equally belong to pain or to pleasure. But in reality, the affection, arising from the idea of vast power, is extremely remote from that neutral character. For first, we must remember, that the idea of pain, in its highest degree, is much stronger than the highest degree of pleasure; and that it preserves the same superiority through all the subordinate gradations. From hence it is, that where the chances for equal degrees of suffering or enjoyment are in any sort equal, the idea of the suffering must always be prevalent. And indeed the ideas of pain, and, above all of death, are so very affecting, that whilst we remain in the presence of whatever is supposed to have the power of inflicting either, it is impossible to be perfectly free from terror. Again, we know by experience, that, for the enjoyment of pleasure, no great efforts of power are at all necessary; nay we know, that such efforts would go a great way towards destroying our satisfaction: for pleasure must be stolen, and not forced upon us; pleasure follows the will; and therefore we are generally affected with it by many things of a force greatly inferior to our own. But pain is always inflicted by a power in some way superior, because we never submit to pain willingly. So that strength, violence, pain, and terror, are ideas that rush in upon the mind together. Look at a man, or any other animal of prodigious strength, and what is your idea before reflection? Is it that this strength will be subservient to you, to your ease, to your pleasure, to your interest in any sense? No; the emotion you feel is, lest this enormous strength should be employed to the purposes of rapine and destruction. That power derives all its sublimity from the terror with which it is generally accompanied, will appear evidently from its effect in the very few cases, in which it may be possible to strip a considerable degree of strength of its ability to hurt. When you do this, you spoil it of everything sublime, and it immediately becomes contemptible. An ox is a creature of vast strength; but he is an innocent creature, extremely serviceable, and not at all dangerous; for which reason the idea of an ox is by no means grand. A bull is strong too: but his strength is of another kind; often very destructive, seldom (at least amongst us) of any use in our business; the idea of a bull is therefore great, and it has frequently a place in sublime descriptions, and elevating comparisons. Let us look at another strong animal in the two distinct lights in which we may consider him. The horse in the light of an useful beast, fit for the plough, the road, the draught, in every social useful light the horse has nothing of the sublime; but is it thus that we are affected with him, *whose neck is clothed with thunder, the glory of whose nostrils is terrible, who swalloweth the ground with fierceness and rage, neither believeth that it is the sound of the trumpet?*[1] In this description the useful character of the horse entirely disappears, and the terrible and sublime blaze out together. We have continually about us animals of a strength that is considerable, but not pernicious. Amongst these we never look for the sublime: it comes upon us in the gloomy forest, and in the howling wilderness, in the form of the lion, the tiger, the panther, or rhinoceros. Whenever strength is only useful, and employed for our benefit or our pleasure, then it is never sublime; for nothing can act agreeably to us, that does not act in conformity to our will; but to act agreeably to our will, it must be subject to us, and therefore can never be the cause of a grand and commanding conception. The description of the wild ass, in Job, is worked up into no small sublimity, merely by insisting on his freedom, and his setting mankind at defiance; otherwise the description of such an animal could have had nothing noble in it....

SECTION VIII. – VASTNESS

Greatness of dimension is a powerful cause of the sublime. This is too evident, and the observation too common, to need any illustration: it is not so common, to consider in what ways greatness of dimension, vastness of extent, or quantity, has the most striking effect. For certainly, there are ways, and modes, wherein the same quantity of extension shall produce greater effects than it is found to do in others. Extension is either in length, height, or depth. Of these the length strikes least; an hundred yards of even ground will never work such an effect as a tower an hundred yards high, or a rock or mountain of that altitude. I am apt to imagine likewise, that height is less grand than depth; and that we are more struck at looking down from a precipice, than at looking up at an object of equal height, but of that I am not very positive. A perpendicular has more force in forming the sublime, than an inclined plane; and the effects of a rugged and broken surface seem stronger than where it is smooth and polished. It would carry us out of our way to enter in this place into the cause of these appearances; but certain it is they afford a large and fruitful field of speculation. However, it may not be amiss to add to these remarks upon magnitude; that, as the great

---

1 *neck clothed with thunder ... trumpet*: imagery taken from Job 39. 19–24.

extreme of dimension is sublime, so the last extreme of littleness is in some measure sublime likewise: when we attend to the infinite divisibility of matter, when we pursue animal life into these excessively small, and yet organised beings, that escape the nicest inquisition of the sense, when we push our discoveries yet downward, and consider those creatures so many degrees yet smaller, and the still diminishing scale of existence, in tracing which the imagination is lost as well as the sense, we become amazed and confounded at the wonders of minuteness; nor can we distinguish in its effects this extreme of littleness from the vast itself. For division must be infinite as well as addition; because the idea of a perfect unity can no more be arrived at, than that of a complete whole to which nothing may be added.

SECTION IX. – INFINITY

Another source of the sublime is *infinity*; if it does not rather belong to the last. Infinity has a tendency to fill the mind with that sort of delightful horror, which is the most genuine effect and truest test of the sublime. There are scarce any things which can become the objects of our senses that are really, and in their own nature infinite. But the eye not being able to perceive the bounds of many things, they seem to be infinite, and they produce the same effects as if they were really so. We are deceived in the like manner, if the parts of some large object are so continued to any indefinite number, that the imagination meets no check which may hinder its extending them at pleasure.

Whenever we repeat any idea frequently, the mind, by a sort of mechanism, repeats it long after the first cause has ceased to operate. After whirling about; when we sit down, the objects about us still seem to whirl. After a long succession of noises, as the fall of waters, or the beating of forge hammers, the hammers beat and the water roars in the imagination long after the first sounds have ceased to affect it; and they die away at last by gradations which are scarcely perceptible.

From *Reflections on the Revolution in France*

... I hear, and I rejoice to hear, that the great lady, the other object of the triumph, has borne that day (one is interested that beings made for suffering should suffer well), and that she bears all the succeeding days, that she bears the imprisonment of her husband, and her own captivity, and the exile of her friends, and the insulting adulation of addresses, and the whole weight of her accumulated wrongs, with a serene patience, in a manner suited to her rank and race, and becoming the offspring of a sovereign distinguished for her piety and her courage; that, like her, she has lofty sentiments; that she feels with the dignity of a Roman matron; that in the last extremity she will save herself from the last disgrace; and that, if she must fall, she will fall by no ignoble hand.

It is now sixteen or seventeen years since I saw the queen of France, then the dauphiness, at Versailles; and surely never lighted on this orb, which she hardly seemed to touch, a more delightful vision. I saw her just above the horizon, decorating and cheering the elevated sphere she just began to move in, – glittering like the morning-star, full of life, and splendour, and joy. Oh! what a revolution! and what a heart must I have, to contemplate without emotion that elevation and that fall! Little did I dream when she added titles of veneration to those of enthusiastic, distant, respectful love, that she should ever be obliged to carry the sharp antidote against disgrace concealed in that bosom; little did I dream that I should have lived to see such disasters fallen upon her in a nation of gallant men, in a nation of men of honour, and of cavaliers. I thought ten thousand swords must have leaped from their scabbards to avenge even a look that threatened her with insult. But the age of chivalry is gone. That of sophisters, economists, and calculators, has succeeded; and the glory of Europe is extinguished for ever. Never, never more, shall we behold that generous loyalty to rank and sex, that proud submission, that dignified obedience, that subordination of the heart, which kept alive, even in servitude itself, the spirit of an exalted freedom. The unbought grace of life, the cheap defence of nations, the nurse of manly sentiment and heroic enterprise is gone! It is gone, that sensibility of principle, that charity of honour, which felt a stain like a wound, which inspired courage whilst it mitigated ferocity, which ennobled whatever it touched, and under which vice itself lost half its evil, by losing all its grossness.

This mixed system of opinion and sentiment had its origin in the ancient chivalry; and the principle, though varied in its appearance by the varying state of human affairs, subsisted and influenced through a long succession of generations, even to the time we live in. If it should ever be totally extinguished, the loss I fear will be great. It is this which has given its character to modern Europe....

... But now all is to be changed. All the pleasing illusions, which made power gentle and obedience liberal, which harmonized the different shades of life, and which, by a bland assimilation, incorporated into politics the sentiments which beautify and soften private society, are to be dissolved by this new conquering empire of light and reason. All the decent drapery of life is to be rudely torn off. All the superadded ideas, furnished from the wardrobe of a moral imagination, which the heart owns, and the understanding ratifies, as necessary to cover the defects of our naked, shivering nature, and to raise it to dignity in our own estimation, are to be exploded as a ridiculous, absurd, and antiquated fashion.

On this scheme of things, a king is but a man, a queen is but a woman; a woman is but an animal; and an animal not of the highest order. All homage paid to the sex in general as such, and without distinct views, is to be regarded as romance and folly. Regicide, and parricide, and sacrilege, are but fictions of superstition, corrupting jurisprudence by destroying its simplicity. The murder of a king, or a queen, or a bishop, or a father, are only common homicide; and if the people are by any chance, or in any way, gainers by it, a sort of homicide much the most pardonable, and into which we ought not to make too severe a scrutiny.

On the scheme of this barbarous philosophy, which is the offspring of cold hearts and muddy understandings, and which is as void of solid wisdom as it is destitute of all taste and elegance, laws are to be supported only by their own terrors, and by the concern which each individual may find in them, from his own private speculations, or can spare to them from his own private interests. In the groves of *their* academy, at the end of every vista, you see nothing but the gallows. Nothing is left which engages the affections on the part of the commonwealth. On the principles of this mechanic philosophy, our institutions can never be embodied, if I may use the expression, in persons; so as to create in us love, veneration, admiration, or attachment. But that sort of reason which banishes the affections is incapable of filling their place. These public affections, combined with manners, are required sometimes as supplements, sometimes as correctives, always as aids to law. The precept given by a wise man, as well as a great critic, for the construction of poems, is equally true as to states: – *Non satis est pulchra esse poemata, dulcia sunto.*[1] There ought to be a system of manners in every nation, which a well-formed mind would be disposed to relish. To make us love our country, our country ought to be lovely....

---

1 *Non satis ... dulcia sunto:* 'It is not enough for poems to be fine; they must be sweet' (Horace, *Ars Poetica*. 1. 99).

...When ancient opinions and rules of life are taken away, the loss cannot possibly be estimated. From that moment we have no compass to govern us; nor can we know distinctly to what port we steer. Europe, undoubtedly, taken in a mass, was in a flourishing condition the day on which your revolution was completed. How much of that prosperous state was owing to the spirit of our old manners and opinions is not easy to say; but as such causes cannot be indifferent in their operation, we must presume, that, on the whole, their operation was beneficial.

We are but too apt to consider things in the state in which we find them, without sufficiently adverting to the causes by which they have been produced, and possibly may be upheld. Nothing is more certain than that our manners, our civilization, and all the good things which are connected with manners, and with civilization, have, in this European world of ours, depended for ages upon two principles; and were indeed the result of both combined; I mean the spirit of a gentleman, and the spirit of religion. The nobility and the clergy, the one by profession, the other by patronage, kept learning in existence, even in the midst of arms and confusions, and whilst governments were rather in their causes than formed. Learning paid back what it received to nobility and to priesthood; and paid it with usury, by enlarging their ideas, and by furnishing their minds. Happy if they had all continued to know their indissoluble union, and their proper place! Happy if learning, not debauched by ambition, had been satisfied to continue the instructor, and not aspired to be the master! Along with its natural protectors and guardians, learning will be cast into the mire, and trodden down under the hoofs of a swinish multitude.[1]

If, as I suspect, modern letters owe more than they are always willing to own to ancient manners, so do other interests which we value full as much as they are worth. Even commerce, and trade, and manufacture, the gods of our economical politicians, are themselves perhaps but creatures; are themselves but effects, which as first causes, we choose to worship. They certainly grew under the same shade in which learning flourished. They too may decay with their natural protecting principles. With you, for the present at least, they all threaten

---

1 *Along with its natural protectors ... mulitude*: Burke is supposedly alluding to the fate of Jean Sylvain Bailly (1736–1793), president of the National Assembly and mayor of Paris, author of *Histoire de l'Astronomie*, and Marie Jean de Caritat, Marquis de Condorcet (1743–1794), mathematician and philosopher, author of *Essay on the Application of Analysis to the Probability of Majority Decisions* – the former was guillotined, the latter was found dead in his prison cell.

to disappear together. Where trade and manufacturers are wanting to a people, and the spirit of nobility and religion remains, sentiment supplies, and not always ill supplies, their place; but if commerce and the arts should be lost in an experiment to try how well a state may stand without these old fundamental principles, what sort of a thing must be a nation of gross, stupid, ferocious, and, at the same time, poor and sordid, barbarians, destitute of religion, honour, or manly pride, possessing nothing at present, and hoping for nothing hereafter?

I wish you may not be going fast, and by the shortest cut, to that horrible and disgustful situation. Already there appears a poverty of conception, a coarseness and a vulgarity, in all the proceedings of the assembly and of all their instructors. Their liberty is not liberal. Their science is presumptuous ignorance. Their humanity is savage and brutal....

From *A Letter to a Noble Lord* (1796)

[*In accepting a pension granted by Pitt's government, Burke was said to have belied his own dictates on economy. The chief critics of the pension in the House of Lords were the Duke of Bedford and the Duke of Lauderdale. This is Burke's reply to them.*]

... Had it pleased God to continue to me the hopes of succession, I should have been, according to my mediocrity, and the mediocrity of the age I live in, a sort of founder of a family: I should have left a son, who, in all the points in which personal merit can be viewed, in science, in erudition, in genius, in taste, in honour, in generosity, in humanity, in every liberal sentiment, and every liberal accomplishment, would not have shown himself inferior to the Duke of Bedford or to any of those whom he traces in his line. His Grace very soon would have wanted all plausibility in his attack upon that provision which belonged more to mine than to me. HE would soon have supplied every deficiency, and symmetrized every disproportion. It would not have been for that successor to resort to any stagnant wasting reservoir of merit in me, or in any ancestry. He had in himself a salient, living spring of generous and manly action. Every day he lived he would have re-purchased the bounty of the crown, and ten times more, if ten times more he had received. He was made a public creature; and had no enjoyment whatever but in the performance of some duty. At this exigent moment, the loss of a finished man is not easily supplied.

But a Disposer whose power we are little able to resist, and whose wisdom it behoves us not at all to dispute, has ordained it in another manner, and (whatever my querulous weakness might suggest) a far better. The storm has gone over me; and I lie like one of those old oaks which the late hurricane has scattered about me. I am stripped of all my honours, I am torn up by the roots, and lie prostrate on the earth! There, and prostrate there, I most unfeignedly recognize the Divine justice, and in some degree submit to it. But whilst I humble myself before God, I do not know that it is forbidden to repel the attacks of unjust and inconsiderate men. The patience of Job is proverbial. After some of the convulsive struggles of our irritable nature, he submitted himself, and repented in dust and ashes. But even so, I do not find him blamed for reprehending, and with a considerable degree of verbal asperity, those ill-natured neighbours of his, who visited his dunghill to read moral, political, and economical lectures on his misery. I am alone, I have none to meet my enemies in the gate. Indeed, my Lord, I greatly deceive myself, if in this hard season I would give a peck of refuse wheat for all that is called fame and honour in the world. This is the appetite but of a few. It is a luxury, it is a privilege, it is an indulgence for those who are at their ease. But we are all of us made to shun disgrace, as we are made to shrink from pain, and poverty, and disease. It is an instinct; and under the direction of reason, instinct is always in the right. I live in an inverted order. They who ought to have succeeded me have gone before me.[1] They who should have been to me as posterity are in the place of ancestors. I owe to the dearest relation (which ever must subsist in memory) that act of piety, which he would have performed to me; I owe it to him to show that he was not descended, as the Duke of Bedford would have it, from an unworthy parent.

The Crown has considered me after long service: the Crown has paid the Duke of Bedford by advance. He has had a long credit for any service which he may perform hereafter. He is secure, and long may he be secure, in his advance, whether he performs any services or not. But let him take care how he endangers the safety of that constitution which secures his own utility or his own insignificance; or how he discourages those, who take up even puny arms to defend an order of things, which, like the sun of heaven, shines alike on the useful and the worthless. His grants are engrafted on the public law of Europe, covered with the awful hoar of innumerable ages. They are guarded by the sacred rules of prescription, found in that full treasury of jurisprudence from which the jejuneness and penury of our municipal

---

1 *They ... before me*: a reference to the death in 1794 of Burke's only son Richard.

law has, by degrees, been enriched and strengthened. This prescription I had my share (a very full share) in bringing to its perfection.[1] The Duke of Bedford will stand as long as prescriptive law endures: as long as the great, stable laws of property, common to us with all civilized nations, are kept in their integrity, and without the smallest intermixture of laws, maxims, principles, or precedents of the grand Revolution. They are secure against all changes but one. The whole revolutionary system, institutes, digest, code, novels, text, gloss, comment, are, not only not the same, but they are the very reverse, and the reverse fundamentally, of all the laws, on which civil life has hitherto been upheld in all the governments of the world. The learned professors of the rights of man regard prescription, not as a title to bar all claim, set up against all possession – but they look on prescription as itself a bar against the possessor and proprietor. They hold an immemorial possession to be no more than a long-continued, and therefore an aggravated injustice.

Such are *their* ideas; such *their* religion; and such *their* law. But as to *our* country and *our* race, as long as the well-compacted structure of our church and state, the sanctuary, the holy of holies of that ancient law, defended by reverence, defended by power, a fortress at once and a temple,[2] shall stand inviolate on the brow of the British Sion – as long as the British monarchy, not more limited than fenced by the orders of the state, shall, like the proud Keep of Windsor, rising in the majesty of proportion, and girt with the double belt of its kindred and coeval towers, as long as this awful structure shall oversee and guard the subject land – so long the mounds and dykes of the low, fat Bedford level will have nothing to fear from the pickaxes of all the levellers of France. As long as our sovereign lord the king, and his faithful subjects, the Lords and Commons of this realm, – the triple cord, which no man can break; the solemn, sworn, constitutional frank-pledge of this nation; the firm guarantees of each others' being, and each others' rights; the joint and several securities, each in its place and order, for every kind and every quality, of property and of dignity: – as long as these endure, so long the Duke of Bedford is safe: and we are all safe together – the high from the blights of envy and the spoliations of rapacity; the low from the iron hand of oppression and the insolent spurn of contempt. Amen! and so be it: and so it will be,

---

1 *This prescription ... perfection*: this was the *Nullum Tempus* Act, passed in 1769. It limited the claims of the crown against private property possessed for over a certain length of time.
2 *temple*: 'templum in modem arcis' (Tacitus [*Histories*, v. 12], of the Temple of Jerusalem). [*Burke's note.*]

Dum domus Æneæ Capitoli immobile saxum
Accolet; imperiumque pater Romanus habebit.[1]

But if the rude inroad of Gallic tumult, with its sophistical rights of man, to falsify the account, and its sword as a makeweight to throw into the scale, shall be introduced into our city by a misguided populace, set on by proud great men, themselves blinded and intoxicated by a frantic ambition, we shall, all of us, perish and be overwhelmed in a common ruin. If a great storm blow on our coast, it will cast the whales on the strand as well as the periwinkles. His Grace will not survive the poor grantee he despises, no, not for a twelvemonth. If the great look for safety in the services they render to this Gallic cause, it is to be foolish, even above the weight of privilege allowed to wealth. If his Grace be one of these whom they endeavour to proselytize, he ought to be aware of the character of the sect whose doctrines he is invited to embrace. With them insurrection is the most sacred of revolutionary duties to the state. Ingratitude to benefactors is the first of revolutionary virtues. Ingratitude is indeed their four cardinal virtues compacted and amalgamated into one; and he will find it in everything that has happened since the commencement of the philosophic Revolution to this hour. If he pleads the merit of having performed the duty of insurrection against the order he lives (God forbid he ever should), the merit of others will be to perform the duty of insurrection against him. If he pleads (again God forbid he should, and I do not suspect he will) his ingratitude to the Crown for its creation of his family, others will plead their right and duty to pay him in kind. They will laugh, indeed they will laugh, at his parchment and his wax. His deeds will be drawn out with the rest of the lumber of his evidence room, and burnt to the tune of *ça ira*[2] in the courts of Bedford (then Equality) House....

OLIVER GOLDSMITH (?1730-1774)

Born in Pallas, Co. Longford, he was the son of a Church of Ireland clergyman who moved his family to Lissoy, near Ballymahon, Co. Westmeath, when Goldsmith was young. He was educated there and at Athlone before going to Trinity College as a sizar (receiving his board and tuition in exchange for carrying out vari-

---

1 *Dum domus ... habebit*: 'As long as the house of Æneas shall dwell on the unshakable rock of the Capitol and the Father of Rome will have his empire' (Virgil. *Aeneid*, IX.458–59).
2 *ça ira*: 'that will go'; part of the refrain of a French Revolutionary song.

ous duties). In 1749 he was not accepted for ordination, but then went to Edinburgh in 1752 to study medicine. He made a tour of the continent, supporting himself by debating in universities and by singing and flute playing; he came to London in 1756, undertaking various roles, practising medicine (it is thought he received a medical degree at Leyden) and, having failed to obtain a surgeon's position in India in 1758, he gradually established himself as an author by undertaking miscellaneous hack-work. There was no subject, Dr Johnson wrote in Goldsmith's epitaph, that he did not write on, and none he did not enhance in doing so. He edited *The Bell* in 1759, contributed to various journals, and wrote his satirical *Chinese Letters*, published as *The Citizen of the World* (1762). *The Vicar of Wakefield* (1766), a short novel, succeeds in portraying a good character, a clergyman, experiencing evil; his two comedies, *The Good-natur'd Man* (1767) and *She Stoops to Conquer* (1773) reflect his dislike of sentimental comedy, his enjoyment of natural humour, his sense of fun. Both comedies have remained popular over the years.

His longer poems, *The Traveller* (1764), the first of his writings to appear under his own name, and *The Deserted Village* (1770), dedicated to his friend Sir Joshua Reynolds, convey, in the first, his capacity for appreciating the good in different countries, and, in the second, his childhood memories, tinged with gentle humour, of Ballymahon combined with reflective criticism of the enclosures of land which were leading to rural depopulation in England.

His popularising work, such as his histories of England (1764; 1771), of Rome (1769) and of Greece (1774), and *The History of the Earth and Animated Nature* (1774), lasted well, his easy flowing style, his often ironic attitudes and his awareness of basic moral principles informing them most effectively.

Letter to Robert Bryanton

Edinburgh, Sepr. ye 26th 1753

My dear Bob

How many good excuses (and you know I was ever good at an excuse) might I call up to vindicate my past shamefull silence. I might tell how I wrote a long letter at my first comeing hither, and seem vastly angry at not receiveing an answer; or I might alledge that business, (with business, you know I was always pester'd) had never given me time to finger a pen; but I supress these and twenty more, equally plausible & as easily invented, since they might all be attended with a slight inconvenience of being known to be lies; let me then speak truth; An hereditary indolence (I have it from the Mothers side) has hitherto prevented my writing to you, and still prevents my writing at least twenty five letters more, due to my friends in Ireland – no turnspit gets up into his wheel with more reluctance, than I sit down to write, yet no dog ever loved the roast meat he turns, better than I do him I now address; yet what shall I say now I am enter'd? Shall I tire you with a description of this unfruitfull country? where I must lead you over their hills all brown with heath, or their valleys scarce able to feed a rabbet? Man alone seems to be the only creature who has arived to the naturall size in this poor soil; every part of the country presents the same dismall landscape, no grove nor brook lend their musick to cheer the stranger, or make the inhabitants forget their poverty; yet with all these disadvantages to call him down to humility, a scotchman is one of the proudest things alive. The poor have pride ever ready to releive them; if mankind shou'd happen to despise them, they are masters of their own admiration; and that they can plentifully bestow on themselves: from their pride and poverty as I take it results one advantage this country enjoys, namely the Gentlemen here are much better bred than among us; no such character here as our Fox-hunter; and they have expresed great surprize when I informed them that some men of a thousand pound a year in Ireland spend their whole lives in runing after a hare, drinking to be drunk, and getting every Girl with Child, that will let them; and truly if such a being, equiped in his hunting dress, came among a circle of scots Gentlemen, they wou'd behold him with the same astonishment that a Country man does King George on horseback; the men here have Gennerally high cheek bones, and are lean, and swarthy; fond of action; Danceing in particular: tho' now I have mention'd danceing, let me say something of their balls which are very frequent here; when a stranger enters the danceing-hall he sees one end of the room taken up by the Lady's, who sit dismally in a Groupe by themselves. On the other end stand their pensive partners, that are to be, but no more intercourse between the sexes than there is between two Countrys at war, the Ladies indeed may ogle, and the Gentlemen sigh, but an embargo is laid on any closer commerce; at length, to interrupt hostility's, the Lady directeress or intendant, or what you will pitches on a Gentleman and Lady to walk a minuet, which they perform with a formality that aproaches despondence, after five or six couple have thus walked the Gauntlett, all stand up to country dance's, each gentleman furnished with a partner from the afforesaid Lady directress, so they dance much, say nothing, and thus concludes our assembly; I told a scotch Gentleman that such a profound silence resembled the ancient procession of the Roman Matrons in honour of Ceres and the scotch Gentleman told me, (and faith I believe he was right) that I was a very great pedant for my pains: now I am come to the Lady's and

to shew that I love scotland and every thing that belongs to so charming a Country Il insist on it and will give him leave to break my head
that deny's it that the scotch ladys are ten thousand times finer and
handsomer than the Irish. To be sure now I see yr. Sisters Betty &
Peggy vastly surprized at my Partiality but tell ym flatly I don't value
them or their fine skins or Eyes or good sense or – a potatoe for I say
it and and will maintain it and as a convinceing proof of (I am in a
very great passion) of what I assert the scotch Ladies say it themselves,
but to be less serious where will you find a language so prettily
become a pretty mouth as the broad scotch and the women here speak
it in it's highest purity, for instance teach one of the Young Lady's at
home to pronounce the Whoar wull I gong with a beccomeing wide-
ness of mouth and I'll lay my life they'l wound every hearer. We have
no such character here as a coquett but alass how many envious
prudes. Some days ago I walk'd into My Lord Killcoubry's don't be
surpriz'd my Lord is but a Glover, when the Dutchess of Hamilton
(that fair who sacrificed her beauty to ambition and her inward peace
to a title and Gilt equipage) pass'd by in her Chariot, her batter'd husband or more properly the Guardian of her charms sat beside her.
Strait envy began in the shape of no less than three Lady's who sat
with me to find fault's in her faultless form – for my part says the first
I think that I always thought that the dutchess has too much of the
red in her complexion, Madam I am of your opinion says the seccond
and I think her face has a palish cast too much on the delicate order,
and let me tell you adds the third Lady whose mouth was puckered
up to the size of an Issue that the Dutchess has fine lips but she wants
a mouth. At this every Lady drew up her mouth as if going to pronounce the letter P. But how ill my Bob does it become me to ridicule
women with whom I have scarce any correspondence. There are 'tis
certain handsome women here and tis as certain they have handsome
men to keep them company. An ugly and a poor man is society only
for himself and such society the world lets me enjoy in great abundance. Fortune has given you circumstance's and Nature a person to
look charming in the Eyes of the fair world nor do I envy my Dear
Bob such blessings while I may sit down and [laugh at the wor]ld, and
at myself – the most ridiculous object in it. But [you see I am grown
downright] splenetick, and perhaps the fitt may continue till I [receive
an answ]er to this. I know you cant send much news from
[Ballymahon, but] such as it is send it all everything you write will be
agre[eable and entertai]ning to me. Has George Conway put up a
signe yet ha[s John [Bin]ley left off drinking Drams; or Tom Allen g[ot

a new wig?] But I leave to your own choice what to write but [while Noll Goldsmith lives know you have a Friend.

P.S. Give my sincerest regards not [merely my] compliments (do you mind) to your agreeable [family] and Give My service to My Mother if you [see her] for as you express it in Ireland I have a sneaking kindness for her still. Direct to me, Student of Physick in Edinburgh.

From *The Traveller*

(1764)

Remote, unfriended, melancholy, slow,
Or by the lazy Scheld,[1] or wandering Po;[2]
Or onward, where the rude Carinthian[3] boor
Against the houseless stranger shuts the door;
Or where Campania's plain[4] forsaken lies,
A weary waste expanding to the skies;
Where'er I roam, whatever realms to see,
My heart untravelled fondly turns to thee;
Still to my brother turns with ceaseless pain,
And drags at each remove a lengthening chain.
    Eternal blessings crown my earliest friend,
And round his dwelling guardian saints attend:
Blest be that spot, where cheerful guests retire
To pause from toil, and trim their evening fire:
Blest that abode, where want and pain repair,
And every stranger finds a ready chair:
Blest be those feasts, with simple plenty crowned,
Where all the ruddy family around
Laugh at the jests or pranks that never fail,
Or sigh with pity at some mournful tale;
Or press the bashful stranger to his food,
And learn the luxury of doing good.

---

1 *Scheld*: a river rising in France which flows through Belgium and the Netherlands to reach the North Sea.
2 *Po*: an Italian river, rising in the Alps, which flows accross northern Italy to reach the Adriatic.
3 *Carinthian*: Carinthia, a mountainous area in Austria which has a reputation for inhospitality.
4 *Campania's plain*: probably the Roman campagna, affected by malaria before the drainage of its swamps in the twentieth century.

But me, not destined such delights to share,
My prime of life in wandering spent and care,
Impelled, with steps unceasing, to pursue
Some fleeting good, that mocks me with the view;
That, like the circle bounding earth and skies,
Allures from afar, yet, as I follow, flies;
My fortune leads to traverse realms alone,
And find no spot of all the world my own.

  E'en now, where Alpine solitudes ascend,
I sit me down a pensive hour to spend;
And placed on high above the storm's career,
Look downward where a hundred realms appear;
Lakes, forests, cities, plains, extending wide,
The pomp of Kings, the shepherd's humbler pride.

  When thus Creation's charms around combine,
Amidst the store, should thankless pride repine?
Say, should the philosophic mind disdain
That good which makes each humbler bosom vain?
Let school-taught pride dissemble all it can,
These little things are great to little man;
And wiser he, whose sympathetic mind
Exults in all the good of all mankind.
Ye glittering towns, with wealth and splendour crowned,
Ye fields, where summer spreads profusion round,
Ye lakes, whose vessels catch the busy gale,
Ye bending swains, that dress the flowery vale,
For me your tributary stores combine;
Creation's heir, the world, the world is mine.

* * *

  To kinder skies, where gentler manners reign,
I turn; and France displays her bright domain.
Gay sprightly land of mirth and social ease,
Pleased with thyself, whom all the world can please,
How often have I led thy sportive choir,
With tuneless pipe, beside the murmuring Loire!
Where shading elms along the margin grew,
And freshened from the wave the zephyr flew;
And haply, though my harsh touch, faltering still,
But mocked all tune, and marred the dancer's skill,
Yet would the village praise my wondrous power,

And dance, forgetful of the noon-tide hour.
Alike all ages. Dames of ancient days
Have led their children through the mirthful maze,
And the gay grandsire, skilled in gestic lore,
Has frisked beneath the burthen of threescore.

* * *

To men of other minds my fancy flies,
Embosomed in the deep where Holland lies.
Methinks her patient sons before me stand,
Where the broad ocean leans against the land,
And, sedulous to stop the coming tide,
Lift the tall rampire's artificial pride.
Onward, methinks, and diligently slow,
The firm-connected bulwark seems to grow;
Spreads its long arms amidst the watery roar,
Scoops out an empire, and usurps the shore;
While the pent ocean rising o'er the pile,
Sees an amphibious world beneath him smile;
The slow canal, the yellow-blossomed vale,
The willow-tufted bank, the gliding sail,
The crowded mart, the cultivated plain, –
A new creation rescued from his reign.

* * *

Fired at the sound, my genius spreads her wing,
And flies where Britain courts the western spring;
Where lawns extend that scorn Arcadian pride,
And brighter streams than famed Hydaspes[1] glide.
There all around the gentlest breezes stray;
There gentle music melts on every spray;
Creation's mildest charms are there combined,
Extremes are only in the master's mind!
Stern o'er each bosom Reason holds her state,
With daring aims irregularly great;
Pride in their port, defiance in their eye,
I see the lords of human kind pass by,
Intent on high designs, a thoughtful band,
By forms unfashioned, fresh from Nature's hand,

---

1 *Hydaspes*: a river in Asia

Fierce in their native hardiness of soul,
True to imagined right, above control,
While e'en the peasant boasts these rights to scan,
And learns to venerate himself as man.

* * *

Yes, brother, curse with me that baleful hour,
When first ambition struck at regal power;
And thus polluting honour in its source,
Gave wealth to sway the mind with double force.
Have we not seen, round Britain's peopled shore,
Her useful sons exchanged for useless ore?
Seen all her triumphs but destruction haste,
Like flaring tapers brightening as they waste;
Seen opulence, her grandeur to maintain,
Lead stern depopulation in her train,
And over fields where scattered hamlets rose,
In barren solitary pomp repose?
Have we not seen, at pleasure's lordly call,
The smiling long-frequented village fall?
Beheld the duteous son, the sire decay'd,
The modest matron, and the blushing maid,
Forced from their homes, a melancholy train,
To traverse climes beyond the western main;
Where wild Oswego[1] spreads her swamps around,
And Niagara stuns with thundering sound?...

From *The Vicar of Wakefield*

(1766)

[*The continuity of an orderly Christian pastoral life.*]

The little republic to which I gave laws was regulated in the following manner: by sunrise we all assembled in our common apartment, the fire being previously kindled by the servant; after we had saluted each other with proper ceremony, for I always thought fit to keep up some mechanical forms of good breeding, without which freedom ever destroys friendship, we all bent in gratitude to that Being who gave us

---

1 *Oswego*: a river in New York state, flowing into Lake Ontario.

another day. This duty being performed, my son and I went to pursue our usual industry abroad, while my wife and daughters employed themselves in providing breakfast, which was always ready at a certain time. I allowed half an hour for this meal, and an hour for dinner; which time was taken up in innocent mirth between my wife and daughters, and in philosophical arguments between my son and me.

* * *

The place of our retreat was in a little neighbourhood, consisting of farmers who tilled their own grounds, and were equal strangers to opulence and poverty. As they had almost all the conveniences of life within themselves, they seldom visited towns or cities in search of superfluity. Remote from the polite, they still retained the primeval simplicity of manners; and frugal by habit, they scarce knew that temperance was a virtue. They wrought with cheerfulness on days of labour; but observed festivals as intervals of idleness and pleasure. They kept up the Christmas carol, sent true love-knots on Valentine's morning, ate pancakes on Shrovetide, showed their wit on the first of April, and religiously cracked nuts on Michaelmas eve.

[*And its sudden disruption*]

... 'We are descended from ancestors that knew no stain, and we shall leave a good and virtuous race of children behind us. While we live they will be our support and our pleasure here, and when we die they will transmit our honour untainted to posterity. Come, my son, we wait for a song; let us have a chorus. But where is my darling Olivia? That little cherub's voice is always sweetest in the concert.' Just as I spoke Dick came running in. – 'O papa, papa, she is gone from us – she is gone from us, my sister Livy is gone from us for ever' – 'Gone, child!' – 'Yes; she is gone off with two gentlemen in a postchaise, and one of them kissed her and said he would die for her; and she cried very much and was for coming back; but he persuaded her again, and she went into the chaise, and said, "O! What will my poor pappa do when he knows I am undone?"' – 'Now then,' cried I, 'my children, go and be miserable; for we shall never enjoy one hour more. And O may heaven's everlasting fury light upon him and his! Thus to rob me of my child! And sure it will, for taking back my sweet innocent that I was leading up to heaven. Such sincerity as my child was possessed of! But all our earthly happiness is now over! Go, my children, go, and be miserable and infamous; for my heart is broken within me!'

Oliver Goldsmith

The Deserted Village
(1770)

Sweet Auburn! loveliest village of the plain,
Where health and plenty cheered the laboring swain,
Where smiling spring its earliest visit paid,
And parting summer's lingering blooms delayed:
Dear lovely bowers of innocence and ease,
Seats of my youth, when every sport could please,
How often have I loitered o'er thy green,
Where humble happiness endeared each scene;
How often have I paused on every charm,
The sheltered cot, the cultivated farm,
The never-failing brook, the busy mill,
The decent church that topped the neighboring hill,
The hawthorn bush, with seats beneath the shade,
For talking age and whispering lovers made;
How often have I blessed the coming day,
When toil remitting lent its turn to play,
And all the village train, from labor free,
Led up their sports beneath the spreading tree,
While many a pastime circled in the shade,
The young contending as the old surveyed;
And many a gambol frolick'd o'er the ground,
And sleights of art and feats of strength went round;
And still as each repeated pleasure tired,
Succeeding sports the mirthful band inspired;
The dancing pair that simply sought renown,
By holding out to tire each other down;
The swain mistrustless of his smutted face,
While secret laughter tittered round the place;
The bashful virgin's sidelong looks of love,
The matron's glance that would those looks reprove:
These were thy charms, sweet village; sports like these,
With sweet succession, taught e'en toil to please;
These round thy bowers their cheerful influence shed,
These were thy charms – But all these charms are fled.
    Sweet smiling village, loveliest of the lawn,
Thy sports are fled, and all thy charms withdrawn;
Amidst thy bowers the tyrant's hand is seen,
And desolation saddens all thy green:

One only master grasps the whole domain,
And half a tillage stints thy smiling plain:
No more thy glassy brook reflects the day,
But choked with sedges, works its weedy way.
Along thy glades, a solitary guest,
The hollow-sounding bittern guards its nest;
Amidst thy desert walks the lapwing flies,
And tires their echoes with unvaried cries.
Sunk are thy bowers in shapeless ruin all,
And the long grass o'ertops the mouldering wall;
And trembling, shrinking from the spoiler's hand,
Far, far away, thy children leave the land.

   Ill fares the land, to hastening ills a prey,
Where wealth accumulates, and men decay:
Princes and lords may flourish, or may fade;
A breath can make them, as a breath has made;
But a bold peasantry, their country's pride,
When once destroyed, can never be supplied.

   A time there was, ere England's griefs began,
When every rood of ground maintained its man;
For him light labor spread her wholesome store,
Just gave what life required, but gave no more:
His best companions, innocence and health;
And his best riches, ignorance of wealth.

   But times are altered; Trade's unfeeling train
Usurp the land and dispossess the swain;
Along the lawn, where scattered hamlets rose,
Unwieldy wealth, and cumbrous pomp repose;
And every want to opulence allied,
And every pang that folly pays to pride.
Those gentle hours that plenty bade to bloom,
Those calm desires that asked but little room,
Those healthful sports that graced the peaceful scene,
Lived in each look, and brightened all the green;
These, far departing, seek a kinder shore,
And rural mirth and manners are no more.

   Sweet Auburn! parent of the blissful hour,
Thy glades forlorn confess the tyrant's power.
Here as I take my solitary rounds,
Amidst thy tangling walks, and ruined grounds,
And, many a year elapsed, return to view

Where once the cottage stood, the hawthorn grew,
Remembrance wakes with all her busy train,
Swells at my breast, and turns the past to pain.

   In all my wanderings round this world of care,
In all my griefs – and GOD has given my share –
I still had hopes my latest hours to crown,
Amidst these humble bowers to lay me down;
To husband out life's taper at the close,
And keep the flame from wasting by repose.
I still had hopes, for pride attends us still,
Amidst the swains to show my book-learned skill,
Around my fire an evening group to draw,
And tell of all I felt, and all I saw;
And, as a hare, whom hounds and horns pursue,
Pants to the place from whence at first she flew,
I still had hopes, my long vexations past,
Here to return – and die at home at last.

   O blest retirement, friend to life's decline,
Retreats from care, that never must be mine,
How happy he who crowns in shades like these,
A youth of labor with an age of ease;
Who quits a world where strong temptations try,
And, since 'tis hard to combat, learns to fly!
For him no wretches, born to work and weep,
Explore the mine, or tempt the dangerous deep;
No surly porter stands in guilty state
To spurn imploring famine from the gate;
But on he moves to meet his latter end,
Angels around befriending virtue's friend;
Bends to the grave with unperceived decay,
While Resignation gently slopes the way;
And, all his prospects bright'ning to the last,
His Heaven commences ere the world be passed!

   Sweet was the sound, when oft at evening's close
Up yonder hill the village murmur rose;
There, as I passed with careless steps and slow,
The mingling notes came softened from below;
The swain responsive as the milkmaid sung,
The sober herd that lowed to meet their young;
The noisy geese that gabbled o'er the pool,
The playful children just let loose from school;

The watchdog's voice that bayed the whisp'ring wind,
And the loud laugh that spoke the vacant mind;
These all in sweet confusion sought the shade,
And filled each pause the nightingale had made.
But now the sounds of population fail,
No cheerful murmurs fluctuate in the gale,
No busy steps the grass-grown foot-way tread,
For all the bloomy flush of life is fled.
All but yon widowed, solitary thing
That feebly bends beside the plashy spring;
She, wretched matron, forced in age, for bread,
To strip the brook with mantling cresses spread,
To pick her wintry faggot from the thorn,
To seek her nightly shed, and weep till morn;
She only left of all the harmless train,
The sad historian of the pensive plain.

   Near yonder copse, where once the garden smiled,
And still where many a garden flower grows wild;
There, where a few torn shrubs the place disclose,
The village preacher's modest mansion rose.
A man he was to all the country dear,
And passing rich with forty pounds a year;
Remote from towns he ran his godly race,
Nor e'er had changed, nor wished to change his place;
Unpractised he to fawn, or seek for power,
By doctrines fashioned to the varying hour;
Far other aims his heart had learned to prize,
More skilled to raise the wretched than to rise.
His house was known to all the vagrant train,
He chid their wand'rings, but relieved their pain;
The long-remembered beggar was his guest,
Whose beard descending swept his aged breast;
The ruined spendthrift, now no longer proud,
Claimed kindred there, and had his claims allowed;
The broken soldier, kindly bade to stay,
Sat by his fire, and talked the night away;
Wept o'er his wounds, or tales of sorrow done,
Shouldered his crutch, and showed how fields were won.
Pleased with his guests, the good man learned to glow,
And quite forgot their vices in their woe;
Careless their merits, or their faults to scan,

His pity gave ere charity began.

    Thus to relieve the wretched was his pride,
And e'en his failings leaned to Virtue's side;
But in his duty prompt at every call,
He watched and wept, he prayed and felt, for all.
And, as a bird each fond endearment tries
To tempt its new-fledged offspring to the skies,
He tried each art, reproved each dull delay,
Allured to brighter worlds, and led the way.

    Beside the bed where parting life was laid,
And sorrow, guilt, and pain, by turns dismayed,
The reverend champion stood. At his control,
Despair and anguish fled the struggling soul;
Comfort came down the trembling wretch to raise,
And his last falt'ring accents whispered praise.

    At church, with meek and unaffected grace,
His looks adorned the venerable place;
Truth from his lips prevailed with double sway,
And fools, who came to scoff, remained to pray.
The service past, around the pious man,
With steady zeal each honest rustic ran;
Even children followed with endearing wile,
And plucked his gown, to share the good man's smile.
His ready smile a parent's warmth expressed,
Their welfare pleased him, and their cares distressed;
To them his heart, his love, his griefs were given,
But all his serious thoughts had rest in Heaven.
As some tall cliff, that lifts its awful form,
Swells from the vale, and midway leaves the storm,
Though round its breast the rolling clouds are spread,
Eternal sunshine settles on its head.

    Beside yon straggling fence that skirts the way,
With blossomed furze unprofitably gay,
There, in his noisy mansion, skilled to rule,
The village master taught his little school;
A man severe he was, and stern to view;
I knew him well, and every truant knew;
Well had the boding tremblers learned to trace
The day's disasters in his morning face;
Full well they laughed, with counterfeited glee,
At all his jokes, for many a joke had he;

Full well the busy whisper, circling round,
Conveyed the dismal tidings when he frowned;
Yet he was kind; or if severe in aught,
The love he bore to learning was in fault;
The village all declared how much he knew;
'Twas certain he could write, and cypher too;
Lands he could measure, terms and tides¹ presage,
And e'en the story ran that he could gauge.
In arguing too, the parson owned his skill,
For e'en though vanquished, he could argue still;
While words of learned length and thund'ring sound
Amazed the gazing rustics ranged around,
And still they gazed, and still the wonder grew,
That one small head could carry all he knew.

    But past is all his fame. The very spot
Where many a time he triumphed, is forgot.
Near yonder thorn, that lifts its head on high,
Where once the sign-post caught the passing eye,
Low lies that house where nut-brown draughts inspired,
Where grey-beard Mirth and smiling Toil retired,
Where village statesmen talked with looks profound,
And news much older than their ale went round.
Imagination fondly stoops to trace
The parlour splendors of that festive place;
The white-washed wall, the nicely sanded floor,
The varnished clock that clicked behind the door;
The chest contrived a double debt to pay,
A bed by night, a chest of drawers by day;
The pictures placed for ornament and use,
The twelve good rules,² the royal game of goose;³
The hearth, except when winter chilled the day,
With aspen boughs, and flowers, and fennel gay;
While broken tea-cups, wisely kept for show,
Ranged o'er the chimney, glistened in a row.

    Vain, transitory splendors! Could not all
Reprieve the tottering mansion from its fall!

---

1 *terms and tides*: 'terms' are dates on which payments were due; 'tides' are holy days in the church calendar.
2 *The twelve good rules*: rules of conduct, attributed to Charles I. On broadsides, they adorned many a tavern wall.
3 *the royal game of goose*: a game in which counters were moved on a board according to the throw of the dice.

Oliver Goldsmith

Obscure it sinks, nor shall it more impart
An hour's importance to the poor man's heart;
Thither no more the peasant shall repair
To sweet oblivion of his daily care;
No more the farmer's news, the barber's tale,
No more the woodman's ballad shall prevail;
No more the smith his dusky brow shall clear,
Relax his pond'rous strength, and lean to hear;
The host himself no longer shall be found
Careful to see the mantling bliss go round;
Nor the coy maid, half willing to be pressed,
Shall kiss the cup to pass it to the rest.

   Yes! let the rich deride, the proud disdain,
These simple blessings of the lowly train;
To me more dear, congenial to my heart,
One native charm, than all the gloss of art;
Spontaneous joys, where nature has its play,
The soul adopts, and owns their first-born sway;
Lightly they frolic o'er the vacant mind,
Unenvied, unmolested, unconfined:
But the long pomp, the midnight masquerade,
With all the freaks of wanton wealth arrayed,
In these, ere triflers half their wish obtain,
The toiling pleasure sickens into pain;
And, e'en while fashion's brightest arts decoy,
The heart distrusting asks, if this be joy.

   Ye friends to truth, ye statesmen, who survey
The rich man's joys increase, the poor's decay,
'Tis yours to judge, how wide the limits stand
Between a splendid and an happy land.
Proud swells the tide with loads of freighted ore,
And shouting Folly hails them from her shore;
Hoards, e'en beyond the miser's wish abound,
And rich men flock from all the world around.
Yet count our gains. This wealth is but a name
That leaves our useful products still the same.
Not so the loss. The man of wealth and pride
Takes up a space that many poor supplied;
Space for his lake, his park's extended bounds,
Space for his horses, equipage, and hounds;
The robe that wraps his limbs in silken sloth

Has robbed the neighboring fields of half their growth;
His seat, where solitary sports are seen,
Indignant spurns the cottage from the green;
Around the world each needful product flies,
For all the luxuries the world supplies:
While thus the land adorned for pleasure, all
In barren splendor feebly waits the fall.

    As some fair female unadorned and plain,
Secure to please while youth confirms her reign,
Slights every borrowed charm that dress supplies,
Nor shares with art the triumph of her eyes:
But when those charms are past, for charms are frail,
When time advances, and when lovers fail,
She then shines forth, solicitous to bless,
In all the glaring impotence of dress.
Thus fares the land, by luxury betrayed,
In nature's simplest charms at first arrayed;
But verging to decline, its splendors rise,
Its vistas strike, its palaces surprise;
While scourged by famine from the smiling land,
The mournful peasant leads his humble band;
And while he sinks, without one arm to save,
The country blooms – a garden, and a grave.

    Where then, ah! where, shall Poverty reside,
To 'scape the pressure of continuous Pride?
If to some common's fenceless limits strayed,
He drives his flock to pick the scanty blade,
Those fenceless fields the sons of wealth divide,
And e'en the bare-worn common is denied.

    If to the city sped – What waits him there?
To see profusion that he must not share;
To see ten thousand baneful arts combined
To pamper luxury, and thin mankind;
To see those joys the sons of pleasure know
Extorted from his fellow creature's woe.
Here, while the courtier glitters in brocade,
There the pale artist plies the sickly trade;
Here, while the proud their long-drawn pomps display,
There the black gibbet glooms beside the way.
The dome where Pleasure holds her midnight reign
Here, richly decked, admits the gorgeous train;

Tumultuous grandeur crowds the blazing square,
The rattling chariots clash, the torches glare.
Sure scenes like these no troubles e'er annoy!
Sure these denote one universal joy!
Are these thy serious thoughts? – Ah, turn thine eyes
Where the poor houseless shiv'ring female lies.
She once, perhaps, in village plenty blest,
Has wept at tales of innocence distressed;
Her modest looks the cottage might adorn,
Sweet as the primrose peeps beneath the thorn;
Now lost to all; her friends, her virtue fled,
Near her betrayer's door she lays her head,
And, pinched with cold and shrinking from the shower,
With heavy heart deplores that luckless hour,
When idly first, ambitious of the town,
She left her wheel and robes of country brown.

    Do thine, sweet Auburn, thine, the loveliest train,
Do thy fair tribes participate her pain?
E'en now, perhaps; by cold and hunger led,
At proud men's doors they ask a little bread!

    Ah, no! To distant climes, a dreary scene,
Where half the convex world intrudes between,
Through torrid tracts with fainting steps they go,
Where wild Altama[1] murmurs to their woe.
Far different there from all that charmed before,
The various terrors of that horrid shore;
Those blazing suns that dart a downward ray,
And fiercely shed intolerable day;
Those matted woods where birds forget to sing,
But silent bats in drowsy clusters cling;
Those pois'nous fields with rank luxuriance crowned,
Where the dark scorpion gathers death around;
Where at each step the stranger fears to wake
The rattling terrors of the vengeful snake;
Where crouching tigers wait their hapless prey,
And savage men more murd'rous still than they;
While oft in whirls the mad tornado flies,
Mingling the ravaged landscape with the skies.
Far different these from every former scene,

---

1 *Altama*: the Altamaha, a river in Georgia.

The cooling brook, the grassy-vested green,
The breezy covert of the warbling grove,
That only sheltered thefts of harmless love.
   Good Heaven! what sorrows gloomed that parting day,
That called them from their native walks away;
When the poor exiles, every pleasure past,
Hung round their bowers, and fondly looked their last,
And took a long farewell, and wished in vain
For seats like these beyond the western main;
And shudd'ring still to face the distant deep,
Returned and wept, and still returned to weep.
The good old sire, the first prepared to go
To new-found worlds, and wept for others' woe;
But for himself, in conscious virtue brave,
He only wished for worlds beyond the grave.
His lovely daughter, lovelier in her tears,
The fond companion of his helpless years,
Silent went next, neglectful of her charms,
And left a lover's for a father's arms.
With louder plaints the mother spoke her woes,
And blessed the cot where every pleasure rose
And kissed her thoughtless babes with many a tear,
And clasped them close, in sorrow doubly dear;
Whilst her fond husband strove to lend relief
In all the silent manliness of grief.
   O luxury! thou cursed by Heaven's decree,
How ill exchanged are things like these for thee!
How do thy potions, with insidious joy,
Diffuse their pleasures only to destroy!
Kingdoms, by thee, to sickly greatness grown,
Boast of a florid vigour not their own:
At every draught more large and large they grow,
A bloated mass of rank unwieldy woe;
Till sapped their strength, and every part unsound,
Down, down they sink, and spread a ruin round.
   E'en now the devastation is begun,
And half the business of destruction done;
E'en now, methinks, as pond'ring here I stand,
I see the rural Virtues leave the land:
Down where yon anchoring vessel spreads the sail,
That idly waiting flaps with ev'ry gale,

Downward they move, a melancholy band,
Pass from the shore, and darken all the strand.
Contented Toil, and hospitable Care,
And kind connubial tenderness are there;
And piety, with wishes placed above,
And steady Loyalty, and faithful Love.
And thou, sweet Poetry, thou loveliest maid,
Still first to fly where sensual joys invade;
Unfit in these degenerate times of shame,
To catch the heart, or strike for honest fame;
Dear charming Nymph, neglected and decried,
My shame in crowds, my solitary pride;
Thou source of all my bliss, and all my woe,
That found'st me poor at first, and keep'st me so;
Thou guide by which the nobler arts excel,
Thou nurse of every virtue, fare thee well!
Farewell, and Oh! where'er thy voice be tried,
On Torno's cliffs, or Pambamarca's side,[1]
Whether where equinoctial fervors glow,
Or winter wraps the polar world in snow,
Still let thy voice, prevailing over time,
Redress the rigours of th' inclement clime;
Aid slighted truth; with thy persuasive strain
Teach erring man to spurn the rage of gain;
Teach him, that states of native strength possessed,
Though very poor, may still be very blest;
That Trade's proud empire hastes to swift decay,
As ocean sweeps the labored mole away;
While self-dependent power can time defy,
As rocks resist the billows and the sky.

The Gift

To Iris, in Bow Street, Convent Garden
(imitated from the French)

Say, cruel Iris, pretty rake,
Dear mercenary beauty,
What annual offering shall I make,

---

1 *Torno's cliffs ... side*: the Torne is a river in Sweden; Pambamarca is a mountain in Ecuador.

Expressive of my duty?

My heart, a victim to thine eyes,
Should I at once deliver,
Say, would the angry fair one prize
The gift, who slights the giver?

A bill, a jewel, watch, or toy,
My rivals give – and let 'em;
If gems, or gold, impart a joy,
I'll give them – when I get 'em.

I'll give – but not the full-blown rose,
Or rose-bud more in fashion:
Such short-liv'd offerings but disclose
A transitory passion.

I'll give thee something yet unpaid,
Not less sincere, than civil,
I'll give thee – ah! too charming maid,
I'll give thee – to the Devil.

Song

Intended for *She Stoops to Conquer*

Ah me! when shall I marry me?
Lovers are plenty; but fail to relieve me.
He, fond youth, that could carry me,
Offers to love, but means to deceive me.

But I will rally, and combat the ruiner:
Not a look, not a smile shall my passion discover:
She that gives all to the false one pursuing her,
Makes but a penitent, loses a lover.

Song

From *The Vicar Of Wakefield*

When lovely woman stoops to folly,

And finds too late that men betray,
What charm can soothe her melancholy,
What art can wash her guilt away?

The only art her guilt to cover,
To hide her shame from every eye,
To give repentance to her lover,
And wring his bosom, is – to die.

Elegy on the Death of a Mad Dog

Good people all, of every sort,
Give ear unto my song;
And if you find it wond'rous short,
It cannot hold you long.

In Islington there was a man,
Of whom the world might say,
That still a godly race he ran,
Whene'er he went to pray.

A kind and gentle heart he had,
To comfort friends and foes;
The naked every day he clad,
When he put on his clothes.

And in that town a dog was found,
As many dogs there be,
Both mongrel, puppy, whelp, and hound,
And curs of low degree.

This dog and man at first were friends;
But when a pique began,
The dog, to gain some private ends,
Went mad and bit the man.

Around from all the neighbouring streets
The wond'ring neighbours ran,
And swore the dog had lost his wits,
To bite so good a man.

The wound it seemed both sore and sad
    To every Christian eye;
And while they swore the dog was mad,
    They swore the man would die.

But soon a wonder came to light,
    That showed the rogues they lied:
The man recovered of the bite,
    The dog it was that died.

From *She Stoops to Conquer*

(1772)

ACT I, SCENE II

An Alehouse Room.
Several shabby Fellows with punch and tobacco.
TONY *at the head of the table, a little higher than*
the rest, a mallet in his hand.

OMNES.	Hurrea! hurrea! hurrea! bravo!
FIRST FELLOW.	Now, gentlemen, silence for a song. The 'Squire is going to knock himself down for a song.[1]
OMNES.	Ay, a song, a song!
TONY.	Then I'll sing you, gentlemen, a song I made upon this alehouse, the Three Pigeons.

SONG.

Let schoolmasters puzzle their brain
    With grammar, and nonsense, and learning,
Good liquor, I stoutly maintain,
    Gives GENUS *a better discerning.*
Let them brag of their Heathenish Gods,
    Their Lethes, their Styxes, and Stygians,
Their Quis, and their Quaes, and their Quods,
    They're all but a parcel of Pigeons.
                Toroddle, toroddle, toroll.

---

1 *knock ... down for a song*: to sell at auction for a low price.

When methodist preachers come down,
    A-preaching that drinking is sinful,
I'll wager the rascals a crown,
    They always preach best with a skinful.
But when you come down with your pence,
    For a slice of their scurvy religion,
I'll leave it to all men of sense,
    But you, my good friend, are the pigeon.
                Toroddle, toroddle, toroll.

Then come, put the jorum about,
    And let us be merry and clever,
Our hearts and our liquors are stout,
    Here's the Three Jolly Pigeons for ever.
Let some cry up woodcock or hare,
    Your bustards, your ducks, and your widgeons;
But of all the GAY *birds in the air,*
    Here's a health to the Three Jolly Pigeons.
                Toroddle, toroddle, toroll.

OMNES.	Bravo, bravo!
FIRST FELLOW.	The 'Squire has got spunk in him.
SECOND FELLOW.	I loves to hear him sing, bekeays he never gives us nothing that's *low*.
THIRD FELLOW.	O damn anything that's *low*, I cannot bear it.
FOURTH FELLOW.	The genteel thing is the genteel thing any time. If so be that a gentleman bees in a concatenation accordingly.
THIRD FELLOW.	I likes the maxum of it, Master Muggins. What, tho' I am obligated to dance a bear, a man may be a gentleman for all that. May this be my poison, if my bear ever dances but to the very genteelest of tunes; Water Parted, or The minuet in Ariadne.[1]
SECOND FELLOW.	What a pity it is the 'Squire is not come to his own. It would be well for all the publicans within ten miles round of him.
TONY.	Ecod, and so it would, Master Slang. I'd then show

---

1 *Water Parted ... Ariadne*: 'Water Parted' is a minuet in Thomas Arne's opera *Artaxerxes* (1762); *Ariadne in Crete* is an opera by Handel (1734).

267

what it was to keep choice of company.

SECOND FELLOW. O he takes after his own father for that. To be sure old 'Squire Lumpkin was the finest gentleman I ever set my eyes on. For winding the straight horn, or beating a thicket for a hare, or a wench, he never had his fellow. It was a saying in the place, that he kept the best horses, dogs, and girls, in the whole county.

TONY. Ecod, and when I'm of age, I'll be no bastard, I promise you. I have been thinking of Bet Bouncer and the miller's gray mare to begin with. But come, my boys, drink about and be merry, for you pay no reckoning. Well, Stingo, what's the matter?

Enter LANDLORD.

LANDLORD. There be two gentlemen in a post-chaise at the door. They have lost their way upo' the forest; and they are talking something about Mr. Hardcastle.

TONY. As sure as can be, one of them must be the gentleman that's coming down to court my sister. Do they seem to be Londoners?

LANDLORD. I believe they may. They look woundily like Frenchmen.

TONY. Then desire them to step this way, and I'll set them right in a twinkling. (*Exit* LANDLORD.) Gentlemen, as they mayn't be good enough company for you, step down for a moment, and I'll be with you in the squeezing of a lemon.

[*Exeunt* mob.

TONY. (*Solus*). Father-in-law has been calling me whelp and hound this half year. Now, if I pleased, I could be so revenged upon the old grumbletonian. But then I'm afraid – afraid of what? I shall soon be worth fifteen hundred a year, and let him frighten me out of *that* if he can.

Enter LANDLORD, conducting MARLOW and HASTINGS.

MARLOW. What a tedious uncomfortable day have we had of it! We were told it was but forty miles across the country, and we have come above threescore.

HASTINGS. And all, Marlow, from that unaccountable reserve of

	yours, that would not let us inquire more frequently on the way.
MARLOW.	I own, Hastings, I am unwilling to lay myself under an obligation to every one I meet, and often stand the chance of an unmannerly answer.
HASTINGS.	At present, however, we are not likely to receive any answer.
TONY.	No offence, gentlemen. But I'm told you have been inquiring for one Mr. Hardcastle, in these parts. Do you know what part of the country you are in?
HASTINGS.	Not in the least, Sir, but should thank you for information.
TONY.	Nor the way you came?
HASTINGS.	No, Sir: but if you can inform us –
TONY.	Why, gentlemen, if you know neither the road you are going, nor where you are, nor the road you came, the first thing I have to inform you is, that – you have lost your way.
MARLOW.	We wanted no ghost to tell us that.
TONY.	Pray, gentlemen, may I be so bold so as to ask the place from whence you came?
MARLOW.	That's not necessary towards directing us where we are to go.
TONY.	No offence; but question for question is all fair, you know. Pray, gentlemen, is not this same Hardcastle a cross-grained, old-fashioned, whimsical fellow, with an ugly face, a daughter, and a pretty son?
HASTINGS.	We have not seen the gentleman; but he has the family you mention.
TONY.	The daughter, a tall, trapesing, trolloping, talkative maypole; the son, a pretty, well-bred, agreeable youth, that everybody is fond of.
MARLOW.	Our information differs in this. The daughter is said to be well-bred and beautiful; the son an awkward booby, reared up and spoiled at his mother's apron-string.
TONY.	He-he-hem! – Then, gentlemen, all I have to tell you is, that you won't reach Mr. Hardcastle's house this night, I believe.
HASTINGS.	Unfortunate!
TONY.	It's a damn'd long, dark, boggy, dirty, dangerous

	way. Stingo, tell the gentlemen the way to Mr. Hardcastle's! (*Winking upon the* LANDLORD.) Mr. Hardcastle's, of Quagmire Marsh, you understand me.
LANDLORD.	Master Hardcastle's! Lock-a-daisy, my masters, you're come a deadly deal wrong! When you came to the bottom of the hill, you should have cross'd down Squash-Lane.
MARLOW.	Cross down Squash-lane!
LANDLORD.	Then you were to keep streight forward, 'till you came to four roads.
MARLOW.	Come to where four roads meet?
TONY.	Ay; but you must be sure to take only one of them.
MARLOW.	O, Sir, you're facetious.
TONY.	Then keeping to the right, you are to go side-ways till you come upon Crack-skull Common: there you must look sharp for the track of the wheel, and go forward 'till you come to farmer Murrain's barn. Coming to the farmer's barn, you are to turn to the right, and then to the left, and then to the right about again, till you find out the old mill –
MARLOW.	Zounds, man! we could as soon find out the longitude!
HASTINGS.	What's to be done, Marlow?
MARLOW.	This house promises but a poor reception; though perhaps the landlord can accommodate us.
LANDLORD.	Alack, master, we have but one spare bed in the whole house.
TONY.	And to my knowledge, that's taken up by three lodgers already. (*After a pause, in which the rest seem disconcerted.*) I have hit it. Don't you think, Stingo, our landlady could accommodate the gentlemen by the fire-side, with——three chairs and a bolster?
HASTINGS.	I hate sleeping by the fire-side.
MARLOW.	And I detest your three chairs and a bolster.
TONY.	You do, do you? – then, let me see – what – if you go on a mile further, to the Buck's Head; the old Buck's Head on the hill, one of the best inns in the whole county?
HASTINGS.	O ho! so we have escaped an adventure for this

night, however.

LANDLORD. *(apart to* TONY). Sure, you ben't sending them to your father's as an inn, be you?

TONY. Mum, you fool you. Let *them* find that out. (*To them*.) You have only to keep on streight forward, till you come to a large old house by the road side. You'll see a pair of large horns over the door. That's the sign. Drive up the yard, and call stoutly about you.

HASTINGS. Sir, we are obliged to you. The servants can't miss the way?

TONY. No, no: but I tell you, though, the landlord is rich, and going to leave off business; so he wants to be thought a gentleman, saving your presence, he! he! he! He'll be for giving you his company; and, ecod, if you mind him, he'll persuade you that his mother was an alderman, and his aunt a justice of peace.

LANDLORD. A troublesome old blade, to be sure; but a keeps as good wines and beds as any in the whole country.

MARLOW. Well, if he supplies us with these, we shall want no farther connexion. We are to turn to the right, did you say?

TONY. No, no; streight forward. I'll just step myself, and show you a piece of the way. (*To the* LANDLORD.) Mum.

LANDLORD. Ah, bless your heart, for a sweet, pleasant – damn'd mischievous son of a whore.
[*Exeunt*.

ACT II.

An old-fashioned house.

Enter HARDCASTLE, *followed by three or four awkward Servants.*

HARDCASTLE. Well, I hope you are perfect in the table exercise I have been teaching you these three days. You all know your posts and your places, and can shew that you have been used to good company, without ever stirring from home.

OMNES. Ay, ay.

HARDCASTLE. When company comes you are not to pop out and

	stare, and then run in again, like frightened rabbits in a warren.
OMNES.	No, no.
HARDCASTLE.	You, Diggory, whom I have taken from the barn, are to make a show at the side-table; and you, Roger, whom I have advanced from the plow, are to place yourself behind *my* chair. But you're not to stand so, with your hands in your pockets. Take your hands from your pockets, Roger; and from your head, you blockhead you. See how Diggory carries his hands. They're a little too stiff, indeed, but that's no great matter.
DIGGORY.	Ay, mind how I hold them. I learned to hold my hands this way when I was upon drill for the militia. And so being upon drill –
HARDCASTLE.	You must not be so talkative, Diggory. You must be all attention to the guests. You must hear us talk, and not think of talking; you must see us drink, and not think of drinking; you must see us eat, and not think of eating.
DIGGORY.	By the laws, your worship, that's parfectly unpossible. Whenever Diggory sees yeating going forward, ecod, he's always wishing for a mouthful himself.
HARDCASTLE.	Blockhead! Is not a belly full in the kitchen as good as a belly full in the parlour? Stay your stomach with that reflection.
DIGGORY.	Ecod, I thank your worship, I'll make a shift to stay my stomach with a slice of cold beef in the pantry.
HARDCASTLE.	Diggory, you are too talkative. – Then, if I happen to say a good thing, or tell a good story at table, you must not all burst out a-laughing, as if you made part of the company.
DIGGORY.	Then ecod your worship must not tell the story of Ould Grouse in the gun-room: I can't help laughing at that – he! he! he! – for the soul of me. We have laughed at that these twenty years – ha! ha! ha!
HARDCASTLE.	Ha! ha! ha! The story is a good one. Well, honest Diggory, you may laugh at that – but still remember to be attentive. Suppose one of the company should call for a glass of wine, how will you behave? A glass of wine, sir, if you please (*to* DIGGORY). – Eh, why

	don't you move?
DIGGORY.	Ecod, your worship, I never have courage till I see the eatables and drinkables brought upo' the table, and then I'm as bauld as a lion.
HARDCASTLE.	What, will no body move?
FIRST SERVANT.	I'm not to leave this pleace.
SECOND SERVANT.	I'm sure it's no pleace of mine.
THIRD SERVANT.	Nor mine, for sartain.
DIGGORY.	Wauns, and I'm sure it canna be mine.
HARDCASTLE.	You numbskulls! and so while, like your betters, you are quarrelling for places, the guests must be starved. O you dunces! I find I must begin all over again — But don't I hear a coach drive into the yard? To your posts, you blockheads. I'll go in the mean time and give my old friend's son a hearty reception at the gate.

[*Exit* HARDCASTLE.

DIGGORY.	By the elevens, my pleas is gone quite out of my head.
ROGER.	I know that my pleas is to be everywhere.
FIRST SERVANT.	Where the devil is mine?
SECOND SERVANT.	My pleas is to be nowhere at all; and so Ize go about my business.

[*Exeunt* SERVANTS, *running about as if frightened, different ways.*

Enter SERVANT *with candles, shewing in* MARLOW *and* HASTINGS.

SERVANT.	Welcome, gentlemen, very welcome! This way.
HASTINGS.	After the disappointments of the day, welcome once more, Charles, to the comforts of a clean room and a good fire. Upon my word, a very well-looking house; antique but creditable.
MARLOW.	The usual fate of a large mansion. Having first ruined the master by good housekeeping, it at last comes to levy contributions as an inn.
HASTINGS.	As you say, we passengers are to be taxed to pay all these fineries. I have often seen a good sideboard, or a marble chimney-piece, tho' not actually put in the bill, inflame a reckoning confoundedly.
MARLOW.	Travellers, George, must pay in all places: the only

difference is, that in good inns you pay dearly for luxuries; in bad inns you are fleeced and starved.

HASTINGS. You have lived pretty much among them. In truth, I have been often surprized, that you who have seen so much of the world, with your natural good sense, and your many opportunities, could never yet acquire a requisite share of assurance.

MARLOW. The Englishman's malady. But tell me, George, where could I have learned that assurance you talk of? My life has been chiefly spent in a college, or an inn, in seclusion from that lovely part of the creation that chiefly teach men confidence. I don't know that I was ever familiarly acquainted with a single modest woman – except my mother – But among females of another class, you know —

HASTINGS. Ay, among them you are impudent enough of all conscience.

MARLOW. They are of *us*, you know.

HASTINGS. But in the company of women of reputation I never saw such an idiot, such a trembler; you look for all the world as if you wanted an opportunity of stealing out of the room.

MARLOW. Why, man, that's because I *do* want to steal out of the room. Faith, I have often formed a resolution to break the ice, and rattle away at any rate. But I don't know how, a single glance from a pair of fine eyes has totally overset my resolution. An impudent fellow may counterfeit modesty, but I'll be hanged if a modest man can ever counterfeit impudence.

HASTINGS. If you could but say half the fine things to them that I have heard you lavish upon the bar-maid of an inn, or even a college bed-maker —

MARLOW. Why, George, I can't say fine things to them; they freeze, they petrify me. They may talk of a comet, or a burning mountain, or some such bagatelle; but, to me, a modest woman, drest out in all her finery, is the most tremendous object of the whole creation.

HASTINGS. Ha! ha! ha! At this rate, man, how can you ever expect to marry?

MARLOW. Never, unless, as among kings and princes, my bride were to be courted by proxy. If, indeed, like an

Eastern bridegroom, one were to be introduced to a wife he never saw before, it might be endured. But to go through all the terrors of a formal courtship, together with the episode of aunts, grandmothers, and cousins, and at last to blurt out the broad staring question of, *madam, will you marry me?* No, no, that's a strain much above me, I assure you.

HASTINGS.

I pity you. But how do you intend behaving to the lady you are come down to visit at the request of your father?

MARLOW.

As I behave to all other ladies. Bow very low, answer yes or no to all her demands – But for the rest, I don't think I shall venture to look in her face till I see my father's again.

HASTINGS.

I'm surprized that one who is so warm a friend can be so cool a lover.

MARLOW.

To be explicit, my dear Hastings, my chief inducement down was to be instrumental in forwarding your happiness, not my own. Miss Neville loves you, the family don't know you; as my friend you are sure of a reception, and let honour do the rest.

HASTINGS.

My dear Marlow! But I'll suppress the emotion. Were I a wretch, meanly seeking to carry off a fortune, you should be the last man in the world I would apply to for assistance. But Miss Neville's person is all I ask, and that is mine, both from her deceased father's consent, and her own inclination.

MARLOW.

Happy man! You have talents and art to captivate any woman. I'm doom'd to adore the sex, and yet to converse with the only part of it I despise. This stammer in my address, and this awkward prepossessing visage of mine, can never permit me to soar above the reach of a milliner's 'prentice, or one of the duchesses of Drury-lane. Pshaw! this fellow here to interrupt us.

Enter HARDCASTLE.

HARDCASTLE.

Gentlemen, once more you are heartily welcome. Which is Mr. Marlow? Sir, you are heartily welcome. It's not my way, you see, to receive my friends with my back to the fire. I like to give them a hearty

	reception in the old style at my gate. I like to see their horses and trunks taken care of.
MARLOW.	(*Aside.*) He has got our names from the servants already. (*To him.*) We approve your caution and hospitality, sir. (*To* HASTINGS.) I have been thinking, George, of changing our travelling dresses in the morning. I am grown confoundedly ashamed of mine.
HARDCASTLE.	I beg, Mr. Marlow, you'll use no ceremony in this house.
HASTINGS.	I fancy, Charles, you're right: the first blow is half the battle. I intend opening the campaign with the white and gold.
HARDCASTLE.	Mr. Marlow – Mr. Hastings – gentlemen – pray be under no constraint in this house. This is Liberty-hall, gentlemen. You may do just as you please here.
MARLOW.	Yet, George, if we open the campaign too fiercely at first, we may want ammunition before it is over. I think to reserve the embroidery to secure a retreat.
HARDCASTLE.	Your talking of a retreat, Mr. Marlow, puts me in mind of the Duke of Marlborough, when we went to besiege Denain.[1] He first summoned the garrison.
MARLOW.	Don't you think the *ventre d'or*[2] waistcoat will do with the plain brown?
HARDCASTLE.	He first summoned the garrison, which might consist of about five thousand men –
HASTINGS.	I think not: Brown and yellow mix but very poorly.
HARDCASTLE.	I say, gentlemen, as I was telling you, he summoned the garrison, which might consist of about five thousand men –
MARLOW.	The girls like finery.
HARDCASTLE.	Which might consist of about five thousand men, well appointed with stores, ammunition, and other implements of war. Now, says the Duke of Marlborough to George Brooks, that stood next to him – you must have heard of George Brooks; I'll pawn my dukedom, says he, but I take that garrison without spilling a drop of blood. So —

---

1 *Denain*: village in France where allied forces were defeated by the French in 1712.
2 *ventre d'or*: gold-fronted.

MARLOW.	What, my good friend, if you gave us a glass of punch in the mean time; it would help us to carry on the siege with vigour.
HARDCASTLE.	Punch, sir! (*Aside.*) This is the most unaccountable kind of modesty I ever met with.
MARLOW.	Yes, Sir, Punch. A glass of warm punch, after our journey, will be comfortable. This is Liberty-hall, you know.
HARDCASTLE.	Here's cup, sir.
MARLOW.	(*Aside.*)So this fellow, in his Liberty-hall, will only let us have just what he pleases.
HARDCASTLE.	(*Taking the Cup.*) I hope you'll find it to your mind. I have prepared it with my own hands, and I believe you'll own the ingredients are tolerable. Will you be so good as to pledge me, Sir? Here, Mr. Marlow, here is to our better acquaintance. [*Drinks.*]
MARLOW.	(*Aside.*) A very impudent fellow this! but he's a character, and I'll humour him a little. Sir, my service to you. [*Drinks.*]
HASTINGS.	(*Aside.*) I see this fellow wants to give us his company, and forgets that he's an innkeeper, before he has learned to be a gentleman.
MARLOW.	From the excellence of your cup, my old friend, I suppose you have a good deal of business in this part of the country. Warm work, now and then, at elections, I suppose.
HARDCASTLE.	No, Sir, I have long given that work over. Since our betters have hit upon the expedient of electing each other, there is no business *for us that sell ale*.
HASTINGS.	So, then you have no turn for politics I find.
HARDCASTLE.	Not in the least. There was a time, indeed, I fretted myself about the mistakes of government, like other people; but finding myself every day grow more angry, and the government growing no better, I left it to mend itself. Since that, I no more trouble my head about *Heyder Ally*, or *Ally Cawn*, than about *Ally Croaker*.[1] Sir, my service to you.
HASTINGS.	So that with eating above stairs, and drinking below,

---

1 *Heyder Ally … Ally Croaker*: Haidar Ally Cawn, shrewd illiterate administrator of Mysore, renowed for his detection of fraud. In 1767 he challenged the British to the first of four Mysore Wars. Ally Croaker is a fickle girl in a popular Irish song.

with receiving your friends within, and amusing them without, you lead a good pleasant bustling life of it.

HARDCASTLE. I do stir about a great deal, that's certain. Half the differences of the parish are adjusted in this very parlour.

MARLOW. (*After drinking.*) And you have an argument in your cup, old gentleman, better than any in Westminster-hall.

HARDCASTLE. Ay, young gentleman, that, and a little philosophy.

MARLOW. (*Aside.*) Well, this is the first time I ever heard of an innkeeper's philosophy.

HASTINGS. So then, like an experienced general, you attack them on every quarter. If you find their reason man-ageable, you attack it with your philosophy; if you find they have no reason, you attack them with this. Here's your health, my philosopher. [*Drinks.*]

HARDCASTLE. Good, very good, thank you; ha! ha! Your Generalship puts me in mind of Prince Eugene, when he fought the Turks at the battle of Belgrade. You shall hear.

MARLOW. Instead of the battle of Belgrade, I believe it's almost time to talk about supper. What has your philoso-phy got in the house for supper?

HARDCASTLE. For Supper, Sir! (*Aside.*) Was ever such a request to a man in his own house?

MARLOW. Yes, sir, supper, sir; I begin to feel an appetite. I shall make devilish work to-night in the larder, I promise you.

HARDCASTLE. (*Aside.*) Such a brazen dog sure never my eyes beheld. (*To him.*) Why, really, Sir, as for supper I can't well tell. My Dorothy and the cook maid set-tle these things between them. I leave these kind of things entirely to them.

MARLOW. You do, do you?

HARDCASTLE. Entirely. By-the-bye, I believe they are in actual con-sultation upon what's for supper this moment in the kitchen.

MARLOW. Then I beg they'll admit *me* as one of their privy council. It's a way I have got. When I travel, I always chuse to regulate my own supper. Let the cook be called. No offence I hope, Sir.

HARDCASTLE.	O no, Sir, none in the least; yet I don't know how: our Bridget, the cook maid, is not very communicative upon these occasions. Should we send for her, she might scold us all out of the house.
HASTINGS.	Let's see your list of the larder then. I ask it as a favour. I always match my appetite to my bill of fare.
MARLOW.	(To HARDCASTLE, *who looks at them with surprize.*) Sir, he's very right, and it's my way too.
HARDCASTLE.	Sir, you have a right to command here. Here, Roger, bring us the bill of fare for to-night's supper. I believe it's drawn out. Your manner, Mr. Hastings, puts me in mind of my uncle, Colonel Wallop. It was a saying of his, that no man was sure of his supper till he had eaten it.
HASTINGS.	(*Aside.*) All upon the high ropes! His uncle a Colonel! We shall soon hear of his mother being a justice of the peace. But let's hear the bill of fare.
MARLOW.	(*Perusing.*) What's here? For the first course; for the second course; for the dessert. The devil, Sir, do you think we have brought down a whole Joiners Company, or the Corporation of Bedford, to eat up such a supper? Two or three little things clean and comfortable, will do.
HASTINGS.	But let's hear it.
MARLOW.	(*Reading.*) For the first course, at the top, a pig and pruin sauce.
HASTINGS.	Damn your pig, I say.
MARLOW.	And damn your pruin sauce, say I.
HARDCASTLE.	And yet, gentlemen, to men that are hungry, pig, with pruin sauce is very good eating.
MARLOW.	At the bottom, a calve's tongue and brains.
HASTINGS.	Let your brains be knock'd out, my good Sir; I don't like them.
MARLOW.	Or you may clap them on a plate by themselves. I do.
HARDCASTLE.	(*Aside.*) Their impudence confounds me. (*To them.*) Gentlemen, you are my guests, make what alterations you please. Is there any thing else you wish to retrench or alter, gentlemen?
MARLOW.	Item, a pork pie, a boiled rabbet and sausages, a

florentine,[1] a shaking pudding, and a dish of tiff – taff – taffety cream.

HASTINGS. Confound your made dishes, I shall be as much at a loss in this house as at a green and yellow dinner at the French ambassador's table. I'm for plain eating.

HARDCASTLE. I'm sorry, gentlemen, that I have nothing you like, but if there be any thing you have a particular fancy to –

MARLOW. Why, really, Sir, your bill of fare is so exquisite, that any one part of it is full as good as another. Send us what you please. So much for supper. And now to see that our beds are air'd, and properly taken care of.

HARDCASTLE. I entreat you'll leave all that to me. You shall not stir a step.

MARLOW. Leave that to you! I protest, Sir, you must excuse me, I always look to these things myself.

HARDCASTLE. I must insist, Sir, you'll make yourself easy on that head.

MARLOW. You see I'm resolved on it. (*Aside.*) A very troublesome fellow this, as I ever met with.

HARDCASTLE. Well, sir, I'm resolved at least to attend you. (*Aside.*) This may be modern modesty, but I never saw any thing look so like old-fashioned impudence.

[*Exeunt* MARLOW *and* HARDCASTLE.

HASTINGS. (*Solus.*) So I find this fellow's civilities begin to grow troublesome. But who can be angry at those assiduities which are meant to please him? Ha! what do I see? Miss Neville, by all that's happy!

Enter MISS NEVILLE.

MISS NEVILLE. My dear Hastings! To what unexpected good fortune, to what accident, am I to ascribe this happy meeting?

HASTINGS. Rather let me ask the same question, as I could never have hoped to meet my dearest Constance at an inn.

MISS NEVILLE. An inn! sure you mistake! my aunt, my guardian,

---

1 *florentine*: a meat pie.

lives here. What could induce you to think this house an inn?

HASTINGS. My friend, Mr. Marlow, with whom I came down, and I, have been sent here as to an inn, I assure you. A young fellow, whom we accidentally met at a house hard by, directed us hither.

MISS NEVILLE. Certainly it must be one of my hopeful cousin's tricks, of whom you have heard me talk so often, ha! ha! ha!

HASTINGS. He whom your aunt intends for you? He of whom I have such just apprehensions?

MISS NEVILLE. You have nothing to fear from him, I assure you. You'd adore him, if you knew how heartily he despises me. My aunt knows it too, and has undertaken to court me for him, and actually begins to think she has made a conquest.

HASTINGS. Thou dear dissembler! You must know, my Constance, I have just seized this happy opportunity of my friend's visit here to get admittance into the family. The horses that carried us down are now fatigued with their journey, but they'll soon be refreshed; and then, if my dearest girl will trust in her faithful Hastings, we shall soon be landed in France, where even among slaves the laws of marriage are respected.

MISS NEVILLE. I have often told you, that though ready to obey you, I yet should leave my little fortune behind with reluctance. The greatest part of it was left me by my uncle, the India Director, and chiefly consists in jewels. I have been for some time persuading my aunt to let me wear them. I fancy I'm very near succeeding. The instant they are put into my possession, you shall find me ready to make them and myself yours.

HASTINGS. Perish the baubles! Your person is all I desire. In the mean time, my friend Marlow must not be let into his mistake. I know the strange reserve of his temper is such, that if abruptly informed of it, he would instantly quit the house before our plan was ripe for execution.

MISS NEVILLE. But how shall we keep him in the deception? Miss

Hardcastle is just returned from walking; what if we still continue to deceive him? – This, this way – [*They confer.*]

Enter MARLOW.

MARLOW. The assiduities of these good people teaze me beyond bearing. My host seems to think it ill manners to leave me alone, and so he claps not only himself, but his old-fashioned wife, on my back. They talk of coming to sup with us too; and then, I suppose, we are to run the gauntlet thro' all the rest of the family. – What have we got here! –

HASTINGS. My dear Charles! Let me congratulate you! – The most fortunate accident! – Who do you think is just alighted?

MARLOW. Cannot guess.

HASTINGS. Our mistresses, boy, Miss Hardcastle and Miss Neville. Give me leave to introduce Miss Constance Neville to your acquaintance. Happening to dine in the neighbourhood, they called, on their return to take fresh horses, here. Miss Hardcastle has just stept into the next room, and will be back in an instant. Wasn't it lucky? eh!

MARLOW. (*Aside.*) I have just been mortified enough of all conscience, and here comes something to complete my embarrassment.

HASTINGS. Well, but wasn't it the most fortunate thing in the world?

MARLOW. Oh! yes. Very fortunate – a most joyful encounter – But our dresses, George, you know are in disorder – What if we should postpone the happiness till to-morrow? – To-morrow at her own house – It will be every bit as convenient – and rather more respectful – To-morrow let it be. [*Offering to go.*]

MISS NEVILLE. By no means, Sir. Your ceremony will displease her. The disorder of your dress will show the ardour of your impatience. Besides, she knows you are in the house, and will permit you to see her.

MARLOW. O! the devil! how shall I support it? Hem! hem! Hastings, you must not go. You are to assist me, you know. I shall be confoundedly ridiculous. Yet, hang

	it! I'll take courage. Hem!
HASTINGS.	Pshaw, man! it's but the first plunge, and all's over. She's but a woman, you know.
MARLOW.	And, of all women, she that I dread most to encounter!

Enter MISS HARDCASTLE, *as returned from walking, a bonnet, &c.*

HASTINGS.	(*Introducing them.*) Miss Hardcastle, Mr. Marlow. I'm proud of bringing two persons of such merit together, that only want to know, to esteem each other.
MISS HARDCASTLE.	(*Aside.*) Now, for meeting my modest gentleman with a demure face, and quite in his own manner. (*After a pause, in which he appears very uneasy and disconcerted.*) I'm glad of your safe arrival, Sir – I'm told you had some accidents by the way.
MARLOW.	Only a few, Madam. Yes, we had some. Yes, Madam, a good many accidents, but should be sorry – Madam – or rather glad of any accidents – that are so agreeably concluded. Hem!
HASTINGS.	(*To him.*) You never spoke better in your whole life. Keep it up, and I'll insure you the victory.
MISS HARDCASTLE.	I'm afraid you flatter, Sir. You that have seen so much of the finest company, can find little entertainment in an obscure corner of the country.
MARLOW.	(*Gathering courage.*) I have lived, indeed, in the world, Madam; but I have kept very little company. I have been but an observer upon life, Madam, while others were enjoying it.
MISS NEVILLE.	But that, I am told, is the way to enjoy it at last.
HASTINGS.	(*To him.*) Cicero never spoke better. Once more, and you are confirmed in assurance for ever.
MARLOW.	(*To him.*) Hem! Stand by me, then, and when I'm down, throw in a word or two, to set me up again.
MISS HARDCASTLE.	An observer, like you, upon life, were, I fear, disagreeably employed, since you must have had much more to censure than to approve.
MARLOW.	Pardon me, Madam. I was always willing to be amused. The folly of most people is rather an object of mirth than uneasiness.
HASTINGS.	(*To him.*) Bravo, Bravo. Never spoke so well in your

whole life. Well! Miss Hardcastle, I see that you and Mr. Marlow are going to be very good company. I believe our being here will but embarrass the interview.

MARLOW. Not in the least, Mr. Hastings. We like your company of all things. (*To him.*) Zounds! George, sure you won't go? How can you leave us?

HASTINGS. Our presence will but spoil conversation, so we'll retire to the next room. (*To him.*) You don't consider, man, that we are to manage a little tête-à-tête of our own.

[*Exeunt.*

MISS HARDCASTLE. (*after a pause*). But you have not been wholly an observer, I presume, Sir: The ladies I should hope have employed some part of your addresses.

MARLOW. (*Relapsing into timidity.*) Pardon me, Madam, I – I – I as yet have studied – only – to – deserve them.

MISS HARDCASTLE. And that, some say, is the very worst way to obtain them.

MARLOW. Perhaps so, Madam. But I love to converse only with the more grave and sensible part of the sex. – But I'm afraid I grow tiresome.

MISS HARDCASTLE. Not at all, Sir; there is nothing I like so much as grave conversation myself; I could hear it for ever. Indeed, I have often been surprised how a man of *sentiment* could ever admire those light airy pleasures, where nothing reaches the heart.

MARLOW. It's – a disease – of the mind, Madam. In the variety of tastes there must be some who, wanting a relish – for – um – a – um.

MISS HARDCASTLE. I understand you, sir. There must be some, who, wanting a relish for refined pleasures, pretend to despise what they are incapable of tasting.

MARLOW. My meaning, madam, but infinitely better expressed. And I can't help observing – a –

MISS HARDCASTLE. (*Aside.*) Who could ever suppose this fellow impudent upon some occasions. (*To him.*) You were going to observe, Sir –

MARLOW. I was observing, Madam – I protest, Madam, I forget what I was going to observe.

MISS HARDCASTLE. (*Aside.*) I vow and so do I. (*To him.*) You were observing, Sir, that in this age of hypocrisy – something about hypocrisy, Sir.

MARLOW. Yes, Madam. In this age of hypocrisy there are few who upon strict inquiry do not – a – a – a –

MISS HARDCASTLE. I understand you perfectly, Sir.

MARLOW. (*Aside.*) Egad! and that's more than I do myself.

MISS HARDCASTLE. You mean that in this hypocritical age there are few that do not condemn in public what they practise in private, and think they pay every debt to virtue when they praise it.

MARLOW. True, Madam; those who have most virtue in their mouths, have least of it in their bosoms. But I'm sure I tire you, Madam.

MISS HARDCASTLE. Not in the least, Sir; there's something so agreeable and spirited in your manner, such life and force – pray, Sir, go on.

MARLOW. Yes, Madam. I was saying – that there are some occasions – when a total want of courage, Madam, destroys all the – and puts us – upon a – a – a –

MISS HARDCASTLE. I agree with you entirely; a want of courage upon some occasions assumes the appearance of ignorance, and betrays us when we most want to excel. I beg you'll proceed.

MARLOW. Yes, Madam. Morally speaking, Madam – But I see Miss Neville expecting us in the next room. I would not intrude for the world.

MISS HARDCASTLE. I protest, Sir, I never was more agreeably entertained in all my life. Pray go on.

MARLOW. Yes, Madam, I was — But she beckons us to join her. Madam, shall I do myself the honour to attend you?

MISS HARDCASTLE. Well, then, I'll follow.

MARLOW. (*Aside.*) This pretty smooth dialogue has done for me.

[*Exit.*

From ACT III.

Enter MISS HARDCASTLE *and* MAID.

MISS HARDCASTLE. What an unaccountable creature is that brother of mine, to send them to the house as an inn! ha! ha! I don't wonder at his impudence.

MAID. But what is more, madam, the young gentleman as you passed by in your present dress, ask'd me if you were the bar maid? He mistook you for the bar maid, madam.

MISS HARDCASTLE. Did he? Then as I live I'm resolved to keep up the delusion. Tell me, Pimple, how do you like my present dress? Don't you think I look something like Cherry in the Beaux Stratagem?[1]

MAID. It's the dress, madam, that every lady wears in the country, but when she visits or receives company.

MISS HARDCASTLE. And are you sure he does not remember my face or person?

MAID. Certain of it.

MISS HARDCASTLE. I vow I thought so; for though we spoke for some time together, yet his fears were such, that he never once looked up during the interview. Indeed if he had, my bonnet would have kept him from seeing me.

MAID. But what do you hope from keeping him in his mistake?

MISS HARDCASTLE. In the first place, I shall be *seen*, and that is no small advantage to a girl that brings her face to market. Then I shall perhaps make an acquaintance, and that's no small victory gained over one who never addresses any but the wildest of her sex. But my chief aim is to take my gentleman off his guard, and, like an invisible champion of romance, examine the giant's force before I offer to combat.

MAID. But you are sure you can act your part, and disguise your voice, so that he may mistake that, as he has already mistaken your person?

MISS HARDCASTLE. Never fear me. I think I have got the true bar cant – Did your honour call? – Attend the Lion there – Pipes and tobacco for the Angel. – The Lamb has been outrageous this half-hour.

MAID. It will do, madam. But he's here.

[*Exit* MAID.

Enter MARLOW.

MARLOW. What a bawling in every part of the house; I have

---

1 *Cherry in the Beaux Stratagem*: Cherry is the landlord's daughter in George Farquhar's comedy *The Beaux Stratagem*.

scarce a moment's repose. If I go to the best room, there I find my host and his story. If I fly to the gallery, there we have my hostess with her curtesy down to the ground. I have at last got a moment to myself, and now for recollection. [*Walks and muses.*]

MISS HARDCASTLE. Did you call, Sir? Did your honour call?

MARLOW. (*Musing.*) As for Miss Hardcastle, she's too grave and sentimental for me.

MISS HARDCASTLE. Did your honour call? (*She still places herself before him, he turning away.*)

MARLOW. No, child. (*Musing.*) Besides, from the glimpse I had of her, I think she squints.

MISS HARDCASTLE. I'm sure, sir, I heard the bell ring.

MARLOW. No, no. (*Musing.*) I have pleased my father, however, by coming down, and I'll to-morrow please myself by returning. [*Taking out his tablets, and perusing.*]

MISS HARDCASTLE. Perhaps the other gentleman called, Sir?

MARLOW. I tell you, no.

MISS HARDCASTLE. I should be glad to know, Sir. We have such a parcel of servants!

MARLOW. No, no, I tell you. (*Looks full in her face.*) Yes, child, I think I did call. I wanted – I wanted —— I vow, child you are vastly handsome.

MISS HARDCASTLE. O la, Sir, you'll make one asham'd.

MARLOW. Never saw a more sprightly malicious eye. Yes, yes, my dear, I did call. Have you got any of your – a – what d'ye call it in the house?

MISS HARDCASTLE. No, Sir, we have been out of that these ten days.

MARLOW. One may call in this house, I find, to very little purpose. Suppose I should call for a taste, just by way of a trial, of the nectar of your lips; perhaps I might be disappointed in that too.

MISS HARDCASTLE. Nectar! nectar! That's a liquor there's no call for in these parts. French, I suppose. We sell no French wines here, Sir.

MARLOW. Of true English growth, I assure you.

MISS HARDCASTLE. Then it's odd I should not know it. We brew all sorts of wines in this house, and I have lived here these eighteen years.

MARLOW. Eighteen years! Why, one would think, child, you

kept the bar before you were born. How old are you?

MISS HARDCASTLE. O! Sir, I must not tell my age. They say women and music should never be dated.

MARLOW. To guess at this distance, you can't be much above forty (*approaching*). Yet, nearer, I don't think so much (*approaching*). By coming close to some women they look younger still; but when we come very close indeed – (*attempting to kiss her*).

MISS HARDCASTLE. Pray, Sir, keep your distance. One would think you wanted to know one's age, as they do horses, by mark of mouth.

MARLOW. I protest, child, you use me extremely ill. If you keep me at this distance, how is it possible you and I can be ever acquainted?

MISS HARDCASTLE. And who wants to be acquainted with you? I want no such acquaintance, not I. I'm sure you did not treat Miss Hardcastle, that was here awhile ago, in this obstropalous manner. I'll warrant me, before her you look'd dash'd, and kept bowing to the ground, and talk'd, for all the world, as if you was before a justice of peace.

MARLOW. (*Aside*.) Egad, she has hit it, sure enough. (*To her*.) In awe of her, child? Ha! ha! ha! A mere awkward squinting thing, no, no. I find you don't know me. I laugh'd and rallied her a little; but I was unwilling to be too severe. No, I could not be too severe, *curse me!*

MISS HARDCASTLE. O! then, Sir, you are a favourite, I find, among the ladies?

MARLOW. Yes, my dear, a great favourite. And yet, hang me, I don't see what they find in me to follow. At the Ladies Club in town I'm called their agreeable Rattle. Rattle, child, is not my real name, but one I'm known by. My name is Solomons. Mr. Solomons, my dear, at your service. (*Offering to salute her*.)

MISS HARDCASTLE. Hold, Sir; you were introducing me to your club, not to yourself. And you're so great a favourite there you say?

MARLOW. Yes, my dear. There's Mrs. Mantrap, Lady Betty

Blackleg, the Countess of Sligo, Mrs. Langhorns, old Miss Biddy Buckskin, and your humble servant, keep up the spirit of the place.

MISS HARDCASTLE. Then it's a very merry place, I suppose?

MARLOW. Yes, as merry as cards, supper, wine, and old women can make us.

MISS HARDCASTLE. And their agreeable Rattle, ha! ha! ha!

MARLOW. (*Aside.*) Egad! I don't quite like this chit. She looks knowing, methinks. You laugh, child?

MISS HARDCASTLE. I can't but laugh, to think what time they all have for minding their work or their family.

MARLOW. (*Aside.*) All's well, she don't laugh at me. (*To her.*) Do you ever work, child?

MISS HARDCASTLE. Ay, sure. There's not a screen or quilt in the whole house but what can bear witness to that.

MARLOW. Odso! then you must shew me your embroidery. I embroider and draw patterns myself a little. If you want a judge of your work, you must apply to me. (*Seizing her hand.*)

MISS HARDCASTLE. Ay, but the colours do not look well by candlelight. You shall see all in the morning. (*Struggling.*)

MARLOW. And why not now, my angel? Such beauty fires beyond the power of resistance. – Pshaw! the father here! My old luck: I never nicked seven that I did not throw ames ace three times following.[1]

[*Exit* MARLOW.

Enter HARDCASTLE, *who stands in surprise.*

HARDCASTLE. So, madam. So, I find *this* is your *modest* lover. This is your humble admirer, that kept his eyes fixed on the ground, and only ador'd at humble distance. Kate, Kate, art thou not asham'd to deceive your father so?

MISS HARDCASTLE. Never trust me, dear papa, but he's still the modest man I first took him for; you'll be convinced of it as well as I.

HARDCASTLE. By the hand of my body, I believe his impudence is infectious! Didn't I see him seize your hand? Didn't I see him haul you about like a milkmaid? And now you talk of his respect and his modesty, forsooth!

---

1 *throw ames ace*: in dice, ames or double ace is the lowest possible throw; seven is the highest.

MISS HARDCASTLE. But if I shortly convince you of his modesty, that he has only the faults that will pass off with time, and the virtues that will improve with age, I hope you'll forgive him.

HARDCASTLE. The girl would actually make one run mad! I tell you, I'll not be convinced. I am convinced. He has scarce been three hours in the house, and he has already encroached on all my prerogatives. You may like his impudence, and call it modesty. But my son-in-law, Madam, must have very different qualifications.

MISS HARDCASTLE. Sir, I ask but this night to convince you.

HARDCASTLE. You shall not have half the time, for I have thoughts of turning him out this very hour.

MISS HARDCASTLE. Give me that hour then, and I hope to satisfy you.

HARDCASTLE. Well, an hour let it be then. But I'll have no trifling with your father. All fair and open, do you mind me.

MISS HARDCASTLE. I hope, Sir, you have ever found that I considered your commands as my pride; for your kindness is such, that my duty as yet has been inclination.

[Exeunt.]

From *The Grecian History from the Earliest Days to the Death of Alexander the Great*

(1774)

THE DEATH OF SOCRATES

In the mean time, while Greece was gaining fame in Persia, Athens was losing its honour at home. Though it had now some breathing time to recover from its late confusions, yet still there were the seeds of rancour remaining, and the citizens opposed each other with unremitting malice. Socrates was the first object that fell sacrifice to these popular dissentions. We have already seen this great man, who was the son of an obscure citizen at Athens, emerging from the mean-ness of his birth, and giving examples of courage, moderation, and wisdom; we have seen him saving the life of Alcibiades in battle, refusing to concur in the edict which unjustly doomed the six Athenian generals to death, withstanding the thirty tyrants, and spurning the bigotry and persecution of the times with the most acute penetration, and the most caustic raillery. He possessed unexampled good-nature, and an universal love to mankind; he was ready to pity vices in others, while he was, in a great measure, free from them himself; however, he knew his own defects, and if he was proud of any thing, it was in the being thought to have none. He seemed, says Libanius, the common father of their public, so attentive was he to the happiness and advantage of his whole country. But as it is very difficult to correct the aged, and to make people change principles, who revere the errors in which they have grown grey, he devoted his labours principally to the instruction of youth, in order to sow the seeds of virtue in a soil more fit to produce the fruits of it. He had no open school, like the rest of the philosophers, nor set times for his lessons; he had no benches prepared nor ever mounted a professor's chair; he was the philosopher of all times and seasons; he taught in all places, and upon all occasions; in walking, conversation at meals, in the army, and in the midst of the camp, in the public assemblies of the senate or people. Such was the man whom a faction in the city had long devoted to destruction: he had been, for many years before his death, the object of their satire and ridicule. Aristophanes, the comic poet, was engaged to expose him upon the stage: he composed a piece called the Clouds, wherein he introduced the philosopher in a basket, uttering the most ridiculous absurdities. Socrates, who was present at the exhibition of his own character, seemed not to feel the least emotion; and, as some strangers were present, who desired to know the original for whom the play was intended, he rose up from his seat, and showed himself during the whole representation. This was the first blow struck at him; and it was not till twenty years after that Melitus appeared in a more formal manner as his accuser, and entered a regular process against him. His accusation consisted of two heads; the first was, that he did not admit the gods acknowledged by the republic, and introduced new divinities; the second, that he corrupted the youth of Athens; and concluded with inferring, that sentence of death ought to pass against him. How far the whole charge affected him is not easy to determine; it is certain, that amidst so much zeal and superstition as then reigned in Athens, he never durst openly oppose the received religion, and was, therefore, forced to preserve an outward show of it; but it is very probable, from the discourses he frequently held with his friends, that in his heart he despised and laughed at their monstrous opinions and ridiculous mysteries, as having no other foundation than the fables of the poets; and that he had attained to the notion of the one only true God, insomuch, that upon the account both of his belief of the Deity, and the exemplariness of his life, some have thought fit to rank him with the Christian philosophers.

As soon as the conspiracy broke out, the friends of Socrates prepared for his defence. Lycias, the most able orator of his time, brought him an elaborate discourse of his own composing, wherein he had set forth the reasons and measures of Socrates in their full force, and interspersed the whole with tender and pathetic strokes, capable of moving the most obdurate hearts. Socrates read it with pleasure, and approved it very much; but, as it was more conformable to the rules of rhetoric, than the sentiments and fortitude of a philosopher, he told him frankly, that it did not suit him. Upon which Lycias having asked him how it was possible to be well done, and at the same time not suit him? In the same manner, said he, using, according to the custom, a vulgar comparison, that an excellent workman might bring me magnificent apparel, or shoes embroidered with gold, to which nothing would be wanting on his part, but which, however, would not suit me. He persisted, therefore, inflexibly in the resolution, not to demean himself by begging suffrages in the low, abject manner common at that time. He employed neither artifice, nor the glitter of eloquence; he had no recourse either to solicitation or entreaty; he brought neither his wife nor children to incline the judges in his favour by their sighs and tears: nevertheless, though he firmly refused to make use of any other voice but his own in his defence, and to appear before his judges in the submissive posture of a suppliant, he did not behave in that manner out of pride, or contempt of the tribunal; it was from a noble and intrepid assurance, resulting from greatness of soul, and the consciousness of his truth and innocence; so that his defence had nothing weak or timorous in it: his discourse was bold, manly, generous, without passion, without emotion, full of the noble liberty of a philosopher, with no other ornament than the truth, and brightened universally with the character and language of innocence.... Socrates pronounced this discourse with a firm and intrepid tone: his air, his action, his visage, expressed nothing of the accused; he seemed the master of his judges from the assurance and greatness of soul with which he spoke, without, however, losing any thing of the modesty natural to him. But how slight soever the proofs were against him, the faction was powerful enough to find him guilty. There was the form of a process against him, and his irreligion was the pretence upon which it was grounded, but his death was certainly a concerted thing. His steady uninterrupted course of obstinate virtue, which had made him in many cases appear singular, and oppose whatever he thought illegal or unjust, without any regard to times or persons, had procured him a great deal of envy and ill-will.

By his first sentence the judges only declared Socrates guilty; but when, by his answer, he appeared to appeal from their tribunal to that of justice and posterity; when, instead of confessing himself guilty, he demanded rewards and honours from the state, the judges were so very much offended, that they condemned him to drink hemlock, a method of execution then in use amongst them.

Socrates received this sentence with the utmost composure. Apollodorus, one of his disciples, launching out into bitter invectives and lamentations that his master should die *innocent*: 'What,' replied Socrates with a smile, 'would you have me die guilty? Melitus and Anytus may kill, but they cannot hurt me.'

After his sentence, he still continued with the same serene and intrepid aspect with which he had long enforced virtue, and held tyrants in awe. When he entered his prison, which now became the residence of virtue and probity, his friends followed him thither, and continued to visit him during the interval between his condemnation and his death, which lasted for thirty days. The cause of that long delay was, the Athenians sent every year a ship to the isle of Delos, to offer certain sacrifices, and it was prohibited to put any person to death in the city from the time the priest of Apollo had crowned the poop of this vessel as a signal of its departure, till the same vessel should return: so that sentence having been passed upon Socrates the day after that ceremony began, it was necessary to defer the execution of it for thirty days, during the continuance of this voyage.

In this long interval, death had sufficient opportunities to present itself before his eyes in all its terrors, and to put his constancy to the proof, not only by the severe rigour of a dungeon, and the irons upon his legs, but by the continual prospect and cruel expectation of an event of which nature is always abhorrent. In this sad condition he did not cease to enjoy that profound tranquillity of mind which his friends had always admired in him. He entertained them with the same temper he had always expressed; and Crito observes that the evening before his death, he slept as peaceably as at any other time. He composed also an hymn in honour of Apollo and Diana, and turned one of Aesop's fables into verse.

The day before, or the same day that the ship was to arrive from Delos, the return of which was to be followed by the death of Socrates, Crito, his intimate friend, came to him early in the morning, to let him know that bad news, and, at the same time, that it depended only upon himself to quit the prison; that the jailor was gained; that he would find the doors open, and offered him a safe retreat in Thessaly. Socrates laughed at this proposal, and asked him, whether he knew any place out of Attica where people did not die? Crito urged the thing very seriously, and pressed him to take the advantage of so precious an opportunity, adding argument upon argument, to induce his consent, and to engage him to resolve upon escape: without mentioning the inconsolable grief he should suffer for the death of such a friend, how should he support the reproaches of an infinity of people, who would believe it was in his power to have saved him, but that he would not sacrifice a small part of his wealth for that purpose: can the people ever be persuaded that so wise a man as Socrates would not quit his prison, when he might do it with all possible security? Perhaps he might fear to expose his friends, or to occasion the loss of their fortunes, or even of their lives or liberty: ought there to be any thing more dear and precious to them than the preservation of Socrates? Even strangers themselves dispute that honour with them, many of whom have come expressly with considerable sums of money to purchase his escape; and declare that they should think themselves highly honoured to receive him amongst them, and to supply him abundantly with all he should have occasion for: ought he to abandon himself to enemies who have occasioned his being condemned unjustly; and can he think it allowable to betray his own cause? Is it not essential to his goodness and justness to spare his fellow citizens the guilt of innocent blood; but if all these motives cannot alter him, and he is not concerned in regard to himself, can he be insensible to the interests of his children? In what a condition does he leave them: and can he forget the father, to remember only the philosopher?

Socrates, after having heard him with attention, praised his zeal and expressed his gratitude; but before he could give in to his opinion, was for examining whether it was just for him to depart out of prison without the consent of the Athenians. The question, therefore, here is, to know whether a man condemned to die, though unjustly, can, without a crime, escape from justice and the laws. Socrates held it was unjust; and therefore nobly refused to escape from prison. He reverenced the laws of his country, and resolved to obey them in all things, even in his death.

At length the fatal ship returned to Athens, which was, in a manner, the signal for the death of Socrates. The next day all his friends, except Plato, who was sick, repaired to the prison early in the morning. The jailor desired them to wait a little, because the eleven magistrates (who had the direction of the prisons) were at that time signifying to the prisoner that he was to die the same day. Presently after they entered, and found Socrates, whose chains had been taken off, sitting by Xantippe, his wife, who held one of his children in her arms; as soon as she perceived them, setting up great cries, sobbing, and tearing her face and hair, she made the prison resound with her complaints. Oh, my dear Socrates! your friends are come to see you this day for the last time! He desired she might be taken away; and she was immediately carried home.

Socrates passed the rest of the day with his friends, and discoursed with them with his usual cheerfulness and tranquillity. The subject of conversation was the most important, and adapted to the present conjuncture; that is to say, the mortality of the soul. What gave occasion to this discourse was, a question introduced in a manner by chance, Whether a true philosopher ought not to desire, and take pains to die? This proposition taken too literally, implied an opinion, that a philosopher might kill himself. Socrates shows that nothing is more unjust than this notion; and that man appertaining to God, who formed and placed him with his own hand in the post he possesses, cannot abandon it without his permission, nor depart from life without his order. What is it then that can induce a philosopher to entertain this love for death? It can be only the hope of that happiness which he expects in another life, and that hope can be founded only upon the opinion of the soul's immortality.

Socrates employed the last day of his life in entertaining his friends upon this great and important subject; from which conversation Plato's admirable dialogue, entitled the *Phaedon,* is wholly taken. He explains to his friends all the arguments for believing the soul immortal, and refutes all the objections against it, which are very nearly the same as are made at this day.

When Socrates had done speaking, Crito desired him to give him, and the rest of his friends, his last instructions in regard to his children and other affairs, that by executing them they might have the consolation of doing him some pleasure. I shall recommend nothing to you this day, replied Socrates, more than I have already done, which is to take care of yourselves. You cannot do yourselves a greater service, nor do me and my family a greater pleasure. Crito having asked him afterwards in what manner he thought fit to be buried: – As you please, said Socrates, if you can lay hold of me, and I escape not out of your hands. At the same time, looking on his friends with a smile, I can never persuade Crito, that Socrates is he who converses with you, and disposes the several parts of his discourse, for he always imagines that I am what he is going to see dead in a little while; he confounds me with my carcase, and therefore asks me how I would be interred. On finishing these words he rose up, and went to bathe himself in a chamber adjoining. After he came out of the bath his children were brought to him; for he had three, two very little, and the other grown up. He spoke to them for some time, gave his orders to the women who took care of them, and then dismissed them. Being returned into his chamber, he laid himself down upon his bed.

The servant of the eleven entered at the same instant, and having informed him that the time for drinking the hemlock was come (which was at sun-set), the servant was so much afflicted with sorrow, that he turned his back, and fell a-weeping. See, said Socrates, the good heart of this man: since my imprisonment he has often come to see me, and to converse with me; he is more worthy than all his fellows; how heartily the poor man weeps for me. This is a remarkable example, and might teach those in an office of this kind how they ought to behave to all prisoners, but more especially to persons of merit, when they are so unhappy as to fall into their hands. The fatal cup was brought. Socrates asked what it was necessary for him to do? Nothing more, replied the servant, than as soon as you have drank off the draught to walk about till you find your legs grow weary, and afterwards lie down upon your bed. He took the cup without any emotion, or change in his colour or countenance; and, regarding the man with a steady and assured look – 'Well,' said he, 'what say you of this drink; may one make a libation out of it?' Upon being told there was only enough for one dose: – 'At least,' continued he, 'we may say our prayers to the gods, as it is our duty, and implore them to make our exit from this world, and our last stage happy, which is what I most ardently beg of them.' After having spoken these words he kept silence for some time, and then drank off the whole draught with an amazing tranquillity and serenity of aspect, not to be expressed or conceived.

Till then his friends, with great violence to themselves, had refrained from tears; but after he had drank the potion, they were no longer their own masters, and wept abundantly. Apollodorus, who had been in tears almost the whole conversation, began then to raise great cries, and to lament with such excessive grief, as pierced the hearts of all that were present. Socrates alone remained unmoved, and even reproved his friends, though with his usual mildness and good nature. 'What are you doing?' said he to them: 'I wonder at you! Oh! What is become of your virtue! Was it not for this I sent away the women, that they might not fall into these weaknesses; for I have always heard you say that we ought to die peaceably, and blessing the gods. Be at ease, I beg you, and show more constancy and resolution.' He then obliged them to restrain their tears.

In the mean time, he kept walking to and fro, and when he found his legs grow weary, he laid down upon his back, as he had been directed.

The poison then operated more and more. When Socrates found it began to gain upon the heart, uncovering his face, which had been covered, without doubt to prevent any thing from disturbing him in his last moments, – 'Crito,' said he, 'we owe a cock to Esculapius; discharge that vow for me, and pray do not forget it.' Soon after which he breathed his last. Crito went to his body, and closed his mouth and eyes. Such was the end of Socrates, in the first year of the ninety-fifth Olympiad, and the seventieth of his age.

CHARLOTTE BROOKE (?1740-1793)

Charlotte Brooke, daughter of the poet and novelist Henry Brooke, was born in Rantavan, Co. Cavan. She contributed translations anonymously to Joseph Cooper Walker's *Historical Memoirs of the Irish Bards* (1786). Encouraged by her father and Walker, she published her *Reliques of Irish Poetry* (1789), influenced by Bishop Thomas Percy's *Reliques of Ancient English Poetry* (1765). In her book she translated Irish originals, her delight in the Irish language conveyed in her Preface. Her renderings of the Red Branch and Fenian material, reinforced by her knowledge of Celtic antiquities, were an extremely influential part of the general antiquarian movement of the later eighteenth century. She translated heroic poems, odes, elegies and songs, providing texts of the originals so that her translations could be assessed. Her work aroused much interest in not only the language but the customs and culture of Gaelic Ireland. Her translation of Carolan's 'Song for Gracey Nugent' is included here; she added a literal translation of the original. Turlough Carolan (Toirdhealbhach Ó Cearbhallaín, 1670-1738), harper, composer and poet, was born near Nobber, Co. Meath and grew up in Ballyfarnan, Co. Roscommon. Blinded by smallpox at eighteen, he was trained as a harper and became an itinerant player. He married and settled for a time in Co. Leitrim; after his wife's death he resumed his itinerant life, popular with different patrons who accorded him the social status enjoyed by Gaelic harpers. Swift translated his Pléaráca na Ruarcach (O'Rourke's Irish Feast*).

Song for Gracey Nugent[1]

By CAROLAN.

Of Gracey's charms enraptur'd will I sing!
Fragrant and fair, as blossoms of the spring;
To her sweet manners, and accomplish'd mind,
Each rival Fair the palm of Love resign'd.

How blest her sweet society to share!
To mark the ringlets of her flowing hair;[2]
Her gentle accents, – her complacent mien! –
Supreme in charms, she looks – she reigns a Queen!
That alabaster form – that graceful neck,
How do the Cygnet's down and whiteness deck! –
How does that aspect shame the cheer of day,
When summer suns their brightest beams display.

---

1 *Song for Gracey Nugent*: The fair subject of this Song was sister to the late John Nugent, Esq; of Castle-Nugent, Culambre. She lived with her sister, Mrs. Conmee, near Belanagar, in the county of Roscommon, at the time she inspired our Bard. [*Brooke's note.*]

2 *her flowing hair*: Hair is a favourite object with all the Irish Poets, and endless is the variety of their description:—'Soft misty curls.'— 'Thick branching tresses of bright redundance.'— 'Locks of fair waving beauty.'—'Tresses flowing on the wind like the bright waving of an inverted torch.' They even affect to inspire it with expression:—as `Locks of *gentle* lustre.'— 'Tresses of tender beauty.'—'The Maid with the *mildly* flowing hair,' &c. &c.

A friend to whom I shewed this Song, observed, that I had omitted a very lively thought in the conclusion, which they had seen in Mr. WALKER's Memoirs. As that version has been much read and admired, it may perhaps be necessary, to vindicate my fidelity, as a translator, that I should here give a literal translation of the Song, to shew that the thoughts have suffered very little, either of encrease or diminution from the poetry.

I will sing with rapture of the Blossom of Whiteness! Gracey, the young and beautiful woman, who bore away the palm of excellence in sweet manners and accomplishments, from all the Fair-ones of the provinces.

Whoever enjoys her constant society, no apprehension of any ill can assail him.—The Queen of soft and winning mind and manners, with her fair branching tresses flowing in ringlets.

Her side like alabaster, and her neck like the swan, and her countenance like the Sun in summer. How blest is it for him who is promised, as riches, to be united to her, the branch of fair curling tendrils.

Sweet and pleasant is your lovely conversation!—bright and sparkling your blue eyes! and every day do I hear all tongues declare your praises, and how gracefully your bright tresses wave down your neck!

I say to the Maid of youthful mildness, that her voice and her converse are sweeter than the songs of the birds! There is no delight or charm that imagination can conceive but what is found ever attendant on Gracey.

Her teeth arranged in beautiful order, and her locks flowing in soft waving curls! But though it delights me to sing of thy charms, I must quit my theme!—With a sincere heart I fill to thy health!

The reader will easily perceive that in this literal translation, I have not sought for elegance of expression, my only object being to put it in his power to judge how closely my version has adhered to my original. [*Brooke's note.*]

Blest is the young whom fav'ring fates ordain
The treasure of her love, and charms to gain!
The fragrant branch, with curling tendrils bound,
With breathing odours – blooming beauty crown'd.

Sweet is the cheer her sprightly wit supplies!
Bright is the sparkling azure of her eyes!
Soft o'er her neck her lovely tresses flow!
Warm in her praise the tongues of rapture glow!

Her's is the voice – tun'd by harmonious Love,
Soft as the Songs that warble through the grove!
Oh! sweeter joys her converse can impart!
Sweet to the *sense*, and grateful to the *heart*!

Gay pleasures dance where'er her foot-steps bend;
And smiles and rapture round the fair attend:
Wit forms her speech, and Wisdom fills her mind,
And *sight* and *soul* in their object find.

Her pearly teeth, in beauteous order plac'd;
Her neck with bright, and curling tresses grac'd: –
But ah, so fair! – in wit and charms supreme,
Unequal Song must quit its darling theme.

Here break I off; – let sparkling goblets flow,
And my full heart its cordial wishes show:
To her dear health this friendly draught I pour,
Long be her life, and blest its every hour! –

GEORGE OGLE (?1740/42-1814)

Like his father, George Ogle the Elder (1704-1746), who was a poet, translator and engraver, George Ogle was born in Co. Wexford. Himself a poet, song writer and politician, he represented Wexford from 1768 to 1796 and Dublin from 1798 to 1800 in the Irish parliament. A Colonel in the Volunteers in 1782, he strongly supported legislative independence for Ireland. After the Union he represented Dublin in the Westminster parliament from 1801 to 1804. His poetry is uncollected but several of his popular songs are included in *Popular Songs of Ireland*, ed. T. Crofton Croker (1839).

Mailigh Mo Stór

[My Darling Molly]

As down by Banna's banks I strayed,
   One evening in May,
The little birds with blithest notes,
   Made vocal every spray;
They sung their little notes of love,
   They sung them o'er and o'er.
Ah! grádh mo chroídhe, mo cailín og,
   'Si Mailligh mo stór.

The daisy pied, and all the sweets
   The dawn of Nature yields –
The primrose pale, and violet blue,
   Lay scattered o'er the fields;
Such fragrance in the bosom lies
   Of her whom I adore.
Ah! grádh mo chroídhe, mo cailín og,
   'Si Mailligh mo stór.

I laid me down upon a bank,
   Bewailing my sad fate,
That doomed me thus the slave of love
   And cruel Molly's hate;
How can she break the honest heart
   That wears her in its core?
Ah! grádh mo chroídhe, mo cailín og,
   'Si Mailligh mo stór.

You said you loved me, Molly dear!
   Ah! why did I believe?
Yet who could think such tender words
   Were meant but to deceive?
That love was all I asked on earth –
   Nay, heaven could give no more.
Ah! grádh mo chroídhe, mo cailín og,
   'Si Mailligh mo stór.

Oh! had I all the flocks that graze
   On yonder yellow hill,

Or lowed for me the numerous herds
    That yon green pasture fill –
With her I love I'd gladly share
    My kine and fleecy store
Ah! grádh mo chroídhe, mo cailín og,
    'Si Mailligh mo stór.

Two turtle-doves, above my head,
    Sat courting on a bough;
I envied them their happiness,
    To see them bill and coo.
Such fondness once for me was shewn,
    But now, alas! 'tis o'er!
Ah! grádh mo chroídhe, mo cailín og,
    'Si Mailligh mo stór.

Then fare thee well, my Molly dear!
    Thy loss I e'er shall moan,
While life remains in my poor heart,
    'Twill beat for thee alone:
Though thou art false, may heaven on thee
    Its choicest blessings pour.
Ah! grádh mo chroídhe, mo cailín og,
    'Si Mailligh mo stór.

RICHARD LOVELL EDGEWORTH (1744-1817)

Edgeworth was outspoken, outgoing, progressive and practical, enjoying the friendship of Humphry Davy, Josiah Wedgewood and Thomas Day (like Edgeworth an admirer of Rousseau, he also wrote *The History of Sandford and Merton* for children – 3 vols, 1738-9). He wrote directly and described some of his numerous inventions and his feats of engineering well. They included hauling a thirty-foot steeple into place with balancing weights from the inside of a church tower; he invented a 'tellograph', an early form of semaphore; he argued that carriages should be sprung to ease the burden on the horses that drew them; his turnip cutter eased the burden of work for his farm labourers; he developed practical theories about draining bogs and making roads. In fact practicability was one of the main virtues he exhibited in running his estate. His *Memoirs*, from which the following extracts are taken, relate largely to his experiences in the eighteenth century. They were concluded by his daughter Maria who inherited his narrative gifts.

From *Memoirs of Richard Lovell Edgeworth*
(1820)

[*THE EFFECT OF EARLY READING*]

...When I was about five years old, I was taught my alphabet: I remember well the appearance of my hornbook; and once I was beaten for not knowing the word *instep*. I recollect as distinctly as if it happened yesterday, that I had never before heard or spelled that word. This unjust chastisement put me back a little in my learning; but as the injustice was afterwards discovered, it saved me in succeeding times from all violence from my teachers. My mother then taught me to read herself. I lent my little soul to the business, and I read fluently before I was six years old. The first books that were put into my hands were the Old Testament, and Æsop's Fables. Æsop's Fables were scarcely intelligible to me: the frogs and their kings, – the fox and the bunch of grapes, confused my understanding; and the satyr and the traveller appeared to me absolute nonsense. I understood the lion and the mouse, and was charmed with the generous conduct of the one, and with the gratitude of the other. When I began to read the Old Testament, the creation made a great impression upon my mind: I personified the Deity, as is usual with ignorance. A particular part of my father's garden was paradise: my imagination represented Adam as walking in this garden; and the whole history became a drama in my mind. I pitied Adam, was angry with Eve, and I most cordially hated the devil. What was meant by Adam's bruising the serpent's head, I could not comprehend, and I frequently asked for explanations. The history of Joseph and his brethren I perfectly understood; it seized fast hold of my imagination, and of my feelings. I admired and loved Joseph with enthusiasm; and I believe, that the impression, which this history made upon my mind, continued for many years to have an influence upon my conduct.

[AN UNUSUAL CURE]

...At the time which I speak of, most families in Ireland dined at three or four o'clock, but Lord Trimblestone never dined till seven or eight in the evening. This arrangement gave an air of mystery to his Lordship's domestic economy, which added perhaps to the influence of his real skill over the minds of his patients. My mother was much struck with the beauty and grace of Lady Trimblestone. She had, I believe, passed the meridian of life: but the glare of a profusion of light; the fine brilliant pendants in her ears; the unchanged colour of her beautiful hair, which fell exuberantly in ringlets upon her neck, – contrary to the fashion of that day, which required that a lady's hair should be powdered and rolled over a cylinder of black silk stuffed with wool, so as to draw the hair almost out by the roots from the forehead; – and above all, an air of ease and dignity which she had acquired in France; made her, at least to the eyes of my mother, a most charming and interesting person. Lord Trimblestone command-ed attention from his high character in the world for medical knowl-edge and philanthropy. They soon set their stranger guests at ease, and both of them amused their auditors with accounts of remarkable patients, diseases, and cures, which they had witnessed. One in par-ticular I will relate.

A very delicate lady of fashion, who had, till her beauty began to decay, been flattered egregiously by one sex, and vehemently envied by the other, began to feel as years approached, that she was shrink-ing into nobody. Disappointment produces ennui, and ennui disease; a train of nervous symptoms succeeded each other with alarming rapidity, and after the advice and the consultations of all the physi-cians in Ireland, and the correspondence of the most eminent in England, this poor lady had recourse in the last resort to Lord Trimblestone. He declined interfering, he hesitated; but at last, after much intercession, he consented to hear the lady's complaints, and to endeavour to effect her cure: this concession was made upon a posi-tive stipulation, that the patient should remain three weeks in his house, without any attendants but those of his own family, and that her friends should give her up entirely to his management. – The case was desperate, and any terms must be submitted to, where there was a prospect of relief. The lady went to Trimblestone, was received with the greatest attention and politeness. Instead of a grave and forbid-ding physician, her host, she found, was a man of most agreeable manners. Lady Trimblestone did every thing in her power to entertain her guest, and for two or three days the demon of ennui was banished. At length the lady's vapours returned; every thing appeared changed. Melancholy brought on a return of alarming nervous complaints – convulsions of the limbs – perversion of the understanding – a horror of society; in short, all the complaints that are to be met with in an advertisement enumerating the miseries of a nervous patient. In the midst of one of her most violent fits, four mutes, dressed in white, entered her apartment; slowly approaching, they took her without violence in their arms, and without giving her time to recollect herself, conveyed her into a distant chamber hung with black, and lighted with green tapers. From the ceiling, which was of a considerable height, a swing was suspended, in which she was placed by the mutes, so as to be seated at some distance from the ground. One of the mutes set the swing in motion; and as it approached one end of the room, she was opposed by a grim menacing figure armed with a huge rod of birch. When she looked behind her, she saw a similar figure at the other end of the room, armed in the same manner. The terror, notwithstanding the strange circumstances which surrounded her, was not of that sort which threatens life; but every instant there was an immediate hazard of bodily pain. After some time, the mutes appeared again, with great composure took the lady out of the swing, and conducted her to her apartment. When she had reposed some time, a servant came to inform her, that tea was ready. Fear of what might be the consequences of a refusal prevented her from declining to appear. No notice was taken of what had happened, and the evening and the next day passed without any attack of her disorder. On the third day the vapours returned – the mutes reappeared – the menacing flagellants again affrighted her, and again she enjoyed a remission of her complaints. By degrees the fits of her disorder became less frequent, the ministration of her tormentors less necessary, and in time, the habits of hypochondriacism were so often interrupted, and such a new series of ideas was introduced into her mind, that she recovered perfect health, and preserved to the end of her life sincere gratitude for her adventurous physician....

[USING HIS HANDS]

...From the remote situation in which we lived, within reach but of few gentry, we had leisure to profit by the excellent library at Brereton Hall. For my own amusement also I procured a few tools, and executed some pieces of machinery, that were indeed more curious than important. I made a clock for the steeple at Brereton; and a chronometer of a singular construction, which I intended to present to the King; not from any peculiar merit, which it possessed as to accuracy, though it was sufficiently accurate for all common purpose; but I thought of presenting it, to add to his Majesty's collection of uncommon clocks and watches, which I had seen at St. James's. It went eight days, shewed the hours, minutes, and seconds on a common dial plate, by common hands, from one common centre; and yet it had no wheels, nor were any of its parts or movements connected by what is technically called *tooth and pinion*.

The power, by which the pendulum was kept in motion, was communicated from the weight, without any friction, except that of small pivots, none of which moved through a space of more than the eight hundredth part of an inch in one second. I mention this as a kind of mechanical paradox; not as a pursuit worthy the attention of any man, who can employ his time in something better than difficult trifles....

[PART OF HIS SON'S EDUCATION IN FRANCE]

[*The boy had been brought up according to Rousseau's precepts, to have 'all the virtues of a child bred in the hut of a savage, and all the knowledge of things which could be aquired by a boy bred in a civilised society'.*]

...In short he [the superior of the Collège des Oratoires] promised not to meddle with my son's religion, and to inform me, if he found that any of his under-masters disobeyed his orders on this subject.

About a month afterwards I paid a visit to the reverend father; he told me, that notwithstanding his injunctions to the contrary, one of the under-masters had endeavoured to teach my son such doctrines, as he thought necessary for his salvation. 'I will tell you,' said the father, 'exactly what passed: Le père Jerome, from the time your son came, had formed the pious design of converting your little gentleman; and for this purpose he had taken particular notice of him, and had from time to time given him bonbons. One day he took your boy between his knees, and began from the beginning of things to teach him what he ought to believe. "My little man," said he, "Did you ever hear of God?"

"Yes."

"You know, that, before he made the world, his spirit brooded over the vast deep, which was a great sea without shores, and *without bottom*. Then he made this world out of earth."

"Where did he find the *earth*?" asked the boy.

"At the bottom of the sea," replied father Jerome.

"But," said the boy, "you told me just now, that the sea had no bottom!"

The Superior of the collége des oratoires concluded, 'You may, Sir, I think, be secure, that your son, when capable of making such a reply, is in no great danger of becoming a catholic from the lectures of such profound teachers as these.'

The Superior kept his word with me, and I never had reason to believe, that any farther attempts at conversion were made upon my son....

[*AN EXPERIMENTAL VELOCIPEDE*]

....During my residence at Hare Hatch, another wager was proposed by me among our acquaintance, the purport of which was, that I undertook to find a man, who should, with the assistance of machinery, walk faster than any other person that could be produced. The machinery which I intended to employ was a huge hollow wheel made very light, within side of which, in a barrel of six feet diameter, a man should walk. Whilst he stepped thirty inches, the circumference of the large wheel, or rather wheels, would revolve five feet on the ground; and as the machine was to roll on planks, and on a plane somewhat inclined, when once the *vis inertiæ* of the machine should be overcome, it would carry on the man within it, as fast as he could possibly walk. I had provided means of regulating the motion, so that the wheel should not run away with its master. I had the wheel made, and when it was so nearly completed as to require but a few hours' work to finish it, I went to London for Lord Effingham, to whom I had promised, that he should be present at the first experiment made with it. But the bulk of and extraordinary appearance of my machine had attracted the notice of the country neighbourhood; and taking advantage of my absence, some idle curious persons went to the carpenter I employed, who lived on Hare Hatch common. From him they obtained the great wheel, which had been left by me in his care. It was not finished. I had not yet furnished it with the means of stopping or moderating its motion. A young lad got into it, his companions launched it on a path which led gently down hill towards a very steep chalk-pit. This pit was at such a distance, as to be out of their thoughts, when they set the wheel in motion. On it ran. The lad within-inside plied his legs with all his might. The spectators, who at first stood still to behold the operation, were soon alarmed by the shouts of their companion, who perceived his danger. The vehicle became quite ungovernable, the velocity increased as it ran down hill. Fortunately the boy contrived to jump from his rolling prison before it reached the chalk-pit; but the wheel went on with such velocity, as to outstrip its pursuers, and, rolling over the edge of the precipice, it was dashed to pieces.

The next day, when I came to look for my machine, intending to try it upon some planks, which had been laid for it, I found to my no small disappointment, that the object of all my labors and my hopes was lying at the bottom of a chalk-pit, broken into a thousand pieces. I could not at that time afford to construct another wheel of this sort, and I cannot therefore determine what might have been the success of my scheme....

[MORE EXPERIMENTS WITH VEHICLES]

...I proceeded to Birmingham. I mentioned that I travelled in a carriage of singular construction. It was a one-wheeled chaise, which I had made for the purpose of going conveniently in narrow roads. It was made fast by shafts to the horse's sides, and was furnished with two weights or counterpoises, that hung below the shafts. The seat was not more than eight and twenty or thirty inches from the ground, in order to bring the centre of gravity of the whole as low as possible. The foot-board turned upon hinges, fastened to the shafts, so that when it met with any obstacle it gave way, and my legs were warned to lift themselves up. In going through water my legs were secured by leathers, which folded up like the sides of bellows; by this means I was pretty safe from wet. On my road to Birmingham I passed through Long-Compton, in Warwickshire, on a Sunday. The people were returning from church, and numbers stopped to gaze at me. There is or was a shallow ford near the town, over which there was a very narrow bridge for horse and foot passengers, but not sufficiently wide for waggons or chaises. Towards this bridge I drove. The people, not perceiving the structure of my one-wheeled vehicle, calling to me with great eagerness to warn me, that the bridge was too narrow for carriages. I had an excellent horse, which went so fast as to give but little time for examination. The louder they called, the faster I drove, and when I had passed the bridge, they shouted after me with surprise. I got on to Shipston upon Stour; but, before I had dined there, I found that my fame had overtaken me. My carriage was put into a coach-house, so that those who came from Long-Compton, not see-ing it, did not recognise me; I therefore had an opportunity of hear-ing all the exaggerations and strange conjectures, which were made by those who related my passage over the narrow bridge. There were posts on the bridge, to prevent, as I suppose, more than one horse-man from passing at once. Some of the spectators asserted, that my carriage had gone over these posts; others said that it had not *wheels*, which was indeed literally true; but they meant to say that it was with-out any wheel. Some were sure that no carriage ever went so fast; and all agreed, that at the end of the bridge, where the floods had laid the road for some way under water, my carriage swam on the surface of the water.

As I am on the subject of carriages, I shall mention a sailing car-riage, that I tried on this common. The carriage was light, steady, and ran with amazing velocity. One day, when I was preparing for a sail in it, with my friend and school-fellow, Mr. William Foster, my wheel-boat escaped from its moorings, just as we were going to step on board. With the utmost difficulty I overtook it, and as I saw three or four stage-coaches on the road, and feared that this sailing chariot might frighten their horses, I, at the hazard of my life, got into my car-riage while it was under full sail, and then, at a favorable part of the road, I used the means I had of guiding it easily out of the way. But the sense of the mischief which must have ensued, if I had not suc-ceeded in getting into the machine at the proper place, and stopping it at the right moment, was so strong, as to deter me from trying any more experiments on this carriage in such a dangerous place.

Such should never be attempted except on a large common, *at a distance from a high road*. It may not however be amiss to suggest, that upon a long extent of iron rail-way, in an open country, carriages properly constructed might make profitable voyages from time to time with sails instead of horses; for though a constant or regular intercourse could not be thus carried on, yet goods of a certain sort, that are saleable at any time, might be stored till wind and weather were favorable....

MARIA EDGEWORTH (1767-1849) AND
RICHARD LOVELL EDGEWORTH (1744-1817)

Maria Edgeworth collaborated with her father on several books. These excerpts are from their *Practical Education* (2 vols, 1798); they also wrote *Essays on Professional Education* (1809) and the *Essay on Irish Bulls* (1802). Maria completed

the *Memoirs of Richard Lovell Edgeworth* (1820) after his death. He encouraged
Maria's writing – she showed rough outlines of her novels to him and he comment-
ed on them, making sure she finished them. It was a fruitful partnership: he also
taught her estate management – she was the eldest of his twenty-two children, the
result of four marriages. These children had to be educated, and Edgeworth was
interested in education, not least in Rousseau's theories. He had many other interests,
engineering perhaps the main one, which led to his inventing self-winding clocks, a
turnip cutter, a land-measurer, a velocipede and a telegraph – an early form of semaphore signalling. He improved his estate, Edgeworthstown in Co. Longford, building roads and draining bogs. His political views were liberal; he supported Catholic
Emancipation and voted against the Union.

From *Practical Education*

(1798)

MEMORY AND INVENTION.

Before we bestow many years of time and pains upon any object, it
may be prudent to afford a few minutes previously to ascertain its precise value. Many persons have a vague idea of the great value of memory, and, without analysing their opinion, they resolve to cultivate the
memories of their children, as much, and as soon as possible. So far
from having determined the value of this talent, we shall find that it
will be difficult to give a popular definition of a good memory. Some
people call that a good memory which retains the greatest number of
ideas for the longest time. Others prefer a recollective, to a retentive
memory, and value not so much the number, as the selection of facts;
not so much the mass, or even the antiquity, of accumulated treasure,
as the power of producing current specie for immediate use. –
Memory is sometimes spoken of as if it were a faculty admirable in
itself, without any union with the other powers of the mind. Amongst
those who allow that memory has no independent claim to regard,
there are yet many who believe, that a superior degree of it is essential to the successful exercise of the higher faculties, such as judgment
and invention. The degree in which it is useful to those powers, has
not, however, been determined. Those who are governed in their
opinions by precedent and authority, can produce many learned
names, to prove that memory was held in the highest estimation
amongst the great men of antiquity; it was cultivated with much anxiety in their public institutions, and in their private education. But
there were many circumstances which formerly contributed to make

a great memory essential to a great man. In civil and military employments, among the ancients, it was in a high degree requisite. Generals
were expected to know by heart the names of the soldiers in their
armies; demagogues, who hoped to please the people, were expected
to know the names of all their fellow citizens.[1] Orators, who did not
speak extempore, were obliged to get their long orations by rote.
Those who studied science or philosophy were obliged to cultivate
their memory with incessant care, because, if they frequented the
schools for instruction, they treasured up the sayings of the masters of
different sects, and learned their doctrines only by oral instruction.
Manuscripts were frequently got by heart by those who were eager to
secure the knowledge they contained, and who had not opportunities
of recurring to the originals. It is not surprising, therefore, that memory, to which so much was trusted, should have been held in such high
esteem.

At the revival of literature in Europe, before the discovery of the
art of printing it was scarcely possible to make any progress in the literature of the age, without possessing a retentive memory. A man who
had read a few manuscripts, and could repeat them, was a wonder
and a treasure; he could travel from place to place, and live by his
learning; he was a circulating library to a nation, and the more books
he could carry in his head the better; he was certain of an admiring
audience if he could repeat what Aristotle or Saint Jerome had written; and he had far more encouragement to engrave the words of others on his memory, than to invent or judge for himself.

In the twelfth century, above six hundred scholars assembled in the
forests of Champagne to hear the lectures of the learned Abeillard;[1]
they made themselves huts of the boughs of trees, and in this new academic grove were satisfied to go almost without the necessaries of life.
In the specimens of Abeillard's composition, which are handed down
to us, we may discover proofs of his having been vain of a surprising
memory; it seems to have been the superior faculty of his mind; his six
hundred pupils could carry away with them only so much of his learning as they could get by heart during his course of lectures; and he who

---

1 *Generals ... fellow citizens*: V. Plutarch, Quintilian. [*Edgeworths' note.*]
2 *Abeillard*: Pierre Abélard or Abailard (1079–1142), a lecturer at the schools of Ste Geneviève
and Notre Dame at Paris, the founder of scholastic theology. He secretly married his pupil
Héloïse; when her Uncle Canon Fulbert found out, Abélard was castrated at his instigation.
Héloïse entered a convent, retaining her devotion for Abélard; she died in 1163, and was buried
beside him at the oratory of the Paraclete, which he had founded. They were later buried in the
same tomb at Père Lachaise in Paris.

had the best memory must have been best paid for his journey.

The art of printing, by multiplying copies so as to put them within the easy reference of all classes of people, has lowered the value of this species of retentive memory. It is better to refer to the book itself, than to the man who has read the book. Knowledge is now ready classed for use, and it is safely stored up in the great common-place books of public libraries. A man of literature need not encumber his memory with whole passages from the author he wants to quote; he need only mark down the page, and the words are safe....

[BOOKS]

... By watching the turn of mind, and by attending the conversation of children, we may perceive exactly what will suit them in books; and we may preserve the connexion of their ideas without fatiguing their attention. A paragraph read aloud from the newspaper of the day, a passage from any book which parents happen to be reading themselves, will catch the attention of the young people in a family, and will perhaps excite more taste and more curiosity, than could be given by whole volumes read at times when the mind is indolent or intent upon other occupations.

The custom of reading aloud for a great while together is extremely fatiguing to children, and hurtful to their understandings; they learn to read on without the slightest attention or thought; the more fluently they read, the worse it is for them; for their preceptors, whilst words and sentences are pronounced with tolerable emphasis, never seem to suspect that the reader can be tired, or that his mind may be absent from his book. The monotonous tones which are acquired by children, who read a great deal aloud, are extremely disagreeable, and the habit cannot easily be broken; we may observe that children who have not acquired bad customs always read as they speak, when they understand what they read; but the moment they come to any sentences which they do not comprehend, their voices alter, and they read with hesitation, or with false emphasis; to these signals a preceptor should always attend, and the passage should be explained before the pupil is taught to read it in a musical tone, or with the proper emphasis; thus children should be taught to read by the understanding, and not merely by the ear. Dialogues, dramas, and well-written narratives, they always read *well*, and these should be their exercises in the art of reading; they should be allowed to put down the book as soon as they are tired; but an attentive tutor will perceive when they ought to be stopped, *before* the utmost point of fatigue. We have heard a boy of nine years old, who had never been taught elocution by any reading-master, read simple, pathetic passages, and natural dialogues in 'Evenings at Home,' in a manner which would have made even Sterne's critic forget his stop-watch.[1] By reading much at a time, it is true, that a great number of books are run through in a few years; but this is not at all our object; on the contrary, our greatest difficulty has been to find a sufficient number of books fit for children to read. If they early acquire a strong taste for literature, no matter how few authors they may have perused. We have often heard young people exclaim, 'I'm glad I have not read such a book. I have "a great pleasure to come!"' Is not this better than to see a child yawn over a work, and count the number of tiresome pages, whilst he says, 'I shall have got through this book by and by; and what must I read when I have done this? I believe I never shall have read all I am to read! What a number of tiresome books there are in the world! I wonder what can be the reason that I must read them all. If I were but allowed to skip the pages that I don't understand, I should be much happier; for when I come to any thing entertaining in a book, I can keep myself awake, and then I like reading as well as any body does.'

Far from forbidding to skip the incomprehensible pages, or to close the tiresome volume, we should exhort our pupils never to read one single page that tires, or that they do not fully understand. We need not fear, that, because an excellent book is not interesting at one period of education, it should not become interesting at another; the child is always the best judge of what is suited to his present capacity. If he says, 'Such a book tires me'; the preceptor should never answer with a forbidding, reproachful look, 'I am surprised at that, it is no great proof of your taste; the book, which you say tires you, is written by one of the best authors in the English language.' The boy is sorry for it, but he cannot help it: and he concludes, if he be of a timid temper, that he has no taste for literature, since the best authors in the English language tire him. It is in vain to tell him that the book is 'universally allowed to be very entertaining.'

> If it be not such to me,
> What care I how fine it be![2]

---

1 *stop-watch*: from Laurence Sterne, *Tristram Shandy*, III, xii: 'Admirable grammarian! ... I looked only at the stop-watch – my Lord. – Excellent observer!'
2 *If it ... fine it be*: George Luthes (1588-1667) 'Shall I wasting in Despair' 15-16: 'If she be not so to me, 'What care I how kind she be?'

The more encouraging, and more judicious parent would answer upon a similar occasion, 'You are right not to read what tires you, my dear; and I am glad that you have sense enough to tell me that this book does not entertain you, though it is written by one of the best authors in the English language. We do not think at all the worse of your taste and understanding; we know that the day will come when this book will probably entertain you; put it by till then, I advise you.'

It may be thought that young people, who read only those parts of books which are entertaining, or those which are selected for them, are in danger of learning a taste for variety and desultory habits which may prevent their acquiring accurate knowledge upon any subject; and which may render them incapable of that literary application, without which nothing can be well learned. We hope the candid preceptor will suspend his judgment till we can explain our sentiments upon this subject more fully, when we examine the nature of Invention and Memory.

The secret fear that stimulates parents to compel their children to constant application to certain books arises, from the opinion, that much chronological and historical knowledge must at all events be acquired during a certain number of years. The knowledge of history is thought a necessary accomplishment in one sex, and an essential part of education in the other. We ought, however, to distinguish between that knowledge of history and of chronology which is really useful, and that which is acquired merely for parade. We must call that useful knowledge which enlarges the view of human life, and of human nature; which teaches by the experience of the past, what we may expect in future. To study history as it relates to these objects, the pupil must have acquired much previous knowledge; the habit of reasoning, and the power of combining distant analogies. The works of Hume,[1] of Robertson,[2] Gibbon,[3] or Voltaire,[4] can be properly understood only by well informed and highly cultivated understandings. Enlarged views of policy, some knowledge of the interests of commerce, of the progress and state of civilization, and literature in dif-

---

1 *Hume:* David Hume (1711-1776), Scottish philosopher; author of A *Treatise of Human Nature* (1739, 1740), *Essays: Moral and Political* (1741, 1742) and *Philosophical Essays Concerning Human Understanding* (1748).
2 *Robertson:* William Robertson (1721-1793), Scottish historian; author of *History of Scotland* (1759).
3 *Gibbon:* Edward Gibbon (1737-1794), English historian; author of *The History of the Decline and Fall of the Roman Empire* (1776-1788).
4 *Voltaire:* François-Marie Arouet (1694-1778), French writer and individualist. His copious writings include *Lettres philosophiques sur les anglais* (1733), *Candide (1759),* and the *Dictionaire philosophique* (1764).

ferent countries, are necessary to whoever studies these authors with real advantage. Without these, the finest sense and the finest writing must be utterly thrown away upon the reader. Children, consequently, under the name of fashionable histories, often read what to them is absolute nonsense: they have very little motive for the study of history, and all that we can say to keep alive their interest, amounts to the common argument, 'that such information will be useful to them hereafter, when they hear history mentioned in conversation.'

Some people imagine, that the memory resembles a storehouse, in which we should early lay up facts; and they assert, that however useless these may appear at the time when they are laid up, they will afterwards be ready for service at our summons. One allusion may be fairly answered by another, since it is impossible to oppose allusion by reasoning. In accumulating facts, as in amassing riches, people often begin by believing that they value wealth only for the use they shall make of it; but it often happens, that during the course of their labours they learn habitually to set a value upon the coin itself, and they grow avaricious of that which they are sensible has little intrinsic value. Young people, who have accumulated a vast number of facts, and names, and dates, perhaps intended originally to make some good use of their treasure; but they frequently forgot their laudable intentions, and conclude by contenting themselves with the display of their nominal wealth. Pedants and misers forget the real use of wealth and knowledge; and they accumulate, without rendering what they acquire useful to themselves or to others.

A number of facts are often stored in the mind, which lie there useless, because they cannot be found at the moment when they are wanted. It is not sufficient in education to store up knowledge; it is essential to arrange facts so that they shall be ready for use, as materials for the imagination, or the judgment, to select and combine. The power of retentive memory is exercised too much, the faculty of recollective memory is exercised too little, by the common modes of education....

HENRY GRATTAN (1746-1820)

A politician, born in Dublin, educated at Trinity College, Dublin and called to the Irish bar in 1772, he entered the Irish parliament in 1773. He carried the amendment for Irish free trade in 1779 and moved addresses in favour of Irish legislative independence unsuccessfully in 1780-81 and successfully in 1782. On his declining office the Irish Parliament voted him £50,000 in appreciation of his efforts. He supported Catholic relief, seceded from the Irish House of Commons in 1797 but returned to oppose the Union in 1800. He then sat in the Parliament of Westminster from 1805 to 1820, supporting proposals for Catholic emancipation.

The Irish Parliament from 1782 to 1800 was generally known as Grattan's Parliament though historians now think Grattan's contemporaries and their predecessors overestimated his achievement. His speeches were most effective and were collected by his son in the *Life and Times of Rt. Hon. Henry Grattan* (1839-1846). The most famous of them is included here. It was on legislative independence and was delivered in the Irish House of Commons in Dublin on 16 April 1782.

Grattan's Speech on Legislative Independence (1782)

Mr. GRATTAN rose, and spoke as follows:

I am now to address a free people: ages have passed away, and this is the first moment in which you could be distinguished by that appellation.

I have spoken on the subject of your liberty so often, that I have nothing to add, and have only to admire by what heaven-directed steps you have proceeded until the whole faculty of the nation is braced up to the act of her own deliverance.

I found Ireland on her knees, I watched over her with an eternal solicitude; I have traced her progress from injuries to arms, and from arms to liberty. Spirit of Swift! spirit of Molyneux! your genius has prevailed! Ireland is now a nation! in that new character I hail her! and bowing to her august presence, I say, *Esto perpetua!*[1]

She is no longer a wretched colony, returning thanks to her governor for his rapine, and to her king for his oppression; nor is she now a squabbling, fretful sectary, perplexing her little wits, and firing her furious statutes with bigotry, sophistry, disabilities, and death, to transmit to posterity insignificance and war.

Look to the rest of Europe, and contemplate yourself, and be satisfied. Holland lives on the memory of past achievement; Sweden has lost her liberty; England has sullied her great name by an attempt to enslave her colonies. You are the only people, – you, of the nations in Europe, are now the only people who excite admiration, and in your present conduct you not only exceed the present generation, but you equal the past. I am not afraid to turn back and look antiquity in the face: the revolution, – that great event, whether you call it ancient or modern I know not, was tarnished with bigotry: the great deliverer

---

1 *Esto perpetua*: 'Long may she live'.

(for such I must ever call the Prince of Nassau)[1] was blemished with oppression; he assented to, he was forced to assent to acts which deprived the Catholics of religious, and all the Irish of civil and commercial rights, though the Irish were the only subjects in these islands who had fought in his defence. But you have sought liberty on her own principle: see the Presbyterians of Bangor petition for the freedom of the Catholics of Munster. You, with difficulties innumerable, with dangers not a few, have done what your ancestors wished, but could not accomplish; and what your posterity may preserve, but will never equal: you have moulded the jarring elements of your country into a nation, and have rivalled those great and ancient commonwealths, whom you were taught to admire, and among whom you are now to be recorded: in this proceeding you had not the advantages that were common to other great countries; no monuments, no trophies, none of those outward and visible signs of greatness, such as inspire mankind and connect the ambition of the age which is coming on with the example of that going off, and forms the descent and concatenation of glory: no; you have not had any great act recorded among all your misfortunes, nor have you one public tomb to assemble the crowd, and speak to the living the language of integrity and freedom.

Your historians did not supply the want of monuments; on the contrary, these narrators of your misfortunes, who should have felt for your wrongs, and have punished your oppressors with oppressions, natural scourges, the moral indignation of history, compromised with public villainy and trembled; they excited your violence, they suppressed your provocation, and wrote in the chain which entrammelled their country. I am come to break that chain, and I congratulate my country, who, without any of the advantages I speak of, going forth as it were with nothing but a stone and a sling, and what oppression could not take away, the favour of Heaven, accomplished her own redemption, and left you nothing to add and every thing to admire.

You want no trophy now; the records of Parliament are the evidence of your glory: I beg to observe, that the deliverance of Ireland has proceeded from her own right hand: I rejoice at it, for had the great requisition of your freedom proceeded from the bounty of England, that great work would have been defective both in renown

---

1 *Prince of Nassau*: William III (1650-1702) born at The Hague, a son of William II of Orange (the House of Orange was a branch of Nassau, a German duchy), landed in England in 1688 and defeated James II at the Battle of the Boyne in 1690.

and security: it was necessary that the soul of the country should have been exalted by the act of her own redemption, and that England should withdraw her claim by operation of treaty, and not of mere grace and condescension; a gratuitous act of parliament, however express, would have been revocable, but the repeal of her claim under operation of treaty is not: in that case, the legislature is put in covenant, and bound by the law of nations, the only law that can legally bind Parliament: never did this country stand so high; England and Ireland treat *ex æquo*. Ireland transmits to the King her claim of right, and requires of the Parliament of England the repeal of her claim of power, which repeal the English Parliament is to make under the force of a treaty which depends on the law of nations, – a law which cannot be repealed by the Parliament of England.

I rejoice that the people are a party to this treaty, because they are bound to preserve it. There is not a man of forty shillings freehold that is not associated in this our claim of right, and bound to die in its defence; cities, counties, associations, Protestants and Catholics; it seems as if the people had joined in one great national sacrament; a flame has descended from heaven on the intellect of Ireland, plays round her head, and encompasses her understanding with a consecrated glory.

There are some who think, and a few who declare, that the associations to which I refer are illegal: come, then, let us try the charge, and state the grievance. And, first, I ask, What were the grievances? an army imposed on us by another country, that army rendered perpetual; the privy-council of both countries made a part of our legislature; our legislature deprived of its originating and propounding power; another country exercising over us supreme legislative authority; that country disposing of our property by its judgments, and prohibiting our trade by its statutes: these were not grievances, but spoliations, which left you nothing. When you contended against them, you contended for the whole of your condition; when the minister asked, by what right? we refer him to our Maker: we sought our privileges by the right which we have to defend our property against a robber, our life against a murderer, our country against an invader, whether coming with civil or military force, – a foreign army, or a foreign legislature. This is a case that wants no precedent; the *revolution* wanted no precedent: for such things arrive to reform a course of bad precedents, and, instead of being founded on precedent, become such: the gazing world, whom they come to save, begins by doubt and concludes by worship. Let other nations be deceived by the sophistry of courts. Ireland has studied politics in the lair of oppression, and, taught by suffering, comprehends the rights of subjects and the duty of kings. Let other nations imagine that subjects are made for the monarch, but we conceive that kings, and parliaments, like kings, are made for the subjects. The House of Commons, honourable and right honourable as it may be; the Lords, noble and illustrious as we pronounce them, are not original but derivative. Session after session they move their periodical orbit about the source of their being, the nation; even the King's Majesty must fulfil his due and tributary course round that great luminary; and created by its beam, and upheld by its attraction, must incline to that light, or go out of the system.

Ministers, we mean the ministers who have gone out, (I rely on the good intentions of the present), former ministers, I say, have put questions to us; we beg to put questions to them. They desired to know by what authority this nation has acted. This nation desires to know by what authority they have acted. By what authority did Government enforce the articles of war? By what authority does Government establish the post-office? By what authority are our merchants bound by the charter of the East India Company? By what authority has Ireland, for near one hundred years been deprived of her export trade? By what authority are her peers deprived of their judicature? By what authority has that judicature been transferred to the peers of Great Britain, and our property in its last resort referred to the decision of a non-resident, unauthorised, and unconstitutional tribunal? Will ministers say it was the authority of the British Parliament? On what ground, then, do they place the question between the Government on one side, and the volunteer on the other? According to their own statement, the government has been occupied in superseding the lawgiver of the country; and the volunteers are here to restore him. The Government has contended for the usurpation, and the people for the laws. His Majesty's late ministers imagined they had quelled the country when they had bought the newspapers; and they represented us as wild men, and our cause as visionary; and they pensioned a set of wretches to abuse both: but we took little account of them or their proceedings, and we waited and we watched, and we moved, as it were, on our native hills, with the minor remains of our parliamentary army, until that minority became Ireland. Let those ministers now go home, and congratulate their king on the redemption of his people. Did you imagine that those little parties whom three years ago you beheld in awkward squads parading in the streets, should have now arrived to such distinction and effect? What was the cause; for it was not the sword of the volunteer, nor his muster, nor his spirit, nor his promptitude to put down accidental disturbance or public disorder, nor his own unblamed and distinguished deportment. This was much; but there was more than this: the upper orders, the property, and the abilities of the country, formed with the volunteer; and the volunteer had sense enough to obey them. This united the Protestant with the Catholic, and the landed proprietor with the people. There was still more than this; there was a continence which confined the corps to limited and legitimate objects; there was a principle which preserved the corps from adultery with French politics; there was a good taste which guarded the corps from the affectation of such folly: this, all this, made them bold; for it kept them innocent, it kept them rational: no vulgar rant against England; no mysterious admiration of France; no crime to conceal, no folly to be ashamed of. They were what they professed to be; and that was nothing less than the society asserting her liberty, according to the frame of the British constitution, her inheritance to be enjoyed in perpetual connection with the British empire.

I do not mean to say that there were not divers violent and unseemly resolutions; the immensity of the means was inseparable from the excess.

Such are the great works of nature: such is the sea; but, like the sea, the waste and excess were lost in the advantage: and now, having given a parliament to the people, the volunteers will, I doubt not, leave the people to Parliament, and thus close, specifically and majestically, a great work, which will place them above censure and above panegyric. These associations, like other institutions, will perish: they will perish with the occasion that gave them being, and the gratitude of their country will write their epitaph, and say, 'This phenomenon, the departed volunteer, justified only by the occasion, the birth of spirit and grievances, with some alloy of public evil, did more public good to Ireland than all her institutions; he restored the liberties of his country, and thus from the grave he answers his enemies.' Connected by freedom as well as by allegiance, the two nations, Great Britain and Ireland, form a constitutional confederacy as well as one empire; the crown is one link, the constitution another; and, in my mind, the latter link is the most powerful.

You can get a king any where, but England is the only country with whom you can participate a free constitution. This makes England your natural connexion, and her king your natural as well as your legal sovereign: this is a connexion, not as Lord Coke[1] has idly said,

---

1 *Coke*: Sir Edward Coke (1552–1634), known for his eleven volumes of *Reports* (1600–1615) and his *Institutes* (1628–1644). He claimed that the history of the Common Law stretched back before the Conquest of 1066.

not as Judge Blackstone[1] has foolishly said, not as other judges have ignorantly said, by conquest; but as Molyneux[2] has said, and as I now say, by compact; and that compact is a free constitution. Suffer me now to state some of the things essential to that free constitution; they are as follows: the independency of the Irish Parliament; the exclusion of the British Parliament from any authority in this realm; the restoration of the Irish judicature, and the exclusion of that of Great Britain. As to the perpetual mutiny bill, it must be more than limited; it must be effaced; that bill must fall, or the constitution cannot stand; that bill was originally limited by this House to two years, and it returned from England without the clause of limitation. What? a bill making the army independent of Parliament, and perpetual! I protested against it then, I have struggled with it since, and I am now come to destroy this great enemy of my country. The perpetual mutiny bill must vanish out of the statute book; the excellent tract of Molyneux was burned; it was not answered; and its flame illumined posterity. This evil paper shall be burned, but burned like a felon, that its execution may be a peace-offering to the people, and that a declaration of right may be planted on its guilty ashes; a new mutiny-bill must be formed after the manner of England, and a declaration of right put in the front of it.

As to the legislative powers of the Privy Councils, I conceive them to be utterly inadmissible against the constitution, against the privileges of Parliament, and against the dignity of the realm. Do not imagine such power to be theoretical; it is in a very high degree a practical evil. I have here an inventory of bills altered and injured by the interference of the Privy Councils; money bills originated by them, protests by the Crown in support of those money bills, prorogation following these protests. I have here a mutiny bill of 1780, altered by the Council, and made perpetual; a Catholic bill in 1778, where the Council struck out the clause repealing the test act; a militia bill, where the Council struck out the compulsory clause requiring the Crown to proceed to form a militia, and left it optional to His Majesty's minister whether there should be a militia, in Ireland. I have

---

1 *Blackstone*: Sir William Blackstone (1723–1780), the Vinerian Professor of Law at Oxford (1758), famed for his *Commentaries on the Laws of England* (4 vols, 1765–1769). He argued that civil society was formed 'sometimes by compulsion and conquest', and that the Common law preceded the Norman Conquest.
2 Molyneux: William Molyneux (1656–1698), a scientist, inventor and writer on politics. A founder of the Dublin Philosophical Society, he wrote *The Case of Ireland's being Bound by Acts of Parliament in England, Stated* (1698), an influential defence of the autonomy of the Irish parliament.

the money bill of 1775, where the Council struck out the clause enabling His Majesty to take a part of our troops for general service, and left it to the minister to withdraw the forces against act of parliament. I have to state the altered money bill of 1771, the altered money bill of 1775, the altered money bill of 1780; the day would expire before I could recount their ill-doings. I will never consent to have men (God knows whom), ecclesiastics, &c. &c., men unknown to the constitution of Parliament, and only known to the minister, who has breathed into their nostrils an unconstitutional existence, steal to their dark divan to do mischief and make nonsense of bills, which their Lordships, the House of Lords, or we, the House of Commons, have thought good and fit for the people. No; those men have no legislative qualifications; they shall have no legislative power.

1st. The repeal of the perpetual mutiny bill, and the dependency of the Irish army on the Irish Parliament.

2nd· The abolition of the legislative power of the Council.

3rd. The abrogation of the claim of England to make law for Ireland.

4th. The exclusion of the English House of Peers, and of the English King's Bench, from any judicial authority in this realm.

5th. The restoration of the Irish Peers to their final judicature. The independency of the Irish Parliament in its sole and exclusive legislature.

These are my terms. I will take nothing from the Crown.

JOHN O'KEEFFE (1747-1833)

Born in Dublin, where he was educated by a Jesuit, he studied painting at the Royal Dublin Society's schools as a pupil of Robert West before spending two years in London. In 1764 he returned to Dublin to act in the Smock Alley Theatre. He wrote many fashionable comedies, some of them including Irish characters and material, among them *Wild Oats* (1791), his most successful play. He also wrote farces, comic operas and other entertainments as well as *Recollections* (2 vols, 1826). His eyesight deteriorated and he became blind by 1800. The poem here was included in his *The Agreeable Surprise* (1781).

Amo, Amas, I Love a Lass

Amo, Amas,
I love a lass,
As a cedar tall and slender!
Sweet cowslips' grace

Is her Nominative Case,
And she's of the Feminine Gender.
Rorum, corum, sunt Divorum!
Harum scarum Divo!
Tag rag, merry derry, periwig and hatband,
Hic, hac, horum Genetivo!

Can I decline
A Nymph divine?
Her voice as a flute is *dulcis*!
Her *oculi* bright!
Her *manus* white!
And soft, when I *tacto,* her pulse is!

Rorum, corum, sunt Divorum!
Harum scarum Divo!
Tag rag, merry derry, periwig and hatband,
Hic, hac, horum Genetivo!

O, how bella
Is my Puella!
I'll kiss s[ae]culorum!
If I've luck, Sir!
She's my Uxor!
O, dies benedictorum!

Rorum, corum, sunt Divorum!
Harum scarum Divo!
Tag rag, merry derry, periwig and hatband,
Hic, hac, horum Genetivo!

JOHN PHILPOT CURRAN (1750-1817)

Born at Newmarket, Co. Cork and educated at Trinity College, Dublin and the Middle Temple in London, Curran was called to the Bar in 1775 and entered the Irish Parliament in 1783, representing Kilbeggan in Co. Westmeath until 1797 when he resigned in disgust at the corrupt measures being used to bring about the Act of Union. A convivial, witty conversationalist, he achieved oratorical fame in his defences of several members of the United Irishmen, including Hamilton Rowan, the Rev. William Jackson, Dr William Drennan and the Sheares brothers, John and Henry. He became Master of the Rolls, but retired in 1814, moving to London. His verse was uncollected. Here we have included his lyric based on Riocard Bairéad's 'Preab san Ól' and part of his speech defending Archibald Hamilton Rowan.

The Deserter's Lamentation

If sadly thinking, with spirits sinking,
    Could, more than drinking, my cares compose,
A cure for sorrow from sighs I'd borrow,
    And hope to-morrow would end my woes.
But as in wailing there's nought availing,
    And Death unfailing will strike the blow,
Then for that reason, and for a season,
    Let us be merry before we go.

To joy a stranger, a wayworn ranger,
    In ev'ry danger my course I've run;
Now hope all ending, and death befriending,
    His last aid lending, my cares are done.
No more a rover, or hapless lover,
    My griefs are over – my glass runs low;
Then for that reason, and for a season,
    Let us be merry before we go.

Curran's Speech Defending Archibald Hamilton Rowan
(1794)

...I would appeal to what fell from the learned counsel for the crown – that notwithstanding the alliance subsisting for two centuries past between the two countries, the date of liberty in one goes no further back than the year 1782.

If it required additional confirmation, I should state the case of the invaded American, and the subjugated Indian, to prove that the policy of England has ever been, to govern her connexions more as colonies than as allies; and it must be owing to the great spirit indeed of Ireland, if she shall continue free. Rely upon it, she shall ever have to hold her course against an adverse current; rely upon it, if the popular spring does not continue strong and elastic, a short interval of debilitated nerve and broken force will send you down the stream again, and re-consign you to the condition of a province ...

You are living in a country where the Constitution is rightly stated to be only ten years old – where the people have not the ordinary rudiments of education. It is a melancholy story that the lower orders of the people here have less means of being enlightened than the same class of people in any other country. If there be no means left by which public measures can be canvassed, what will be the consequences? Where the Press is free and discussion unrestrained, the mind, by the collision of intercourse, gets rid of its own asperities; a sort of insensible perspiration takes place in the body politic, by which those acrimonies, which would otherwise fester and inflame, are quietly dissolved and dissipated. By now, if any aggregate assembly shall meet, they are censured; if a printer publishes their resolutions, he is punished: rightly, to be sure, in both cases, for it has been lately done. If the people say, let us not create tumult, but meet in delegation, they cannot do it, if they are anxious to promote parliamentary reform in that way, they cannot do it, the law of the last session has for the first time declared such meetings to be a crime.[1]

What then remains? The liberty of the Press *only* – that sacred palladium, which no influence, no power, no minister, no government, which nothing but the depravity, or folly, or corruption of a jury, can ever destroy.[2] And what calamities are the people saved from by having public communication left open to them? I will tell you, gentlemen, what they are saved from and what the government is saved from. I will tell you also to what both are exposed by shutting up that communication. In one case sedition speaks aloud and walks abroad; the demagogue goes forth – the public eye is upon him – he frets his busy hour upon the stage;[3] but soon either weariness or bribe, or punishment, or disappointment, bears him down, or drives him off, and he appears no more. In the other case, how does the work of sedition go forward? Night after night the muffled rebel steals forth in the dark, and casts another brand upon the pile, to which, when the hour of fatal maturity shall arrive, he will apply the torch. If you doubt the horrid consequence of suppressing the effusion even of individual discontent, look to those enslaved countries where the protection of despotism is supposed to be secured by such restraints. Even the person of the despot there is never in safety. Neither the fear of the despot, nor the machinations of the slave, have any slumber – the one anticipating

---

1 *the law of the last sesion ... a crime*: the Convention Act of 1793 declared that assemblies appointed to represent the public or sections of it were unlawful.
2 *The liberty of the Press ... destroy*: here Curran is indirectly referring to governmental attempts to suppress the printing of what it considered seditious material.
3 *he frets ... stage*: Shakespeare, *Macbeth*, V. 5. 25: 'A poor player, that struts and frets his hour upon the stage'.

the moment of peril, the other watching the opportunity of aggression. The fatal crisis is equally a surprise upon both, the decisive instant is precipitated without warning – by folly on the one side, or by frenzy on the other; and there is no notice of the treason till the traitor acts. In those unfortunate countries – one cannot read it without horror – there are officers, whose province it is, to have the water which is to be drunk by their rulers, sealed up in bottles, lest some wretched miscreant should throw poison into the draught.

RICHARD BRINSLEY SHERIDAN (1751-1816)

Born in Dublin, Sheridan was educated there at Samuel Whyte's school and later at Harrow School. In 1770 his family moved to Bath. His father was the actor manager and educationalist Thomas Sheridan*, son of Swift's friend Thomas Sheridan*; his mother was Frances* (*nee* Chamberlaine), a successful novelist and playwright.

Sheridan eloped with Elizabeth Ann Linley, fought two duels over her and entered the Middle Temple while she pursued her successful career as a singer; they married in 1773. His first play, *The Rivals* (1775), has proved lastingly popular; he followed it with *St Patrick's Day* (1775); *The Duenna* (1775), a comic opera; *A Trip to Scarborough* (1776), a version of Vanbrugh's *The Relapse*; *The School for Scandal* (1777), his masterpiece; and *The Critic* (1779).

Sheridan bought Garrick's share in the Drury Lane Theatre in 1776 and owned the theatre by 1779. In 1780 he became an MP, making his parliamentary name by his maiden speech in support of Burke's impeachment of Warren Hastings. He held several offices of state. His personal debts increased because of his expensive way of life. His wife died in 1792; three years later he married Elizabeth Jane Ogle, who was nineteen, committing himself to a large marriage settlement. He was financially ruined when the Drury Lane Theatre, rebuilt by him at the then large cost of £150,000, burned down in 1809. He was excluded from any managerial functions in 1811 and failed to be re-elected MP in 1812, was arrested and imprisoned for debt, his final years miserable – his wife dying of cancer. In his last years he had succeeded in reducing his massive debts almost entirely. An easy-going character, charming, with a wide circle of fashionable and aristocratic friends, including the Prince of Wales, he would have preferred political to literary and dramatic success, though he is now remembered for his sparkling comedies, *The Rivals* and *The School for Scandal*.

Thou Canst Not Boast of Fortune's Store

Thou canst not boast of Fortune's store,
My love, while me they wealthy call:
But I was glad to find thee poor,

For with my heart I'd give thee all.
And then the grateful youth shall own
I loved him for himself alone.

But when his worth my hand shall gain,
No word or look of mine shall show
That I the smallest thought retain
Of what my bounty did bestow:
Yet still his grateful heart shall own
I loved him for himself alone.

Dry Be That Tear

Dry be that tear, my gentlest love,
   Be hushed that struggling sigh:
Nor seasons, day, nor fate shall prove
   More fixed, more true, than I:
Hushed be that sigh, be dry that tear,
Cease boding doubt, cease anxious fear –
                Dry be that tear.

Ask'st thou how long my love shall stay,
   When all that's new is past?
How long? ah! Delia, can I say
   How long my life shall last?
Dry be that tear, be hushed that sigh,
At least I'll love thee till I die –
                Hushed be that sigh.

And does that thought affect thee too,
   The thought of Sylvio's death,
That he who only breath'd for you,
   Must yield that faithful breath?
Hushed be that sigh, be dry that tear,
Nor let us lose our heaven here –
                Dry be that tear.

I Ne'er Could Any Lustre See

I ne'er could any lustre see
In eye that would not look on me;

I ne'er saw nectar on a lip,
But where my own did hope to sip.
Has the maid who seeks my heart
Cheeks of rose, untouched by art?
I will own the colour true,
When yielding blushes add their hue.

Is her hand so soft and pure?
I must press it, to be sure;
Nor can I be certain then,
Till it, grateful, press again.
Must I, with attentive eye,
Watch her heaving bosom sigh?
I will do so, when I see
That heaving bosom sigh for me.

Song

[From *The School for Scandal, Act III*, SCENE III.
The song is sung by Sir Toby Bumper at a convival gathering.]

Here's to the maiden of bashful fifteen;
Here's to the widow of fifty;
Here's to the flaunting extravagant quean.
And here's to the housewife that's thrifty.
Chorus.
Let the toast pass, –
Drink to the lass,
I'll warrant she'll prove an excuse for the glass.

Here's to the charmer whose dimples we prize;
Now to the maid who has none, sir:
Here's to the girl with a pair of blue eyes,
And here's to the nymph with but *one,* sir.
Chorus. Let the toast pass, &c.

Here's to the maid with a bosom of snow;
Now to her that's as brown as a berry:
Here's to the wife with a face full of woe,
And now to the girl that is merry.
Chorus. Let the toast pass, &c.

For let 'em be clumsy, or let 'em be slim,
Young or ancient, I care not a feather;
So fill a pint bumper quite up to the brim,
And let us e'en toast them together.
Chorus. Let the toast pass, &c.

From *The Rivals*

(1775)

ACT I, SCENE II

A Dressing-room in Mrs. MALAPROP's *Lodgings.*
LYDIA *sitting on a sofa, with a book in her hand. –*
LUCY, *as just returned from a message.*

LUCY.   Indeed, Ma'am, I traversed half the town in search of it: –
I don't believe there's a circulating library in Bath I ha'n't
been at.

LYD.   And could not you get 'The Reward of Constancy?'

LUCY.   No, indeed, ma'am.

LYD.   Nor 'The Fatal Connexion?'

LUCY.   No, indeed, ma'am.

LYD.   Nor 'The Mistakes of the Heart?'

LUCY.   Ma'am, as ill-luck would have it, Mr. Bull said Miss Sukey
Saunter had just fetch'd it away.

LYD.   Heigh-ho! Did you inquire for 'The Delicate Distress?'

LUCY.   Or, 'The Memoirs of Lady Woodford?' Yes, indeed, Ma'am.
– I asked everywhere for it; and I might have brought it
from Mr. Frederick's, but Lady Slattern Lounger, who had
just sent it home, had so soiled and dog's-ear'd it, it wa'n't
fit for a christian to read.

LYD.   Heigh-ho! – Yes, I always know when Lady Slattern has
been before me. – She has a most observing thumb; and, I
believe, cherishes her nails for the convenience of making
marginal notes. – Well, child, what *have* you brought me?

LUCY.   Oh! here, Ma'am.
[*Taking books from under her cloak and from her pockets.*]
This is 'The Gordian Knot,' – and this 'Peregrine Pickle.' Here
are 'The Tears of Sensibility' and 'Humphrey Clinker.' This is
'The Memoirs of a Lady of Quality, written by herself,' – and
here the second volume of 'The Sentimental Journey.'

LYD.	Heigh-ho! – What are those books by the glass?
LUCY.	The great one is only '*The Whole Duty of Man*,' where I press a few blonds, Ma'am.
LYD.	Very well – give me the *sal volatile*.
LUCY.	Is it in a blue cover, Ma'am?
LYD.	My smelling-bottle, you simpleton!
LUCY.	Oh, the drops! – here, Ma'am.
LYD.	Hold! – here's some one coming – quick! see who it is.——

[*Exit* LUCY.

Surely I heard my cousin Julia's voice.

Re-enter LUCY.

LUCY.	Lud! Ma'am, here is Miss Melville.
LYD.	Is it possible! —

[*Exit* LUCY.

Enter JULIA.

LYD.	My dearest Julia, how delighted am I! – [*Embrace.*] How unexpected was this happiness!
JUL.	True, Lydia – and our pleasure is the greater; – but what has been the matter? – you were denied to me at first!
LYD.	Ah, Julia, I have a thousand things to tell you! – but first inform me, what has conjur'd you to Bath? – Is Sir Anthony here?
JUL.	He is – we are arrived within this hour – and I suppose he will be here to wait on Mrs. Malaprop as soon as he is dress'd.
LYD.	Then before we are interrupted, let me impart to you some of my distress! – I know your gentle nature will sympathize with me, though your prudence may condemn me! – My letters have inform'd you of my whole connexion with Beverley; – but I have lost him, Julia! – my aunt has discovered our intercourse by a note she intercepted, and has confin'd me ever since! —Yet, would you believe it? she has fallen absolutely in love with a tall Irish baronet she met one night since she has been here, at Lady Macshuffle's rout.
JUL.	You jest, Lydia!
LYD.	No, upon my word. – She really carries on a kind of correspondence with him, under a feigned name though, till she chuses to be known to him; — but it is a *Delia* or a *Celia*, I assure you.

JUL.	Then, surely, she is now more indulgent to her niece.
LYD.	Quite the contrary. Since she has discovered her own frailty, she is become more suspicious of mine. Then I must inform you of another plague! – That odious Acres is to be in Bath to-day; so that I protest I shall be teased out of all spirits!
JUL.	Come, come, Lydia, hope the best – Sir Anthony shall use his interest with Mrs. Malaprop.
LYD.	But you have not heard the worst. Unfortunately I had quarrell'd with my poor Beverley, just before my aunt made the discovery, and I have not seen him since, to make it up.
JUL.	What was his offence?
LYD.	Nothing at all! – But, I don't know how it was, as often as we had been together, we had never had a quarrel! – And, somehow I was afraid he would never give me an opportunity. – So, last Thursday, I wrote a letter to myself, to inform myself that Beverley was at that time paying his addresses to another woman. – I sign'd it *your Friend unknown*, shew'd it to Beverley, charg'd him with his falsehood, put myself in a violent passion, and vow'd I'd never see him more.
JUL.	And you let him depart so, and have not seen him since?
LYD.	'Twas the next day my aunt found the matter out. I intended only to have teased him three days and a half, and now I've lost him for ever.
JUL.	If he is as deserving and sincere as you have represented him to me, he will never give you up so. Yet, consider, Lydia, you tell me he is but an ensign, and you have thirty thousand pounds!
LYD.	But you know I lose most of my fortune, if I marry without my aunt's consent, till of age; and that is what I have determin'd to do, ever since I knew the penalty. – Nor could I love the man, who would wish to wait a day for the alternative.
JUL.	Nay, this is caprice!
LYD.	What, does Julia tax me with caprice? – I thought her lover Faulkland had enured her to it.
JUL.	I do not love even *his* faults.
LYD.	But a-propos – you have sent to him, I suppose?
JUL.	Not yet, upon my word – nor has he the least idea of my being in Bath. – Sir Anthony's resolution was so sudden, I could not inform him of it.

LYD.   Well, Julia, you are your own mistress, (though under the
protection of Sir Anthony) yet have you, for this long year,
been a slave to the caprice, the whim, the jealousy of this
ungrateful Faulkland, who will ever delay assuming the
right of a husband, while you suffer him to be equally
imperious as a lover.

JUL.   Nay, you are wrong entirely. – We were contracted before
my father's death. – *That*, and some consequent embar-
rassments, have delay'd what I know to be my Faulkland's
most ardent wish. – He is too generous to trifle on such a
point. – And for his character, you wrong him there, too.
– No, Lydia, he is too proud, too noble to be jealous; if he
is captious, 'tis without dissembling; if fretful, without
rudeness. – Unus'd to the fopperies of love, he is negligent
of the little duties expected from a lover – but being
unhackney'd in the passion, his affection is ardent and sincere; and as it engrosses his whole soul, he expects every
thought and emotion of his mistress to move in unison
with his. – Yet, though his pride calls for this full return –
his humility makes him undervalue those qualities in him,
which would entitle him to it; and not feeling why he
should be lov'd to the degree he wishes, he still suspects
that he is not lov'd enough. – This temper, I must own, has
cost me many unhappy hours; but I have learn'd to think
myself his debtor, for those imperfections which arise from
the ardour of his attachment.

LYD.   Well, I cannot blame you for defending him. – But tell me
candidly, Julia, had he never sav'd your life, do you think
you should have been attach'd to him as you are? – Believe
me, the rude blast that overset your boat was a prosperous
gale of love to him.

JUL.   Gratitude may have strengthened my attachment to Mr.
Faulkland, but I lov'd him before he had preserv'd me; yet
surely that alone were an obligation sufficient.

LYD.   Obligation! – Why a water spaniel would have done as
much! – Well, I should never think of giving my heart to
a man because he could swim!

JUL.   Come, Lydia, you are too inconsiderate.

LYD.   Nay, I do but jest – – What's here?

Enter LUCY *in a hurry*.

LUCY.   O Ma'am, here is Sir Anthony Absolute just come home with your aunt.

LYD.   They'll not come here. – Lucy, do you watch.

[*Exit* LUCY.

JUL.   Yet I must go. – Sir Anthony does not know I am here, and if we meet, he'll detain me, to shew me the town. – I'll take another opportunity of paying my respects to Mrs. Malaprop, when she shall treat me, as long as she chooses, with her select words so ingeniously *misapplied*, without being *mispronounced*.

Re-enter LUCY.

LUCY.   O Lud! Ma'am, they are both coming up stairs.

LYD.   Well, I'll not detain you, Coz. – Adieu, my dear Julia, I'm sure you are in haste to send to Faulkland. – There – through my room you'll find another stair-case.

JUL.   Adieu! —[*Embrace*.]

[*Exit* JULIA.

LYD.   Here, my dear Lucy, hide these books. Quick, quick – Fling *Peregrine Pickle* under the toilet – throw *Roderick Random* into the closet – put *The Innocent Adultery* into *The Whole Duty of Man* – thrust *Lord Aimworth* under the sopha – cram *Ovid* behind the bolster – there – put *The Man of Feeling* into your pocket – so, so – now lay *Mrs. Chapone* in sight, and leave *Fordyce's Sermons* open on the table.

LUCY.   O burn it, Ma'am! the hair-dresser has torn away as far as *Proper Pride*.

LYD.   Never mind – open at *Sobriety*. – Fling me *Lord Chesterfield's Letters*. – Now for 'em.

[*Exit* LUCY.

Enter Mrs. MALAPROP, *and Sir* ANTHONY ABSOLUTE.

MRS. MAL.   There, Sir Anthony, there sits the deliberate Simpleton, who wants to disgrace her family, and lavish herself on a fellow not worth a shilling!

LYD.   Madam, I thought you once –

MRS. MAL.   You thought, Miss! I don't know any business you have to think at all – thought does not become a young woman. But the point we would request of you is, that you will

	promise to forget this fellow – to illiterate him, I say, quite from your memory.
LYD.	Ah! Madam! our memories are independent of our wills. – It is not so easy to forget.
MRS. MAL.	But I say it is, Miss; there is nothing on earth so easy as to *forget*, if a person chooses to set about it. – I'm sure I have as much forgot your poor dear uncle as if he had never existed – and I thought it my duty so to do; and let me tell you, Lydia, these violent memories don't become a young woman.
SIR ANTH.	Why sure she won't pretend to remember what she's order'd not! – aye, this comes of her reading!
LYD.	What crime, Madam, have I committed, to be treated thus?
MRS. MAL.	Now don't attempt to extirpate yourself from the matter; you know I have proof controvertible of it. – But tell me, will you promise to do as you're bid? – Will you take a husband of your friends' choosing?
LYD.	Madam, I must tell you plainly, that had I no preference for any one else, the choice you have made would be my aversion.
MRS. MAL.	What business have you, miss, with *preference* and *aversion*? They don't become a young woman; and you ought to know, that as both always wear off, 'tis safest in matrimony to begin with a little *aversion*. I am sure I hated your poor dear uncle before marriage as if he'd been a black-a-moor – and yet, Miss, you are sensible what a wife I made! – and when it pleas'd Heav'n to release me from him, 'tis unknown what tears I shed! – But suppose we were going to give you another choice, will you promise us to give up this Beverley?
LYD.	Could I belie my thoughts so far, as to give that promise, my actions would certainly as far belie my words.
MRS. MAL.	Take yourself to your room. – You are fit company for nothing but your own ill-humours.
LYD.	Willingly, Ma'am – I cannot change for the worse.

[*Exit* LYDIA.

MRS. MAL.	There's a little intricate hussy for you!
SIR ANTH.	It is not to be wonder'd at, Ma'am, – all this is the natural consequence of teaching girls to read. – Had I a thousand daughters, by Heaven! I'd as soon have them taught the black art as their alphabet!

MRS. MAL. Nay, nay, Sir Anthony, you are an absolute misanthropy.

SIR ANTH. In my way hither, Mrs. Malaprop, I observed your niece's maid coming forth from a circulating library! – She had a book in each hand – they were half-bound volumes, with marble covers! – From that moment I guess'd how full of duty I should see her mistress!

MRS. MAL. Those are vile places, indeed!

SIR ANTH. Madam, a circulating library in a town is as an ever-green tree of diabolical knowledge! – It blossoms through the year! – And depend on it, Mrs. Malaprop, that they who are so fond of handling the leaves, will long for the fruit at last.

MRS. MAL. Fie, fie, Sir Anthony, you surely speak laconically!

SIR ANTH. Why, Mrs. Malaprop, in moderation, now, what would you have a woman know?

MRS. MAL. Observe me, Sir Anthony. – I would by no means wish a daughter of mine to be a progeny of learning; I don't think so much learning becomes a young woman; for instance, I would never let her meddle with Greek, or Hebrew, or Algebra, or Simony, or Fluxions, or Paradoxes, or such inflammatory branches of learning – neither would it be necessary for her to handle any of your mathematical, astronomical, diabolical instruments; – But, Sir Anthony, I would send her, at nine years old, to a boarding-school, in order to learn a little ingenuity and artifice. – Then, Sir, she should have a supercilious knowledge in accounts; – and as she grew up, I would have her instructed in geometry, that she might know something of the contagious countries; – but above all, Sir Anthony, she should be mistress of ortho-doxy, that she might not mis-spell, and mis-pronounce words so shamefully as girls usually do; and likewise that she might reprehend the true meaning of what she is saying. – This, Sir Anthony, is what I would have a woman know; – and I don't think there is a superstitious article in it.

SIR ANTH. Well, well, Mrs. Malaprop, I will dispute the point no fur-ther with you; though I must confess that you are a truly moderate and polite arguer, for almost every third word you say is on my side of the question. – But, Mrs. Malaprop, to the more important point in debate, – you say, you have no objection to my proposal?

MRS. MAL. None, I assure you. – I am under no positive engagement with Mr. Acres, and as Lydia is so obstinate against him, perhaps your son may have better success.

SIR ANTH. Well, Madam, I will write for the boy directly. – He knows not a syllable of this yet, though I have for some time had the proposal in my head. He is at present with his regiment.

MRS. MAL. We have never seen your son, Sir Anthony; but I hope no objection on his side,

SIR ANTH. Objection! – let him object if he dare! – No, no, Mrs. Malaprop, Jack knows that the least demur puts me in a frenzy directly. – My process was always very simple – in their younger days, 'twas 'Jack do this;' – if he demur'd – I knock'd him down – and if he grumbled at that – I always sent him out of the room.

MRS. MAL. Aye, and the properest way, o' my conscience! – nothing is so conciliating to young people as severity. – Well, Sir Anthony, I shall give Mr. Acres his discharge, and prepare Lydia to receive your son's invocations; – and I hope you will represent *her* to the Captain as an object not altogether illegible.

SIR ANTH. Madam, I will handle the subject prudently. – Well, I must leave you – and let me beg you, Mrs. Malaprop, to enforce this matter roundly to the girl; – take my advice – keep a tight hand – if she rejects this proposal – clap her under lock and key: – and if you were just to let the servants forget to bring her dinner for three or four days, you can't conceive how she'd come about!

[*Exit Sir* ANTH.

MRS. MAL. Well, at any rate, I shall be glad to get her from under my intuition. – She has somehow discovered my partiality for Sir Lucius O'Trigger – sure, Lucy can't have betray'd me! – No, the girl is such a simpleton, I should have made her confess it. – Lucy! – Lucy! – [*calls.*] Had she been one of your artificial ones, I should never have trusted her.

Enter LUCY.

LUCY. Did you call, Ma'am?

MRS. MAL. Yes, girl. – Did you see Sir Lucius while you was out?

LUCY. No, indeed, Ma'am, not a glimpse of him.

MRS. MAL. You are sure, Lucy, that you never mention'd —

LUCY. Oh, Gemini! I'd sooner cut my tongue out.

MRS. MAL. Well, don't let your simplicity be impos'd on.

LUCY. No Ma'am.

MRS. MAL. So, come to me presently, and I'll give you another letter to Sir Lucius; – but mind, Lucy – if ever you betray what you are entrusted with – (unless it be other people's secrets to me) you forfeit my malevolence for ever: – and your being a simpleton shall be no excuse for your locality.

[*Exit Mrs.* MALAPROP.

LUCY. Ha! ha! ha! – So, my dear *simplicity*, let me give you a little respite. – [*altering her manner*] – let girls in my station be as fond as they please of appearing expert, and knowing in their trusts; – commend me to a mask of *silliness*, and a pair of sharp eyes for my own interest under it! – Let me see to what account have I turned my *simplicity* lately. –

[*looks at a paper.*]

For *abetting Miss Lydia Languish in a design of running away with an Ensign! – in money – sundry times – twelve pound twelve – gowns, five – hats, ruffles, caps,* etc. etc. – *numberless! – From the said Ensign, within this last month, six guineas and a half.* – About a quarter's pay! – Item, *from Mrs. Malaprop, for betraying the young people to her* – when I found matters were likely to be discovered – *two guineas, and a black paduasoy.* – Item, *from Mr. Acres, for carrying divers letters* – which I never deliver'd – *two guineas, and a pair of buckles* – Item, *from Sir Lucius O'Trigger – three crowns – two gold pocket-pieces – and a silver snuff-box!* – Well done, *simplicity!* – yet I was forced to make my Hibernian believe, that he was corresponding, not with the *Aunt*, but with the *Niece*; for, though not over rich, I found he had too much pride and delicacy to sacrifice the feelings of a gentleman to the necessities of his fortune.

[*Exit.*

END OF THE FIRST ACT

From *The School for Scandal*

(1777)

ACT II. SCENE I.
SIR PETER TEAZLE's *house.*

Enter SIR PETER *and* LADY TEAZLE.

SIR PETER. Lady Teazle, Lady Teazle, I'll not bear it.

LADY TEAZLE. Sir Peter, Sir Peter, you may bear it or not, as you please; but I ought to have my own way in everything, and what's more, I *will* too. – What! though I was educated in the country, I know very well that women of Fashion in London are accountable to nobody after they are married.

SIR PETER. Very well! ma'am very well, – so a husband is to have no influence, no authority?

LADY TEAZLE. Authority! No, to be sure – if you wanted authority over me, you should have adopted me, and not married me, I am sure you were old enough.

SIR PETER. Old enough! – aye, there it is! – Well, well, Lady Teazle, though my life may be made unhappy by your temper, I'll not be ruined by your extravagance.

LADY TEAZLE. My extravagance! I'm sure I'm not more extravagant than a woman of fashion ought to be.

SIR PETER. No, no, madam, you shall throw away no more sums on such unmeaning luxury – 'Slife! to spend as much to furnish your dressing-room with flowers in winter as would suffice to turn the Pantheon into a greenhouse, and give a *fête champêtre* at Christmas!

LADY TEAZLE. Lord, Sir Peter, am I to blame because flowers are dear in cold weather? You should find fault with the climate, and not with me. For my part, I am sure I wish it was spring all the year round, and that roses grew under one's feet!

SIR PETER. Oons! madam – if you had been born to this, I shouldn't wonder at your talking thus. – But you forget what your situation was when I married you.

LADY TEAZLE. No, no, I don't; 'twas a very disagreeable one, or I should never have married *you.*

SIR PETER. Yes, yes, madam, you were then in somewhat a humbler style – the daughter of a plain country squire. Recollect, Lady Teazle, when I saw you first, sitting at your tambour, in a pretty figured linen gown, with a bunch of keys by your side, your hair combed smooth over a roll, and your apartment hung round with fruits in worsted, of your own working.

LADY TEAZLE. O yes! I remember it very well, and a curious life I led –

	my daily occupation to inspect the dairy, superintend the poultry, make extracts from the family receipt-book, and comb my aunt Deborah's lap-dog.
SIR PETER.	Yes, yes ma'am, 'twas so indeed.
LADY TEAZLE.	And then, you know, my evening amusements! To draw patterns for ruffles, which I had not the materials to make; play Pope Joan[1] with the Curate; to read a novel to my aunt; or to be stuck down to an old spinet to strum my father to sleep after a fox-chase.
SIR PETER.	I am glad you have so good a memory. Yes, madam, these were the recreations I took you from; but now you must have your coach – *vis-à-vis* – and three powdered foot-men before your chair and, in summer, a pair of white cats to draw you to Kensington Gardens. – No recollection, I suppose, when you were content to ride double behind the butler on a docked coach-horse?
LADY TEAZLE.	No – I swear I never did that – I deny the butler, and the coach-horse.
SIR PETER.	This, madam, was your situation – and what have I not done for you? I have made you a woman of fashion, of fortune, of rank – in short, I have made you my wife.
LADY TEAZLE.	Well, then, and there is but one thing more you can make me to add to the obligation – and that is –
SIR PETER.	My widow, I suppose?
LADY TEAZLE.	Hem! hem!
SIR PETER.	Thank you, madam – but don't flatter yourself; for though your ill-conduct may disturb my peace, it shall never break my heart, I promise you; however, I am equally obliged to you for the hint.
LADY TEAZLE.	Then why will you endeavour to make yourself so dis-agreeable to me, and thwart me in every little elegant expense?
SIR PETER.	'Slife, madam, I say, had you any of these elegant expens-es when you married me?
LADY TEAZLE.	Lud, Sir Peter! would you have me be out of the fashion?
SIR PETER.	The fashion, indeed! what had you to do with the fash-ion before you married me?
LADY TEAZLE.	For my Part, I should think you would like to have your wife thought a woman of taste.

1 *Pope Joan*: a card game said to be called after a fabulous female Pope, but its French name, *nain Jaune*, or yellow dwarf, may indicate its real origin.

SIR PETER. Aye – there again – taste! Zounds! madam, you had no taste when you married *me*.

LADY TEAZLE. That's very true, indeed, Sir Peter! and, *after* having married you, I am sure I should never pretend to taste again! But now, Sir Peter, if we have finished our daily jangle, I presume I may go to my engagement of Lady Sneerwell's?

SIR PETER. Aye – there's another precious circumstance! – a charming set of acquaintance you have made there!

LADY TEAZLE. Nay, Sir Peter, they are people of rank and fortune, and remarkably tenacious of reputation.

SIR PETER. Yes, egad, they are tenacious of reputation with a vengeance; for they don't choose anybody should have a Character but themselves! Such a crew! Ah! many a wretch has rid on hurdles who has done less mischief than those utterers of forged tales, coiners of scandal, – and clippers of reputation.

LADY TEAZLE. What! would you restrain the freedom of speech?

SIR PETER. Oh! they have made you just as bad as any one of the society.

LADY TEAZLE. Why – I believe I do bear a part with a tolerable grace. But I vow I bear no malice against the people I abuse; when I say an ill-natured thing, 'tis out of pure good humour – and I take it for granted they deal exactly in the same manner with me. But, Sir Peter, you know you promised to come to Lady Sneerwell's too.

SIR PETER Well well, I'll call in just to look after my own character.

LADY TEAZLE. Then, indeed, you must make haste after me or you'll be too late – so good bye to ye.

[*Exit* LADY TEAZLE.

SIR PETER. So – I have gained much by my intended expostulations! Yet with what a charming air she contradicts everything I say, and how pleasingly she shows her contempt of my authority! Well, though I can't make her love me, there is a great satisfaction in quarrelling with her, and I think she never appears to such advantage as when she's doing everything in her power to plague me.

[*Exit.*

ACT V. scene ii.
At sir peter's

Enter mrs. candour *and* maid.

MAID	Indeed, ma'am, my lady will see nobody at present.
MRS. CANDOUR.	Did you tell her it was her friend Mrs. Candour?
MAID	Yes, ma'am; but she begs you will excuse her.
MRS. CANDOUR.	Do go again; I shall be glad to see her, if it be only for a moment, for I am sure she must be in great distress. –

[*Exit* MAID.

Dear heart, how provoking! – I'm not mistress of half the circumstances! – We shall have the whole affair in the newspapers, with the names of the parties at length, before I have dropped the story at a dozen houses.

Enter sir benjamin backbite.

	O dear Sir Benjamin! you have heard, I suppose —
SIR BENJAMIN.	Of Lady Teazle and Mr. Surface —
MRS. CANDOUR.	And Sir Peter's discovery —
SIR BENJAMIN.	Oh, the strangest piece of business, to be sure!
MRS. CANDOUR.	Well, I never was so surprised in my life. I am so sorry for all parties, indeed, I am.
SIR BENJAMIN.	Now, I don't pity Sir Peter at all – he was so extravagantly partial to Mr. Surface.
MRS. CANDOUR.	Mr. Surface! Why, 'twas with Charles Lady Teazle was detected —
SIR BENJAMIN.	No such thing – Mr. Surface is the gallant —
MRS. CANDOUR.	No, no – Charles is the man – 'Twas Mr. Surface brought Sir Peter on purpose to discover them.
SIR BENJAMIN.	I tell you I have it from one —
MRS. CANDOUR.	And I have it from one —
SIR BENJAMIN.	Who had it from one, who had it —
MRS. CANDOUR.	From one immediately — But here's Lady Sneerwell; perhaps she knows the whole affair.

Enter lady sneerwell.

LADY SNEERWELL.	So, my dear Mrs. Candour, here's a sad affair of our friend Lady Teazle —

MRS. CANDOUR. Aye, my dear friend, who could have thought it——

LADY SNEERWELL. Well, there's no trusting appearances; though, indeed, she was always too lively for me.

MRS. CANDOUR. To be sure, her manners were a little too free – but she was very young.

LADY SNEERWELL. And had, indeed, some good qualities.

MRS. CANDOUR. So she had, indeed, but have you heard the particulars?

LADY SNEERWELL. No; but everybody says that Mr. Surface ——

SIR BENJAMIN. Aye, there, I told you – Mr. Surface was the man.

MRS. CANDOUR. No, no, indeed – the assignation was with Charles.

LADY SNEERWELL. With Charles! You alarm me, Mrs. Candour.

MRS. CANDOUR. Yes, yes, he was the lover – Mr. Surface – do him justice – was only the informer.

SIR BENJAMIN. Well, I'll not dispute with you, Mrs. Candour; but, be it which it may, I hope that Sir Peter's wound will not ——

MRS. CANDOUR. Sir Peter's wound! – Oh, mercy! I didn't hear a word of their fighting.

LADY SNEERWELL. Nor I, a syllable.

SIR BENJAMIN. No! what, no mention of the duel?

MRS. CANDOUR. Not a word.

SIR BENJAMIN. O, Lord – yes, yes – they fought before they left the room.

LADY SNEERWELL. Pray let us hear.

MRS. CANDOUR. Aye, do oblige us with the duel.

SIR BENJAMIN. 'Sir,' says Sir Peter – immediately after the discovery – 'you are a most ungrateful fellow.'

MRS. CANDOUR. Aye, to Charles ——

SIR BENJAMIN. No, no, to Mr. Surface – 'a most ungrateful fellow; and, old as I am, sir,' says he, 'I insist on immediate satisfaction.'

MRS. CANDOUR. Aye, that must have been to Charles, for 'tis very unlikely Mr. Surface should go to fight in his own house.

SIR BENJAMIN. Gad's life, ma'am, not at all – 'giving me immediate satisfaction.' – On this, madam, Lady Teazle, seeing Sir Peter in such danger, ran out of the room in strong hysterics, and Charles after her, calling out for hartshorn and water! – Then, madam, they began to fight with swords –

Enter CRABTREE.

CRABTREE.	With pistols, nephew – I have it from undoubted authority.
MRS. CANDOUR.	O Mr. Crabtree, then it is all true!
CRABTREE.	Too true, indeed, ma'am, and Sir Peter dangerously wounded —
SIR BENJAMIN.	By a thrust of in *seconde* – quite through his left side —
CRABTREE.	By a bullet lodged in the thorax.
MRS. CANDOUR.	Mercy on me, poor Sir Peter!
CRABTREE.	Yes, ma'am – though Charles would have avoided the matter, if he could.
MRS. CANDOUR.	I knew Charles was the person.
SIR BENJAMIN.	Oh, my Uncle, I see, knows nothing of the matter.
CRABTREE.	But Sir Peter taxed him with the basest ingratitude —
SIR BENJAMIN	That I told you, you know.
CRABTREE.	Do, nephew let me speak! – and insisted on an immediate –
SIR BENJAMIN.	Just as I said.
CRABTREE.	Odd's life! Nephew, allow others to know something too. – a pair of pistols lay on the bureau, for Mr. Surface, it seems, had come home the night before late from Salt-Hill where he had been to see the Montem[1] with a friend, who has a son at Eton; so, unluckily, the Pistols were left charged.
SIR BENJAMIN.	I heard nothing of this.
CRABTREE.	Sir Peter forced Charles to take one, and they fired, it seems, pretty nearly together – Charles's shot took place, as I tell you, and Sir Peter's missed; – but, what is very extraordinary, the ball struck against a little bronze Pliny that stood over the chimney-piece, grazed out of the window at a right angle, and wounded the postman, who was just coming to the door with a double letter from Northamptonshire.
SIR BENJAMIN.	My uncle's account is more circumstantial, I must confess, but I believe mine is the true one, for all that.

---

1 *the Montem*: a festival celebrated up to 1844 on Whit Tuesday every third year by the scholars of Eton, who went in fancy costumes to a mound (Latin *ad montem*) near Slough, 'Salt Hill',
where they collected money, known as salt, to finance the senior colleger (the 'Captain of
Montem') at King's College, Cambridge.

LADY SNEERWELL   *(aside).* I am more interested in this affair than they imagine, and must have better information.

                                    [*Exit* LADY SNEERWELL.

SIR BENJAMIN   *(after a pause, looking at each other).* Ah! Lady Sneerwell's alarm is very easily accounted for.

CRABTREE.   Yes, yes, they certainly *do* say – but that's neither here nor there.

MRS. CANDOUR.   But, pray, where is Sir Peter at present?

CRABTREE.   Oh! they brought him home, and he is now in the house, though the servants are ordered to deny it.

MRS. CANDOUR.   I believe so, and Lady Teazle, I suppose, attending him.

CRABTREE.   Yes, yes; I saw one of the faculty enter just before me.

SIR BENJAMIN.   Hey! who comes here?

CRABTREE.   Oh, this is he – the physician, depend on't.

MRS. CANDOUR.   Oh, certainly, it must be the physician – and now we shall know.

Enter SIR OLIVER SURFACE.

CRABTREE.   Well, doctor – what hopes?

MRS. CANDOUR.   Aye, doctor! How's your patient?

SIR BENJAMIN.   Now, doctor, isn't it a wound with a small-sword?

CRABTREE.   A bullet lodged in the thorax, for a hundred!

SIR OLIVER.   Doctor! a wound with a small-sword! and a bullet in the thorax! Oons! are you mad, good people?

SIR BENJAMIN.   Perhaps, sir, you are not a doctor.

SIR OLIVER.   Truly, I am to thank you for my degree, if I am.

CRABTREE.   Only a friend of Sir Peter's, then, I presume; but, sir, you must have heard of this accident?

SIR OLIVER.   Not a word!

CRABTREE.   Not of his being dangerously wounded?

SIR OLIVER.   The devil he is!

SIR BENJAMIN.   Run through the body —

CRABTREE.   Shot in the breast —

SIR BENJAMIN.   By one Mr. Surface —

CRABTREE.   Aye, the younger.

SIR OLIVER.   Hey! what the plague! you seem to differ strangely in your accounts – however, you agree that Sir Peter is dangerously wounded.

SIR BENJAMIN.   Oh yes, we agree there.

CRABTREE.   Yes, yes, I believe there can be no doubt of that.

SIR OLIVER. Then, upon my word, for a person in that situation, he is the most imprudent man alive – for here he comes, walking as if nothing at all were the matter.

Enter SIR PETER TEAZLE.

Odd's heart, Sir Peter! you are come in good time, I promise you; for we had just *given you over*.

SIR BENJAMIN. Egad, uncle, this is the most sudden recovery!

SIR OLIVER. Why, man, what do you do out of bed with a small-sword through your body, and a bullet lodged in your thorax!

SIR PETER. A small-sword and a bullet?

SIR OLIVER. Aye; these gentlemen would have killed you without law or physic – and wanted to dub me a doctor – to make me an accomplice.

SIR PETER. Why, what is all this?

SIR BENJAMIN. We rejoice, Sir Peter, that the story of the duel is not true, and are sincerely sorry for your other misfortunes.

SIR PETER (*aside*). So, so; all over the town already!

CRABTREE. Though, Sir Peter, you were certainly vastly to blame to marry at all, at your years.

SIR PETER. Sir, what business is that of yours?

MRS. CANDOUR. Though, indeed, as Sir Peter made so good a husband, he's very much to be pitied!

SIR PETER. Plague on your pity, ma'am, I desire none of it.

SIR BENJAMIN. However, Sir Peter, you must not mind the laughing and jests you will meet with on this occasion.

SIR PETER. Sir, I desire to be master in my own house.

CRABTREE. 'Tis no uncommon case, that's one comfort.

SIR PETER. I insist on being left to myself: without ceremony, I insist on your leaving my house directly!

MRS. CANDOUR. Well, well, we are going, and depend on't, we'll make the best report of you we can.

SIR PETER. Leave my house!

CRABTREE. And tell how hardly you have been treated.

SIR PETER. Leave my house!

SIR BENJAMIN. And how patiently you bear it.

SIR PETER. Fiends! vipers! furies! Oh, that their own venom would choke them!

[*Exeunt* MRS. CANDOUR, SIR BENJAMIN BACKBITE, CRABTREE, &c.

Richard Brinsley Sheridan

From The Speeches

FROM SPEECH OF 19 JUNE 1798 ON THE REBELLION

To keep Ireland against the will of the people is a vain expectation. With eighty thousand troops with arms and discipline against an unarmed and undisciplined multitude!... The struggle is one, not of local discontent and partial disaffection, but it is a contest between the people and the government. In such a state of things, without entering into a particular enquiry, the fair presumption is, that the government is to blame.

FROM SPEECH OPPOSING THE IRISH INSURRECTION BILL

[*The historical causes of disaffection*]

When they express their surprise that the Irish are not contented, while, according to their observation, that people have so much reason to be happy; they betray a total ignorance of their actual circumstances. The fact is, that the tyranny practised upon the Irish has been throughout unremitting. There has been no change but in the manner of inflicting it. They have had nothing but variety in oppression extending to all ranks and degrees of certain description of the people [*i.e.* Catholics]. If you would know what this varied oppression consisted in, I would refer you to the penal statutes you have repealed, and to some of those which still exist. There you will see the high and the low equally subjected to the lash of persecution; and still some effect [*sic*] to be astonished at the discontents of the Irish....

[*On ill-conceived plans for Catholic Emancipation*]

I think they began at the wrong end and commenced the measure of redress in Ireland at the cottage, instead of at the park and the mansion. To have gone first to higher orders of the Catholics; to have sought to make them judges and peers and commoners; I do not know that such a proceeding, had it taken place, would not rather have served to aggravate discontent, as it might have been construed into a design to divide the interests of the Catholics. Sure I am, that with a view to serve or to conciliate the Catholic population, I mean the poor, the peasantry, its effect would be nothing; indeed it would be quite a mockery. It would be like dressing or decorating the top masts of a ship when there were ten feet [of] water in the hold, or putting a laced hat on a man who had not a shoe to his foot. The place to set out to in Ireland for the relief of the people is the cottage....

[*On wrongly blaming the poor for their poverty*]

I have always been shocked at the assertion that the Irish peasantry might be comfortable if they chose to be industrious; and that it is idle to attempt any improvement of their condition. It is abominable to hear blame laid on providence instead of laying it on man. Can any set of men, I would ask, be found who manifest so much of the qualities of which those cruel calumniators would deprive them as the Irish peasantry? But they are only calumniated by those men who would degrade them below the level of the human creation, in order to palliate their own inhumanity towards them. We are told in England that the unhappy Africans were insensible to the ordinary feelings of humanity, in order to render us indifferent to their sufferings, and to the custom of the slave-trade. On similar motives the character of the Irish peasantry is so foully misrepresented by some men in this country and in Ireland also.

A Concern for the Poorer Employees after the Fire at Drury Lane

I am aware that many of the principal performers may get profitable engagements at the different provincial theatres, but what then would become of the inferior ones, some of whom have large families? Heaven forbid that they should be deserted! – No: I most earnestly recommend and entreat, that every individual belonging to the concern should be taken care of. Let us make a long pull, a strong pull, and a pull all together; above all, make the general good our sole consideration. Elect yourselves into a committee; but keep in your remembrance even the poor sweepers of the stage, who, with their children, must starve, if not protected by our fostering care.

WILLIAM DRENNAN (1754-1820)

D rennan, architect of the Society of United Irishmen, 'unbending and eloquent advocate of the Rights of Man', was born in Belfast in 1754, the son of a liberal Presbyterian clergyman. He read medicine in Glasgow and Edinburgh, subsequently practising in Belfast, Newry and Dublin. His radical address to the Irish Volunteers, issued in 1792, led to his being tried for sedition in 1794; he was acquitted largely because of the skill of his counsel John Philpot Curran. His letter to his mother, included here, shows the effect of his trial on him. A nationalist poet, he was probably the first to call Ireland the 'emerald isle' in his poem 'When Erin First Rose.' 'The Wake of William Orr,' a patriotic ballad, dealt with the hanging in 1797 of a member of the United Irishmen. Drennan's poems, published as *Fugitive Pieces* in 1815, also included 'The Wail of the Women after the Battle.'

The Wake of William Orr

There our murdered brother lies;
Wake not him with women's cries;
Mourn the way that manhood ought –
Sit in silent trance of thought.

Write his merits on your mind;
Morals pure and manners kind;
On his head, as on a hill,
Virtue placed her citadel.

Why cut off in palmy youth?
Truth he spoke, and acted truth.
'Countrymen, UNITE,' he cried,
And died for what our Saviour died.

God of peace, and God of love!
Let it not Thy vengeance move –
Let it not Thy lightnings draw –
A Nation guillotined by law.

Hapless Nation, rent and torn,
Thou wert early taught to mourn;
Warfare for six hundred years!
Epochs marked with blood and tears!

Hunted thro' thy native grounds,
Or flung reward to human hounds;
Each one pulled and tore his share,
Heedless of thy deep despair.

Hapless Nation! hapless Land!
Heap of uncementing sand!

Crumbled by a foreign weight:
And by worse, domestic hate.

God of mercy! God of peace!
Make this mad confusion cease;
O'er the mental chaos move,
Through it SPEAK the light of love.

Monstrous and unhappy sight!
Brothers' blood will not unite;
Holy oil and holy water,
Mix, and fill the world with slaughter.

Who is she with aspect wild?
The widowed mother with her child –
Child new stirring in the womb!
Husband waiting for the tomb!

Angel of this sacred place,
Calm her soul and whisper peace –
Cord, or axe, or guillotine,
Make the sentence – not the sin.

Here we watch our brother's sleep:
Watch with us, but do not weep:
Watch with us thro' dead of night –
But expect the morning light.

Conquer fortune, persevere –
Lo! it breaks – the morning clear!
The cheerful cock awakes the skies,
The day is come – arise, arise!

Letter to his Mother

Dublin, June 26 [1794]
Thursday

I was acquitted about half past Eleven o'clock last night, after a trial
which lasted from half after ten in the morning. The jury, by Sir John
Thrale, the foreman, pronounced me not guilty in all the *nine*

counts.... After the charges of the judges, which lasted more than an hour, the jury went out and remained out above an hour, in which time I was a little in suspense by having got some reason for hopes from the opinion of the lawyers around us, for before that time and during the whole day, I was in composed certainty of an unfavourable verdict.... I was like to be smothered with congratulations on all sides, and the difficulty was now to get safe from the mob about the Courts, which was at length done by stealing through a back door and being carried by two friends through bye-allies to Dame Street, where with great difficulty we got into the house, or, rather, were carried, Sam and I, both out of breath, and I with but one shoe on, and the mob shouting and huzzaing at a tremendous rate, I mean, tremendous to Giffard, the Sheriff, who was pursued by the call of 'A Dog in Office,' by barking and whistling, etc. Near 1,000 people were about the Courts at half after eleven at night, and I am sure more than nine-tenths my friends, and even many three-quarter aristocrats expressed much pleasure.

Emmet acted in the shade most zealously and friendly. Fletcher, my other lawyer, had little to say, for Curran took the whole labour on himself for 11 hours....

I am sure, dear mother, this affair will please you in your old days, especially when I tell you that it will operate rather as a quietus in my politics, at least so far as not to dabble in these fugitive and now dangerous papers.... Emmet thinks, and so do all, that I am completely to be freed from apprehension of any farther prosecution, and that there is an end of the whole business about this much-talked-of paper which has served as a pretext for so many prosecutions.

PATRICK O'KELLY (1754-1835?)

O'Kelly was possibly born in Co. Clare; he was a schoolmaster in Galway. His work included *Killarney, A Descriptive Poem*, and his 'Curse of Doneraile' caused much amusement as did his rectraction, 'Blessing on Doneraile,' written when Lady Doneraile gave him a watch and seal to replace the watch and seal lost or pilfered in Doneraile.

The Curse of Doneraile

Alas! how dismal is my tale,
I lost my watch in Doneraile.

My Dublin watch, my chain and seal,
Pilfered at once in Doneraile.
May Fire and Brimstone never fail,
To fall in showers on Doneraile.
May all the leading fiends assail
The thieving town of Doneraile.
As lightnings flash across the vale,
So down to Hell with Doneraile.
The fate of Pompey at Pharsale,
Be that the curse of Doneraile.
May Beef or Mutton, Lamb or Veal
Be never found in Doneraile,
But Garlic Soup and scurvy Kale,
Be still the food for Doneraile.
May Heaven a chosen curse entail,
On rigid, rotten Doneraile.
May Sun and Moon forever fail,
To beam their lights on Doneraile.
May every pestilential gale,
Blast that cursed spot called Doneraile.
May no Cuckoo, Thrush, or Quail,
Be ever heard in Doneraile.
May Patriots, Kings, and Commonweal,
Despise and harass Doneraile.
May ev'ry Post, Gazette, and Mail,
Sad tidings bring of Doneraile.
May loudest thunders ring a peal,
To blind and deafen Doneraile.
May vengeance fall at head and tail,
From North to South at Doneraile.
May profit light and tardy sale,
Still damp the trade of Doneraile.
May Fame resound a dismal tale,
Whene'er she lights on Doneraile.
May Egypt's plagues at once prevail,
To thin the knaves of Doneraile.
May frost and snow, and sleet and hail
Benumb each joint in Doneraile.
May wolves and bloodhounds trace and trail,
The cursed crew of Doneraile.
May every mischief fresh and stale,

Patrick O'Kelly

Abide henceforth in Doneraile.
May all from Belfast to Kinsale,
Scoff, curse, and damn you, Doneraile.
May neither Flow'r nor Oatenmeal,
Be found or known in Doneraile.
May want and woe each joy curtail,
That e'er was known in Doneraile.
May no one coffin want a nail,
That wraps a rogue in Doneraile.
May all the thieves that rob and steal,
The gallows meet in Doneraile.
May all the sons of Granuale,
Blush at the thieves of Doneraile.
May mischief big as Norway whale,
O'erwhelm the knaves of Doneraile.
May curses wholesale and retail,
Pour with full force on Doneraile.
May ev'ry transport want to sail,
A convict bring from Doneraile.
May ev'ry churn and milking pail,
Fall dry to staves in Doneraile.
May cold and hunger still congeal,
The stagnant blood of Doneraile.
May ev'ry hour new woes reveal,
That Hell reserves for Doneraile.
May ev'ry chosen ill prevail,
O'er all the Imps of Doneraile.
May no one wish or prayer avail,
To soothe the woes of Doneraile.
May th'Inquisition straight impale,
The rapparees of Doneraile.
May curse of Sodom now prevail,
And sink to ashes Doneraile.
May Charon's Boat triumphant sail,
Completely manned from Doneraile.
Oh! may my Couplets never fail,
To find new curse for Doneraile.
And may Grim Pluto's inner jail,
For ever groan with Doneraile.

Blessings on Doneraile

How vastly pleasing is my tale
I found my watch in Doneraile.
My Dublin watch, my chain and seal
Were all restored at Doneraile.
May fire and brimstone ever fail
To hurt or injure Doneraile.
May neither friend nor foe assail
The splendid town of Doneraile.
May lightning never singe the vale
That leads to generous Doneraile.
May Pompey's fate[1] and old Pharsale
Be still reversed at Doneraile.
May beef and mutton, lamb and veal
Plentyful be in Doneraile.
May garlic soup and scurvy kale
No palate spoil in Doneraile.
May neither frog nor creeping snail
Subtract the crops of Doneraile.
May Heaven each chosen bliss entail
On honest, friendly Doneraile.
May Sol and Luna never fail
To shed their light on Doneraile.
May every soft ambrosial gale
Waft heavenly bliss to Doneraile.
May every cuckoo, thrush and quail
A concert sing in Doneraile.
May every post, gazette and mail
Glad tidings bring to Doneraile.
May no harsh thunder sound a peal
To incommode sweet Doneraile.
May profit high and speedy sale
Enlarge the trade of Doneraile.
May fame resound a pleasant tale
Of all the joys in Doneraile.
May Egypt's plagues forever fail

---

1 *Pompey's fate*: he was surnamed the Great, a Roman general (106–48BC) who, after a successful military career formed the first triumvirate with Julius Caesar and Crassus. He became the leader of the aristocratic conservative party (after his wife, Caesar's daughter, died) and began the civil war against Caesar in 49BC. He was defeated at Pharsalus in 48BC.

To hurt or injure Doneraile.
May frost and snow, and rain and hail
No mischief do at Doneraile.
May Oscar with his fiery flail
Thrash all the foes of Doneraile.
May all from Belfast to Kinsale
Respect the town of Doneraile.
May choicest flour and oatenmeal
Be still to spare in Doneraile.
May want and woe no joy curtail
That's always known in Doneraile.
No coffin that grim death can nail
May wrap a rogue in Doneraile.
There are no thieves to rob and steal
Within two leagues of Doneraile.
And all the sons of Granuale
Can well be proud of Doneraile.
May no dire monster, shark or whale
Annoy or torture Doneraile.
May no disaster e'er assail
The bliss and peace of Doneraile.
May every transport wont to sail
Increase the wealth of Doneraile.
May every churn and milking pail
O'erflow with cream at Doneraile.
May cold and hunger ne'er congeal
The good rich blood of Doneraile.
May every day new joys reveal
To crown the bliss of Doneraile.
May every soft ambrosial gale
Sweet odours waft to Doneraile.
May no corroding ill prevail
To damp the joys of Doneraile.
May the Inquisition ne'er impale
Or hurt a limb from Doneraile.
May Sodom's curse forever fail
To hurt and injure Doneraile
But may each wish and prayer prevail
To crown with peace sweet Doneraile.

THE ABBÉ EDGEWORTH (1745-1807)

Henry Essex Edgeworth, Abbé de Firmont, was the son of the Rev. Robert Edgeworth, and cousin of Richard Lovell Edgeworth. His father resigned his living of Edgeworthstown, Co. Longford when he became a Roman Catholic, moving with his family to Toulouse. There Henry attended the University, and subsequently the Collège des Trente-trois at Paris before joining the Seminaire des Missions étrangères in the Rue du Bac. Known as the Abbé de Firmont (from Fairmount, a small estate in Co. Longford which provided the family in France with an income) he refused the offer of a Bishopric in Ireland in 1788. Three years later he became the confessor of Madame Elisabeth, the sister of Louis XVI. He continued to visit the court after the Tuilleries had been stormed and the King removed from the Convention Hall to the Temple.

The Abbé's own rooms were raided, a friend of his removed and subsequently murdered, and his papers examined twice. He escaped, but after the Archbishop of Paris invested him with all his powers, the King asked him to assist him in his last moments. After the execution of the King he avoided capture and after various adventures eventually arrived in London in 1796. He then became chaplain to the exiled Louis XVIII at Blankenburg, Brunswick, and then at Mittau (near Riga) where he died in 1807, having caught typhus from some French soldiers he was attending.

The Memoirs of the Abbé Edgeworth (1815) were edited and translated by his cousin C. Sneyd Edgeworth; they contain a long letter to his brother Ussher Edgeworth written on 1 September 1796, giving an account of his various escapes and adventures from 1791 to 1796, as well as his narrative of the last hours of Louis XVI, written at the request of Louis XVIII shortly after the letter to his brother Ussher. The Abbé Gossier contributed an account of the Abbé Edgeworth's career after his escape. *Letters from the Abbé Edgeworth to his Friends*, ed. T.R. England (1817), reveal his sensitive, generous and courageous character.

From *The Memoirs of the Abbé Edgeworth*

[The King] led me into his closet that he might speak more freely; for from his chamber all he said was overheard. This closet had been constructed in one of the turrets of the Temple; it was bare alike of ornament and hangings; a wretched earthenware stove served for a fireplace, and the only furniture was one table and three leathern chairs.

There, making me sit down near him, 'Now, Sir,' said he, 'the great business of my salvation is the one thing which should occupy my thoughts; the one thing of importance. What is all else compared with this? But I must beg a few moments' delay. For my family are coming down to see me. In the meantime, here is a paper which I am glad to be able to communicate to you.' As he spoke, he drew from his pocket a sealed paper and broke it open. It was his will, which he had made as far back as December, that is to say, at a period when he was still uncertain whether any religious assistance would be allowed him in his last necessity. All those who have read this document, so interesting in itself and so worthy of a Christian King, will easily judge what a deep impression it must have made upon me. But what most astonished me was that he had the courage to read it himself, twice over. His voice was firm, his countenance unchanged, save when he read the names most dear to him; then all his tenderness was awakened, he was obliged to pause a moment, and his tears flowed despite his efforts to restrain them. But when he read passages that concerned only himself and his calamities, he seemed no more affected than most men are when they hear of the misfortunes of others.

The Royal Family had not yet come down, when he finished reading, and he at once proceeded to ask news of his clergy and of the position of the French Church. Notwithstanding the strictness of his confinement, he knew something of the facts; he knew, for instance, that the French clergy had been obliged to fly the country and had found a refuge in London; but he was absolutely ignorant of the particulars. The little that I thought it my duty to tell him seemed to make a great impression on his mind; he deplored the fate of his clergy and expressed the greatest admiration for the people of England who had mitigated their sufferings. But he did not confine himself to these general inquiries; he entered into particulars that surprised me; he wished to know what had become of the clergy in whose welfare he took a peculiar interest. He was specially concerned to know the fate of Cardinal de la Rochefoucauld and the Bishop of Clermont, but his interest redoubled at the mere mention of the Archbishop of Paris; he inquired where he was, what he was doing and whether I was in a position to correspond with him. 'Tell him' said the King 'that I die in his communion, and that I have never acknowledged any pastor but him; alas! I fear he is offended because I never answered his last letter. I was then at the Tuileries, but events followed so thick and close upon each other, that I could not find the time. But he has such a good heart that I am sure he will pardon me.' He spoke also of the Abbé de Floirac, whom he had never seen; but he was well acquainted with the services that this noble priest had rendered to the diocese of Paris in times of the greatest difficulty; he asked me what had become of him, and when I told him that he had had the good fortune to escape, he spoke of him in terms which showed the value he attached to his preservation and the esteem in which he held his virtues. I do not know by what chance we came to speak of the Duke of Orleans; the King seemed to be well acquainted with his extravagances and with the abominable part he played at the Convention. But he spoke of him without a shadow of bitterness, in pity rather than in anger. 'What have I done to my Cousin' he exclaimed, 'that he should so persecute me? But why blame him? He is more to be pitied than I. My lot is melancholy enough, but, were it yet worse than it is, I would not change places with him.'

This engrossing conversation was interrupted by one of the commissaries who came to inform the King that his family were come down, and that he was at length permitted to see them. At this he betrayed signs of strong emotion and darted from the room. The interview took place, as far as I could judge, for I was not present at it, in a little room, which was only separated by a glass door from that occupied by the commissaries, so that they could see and hear all that passed. Even I, though shut up in the closet where the King had left me, could easily distinguish their voices, and I was an involuntary witness of the most touching scene it ever was my fate to hear. To give an adequate picture of this heart-breaking interview is beyond the powers of my poor pen. For more than quarter of an hour not a single articulate word reached my ears. There were no sobs, no tears, only piercing cries which were audible as far as the outer court. The King, the Queen, Monseigneur the Dauphin, Madame Elizabeth, Madame Royale, all bewailed themselves at once, and their voices were confounded. At length their tears ceased (for their strength was exhausted) and they spoke together in a low voice and with some degree of tranquillity. The conversation lasted near an hour; the King then dismissed his family, holding out hopes that they might see him in the morning.

He returned at once to me, but in such agitation and distress as shewed that he was wounded to the heart. 'Ah,' he cried, throwing himself into a chair, 'what agony this meeting has caused me! Why must I love so tenderly and be so tenderly beloved! But it is over; let us forget everything else and think only of the one thing that is necessary, that now should occupy all my affections and all my thoughts.' He was continuing in this strain, showing at once his sensibility and his courage, when Cléry came to entreat him to take some refreshment. The King hesitated a moment, but on reflection consented. The supper took but five minutes, and the King returning once more to his closet, begged me to follow him. I could scarcely face the ordeal, but the dread of giving him pain made me comply. One thought had been ever-present in my mind since I had been so near the King, at whatever danger to myself, the resolve to procure for him the Holy Communion of which he had been so long deprived. I might have brought it to him in secret, as we were obliged to do to all the faithful who were detained in their own houses; but the rigorous search imposed on entering the Temple, and the profanation which would infallibly have followed, were reasons more than sufficient to prevent me. The sole resource left me was to say Mass in the King's chamber, if I could find the means. I proposed it to him, but at first he seemed alarmed at the thought. However, seeing that he most ardently desired this means of grace and that his opposition sprang solely from the fear of compromising me, I entreated him to give me his consent, promising that I would conduct myself with prudence and discretion. He at length yielded; 'Go, Sir,' he said, 'but I greatly fear that you will not succeed, for I know the men with whom you have to deal; they will grant nothing which they can refuse.' Armed with this permission, I asked to be conducted to the hall of council, and made my demand in the name of the King. This proposal, for which the commissaries were not prepared, disconcerted them extremely, and they sought for different pretexts to evade it. 'How' they said 'can we find a priest at so late an hour? And if we should find one, how shall we provide all that is necessary?' 'The priest is already found,' I replied, 'for here am I. As for the rest, the nearest church will supply all that is needful, if you will make the application. Further, my demand is just, and it would be against your own principles to refuse it.' One of the commissaries instantly, though in guarded terms, replied that my request might be no more than a trap, and that under pretext of administering the communion to the King, I might poison him. 'History' he added 'has furnished us with examples enough of this kind to make us circumspect.' I looked him steadily in the face and replied, 'The strict search to which I was subjected on my entry, ought to have convinced you that I have no poison about my person. If therefore to-morrow any is found, it is from you that I shall have received it, since all that I require for the celebration of Mass must pass through your hands.'

He would have replied, but the rest commanded him to be silent, and as a last subterfuge they said that, as the council was not complete, they could not take it upon themselves to give any decision; but that they would summon the absent members and acquaint me with the result of their deliberations. A quarter of an hour passed, and I was again brought into their chamber, where the President thus addressed me, 'Citizen minister of worship, the council have considered the request made by you in the name of Louis Capet; his request being conformable to the law, which declares all forms of worship to be free, it has been decided to grant it. Nevertheless we must insist on two conditions; first that you should at once draw up a form of request, stating your demand and signed by yourself; and secondly that your ceremonies should be concluded by seven o'clock to-morrow, at the latest; for at eight precisely Louis Capet must proceed to the place of execution.' These last words were uttered, like all the rest, with a callous composure, revealing a brutality to which the contemplation of the worst of crimes brought not a shadow of remorse. Still I put my request in writing and laid it on the table. I was re-conducted to the King, who was anxiously awaiting the issue of my negotiations. My brief relation of what had taken place (I suppressed all details) seemed to give him the liveliest satisfaction. It was now past ten o'clock, and I remained with the King till the night was far advanced; when, perceiving him to be fatigued, I begged him to take some repose. He consented with his accustomed good humour, and made me promise to do likewise. I went by his desire into the little room occupied by Cléry, which was only separated from the King's room by a thin partition; and whilst I was a party to the most overwhelming reflections, I heard the King calmly giving directions for the next day, after which he lay down to rest.

At five o'clock, he rose and dressed as usual. Soon afterwards he sent for me and spoke with me for nearly an hour in the closet, where he had received me the evening before. On leaving him I found an altar completely prepared in the King's apartment. The commissaries had executed to the letter all that I had required of them; they had even done more than I had asked; for I had only demanded what was absolutely indispensable. The King heard Mass, he knelt on the ground without cushion or desk, he then received the sacrament, after which ceremony I left him for a short time at his prayers; he soon sent for me again; I found him seated near his stove where he could scarcely warm himself. 'I thank God' he said 'for the blessed gift of my religious principles. Without them, what should I now be? But with them how sweet death appears to me. For there dwells on high an incorruptible judge, from whom I shall assuredly receive the justice that is denied me here on earth.'

The sacred nature of the duties which I then performed prevent me from relating more than a few fragments of the many conversations which he held with me during the last sixteen hours of his life. But from the little I have told, it may be seen how much I might have added, were it consistent with my duty to say more. Morning began to dawn, and in every quarter of Paris drums beat to arms. The extraordinary stir in all the city was audible even in the tower, and I confess, it made the blood freeze in my veins. But the King, calmer than I, after listening to it for a moment, said to me without any sign of emotion, 'It must be the National Guard that are beginning to assemble. In a short time detachments of cavalry entered the court-yard of the Temple, and we could distinctly hear the voices of the officers and the trampling of horses. The King listened again and said to me with the same composure, 'They seem to be approaching.' On taking leave of the Queen the evening before, he had promised her that he would see her again in the morning, and he desired passionately to keep his word. But I earnestly entreated him not to subject her to a trial greater than she could bear. He hesitated a moment and then, with an expression of the most profound grief, said, 'You are right, Sir, it would kill her. I must deprive myself of this melancholy consolation, and let her live on hope for a few moments longer.'

From seven o'clock to eight, various persons came frequently, on various pretexts, came and knocked at the door of the closet, and each time I trembled lest is should be the last. But the King, with greater firmness than I could have shown, rose without emotion, went to the door and quietly answered the persons who thus interrupted us. I do not know who they were; but among them was certainly one of the greatest monsters that the Revolution had produced; for I heard him distinctly say to his King, in a tone of mockery, I know not in what connexion, 'Oh, that was all very well when you were King; but you are King no longer.' The King answered not a word, but on returning to me, contented himself with saying, 'You see how these people treat me, but I must know how to endure everything.' Another time, having answered one of the commissaries who came to interrupt us, he returned and said with a smile, 'These people see daggers and poisons everywhere. They are afraid I shall kill myself. Alas! they little know me. To kill myself would be mere weakness. No! Since it must be so, I shall know how to die.' Then came another knock – the last. It was Santerre and his crew. The King opened the door as usual. They announced to him (I could not hear their actual words) that he must go to his death. 'I am busy,' he replied with an air of authority, 'Wait for me; in a few minutes I shall be at your disposal.' So saying, he shut the door and threw himself at my knees. 'It is finished,' he said. 'Give me your last blessing, and pray that it may please God to support me to the end.' He soon rose and, leaving the closet, advanced towards the party who stood in the middle of his bed-chamber. Their faces showed them to be exceeding ill at ease, but not a hat was doffed, and the King, perceiving it, asked for his own. Whilst Cléry, bathed in tears, ran to fetch it, 'Is any of you a Member of the Commune?' said the King, 'I charge him to deposit this paper there.' It was his will. One of the party took it from his hands. 'I also' he continued 'recommend to the Commune, Cléry, my valet-de-chambre. For his services I have nothing but praise. See to it that he has my watch and clothes, not only those which I have here, but those that have been deposited with the Commune. I also desire that, in return for the attachment he has shewn me, he may be allowed to enter into the Queen's – into my wife's service'; for he used both expressions. No one answering, the King cried with a firm voice, 'Let us proceed!' whereupon the escort moved forward; the King crossed the first courtyard, formerly the garden, on foot; he turned back once or twice towards the tower, as if to bid farewell to all that he held most dear on earth; and by his gestures it was plain that he was trying to collect all his strength and courage. At the entrance of the second court, a hackney coach was in waiting, two gendarmes held the door; at the King's approach, one of them entered first and placed himself in front; the King followed and placed me at his side; the second gendarme jumped in last, and shut the door. It is said that one of these men was a priest in disguise; for the honour of the priesthood I hope that this is untrue. It is also said that they had orders to assassinate the King on the slightest movement on the part of the people. I do not know whether these were their instructions or no, but unless they had other concealed weapons about them it seems to me that it would have been difficult to accomplish their purpose; for it would have been impossible for them to have used their muskets, which were the only weapons visible. But the movement which they feared was far from being a figment of their imagination. For a large number of persons devoted to the King had determined to tear him by force from the hands of his guards or to die in the attempt. Two of the principal actors, young men of a well-known family, had come to warn me of their intentions the night before; and I confess that, without being sanguine of their success, even at the scaffold's foot I had still a glimmer of hope. I have since heard that the orders given for this dreadful morning had been planned with such skill and executed with such precision that of four or five hundred loyal and devoted men, twenty-five only reached the rendez-vous. Of the others, as the result of the measures taken at day-break in all the streets of Paris, not a man succeeded in even leaving his house.

Be this as it may, the King finding himself crammed into a carriage, where he could neither speak nor be spoken to without witnesses, decided to say nothing. I at once gave him my breviary, the sole book I had about me, and he seemed to accept it with pleasure. He even appeared anxious that I should show him the psalms best suited to his situation and recited them antiphonally with me. The gendarmes, though they uttered not a word, seemed astonished and confounded at the tranquil piety of a monarch whom they had doubtless never seen at such close quarters. The procession lasted almost two hours. The streets were lined with citizens, two or three deep, and all armed, some with pikes and some with guns, and in addition the carriage was surrounded by an imposing body of troops, composed, I have no doubt, of all the vilest creatures that Paris could produce. As a crowning precaution they had placed before the horses, a multitude of drums, intended to drown any cries that might be uttered in favour of the King; yet how could they have been heard? there was no one at doors or windows, and in the street there was nothing to be seen but citizens in arms, that is to say, citizens who out of weakness, if nothing worse, thronged to the commission of a crime which perhaps they detested in their hearts. Thus in profound silence the carriage proceeded to the Place de Louis XV, and there stopped in a great empty space that had been left round the scaffold; this space was surrounded with cannon, and beyond, as far as eye could reach, there stretched an armed multitude. As soon as the King perceived that the carriage stopped, he turned to me and whispered, 'If I am not mistaken, we are at our journey's end.' My silence answered that we were. One of the guards came at once to open the carriage door, and the gendarmes would have jumped out but the King stopped them, and placing his hand upon my knee, 'Gentlemen,' he said, in a tone of majesty, 'I commend this gentleman to your care; see that after my death no insult is offered to him; I charge you to prevent it.' Neither answered a word, and the King was continuing in a louder tone, when one of them interrupted him, saying, 'Yes, yes, we will take care of him; leave him to us.' I should add that these words were spoken in a tone of voice which must have made my blood run cold, if at such a moment it had been possible for me to have thought of myself.

As soon as the King had left the carriage, three guards surrounded him and would have stripped him, but he repulsed them haughtily, undressing himself, untied his neck-cloth, opened his shirt and arranged it himself. The guards, whom his royal dignity had for a moment disconcerted, seemed to recover their audacity. They surrounded him again and would have seized his hands. 'What do you mean?' cried the King, sharply withdrawing his hands. 'To bind you,' replied one of them. 'To bind me! I shall never consent to that. Carry out your orders. But you shall never bind me. Put that out of your minds.' They insisted, raised their voices and seemed on the point of summoning others to assist them by main force.

This was perhaps the most terrible moment of this most dreadful morning; another instant, and the best of kings would have received, before the eyes of his rebellious subjects, an outrage far more insupportable than death; for they would have laid violent hands upon him. He appeared to fear it himself and, turning to me, looked fixedly at me, as if to ask my advice. Alas! it was impossible for me to give any, and I only answered by silence. But, as he continued to look at me, 'Sire,' I said, 'in this fresh outrage I see only a last trait of resemblance between your Majesty and the God who is soon to be your reward.' At these words, he raised his eyes to heaven with an expression of grief past my powers of description. 'You are right,' he said. 'His example is enough. I will submit even to this'; and turning to his guards, 'Do what you will,' he said, 'I will drink of the cup even to the dregs.'

The steps leading to the scaffold were extremely steep. The King was obliged to lean upon my arm, and from the difficulty which he seemed to feel in the ascent, I feared for a moment that his courage was beginning to fail. But what was my astonishment when, arrived at the last step, I saw him, if I may use the expression, escape from my hands, with a firm step cross the whole breadth of the scaffold, silence by his look alone fifteen or twenty drums that were placed opposite him, and with a voice, so loud that it must have been heard at the Pont Tournant, distinctly pronounce these for ever memorable words: 'I die innocent of all the crimes laid to my charge. I pardon those who have occasioned my death, and I pray to God that the blood which you are now about to shed may never be visited upon France.' He was proceeding to say more, when a man on horseback, wearing the national uniform, suddenly burst forward sword in hand and crying fiercely at the drums, forced them to beat. Many voices were heard at the same time encouraging the executioners. They seemed to rouse themselves, and, laying violent hands on the most virtuous of Kings, dragged him under the axe, which severed his head from his body with a single blow.

All this passed in a moment. The youngest of the executioners (he seemed a boy of eighteen) immediately raised the head and displayed it to the people as he walked round the scaffold. He accompanied this monstrous ceremony with the most atrocious cries and the most indecent gestures. At first a melancholy silence prevailed; at length some cries of 'Vive la Republique' were heard; gradually the voices multiplied, and in less than ten minutes this cry, a thousand times repeated, became the sole cry of the multitude and every hat was in the air.

THEOBALD WOLFE TONE (1763-1798)

Tone, born in Dublin, was educated in Trinity College, Dublin (as an undergraduate he eloped with Matilde Witherington) and was called to the Bar in 1789. Influenced by French revolutionary theories, he became a Republican, founding the society of United Irishmen in 1791. He was associated with William Jackson, sent by the French government to assess the possibilities of an invasion of England. After Jackson's arrest in 1795 Tone was allowed to emigrate to America. He then went to France and persuaded the Directory to undertake an invasion of Ireland: he sailed in the French invasion fleet which bad weather prevented from landing in Bantry Bay in December 1796. After a second failure in 1797 a third expedition was defeated at Lough Swilly, and Tone was captured and coutrmartialled; sentenced to hanging, he committed suicide in prison. His *Journal* was issued by his son in Washington in 1826.

Extract from Tone's Diary, December 1796

December 2nd. – Received my order to embark on board the *Indomptable*, of eighty guns, Captain Bedout…. We have a most magnificent vessel…. I hope to God we are about to set out at last. I see by a proclamation of the Lord-Lieutenant that the North of Ireland is in a flame; if we arrive safe, we shall not do much to extinguish it.

December 4th. – … In the meantime the troops keep up their health and spirits and are at this moment as well as possible and every evening dancing on the quarter-deck. Would to God we were all in Ireland, but when will that be?

December 12th. – The État Major came aboard last night. We are seven in the great cabin, including a lady in boy's clothes – the wife of a Commissaire, one Ragoneau. By what I see we have a little army of commissaries, who are going to Ireland to make their fortunes. If we arrive safe, I think I will keep my eye a little upon these gentlemen.

December 14th. – I must remark the infinite power of female society over our minds, which I see every moment exemplified in the effect which the presence of Madame Ragoneau has on our manners; not that she has any claim to respect other than as she is a woman, for she is not very handsome, she has no talents, and (between friends) she was originally a *fille de joie* at Paris. Yet we are all attentive and studious to please her, and I am glad, in short, she is aboard, as I am satisfied she humanizes us not a little. General Watrin paid us a visit this evening with the band of his regiment, and I went down into the great cabin where all the officers mess and where the music was playing. I was delighted with the effect it seemed to have on them. The cabin was ceiled with the firelocks intended for the expedition; the candlesticks were bayonets stuck in the table. The officers were in their jackets and *bonnets de police,* some playing cards, others singing to the music, others conversing, and all in the highest spirits – once again I was delighted with the scene. At length Watrin and his band went off, and, as it was a beautiful moonlight night, the effect of the music on the water, diminishing as they receded from our vessel, was delicious.

December 15th. – It is most delicious weather and the sun is warm and bright as in the month of May. 'I hope,' as Lord George Brilliant said, 'he may not shine through somebody presently.' We are all in high spirits and the troops are as gay as if they were going to a ball. With our fifteen thousand, or more correctly thirteen thousand and nine hundred and seventy-five men, I would not have the least doubt of our beating thirty thousand of such as will be opposed to us – that is to say if we reach our destination. The signal is now flying to get under way, so one way or other the affair will be at last brought to a decision, and God knows how sincerely I rejoice at it. The wind is right aft. Huzza! At one we got under way and stood out of the Goulet until three, when we cast anchor by signal in the Bay de Camaret, having made about three leagues.

December 16th. – At two signal to get under way. At half after two made sail, the wind still favourable but slack.

December 17th. – Last night passed through the Raz, a most dangerous and difficult pass, wherein we were within an inch of running on a sunken rock, where we must every soul have inevitably perished. I knew nothing about it, for my part, till this morning and I am glad of it ... Ours is the first squadron that has passed through the Raz, which even single ships avoid unless in case of necessity. This morning, to my infinite mortification and anxiety, we are but eighteen sail in company instead of forty-three, which is our number. We conjecture, however, that the remaining twenty-five have made their way through the Yroise and that we shall see them tomorrow morning; at the same time we much fear that some of our companions have perished in that infernal Raz ... Two of the Admirals and the General are with the absent; God send they may have escaped the Raz. Rear-Admiral Bouvet and General Grouchy, Second-in-Command, are with us.

December 18th. – At nine this morning a fog so thick that we cannot see a ship's length before us ... We may be for aught I know within a quarter of a mile of our missing ships without knowing it; it is true we may also by the same means miss the English, so it may be as well for good as evil ... Foggy all day and no appearance of our comrades. I asked General Chérin what we should do in case they did not rejoin us. He said that he supposed General Grouchy would take the command with the troops we had with us, which on examination we found to amount to about 6500 men. I need not say that I supported this idea with all my might. The Captain has opened a packet containing instructions for his conduct in case of separation, which order him to cruise for five days off Mizen Head and, at the end of that time, proceed to the mouth of the Shannon, where he is to remain three more, at the end of which time, if he does not see the fleet or receive further orders by a frigate, he is to make the best of his way back to Brest. But we must see in that case whether Bouvet and Grouchy may not take themselves to land the troops.

December 19th. – This morning at eight signal of a fleet in the offing; *branlebas général*;[1] rose directly and made my toilet, so now I am ready 'ou pour les Anglais ou pour les Anglaises'. I see about a dozen sail, but whether they are friends or enemies God knows. It is a stark calm, so that we do not move an inch even with our studding sails, but here we lie rolling like so many logs on the water ... At half-past ten we floated near enough to recognize the signals and, to my infinite satisfaction, the strange fleet proves to be our comrades, so now 'nous en sommes quittes pour la peur', as the French say ... The wind, which favoured us thus far, is chopped about and is now right in our teeth; that is provoking enough. If we had a fair wind, we should be in Bantry Bay tomorrow morning. At half-past one hailed by a lugger, which informed us of the loss of the *Séduisant*, a seventy-four of our squadron, the first night of our departure, with 550 of the ninety-fourth demi-brigade, of whom she saved 33. It happened near the same spot where we were in such imminent danger.... Admiral Morard de Galles, General Hoche, General Debelle, and Colonel

---

1 *branlebas général*: a general clearing for action.

Shee are aboard the *Fraternité,* and God knows what has become of them. The wind, too, continues against us and altogether I am in terrible low spirits. How if these damned English should catch us at last after having gone on successfully thus far?

December 20th. – Last night in moderate weather we contrived to separate again, and this morning at 8 o'clock we are but fifteen sailing company with a foul wind and hazy. I am in horrible ill humour and it is no wonder. We shall lie beating about here within thirty leagues of Cape Clear until the English come and catch us, which will be truly agreeable. Let me not think; I amuse myself at night, when the rest are at cards, walking alone in the gallery and singing the airs that my poor love used to be fond of:

> The wandering tar, that not for years has prest
> The widowed partner of his day of rest,
> On the cold deck, far from her arms removed,
> Still hums the ditty that his Susan loved.[1]

I feel now the truth of these beautiful lines. Well, hang sorrow! At ten several sail in sight to windward; I suppose they are our stray sheep. It is scandalous to part company twice in four days in such moderate weather as we have had, but sea affairs, I see, are not our forte. Captain Bedout is a seaman, which I fancy is more than can be said for nine-tenths of his confrères.

December 21st. – Stark calm all the fore part of the night. At length a breeze sprung up, and this morning at day-break we are under Cape Clear, distant about four leagues, so I have at all events once more seen my country; but the pleasure I should otherwise feel at this is totally destroyed by the absence of the General, who has not joined us and of whom we know nothing.... It is most delicious weather, with a favourable wind and everything in short that we can desire except our absent comrades. At the moment I write this we are under easy sail, within three leagues of most of the coast, so that I can discover here and there patches of snow on the mountains. What if the General should not join us? If we cruise here five days according to our instructions, the English will be upon us and then all is over. We are thirty-five sail in company and seven or eight absent. Is that such a separation of our force as, under all the circumstances, will warrant our following the letter of our orders to the certain failure of the

---

1 *The wandering tar ... Susan loved*: R. B. Sheridan, *The Rivals*, Epilogue, ll. 34-37.

expedition? If Grouchy and Bouvet be men of spirit and decision, they will land immediately and trust to their success for justification. If they be not, and if this day passes without our seeing the General, I much fear the game is up. I am in undescribable anxiety, and Chérin, who commands aboard, is a poor creature, to whom it is vain to speak; not but I believe he is brave enough, but he has a little mind. There cannot be imagined a situation more provokingly tantalizing than mine at this moment – within view, almost within reach, of my native land, and uncertain whether I shall ever set my foot on it. We are now, nine o'clock, at the rendezvous appointed; stood in for the coast till twelve, when we were near enough to toss a biscuit ashore; at twelve tacked and stood out again, so now we have begun our cruise of five days in all its forms, and shall, in obedience to the letter of our instructions, ruin the expedition and destroy the remnant of the French Navy with a precision and punctuality which will be truly edifying. We opened Bantry Bay and in all my life rage never entered so deeply into my heart as when we turned our backs on the coast. I sounded Chérin as to what Grouchy might do, but he turned the discourse.... At half after one the *Atalante,* one of our missing corvettes, hove in sight, so now again we are in hopes to see the General. Oh, if he were in Grouchy's place, he would not hesitate one moment! Continue making short boards; the wind foul.

December 22nd. This morning at eight we have neared Bantry Bay considerably, but the fleet is terribly scattered. No news of the *Fraternité*; I believe it is the first instance of an Admiral in a clean frigate, with moderate weather and moonlight nights, parting company with his fleet. Captain Grammont, our first lieutenant, told me his opinion is that she is either taken or lost, and in either event it is a terrible blow to us. All rests now upon Grouchy and I hope he may turn out well; he has a glorious game in his hands if he has spirits and talent to play it. If he succeeds, it will immortalize him. I do not at all like the countenance of the État Major in this crisis. When they speak of the expedition, it is in a style of despondency, and, when they are not speaking of it, they are playing cards and laughing. They are every one of them brave of their persons, but I see nothing of that spirit of enterprise, combined with a steady resolution, which our present situation demands. They stared at me this morning when I said that Grouchy was the man in the whole army who had the least reason to regret the absence of the General, and began to talk of responsibility and difficulties, as if any great enterprise was without responsibility and difficulties. I was burning with rage; however I said nothing and will say nothing until I get ashore, if ever I am so happy as to arrive there. We are gaining the Bay by slow degrees, with a head wind at East, where it has hung these five weeks. Tonight we hope, if nothing extraordinary happens, to cast anchor in the mouth of the Bay and work up tomorrow morning. These delays are dreadful to my impatience; I am now so near the shore that I can see distinctly two old castles, yet I am utterly uncertain whether I shall ever set foot on it. According to appearances, Bouvet and Grouchy are resolved to proceed; that is a great point gained, however. Two o'clock; we have been tacking ever since eight this morning and I am sure we have not gained one hundred yards. The wind is right ahead and the fleet dispersed, several being far to leeward. I have been looking over the schedule of our arms, artillery and ammunition. We are well provided.... Messieurs of the État Major continue in the horrors; I find Simon the stoutest of them and Fairin, Chérin's aide-de-camp, the worst; he puts me in mind of David in *The Rivals*: 'But I am fighting Bob and, damn it, I won't be afraid'.[1] I continue very discreetly to say little or nothing, as my situation just now is rather a delicate one. If we were once ashore and things turn out to my mind, I shall soon be out of my trammels, and perhaps in that respect I may be better off with Grouchy than with Hoche. If the people act with spirit, as I hope they will, it is no matter who is General, and, if they do not, all the talents of Hoche would not save us, so it comes to the same thing at last. At half-past six cast anchor off Bere Island, being still four leagues from our landing-place. At work with General Chérin writing and translating proclamations, etc., all our printed papers, including my two pamphlets, being on board the *Fraternité*, which is pleasant.

December 23rd. – Last night it blew a heavy gale from the eastward, with snow, so that the mountains are covered this morning, which will render our bivouacs extremely amusing. It is to be observed that, of the thirty-two points of the compass, the east is precisely the most unfavourable to us. In consequence we are this morning separated for the fourth time; sixteen sail, including nine or ten of the line, with Bouvet and Grouchy, are at anchor with us, and about twenty are blown to sea; luckily the gale set from the shore, so I am in hopes no mischief will ensue. The wind is still high and, as usual, right ahead; and I dread a visit from the English and altogether I am in great uneasiness. Oh that we were once ashore, let what might ensue after! I am sick to the very soul of this suspense. It is curious to

---

1 *I won't be afraid*: probably Tone is confusing David's 'so –we fight' and Acre's later 'Zounds! I won't be afraid' in Act IV, sc. I.

see how things are managed in this best of all possible worlds. We are here, sixteen sail great and small, scattered up and down in a noble Bay and so dispersed that there are not two together in any spot save one, and there they are now so close that, if it blows tonight as it did last night, they will inevitably run foul of each other, unless one of them prefers driving on shore.... The day has passed without the appearance of one vessel; friend or enemy, the wind rather more moderate but still ahead.... I am now so near the shore that I can in a manner touch the sides of Bantry Bay with my right and left hand; yet God knows whether I shall ever tread again on Irish ground. There is one thing which I am surprised at, which is the extreme *sang-froid* with which I view the coast. I expected I should have been violently affected; yet I look at it as if it were the coast of Japan. I do not, however, love my country the less for not having romantic feelings with regard to her. Another thing, we are now three days in Bantry Bay; if we do not land immediately, the enemy will collect a superior force and perhaps repay us our victory of Quiberon. In an enterprise like ours everything depends upon the promptitude and audacity of our first movements, and we are here, I am sorry to say it, most pitifully languid. It is mortifying, but that is too poor a word; I could tear my flesh with rage and vexation, but that advances nothing, and so I hold my tongue in general and devour my melancholy as I can. To come so near and then to fail, if we are to fail! And everyone aboard seems now to have given up all hopes.

December 24th – This morning the whole État Major has been miraculously converted, and it was agreed in full council that General Chérin, Colonel Waudré (Chef d'État Major of the Artillery), and myself should go aboard the *Immortalité* and press General Grouchy in the strongest manner to proceed on the expedition with the ruins of our scattered army. Accordingly, we made a signal to speak with the Admiral, and in about an hour we were aboard. I must do Grouchy the justice of saying that the moment we gave our opinion in favour of proceeding he took his part decidedly and like a man of spirit; he instantly set about preparing the *ordre de bataille* and we finished it without delay. We are not more than 6500 strong, but they are tried soldiers who have seen fire, and I have the strongest hopes that after all we shall bring our enterprise to a glorious termination. It is a bold attempt and truly original. All the time we were preparing the *ordre de bataille* we were laughing most immoderately at the poverty of our means, and I believe, under the circumstances, it was the merriest council of war that was ever held; but 'des chevaliers français tel est le caractère'. Grouchy, the Commander-in-Chief, never had so few men under his orders since he was Adjutant-General; Waudré, who is Lieutenant-Colonel, finds himself now at the head of the artillery, which is a furious park consisting of one piece of eight, one of four, and two six-inch howitzers; when he was a captain, he never commanded fewer than ten pieces, but now that he is in fact General of the Artillery, he prefers taking the field with four. ... We have not one guinea; we have not a tent; we have not a horse to draw our four pieces of artillery; the General-in-Chief marches on foot; we leave all our baggage behind us; we have nothing but the arms in our hands, the clothes on our backs, and a good courage, but that is sufficient. ... But this infernal easterly wind continues without remorse and, though we have been under way three or four hours and made I believe three hundred tacks, we do not seem to my eyes to have gained one hundred yards in a straight line.... Well, let it blow and be hanged! I do not wonder tonight at Xerxes whipping the sea,[1] for I find myself pretty much in the mood to commit some such rational action. To return to our expedition, the more I think of it, the more I find it amusing. As Johnson says, 'the negative catalogue of our means is extremely copious'.[2] In addition to what I have mentioned already, we have no horses for our cavalry. Huzza! I apprehend we are tonight 6000 of the most careless fellows in Europe, for everybody is in the most extravagant of spirits on the eve of an enterprise which, considering our means, would make many people serious. I never liked the French half so well as tonight, and I can scarcely persuade myself that the loungers of the boulevards and the soldiers I see about me are of the same hemisphere. To judge the French rightly, or at least to see the bright part of their character, you must see them not in Paris but in the camp. It is in the armies that the Republic exists. My enemy, the wind, seems just now at 8 o'clock to relent a little, so we may reach Bantry by tomorrow. The enemy has now had four days to recover from his panic and prepare to receive us; so much the worse, but I do not mind it. We purpose to make a race for Cork as if the devil were in our bodies, and, when we are fairly there, we will stop for a day or two to take breath and look about us. From Bantry to Cork is about forty-five miles, which, with all our efforts, will take us three days, and I suppose we may have a brush by the way, but I think we are able

---

1 *Whipping the sea*: Xerxes, king of the Persians, when attacking Greece, was so infuriated when a storm destroyed his bridges over the Hellespont that he commanded the sea to be given three hundred lashes.

2 *'the negative catalogue ... copious'*: Samuel Johnson, *Journey to the Western Isles of Scotland*, comments on an inn's provisions having a copious 'negative catalogue'.

to deal with any force that can at a week's notice be brought against us.... It is inconceivable how well that most inconceivable of all writers, Shakespeare, has hit off the French character in his play of *Henry V.* I have been struck with it fifty times this evening; yet it is highly probable he never saw a French officer in his life.... I presume our arrival has put several respectable characters in no small fuss, but time will show more of that.

December 25th. – Last night I had the strongest expectations that today we should debark, but at two this morning I was awakened by the wind. I rose immediately and, wrapping myself in my greatcoat, walked for an hour in the gallery, devoured by the most gloomy reflections. The wind continues right ahead, so that it is absolutely impossible to work up to the landing-place, and God knows when it will change. The same wind is exactly favourable to bring the English upon us, and these cruel delays give the enemy time to assemble his entire force in this neighbourhood.... Had we been able to land the first day and march directly to Cork, we should have infallibly carried it by a *coup de main;* and then we should have a footing in the country, but, as it is – ? If we are taken, my fate will not be a mild one; the best I can expect is to be shot as an *émigré rentré,* unless I have the good fortune to be killed in the action; for most assuredly if the enemy will have us, he must fight for us. Perhaps I may be reserved for a trial, for the sake of striking terror into others, in which case I shall be hanged as a traitor and embowelled, etc. As to the embowelling, *je m'en fiche;* if ever they hang me, they are welcome to embowel me if they please. These are pleasant prospects! Nothing on earth could sustain me now but the consciousness that I am engaged in a just and righteous cause.... Our first capital error was in setting sail too late from the Bay of Camaret, by which means we were obliged to pass the Raz in the night, which caused the loss of the *Séduisant,* the separation of the fleet ... and, above all, the loss of time resulting from all this and which is never to be recovered. Our second error was in losing an entire day in cruising off the [Bantry] Bay when we might have entered and effected a landing with thirty-five sail, which would have secured everything.... I have a merry Christmas of it today.

December 26th. – Last night at half after six o'clock, a heavy gale of wind still from the east, we were surprised by the Admiral's frigate running under our quarter and hailing the *Indomptable* with orders to cut our cable and put to sea instantly; the frigate then pursued her course, leaving us all in the utmost astonishment. Our first idea was that it might be an English frigate, lurking in the bottom of the Bay, which took advantage of the storm and darkness of the night to make her escape, and wished to separate our squadron by this strategy; for it seems utterly incredible that an Admiral should cut and run in this manner without any previous signal of any kind to warn the fleet, and that the first notice we should have of his intention should be his hailing us in this extraordinary manner with such unexpected and peremptory orders. After a short consultation with his officers (considering the storm, the darkness of the night, that we had two anchors out and only one spare one in the hold), Captain Bedout resolved to wait at all events till tomorrow morning, in order to ascertain whether it was really the Admiral who hailed us. The morning is now come, the gale continues, and the fog is so thick that we cannot see a ship's length ahead; so here we lie in the utmost uncertainty and anxiety. In all probability we are now left without Admiral or General; if so, Chérin will command the troops and Bedout the fleet, but at all events there is an end of the expedition.... Of forty-three sail, of which the expedition consisted, we can muster of all sizes but fourteen. There only wants our falling in with the English to complete our destruction; and, to judge of the future by the past, there is every probability that that will not be wanting. All our hopes are now reduced to get back in safety to Brest and I believe we will set sail for that port the instant the weather will permit.... Notwithstanding all our blunders, it is the dreadful stormy weather and easterly winds, which have been blowing furiously and without intermission since we made Bantry Bay, that have ruined us. Well, England has not had such an escape since the Spanish Armada, and that expedition, like ours, was defeated by the weather.... I hope the Directory will not dismiss me the Service for this unhappy failure, in which certainly I have nothing personally to reproach myself with; and, in that case, I shall be rich enough to live as a peasant. If God Almighty sends me my dearest love and darling babies in safety, I will buy or rent a little spot and have done with the world for ever. I shall neither be great nor famous nor powerful, but I may be happy.... I am as eager to get back to France as I was to come to Ireland.

December 27th. – Yesterday several vessels, including the *Indomptable,* dragged their anchor several times and it was with great difficulty they rode out the gale.... This morning we are reduced to seven sail of the line and one frigate. Any attempt here is now desperate, but I still think if we were debarked at the mouth of the Shannon, we might yet recover all. At 10 o'clock the Commodore made signal to get under way, which was delayed by one of the ships, which required an hour to get ready. This hour we availed ourselves of to hold a council of war.... It was agreed that our force being now reduced to 4168 men, our artillery to two four-pounders, our ammunition to 1,500,000 cartridges and 500 rounds for the artillery with 500 lbs. of powder – this part of the country being utterly wild and savage, furnishing neither provisions nor horses, and especially as the enemy, having seven days' notice; together with three more which it would require to reach Cork, supposing we even met with no obstacle, had time more than sufficient to assemble his forces in numbers sufficient to crush our little army; considering, moreover, that this province is the only one of the four which has testified no disposition to revolt; that it is the most remote from the party which is ready for insurrection; and, finally, Captain Bedout having communicated his instructions, which are to mount as high as the Shannon and cruise there five days; it was unanimously agreed to quit Bantry Bay directly and proceed for the mouth of the Shannon in hopes to rejoin some of our scattered companions; and when we are there we will determine according to the means in our hands what part we shall take.... The wind at last has come round to the southward and the signal is now flying to get underway. At half after four, there being every appearance of a stormy night, three vessels cut their cables and put to sea. The *Indomptable* having with great difficulty weighed one anchor, we were forced at length to cut the cable of the other and make the best of our way out of the Bay, being followed by the whole of our little squadron, now reduced to ten sail.

December 28th. – Last night it blew a perfect hurricane. At one this morning a dreadful sea took the ship in the quarter, stove in the quarter gallery and one of the dead-lights in the great cabin, which was instantly filled with water to the depth of three feet. The cots of the officers were almost all torn down, and themselves and their trunks floated about the cabin. For my part, I had just fallen asleep when awakened by the shock, of which I at first did not comprehend the meaning; but hearing the water distinctly rolling in the cabin beneath me, and two or three of the officers mounting in their shirts as wet as if they had risen from the bottom of the sea, I concluded instantly that the ship had struck and was filling with water and that she would sink directly. As the movements of the mind are as quick as lightning in such perilous moments, it is impossible to describe the infinity of ideas which shot across my mind in an instant. As I knew all notion of saving my life was in vain in such a stormy sea, I took my part instantly and lay down in my hammock, expecting every instant to go to the bottom; but I was soon relieved by the appearance of one of the officers, Baudin, who explained to us the accident. I can safely say that I had perfect command of myself during the few terrible minutes which I passed in this situation, and I was not, I believe, more afraid than any of those about me. I resigned myself to my fate, which I verily thought was inevitable, and I could have died like a man. Immediately after this blow the wind abated, and at daylight, having run nine knots an hour under one jib only during the hurricane, we found ourselves at the rendezvous, having parted with three ships of the line and the frigate, which makes our sixth separation. The frigate *[Coquille]* joined us in the course of the day, which we spent standing off and on the shore, without being joined by any of our missing companions.

December 29th. – At four this morning the Commodore made the signal to steer for France, so there is an end of our expedition for the present – perhaps for ever. I spent all yesterday in my hammock, partly through sea-sickness and much more through vexation. At ten we made prize of an unfortunate brig bound from Lisbon to Cork laden with salt, which we sunk.

December 31st. – On our way to Brest. It will be well supposed I am in no great humour to make memorandums. This is the last day of the year 1796, which has been a very remarkable one in my history.

January 1st. – At eight this morning made for the island of Ushant and at twelve opened the Goulet. We arrived seven sail.... We left Brest forty-three sail, of which seventeen were of the line. I am utterly astonished that we did not see a single English ship of war, going nor coming back. They must have taken their measures very ill not to intercept us, but perhaps they have picked up some of our missing ships. Well, this evening will explain and we shall see now what is become of our four Admirals and of our two Generals-in-Chief.

EDWARD BUNTING (1773-1845)

Born in Armagh, Bunting moved to Drogheda on his father's death, his eldest brother being an organist and music teacher there. Bunting followed a similar career, being apprenticed as an organist in Drogheda in 1784. When the famous Belfast Festival of the Harpers was held in 1792 he transcribed the harpers' airs, and the following year he travelled widely in Ulster, Connacht and Munster collecting sixty-six airs for his *General Collection of the Ancient Music of Ireland* (1796). A second edition of 1809 contained seventy-seven more airs while *The Ancient Music of Ireland* provided a further 120 airs. Bunting stayed in London and Paris before marrying and moving to Dublin where he was organist to St. Stephen's Church.

Preface to A General Collection of the Ancient Irish Music (1796)

It is an extraordinary fact, that although Ireland has from a remote antiquity, been celebrated for its cultivation of Music, and admitted to be one of the parent countries of that delightful art, the present is the first General collection of its national airs. Most of them are of such ancient origin, that the names of their authors, and the era in which they were composed, are alike unknown.

The works of some of its latest composers, as Conolan[1] and Carolan*, have before been selected; but of these it remained to this day to give accurate copies; while the superior productions of their masters, on whom they had formed their style, and of whose excellence they have fallen short, are now only partially known in the very Country where they once flourished. To rescue them from oblivion, and to open a new source of Musical delight, the public are now presented with the first Volume of such a collection, as has for a long time been eagerly desired.

A brief account of the circumstances which led to this Collection will naturally be expected.

The rapid decrease of the number of itinerant Performers on the Irish Harp, with the consequent decline of that tender and expressive Instrument, gave the first idea of assembling the remaining Harpers dispersed over the different Provinces of Ireland. A meeting of them was accordingly procured at a considerable expense, by the Gentlemen of Belfast on the 12th of July 1792, and liberal Premiums were distributed among them, according to their respective merits.

The compiler of this Volume was appointed to attend on that occasion, to take down the various airs played by the different Harpers, and was particularly cautioned against adding a single note to the old melodies, which would seem from inferences, that will afterwards be drawn, to have been preserved pure and handed down unalloyed, through a long succession of ages.

A principal motive to convene this assemblage of the remnant of the

---

1 *Conolan*: a harper born *c.* 1640 in Co. Sligo.

Irish Bards, was to procure, while yet attainable, the most approved copies of tunes already in the hands of practitioners, as well as to revive and perpetuate a variety of others extremely ancient of which there were no copies extant and which were therefore likely to become extinct.

This end was, in a great degree, secured by the meeting alluded to; and it has since been perfected by the editor of the present work, who made a tour through a principal portion of the Kingdom for the purpose of comparing the Music already procured, with that in the possession of Harpers in other parts, and of making such additions as would render the work complete.

The work is now before that tribunal, which is the natural Judge of its merits, it may however without presumption, be alleged, that while public taste shall remain sufficiently pure and unadulterated, to be capable of admiring strains which lead directly to the heart, the ancient Music of Ireland will be studied with increasing delight....

THOMAS DERMODY (1775-1802)

A child prodigy born in Ennis, Co. Clare, he was the son of a schoolmaster whom he assisted in teaching the classics at the age of nine. He subsequently ran away to Dublin where he gained some influential patrons. Their patience inevitably ran out as their efforts to educate him and prevent his heavy drinking proved in vain. He served briefly in the army in France but died penniless in a hut in Sydenham, Kent, his last words 'I am vicious because I like it.' He wrote lyrics with facility, his collected poems appearing as *The Harp of Erin* (2 vols, 1807).

John Baynham's Epitaph[1]

Here lies Hercules the Second,
A penman fine by critics reckon'd;
With back so huge, and brawny neck on't,
      And shrewdish head,
Which oft to smoking hotpot beckon'd:
      John Baynham's dead.

Woe's me! no more shall younkers crowd
About thy hearth, and gabble loud;

---

1 *John Baynham's Epitaph*: Baynham was a parish clerk of Killeigh, Co. Offaly. He wrote letters for the parishioners and was one of Dermody's drinking companions. They met in a pub owned by Lory, as the Postscript tells us.

Thomas Dermody

Where thou, in magistracy proud,
                Nought humbly said:
Alas! we never thought thee good
                Till thou wast dead.

Though, by my soul! still sober, mellow,
I ken'd thee aye a special fellow,
Catches or psalm-staves prompt to bellow,
                O pious breed!
I ween thou'n fixt 'tween heav'n and hell: oh!
                Our comfort's dead.

But for that plaguy profligate,
We early might enjoy and late
The knowledge of thy teeming pate
                From board to bed:
But now thou'rt 'neath a puny slate:
                Droll Johnny's dead.

Full many a hard bout hast thou weather'd:
By merry Bob severely tether'd;
More sadly than if tarr'd and feather'd,
                Like bull-dog led:
Now all my tools are fairly gather'd;
                Blythe Baynham's dead.

Heav'n lend thy soul its surest port,
And introduce thee to the court;
Revive again thy earthly sport
                And melt thy lead!
Alas! we mourn; for, by the mort!
                John Baynham's dead.

No curate now can work thy throat,
And alter clean thy jocund note;
Charon[1] has plump'd thee in his boat,
                And run ahead:
My curse on death, the meddling sot!
                Gay Johnny's dead.

---

1 *Charon*: in Greek mythology, the ferryman who conveyed the dead across the river Styx or Acheron to Hades.

With gills of noblest usquebaugh[1]
Will we anoint thy epitaph;
While thou at the full bowl shalt laugh,
          A precious meed:
At last thou liest in harbour safe;
           Sage Johnny's dead.

News shall no more thy mornings muzzle,
Or schemes good spirit-punch to guzzle;
Wounds! thou art past this mortal bustle,
          With manna fed;
Satan and thou hadst a long tussel;
           At last thou'rt dead.

May blessings light upon thy gloom,
And geese grow fat upon thy tomb!
While no rash scribbler's impious thumb
          Shall maul thy head;
But greet thee soft 'in kingdom come,'
           Though thou art dead.

Postscript

After inditing these sad stories,
I happed to hear some brother tories
Ranting and roaring loud at Lory's',
          Not quite well bred;
I enter'd, and exclaim'd, 'Ye glories,
           John Baynham's dead.'

Scarce had I spoke, when 'neath the table
Something sigh'd out most lamentable:
Anon, to make my song a fable,
          Starts out brave John;
Sitting by Jove above! most stable
           On wicked throne.

They press'd my sitting: marv'lous dull,
I gap'd at Banquo[2] like a fool,

---

1 *usquebaugh*: whiskey (Irish, the water of life).
2 *Banquo*: a Scottish general in Shakespeare's *Macbeth*.

And cried 'Good Sirs, the table's full,
              And there's a spirit,'
'Come reach,' quote sprite, 'an easy stool:'
              And lent a wherret.[1]

'You rogue,' said he, 'how dare you write
Such stuff on me, as dead outright;
I think, by this good candle-light,
You've earn'd a drubbing.'
'Pho! peace,' said I, 'I'll blot it quite;
Aye, by St. Dobbin.'

Witness therefore, by my small finger,
John chooses still on earth to linger
As penman, poet, toper, singer,
In trade full thriving;
Know then, old bellman, barber, tinker
John Baynham's living.

MARIA EDGEWORTH (1767-1849)

The third child of Richard Lovell Edgeworth by the first of his four wives, Maria Edgeworth was born in England, where she was educated. In 1782 she moved with her father to the family estate in Edgeworthstown, Co. Longford. Here she taught her younger stepbrothers and stepsisters, and collaborated with her father in formulating a progressive system of education based on the tenets of Jean Jacques Rousseau (set out in their *Practical Education* of 1798) and on the humane management of the estate. Her father encouraged her writings. In 1800 she published *Castle Rackrent*, which was praised by Sir Walter Scott and her fame (As a regional novel it had been preceded by *Virtue Rewarded: or, The Irish Princess. A New Novel* (1693)) It offers a notoriously unreliable narrator, the servant Thady Quirke. The responsibility of the Irish landed gentry informs her novels *Ennui* (1809), *The Absentee* (1812) and *Ormond* (1817). After her father's death in 1817, she completed his *Memoirs*. During the Famine she worked tirelessly to relieve the plight of the peasants in the area. She died not long after.

---

1 *wherret*: a glow.

Letter to Mrs Ruxton

Edgeworthstown,
Saturday Night, Jan. 1796

... My father is gone to a Longford committee, where he will I suppose hear many dreadful Defender[1] stories: he came home yesterday fully persuaded that a poor man in this neighbourhood, a Mr. Houlton, had been murdered, but he found he was only *kilt*, and 'as well as could be expected,' after being twice robbed and twice cut with a bayonet. You, my dear aunt, who were so brave when the county of Meath was the seat of war, must know that we emulate your courage; and I assure you in your own words, 'that whilst our terrified neighbours see nightly visions of massacres, we sleep with our doors and windows unbarred.'

I must observe though, that it is only those doors and windows which have neither bolts nor bars, that we leave unbarred, and these are more at present than we wish, even for the reputation of our valour. All that I crave for my own part is, that if I am to have my throat cut, it may not be by a man with his face blackened with charcoal. I shall look at every person that comes here very closely, to see if there be any marks of charcoal upon their visages. Old wrinkled offenders I should suppose would never be able to wash out their stains; but in others a very clean face will in my mind be a strong symptom of guilt – clean hands proof positive, and clean nails ought to hang a man.

DOROTHEA HERBERT (1768/1770-1829)

The eldest of the nine children of the Rev. Nicholas Herbert (d. 1803), who married the Hon. Martha Cuffe (d. 1811) in 1766, she described the rudiments of her education as being laid at home 'under Mrs Charles an Anglo-French governess Seignor Tassoni an itinerant Dancing Master and Monsier Dabeard a blind drunken French music master'. A brief spell in Miss English's school at Carrick until Miss English refused to teach her and her companions was followed by an old French woman who had come begging in rags, teaching them French 'capitally' as well as instructing them in the art of making Mushroom soup and Soupe Maigre. There followed a spell in Dublin under the instruction of dancing, music and art masters, who declared her spoiled by her country teachers. The music master said she must unlearn all she had learned from the Carrick Brogueneers.

Dorothea Herbert did not marry, and the 260-page manuscript of the *Retrospections* was first published in 1929, having come through her youngest brother

---

1 *Defender stories*: about an oath-bound secret society, very active in the 1790s. The Defenders were to remain an underground, largely peasant, organisation after the 1798 revolution.

Nicholas, rector of Knockgrafton for forty years, to the Mandeville family. The published version does not include more than half her *Retrospections*, which continued to 1806; it concludes with her account of her unhappy love affair in 1789 ('surely,' she wrote, 'there is in love a mysterious Law that chains the Soul to silent Endurance...'). She mentions also writing *Poems*, *Plays* and *Novels* but these have not come to light. She conveys the tightly knit family life of the time – when she was in Dublin there were 19 or 20 cousins living in three adjacent streets – and she is always interested in family connections and histories.

From Retrospections

FROM CHAPTER THE 12TH [1776]

... After spending three Months very pleasantly My Mother being quite recovered we set out for Lamplighters Hall having engaged one Captain Clevelands Vessel a Trader for return by long Sea – After waiting there three Days, He got other Passengers, and put to Sea unknown to us in a Violent Storm – Vex'd to Death at this disappointment We hired a Boat and follow'd him three long leagues – The Tempest encreasing every Moment, and the Sea mountainous high – We had a Madwoman with us who roared in Our Ears Blow Blow ye Winds Blow – Our Oars broke, and the Boatmen gave us up for lost – However as My Mothers White Handkerchief floated astern – The brutal Captain Cleveland tacked his Ship about and picked us up from the Waves half dead with Terror and fatigue.

His Ship the two Brothers was a dirty dark Vessel laden with Rotten Eggs for the Sugar House – had a quantity of stinking Meat on board – and a dead Corpse to make it more delectable – This last Article was hid under our bed for neither the Sailors or we would have relishd such a Shipmate the former being always superstitious on such Occasions – The Stenches became so intolerable altogether that we kept our Beds from Nausea and only found relief in Embrocations of Vinegar – I was seized with a Vomitting of Blood which was near ending My Existence – From thence I grew quite heavy and Stupid – The honest Tars however forced My Mother much against her Will to pour down my Throat a Whole Bowl of their Brown Pottage which stopd the Vomitting and cured Me – This brought the Pottage into high vogue amongst the Quality and was a most Seasonable discovery as all our Hamper Provisions grew Putrid – To this Day I remember it was the most grateful healing Mess I ever tasted.

We now got Sight of the Irish Coast but the Captain would not put in without a Pilot – The Winds were fierce and changeable the Shore uncertain and dangerous, and the whole Ship Short of Provisions – after a horrid Bandying about amongst the Billows we got into Passage – from thence to Waterford – And on Thursday the Eleventh of June we arrived at Dear dear Carrickonsuir – The Joy at meeting was as great as the Grief at parting our friends – Every thing now promised felicity – My Mother quite recoverd – the Children all in rude health and spirits – All our Friends quite happy to see us, and proud of the Various little Presents we brought over.

CHAPTER THE 13TH [1778]

'The veriest Gluttons do not always cram'[1]

Our Guests were not long gone, when my Aunt Cuffe of Dublin my Fathers Sister and her only Child Grace Cuffe arrived with Mrs Fleming a poor relation of ours – Grace Cuffe was a most accomplishd little Creature and knew it to her comfort – They perswaded my Mother to let me go to them for a twelve month, for the Benefit of Masters in the Metropolis – At this time we were at home as happy as Uncultivated Nature could be – dressing out as Shepherds and Shepherdesses with flower wrought vestments, and Parasoles of Sycamore Leaves studded with Daisies and Buttercups – Here was a groupe of lovely Shepherdesses basking on a Sunny Hillock with two or three pet Kids browzing beside them – There a groupe of Shepherds with their Dogs and Crooks – regaling on a frugal Meal of stolen Cold Meat with a Wretched Sallad – 'Their Drink the Chrystal Well' – Except at the Season the Whiskey Currants were thrown out when we were all as fuddled as Couple Beggars – Nay one time the Pigs, Servants, and Children were reeling about the Yard where the heaps were thrown – Having once got a relish for the delightful Haut gout we often found a pretence to stay at home from Church, when the Jephsons and we used to say family Prayers – dress'd out in our Mothers fine flowerd Damasks with sticks across for large Hoops – We first todds up a Marmalade of orange peels and Stolen Honey – then we got to the Cellar and made a delightful warm jug of Punch in the fine hot Summers Mornings – After that we made Pews with the Chairs and then most devoutly fell to Prayers never missing one Amen – At length our revelry was ended by my Mothers catching us one Sunday Morning in such a State of Intoxication that not one of us could stir from our Chairs or utter a

---

1 *The veryest Gluttons do not always cram*: Robert Blair, *The Grave* (1742), 1. 642.

Monosyllable – This stopd all our future Piety and feasting – Our tastes were indeed rather Eccentric – We would eat nothing but pig Potatoes, Pap or Stirabout for our breakfast and we ended the Day with a Desert of raw Turneps, Cabbage Stumps, or Celery Tops – In this wild state my Aunt Cuffe and her accomplish'd Grace found us – they were much Shocked at first but we soon brought Grace over and conferr'd on her the honour of being head Cook and Confectioner having just Politeness enough to shew our Guest this Mark of Distinction.

Nothing now was heard of but hot Mutton Pies and so forth with all the Varieties of Creams and Candies that the Dairy and Garden could allow – some were contriving small Ovens that we might do without the cross Cook – others Stills, baking Dishes, and Pudding Cloths, till my Aunt Cuffe one Day found our Confectioner regaling under a Tree of green Gooseberries – on which she was confined, and put in Coventry by her Mother and never after allowed to come down till Dinner time – This was a terrible Blow to poor Grace, who almost forgot her Town Education amongst her Country Cousins.

FROM CHAPTER 16TH [1779]

... an awkward Mistake of my Aunt Herberts who joined us there She mistaking Kitty Cut-a-Dash the famous Thaïs[1] of the times for her Daughter Fanny (they being dress'd alike in White Lutestring) made several Promenades leaning on her Arm and Conversing with another Thais her Companion whilst Kitty and her friend acted their Parts to a Miracle – After the late Accident we kept close House for a Long time but at length my Aunt ventured to treat us to a Play – And Announced her Intentions accordingly.

FROM CHAPTER 17TH [1779]

The Play was the Beggars Opera – And it being the first thing of the kind I had ever seen, I did nothing but laugh and cry during the whole representation for which I was rated by Mrs Fleming who declared it was quite against the Rules of Polite Decorum and betrayed a Vulgar Rusticity to laugh or Cry at a Play House – Nor was my Cousin without a Lecture from my Aunt for talking too loud in the Green Room to a Pretty Gentleman who paid her some Compliments....

---

1 *Thaïs*: Greek courtesan (4th c. BC), reputed mistress of Alexander the Great and wife of Ptolemy I.

CHAPTER 35ᵀᴴ [1784]

'To heavenly Themes, sublimer Strains belong'[1]

I had Never heard any powerful Music before – but the Oratorios[2] no sooner began than I felt Myself quite overpower'd – I wept and laughd with secret Rapture – My Head Swam and I found Myself fainting Away and just on the wing to Heaven as it were – I knew not what passd till I found Mrs Hare holding a Smelling Bottle to my Nose which the ArchBishops Lady Mrs Agar had humanely handed over the Pew – I was quite Shocked at My Own behaviour, recollecting the Lecture Mrs Fleming gave me once before on an Occasion somewhat similar – The archbishops Throne was just over our Pew – He noticed all that passd, and seemd delighted at the Effect his Music had on a Novice – After Service Mrs Agar asked My Mother if I was her Daughter declaring herself much pleased with My Sensibility – 'Comfort Ye My people,' 'Every Valley shall be Exalted,' 'and the Trumpet shall sound' were the three principal Oratorios and I do believe there never was a more Capital Performance As the Archbishop spared No cost or pains on it – Mr Hare rallied me a good deal on My feelings, the Effects of which were too obvious not to be seen by the Whole Congregation....

FROM CHAPTER 39ᵀᴴ [1785]

... We were now at full Liberty to follow our Amusements – We had Many flaming Parties this Summer particularly one Given by Mr Simon Osborne of Annfield (a Widower) to a Miss Dodd with whom he flirted, and who pestered him out of a Fete Champêtre – Every one within twenty or thirty Miles was invited – We dined under Tents and Marquees in the Lawn – Nothing could exceed the Elegance of the Entertainment, and there was no counting the Company – But the chief Heroines were two Miss Kennedys both newly Married – They were just come from the assizes of Waterford where they prosecuted to Conviction three Men who ran away with them a Month before from whom they were rescued by their present Bridegrooms – The Men were hanged and every one was disgusted at the Ladies appearing so soon in Public after so horrid a Business – The Eldest Sister at

---

1 'To heavenly Themes ... belong: Pope, 'Messiah. A Sacred Eclogue, in imitation of Virgil's "Pollio"', 1. 2.
2 the Oratorios: Handel's Messiah was widely performed for the 25th anniversary of his death.

the Tryal fainted several Times and wished to evade the Prosecution, but was urged on to it by the Youngest who was hardend and inexorable – This fair Termagant was a very fine handsome Woman and came to the Ball dressed in a great display of Bridal Finery – pure Virgin white, trimmed all over with Silver Coxcomb whilst many cursed her Cruelty in hanging three very handsome young fellows of good Families Who treated her with Respect whilst she was with them – The Eldest a pretty Woman was more Moderately dressd in a brown Lustring quite plain....

FROM CHAPTER 52ND [1786]

... At that time a Miss Howley lived with Mrs English a remarkable fine handsome Young Woman but as remarkably vain proud fierce and intractable – In the Winter I got a little fancy Watch – And the Jephsons immediately after sent to London for one apiece – They bragged so much of them to Miss Howley on Purpose to vex her, that she resolving to outdo them sent to Paris for One – The Officers and we had great laughing about this new prodigy that was to appear to the total Annihilation of our Vanity – April Day I rose early made a very pretty Turnip Watch – and sent it in a nice little packing Box with a Dozen sheets of Brown Paper and as many Seals, with the Box tied and seal'd in like Manner – Round the Watch was a Paper written – A Paris Watch for Miss Howley and lines to the following Effect – 'Beware of the Ides of March' said the Roman Augur to Julius Caesar – 'Beware of the Month of May' said the British Spectator to his fair Country Woman – 'And Beware of the first of April' says the writer of this to the fair Miss Howley having the Honour of calling her – An April fool.

Officers, Jephsons, All were assembled at Mrs Englishes usual Levee when the Packet arrived – Oh God said Miss Howley (bouncing up) 'It's My Watch! – My Paris Watch!' – In transports she began to unpack – Ay! It's easy to know french Packing from english she cried – casting a triumphant Look at the Jephsons – She went on unpacking Paper after Paper till quite out of patience she call'd to Melifont for his Penknife – Words cannot express her Rage at the Disappointment – She Wept, stamp'd and tore her hair nor could be pacified till Mrs English promised to find out the Author of this Insult – Immediately Mrs Bab Butlar was dispatched at the head of half a Dozen Old Cronies to find out who had dared to insult Miss Howley – but hearing of the Racket it caused we let none but the Jephsons into our Secret – They to be sure enjoyed it with mischievous Sport.

They had however Scarce vented their Laughter at Miss Howleys Expence when I play'd them a Trick which though not so vexatious compleatly duped them – I dressed Myself as a raw Country Girl and went in one Night with a Letter which on rapping at the Door I delivered to Old James Meaker the Butlar and he presented to his mistress – In it I complained that I was a poor Country Girl who had the Misfortune of having a Merry begotten Child, That I complained to Mr Cox the Magistrate of the Young Man who had quitted Me – but that he order'd me to be turned out of his House and I threw myself on her Honours Mercy to speak to Mr Cox as I knew she was intimate with him, and he could refuse her Nothing she asked – It was a long Letter and so compleatly disguised in the Hibernian Dialect that She never once suspected the Forgery – Meanwhile James Meagher came to the Door and was very inquisitive to know what brought me there so late at Night – He questioned me so hard, and I made such pert Answers that he called Nurse Dwyer who advised him to kick me out of the Hall – In a little time the Bell rang violently – and I heard Mrs Jephson in the greatest passion crying 'The Audacious Creature! How durst she presume to think I would speak to Mr Cox on such a Business – Our family all drank Tea there on purpose to witness the Joke – When they had worked up Mrs Jephson sufficiently, the Boys came out to me and we had such a Sham Battle of ill Language that James, Nurse, and Mrs Jephson were compleatly transmogrified into Furies – They shook me and threatend Me with so many Grimaces that the Boys and Girls screech'd again with laughter – I was at last kicked out of the House and the Door clap'd in my Face – Mrs Jephson kept the Letter and shew'd it to the Gentlemen about – They offerd a Reward for Apprehension and Not till a long time after did we inform Mrs Jephson who her Petitioner was.

CHAPTER 56TH [1786]

One prospect lost, Another still we gain
And not a Vanity is giv'n in Vain[1]

We arrived at Carrick the Second of August 1786, and then got a New Neighbour whose coming soon alter'd the whole usual course of our

---

1 *One prospect lost … vain*: Alexander Pope, *An Essay on Man* (1733-34), Epistle II – Of the Nature and State of Man with Respect to Himself, as an Individual, 286–287.

Lives – This was my Cousin Edward Eyre Nephew to my Father – One of the greatest Oddities that Nature or Art ever produced – I say Art, because he studied every possible Method to make himself diverse from all Other human Beings – He was Heir to an immense property but spent and dabbled amongst Usurers to the tune of one hundred thousand pounds which kept him at Law and in poverty all his Life – He had a glass Coach and a glass Vis a Vis where he sat dress'd out from Top to Toe in a Suit of the Gayest Colour Silk or Sattin lined with Persian of a different Colour – He wore Sattin Shoes and Set Buckles had two or three sets of paste Buttons that cost an immensity – His Hair was dress'd like a Womans over a Rouleau or Tete, which was then the fashion amongst the Ladies – He sometimes carried a Muff, sometimes a Fan, and was always painted up to the Eyes with the deepest Carmine – His Manners and Actions were as Outré as his Dress and he was for ever engaged in some Novel Enterprize – Every Year he bought 200 pounds worth of Lottery Tickets though he seldom ever got a prize of any Value.

We all doated on him, and his settling here gave us infinite pleasure – After searching out every old ruined Seat about, (for such only would he take) He at length took Linville a beautiful Cottage by the Side of the Suir – Six Miles from our House and half way between Carrick and Clonmell – There he lived in most romantic Retirement with half a dozen favourite Servants and two very large spotted spaniels of the Leopard Breed which He called Miss Dapper and Miss Kitsy and adopted as Daughters and Co Heiresses – His Books, writings and Lottery Tickets engrossing the Hours that he did not spend with those Ladies or at the Card Table with his Mother Aunts, Cousins or Cronies – He was continually planning some ludicrous Exploit or Excursion and spared no Expense in its Execution – We all lived mostly at Linville with him, for he was quite affronted if he had   not two or three of us there Every Week – He kept his Room all the Morning and only came down to Dinner and Cards – Tea and Cold Water were his only Beverage and Sweetmeats or Pickles of every kind his constant food – When he was in good humour we always came in for a share of his Goodies and even when out of Temper he treated us with the utmost Civility, and left us full possession of his House, Gardens and all they contained – He had not been long settled when we determined on a Round of Excursions to all the waste places of the Neighbourhood, where we drove with the coach and vis a vis full and a Cart following with all kind of provision through Bog and Mire, Thick and Thin, and many a disastrous Event we had to encounter to his great Delight.

One of our first visits was to Etm Ville the residence of Old Counsellor Butlar who we heard was from home at that time – The two Carriages and the Cart with provisions drove up to the Door with all immaginable freedom – but to our great Annoyance the Old Counsellor himself was the first Object we met at the Door – He came out, and with his hand to his Eyes very narrowly pored into all the Circumstances of our Visit – after pressing us in vain to alight, for we were rooted to the Carriages with Surprize he questiond to know What brought us there, Where were we going, And Why his friend Mr Herbert would take such a Journey without refreshment – He then hinted that he could Not make out what our Cart meant – And we were so dumbfounded we could not answer a Single cross Question – We departed in a Roar of Laughter, leaving the Old gentleman in uncertainty and Amazement about us....

Ned Eyre had an Estate in the Co Galway which he now determined to Visit – And reading in the Newspaper that his Cousin Giles Eyre of Sporting Memory, had a Horse to run at the Ensuing Races of Loughrea – He resolved that we should Post it off to Galway – pop in on the Races of Loughrea and reimburse the Expence by making up a Match between his Cousin Giles and his Cousin Dolly – The Idea got so strongly in his Head, that he already was busy planning our Cloaths, Equipage, and future Visits....

CHAPTER 57TH [1787]

No vernal Bloom their torpid Rocks display
But Winter lingering chills the Lap of May[1]

Our journey was as curious as Ourselves but we did not feel the tiresomeness of it till we got into the County Galway where the bad Roads and parched fields only bounded by loose stone Walls for many Miles, gave us at once a hearty surfeit of it....

We proceeded on to Galway and had all the Bells in the Town ringing for our Arrival as Ned Eyre was proprietor of great part of the Town – The first thing he did was to Order his family Vault to be opened Where he descended and spent his first morning in paying his Duty to the remains of his great grand Aunt whose carcase he inspected and brought away some of the Sacred Ashes till a Mob began to

---

1 *No vernal blooms their torpid rocks array / But winter ling'ring chills the lap of May*: Oliver Goldsmith, *The Traveller* xiv. 7–8.

gather loudly murmuring at the prophanation and Ned Eyre with difficulty escaped – His Next amusement was treating all the Beggars of Galway to Hot Toast, Tea, and Chocolate – and we had a Publick Breakfast at the Door every Morning where Myriads attended – None were sent empty away and Ned put a Shilling on every Saucer he sent down.

But his general amusement was painting and dressing up one of his Hands as an Infant, and dandling it in the presence of a Nurse and new born Heir that lived Opposite – The fine folks of the Town soon heard of our doings and came in a Body one Sunday to stare and to gaze – But Ned Eyre threw up the Sash and thrusting himself half way out of the Window put out his Tongue at them All on which they retired from the opposite Windows and never after Molested us.

FROM CHAPTER 58TH [1787]

… In short we did many things which I cannot now recollect – and finally quitted Galway swearing Never to enter it again.

Ned Eyre and his Carriage fill'd with the finest ripe Peaches and Apricots but he kept them all for his Dog Lady Dapper and would send us none but the riff raff which we shared with his other Dog Miss Kitsy – However Sim White now and then stole a few good ones for us – Meanwhile Ned Stuffd our Carriage with Galway fish which soon stank so abominably that there was no bearing it – at last we crossd the Ferry near Mr Yelvertons and got out of the Nasty County Galway – the Rain poured down in Cascades and we were forced to enter a wretched Hovel on the Other side where with difficulty we got a few potatoes and Eggs with Rashers to satisfie our ravenous Stomachs.

Nothing else very material happen'd besides common Accidents till we got home when Sim White now overhead and Ears in Love sent in his Proposals for my Sister Fanny – He was then sent off to ask his Mothers Consent who gave a positive Negative – He wanted to carry on a Correspondence which was negatived at our Side and there the Matter dropd but not without Causing very great Vexation and Commotion amongst us – Sim White was a very interesting looking young Man and could make himself very Agreeable when he pleased – but he was very young and had an Artful Mother so could not be trusted.

CHAPTER 60TH [1788]

But our vile Tastes her lawful Charms refuse
And painted Arts depraved Allurements use[1]

We spent the ensuing Week with Ned Eyre amusing him with
Anecdotes about Prince Henry – Our Recluse seldom went to those
places unless some particular Whim occurred to him as once at Cork
when he promised to paint the Cheeks of a very pale Lady for an
assembly – When she came down dressd to the Parlour, He at one side
and Mrs White at the other scrubb'd her Cheeks – one with the deepest Crimson the other with plain Wool, and then hurried her off without letting her go to the Glass – For fear the Joke should light all on
their pale friend, and her odd Cheeks of Various Hue – The Brother
and Sister carried Jalap[2] in their pockets which they secretly mixd
with the Tea and Coffee – So that the Ladies and Gentlemen of the
Ball Room soon found something else to think of besides laughing at
Ned Eyre's pale protégée – The worthy Pair locked the Ball Room
Door and a General Confusion ensued – Some were fainting Some
weeping whilst their wicked Physicians escaped and drove home.

At the Age of fourteen Mrs White then Miss Eyre was devoutly
carried to a Confirmation, but was so vex'd at being forced to take all
her Sins on herself that She stuck her Head full of Iron Pins with the
Points up to annoy the Bishop who was terribly Scratched and torn
when he laid his hands on his Contumelious Disciple...

My Aunt Eyre was even at that Age a beautiful looking Woman,
she was of the largest size and had an Air of Majesty about her that
struck every one – she had all the Pleasing Manners of My Father
except his Meekness and Patience, for when rouzed she was very fiery
and passionate – and being a great family Woman nothing provoked
her so much as Ned Eyres taking up the Almanack and pointing out
where his Cousin the Haberdasher and his Relation the Shoemaker
lived in Dublin – She Always stood up with her Hands clench'd telling
the puppy He was the only Blot in the family from the time they came
over with William the Conqueror and that his Ancestors were the lin-
eal Descendants of Charlemagne and Pepin Kings of France – She was
so like my Father in every thing but her hastiness, that we loved her
greatly and her warm temper made her equally fond of her dear and

---

1 *But our lewd ... Allurements use*': Edward Young, 'Satire V. On Women', 235-236.
2 *Jalap*: a purgative.

now only Brother and his family – Ned who always reflected her Sentiments treated us with the greatest Defference, And let who would be there they were obliged to Make Room for us....

Writing of Plays I shall mention one we acted when Mrs Cooke was here which I forgot to mention in its right place – The Old Garret the scene of most of our childish Pranks was our theatre – The Fair Penitent[1] the play we chose – I had at once the laborious Tasks of painting the Scenes and fitting Myself for the formidable part of Calista – Otway acted Altamont – George Carshore Lothario – Miss Carshore Lavinia – and Tom the brave Horatio – We made the Children act as Snobs, Stage Sweepers Guards Musicians and waiting Maids – All the Money we could rap or run was expended in Canvas, Whiting, Gambouge, Stone Blue and Oil for the Painter – and many a time the poor Boys denied themselves a halfpennyworth of Elecampane or Gingerbread to devote their little pocket Money to the Theatre – We got a friend to dig up a Skull in the Church Yard and ransacked every place for Relicks to make the last Scene as dismal as possible – My Fathers old black Cassocks served for hangings, and his Wig converted Altamont into a venerable Sciolto – We had the whole Stage decorated with Pictures, flower pots Ribbons Shells Moss and Lobster Claws – Calista was dress'd in Virgin White with her beautiful golden Locks hanging in loose Ringlets and festoon'd with penny Rings and two penny Beads &c – Lavinia was dress'd in a Salmon Colour Stuff ornamented with Natural flowers – Great Interest was made by Captain Curtis and Perceval to be admitted as Snobs, but we limited our Audience to the Carshores, Jephsons, Mr Rankin and some Others – Many were our failures and Mischances – Our Prompter not yet out of his spelling Book miscalled his Words or lost his place – The gallant gay Lothario[2] grew sulky and refused to act his Part when the brave Horatio tilted him too roughly – The venerable Sciolto burst out laughing just in the Act of introducing the lost Calista to the dead Body of her Lover – Calista and Lavinia fought desperately behind the scenes about change of Dresses – and finally the Candle snuffers set the Stage on fire.

---

1 *The Fair Penitent*: popular tragedy (1703) by Nicholas Rowe. Its last scene, with charnel house and grave, has all the trappings of gothic melodrama.
2 *gay Lothario*: this became a standard phrase for a heartless libertine.

Index of First Lines

General Index

General Index

'I tell thee, Charmion, could I time
retrieve', **102**
Incognita, 96,
Love for Love, 8, 97,
The Mourning Bride, 8, 97,
The Old Batchelor, 96
The Way of the World, 1, 8, **97-101**
Connellan, Thomas, 375
Convention Act (1793), 324n
Corbet, Peter, 171-173
Corbet, Thomas, 171-173
'Coughing Old Man, The', **228-229**
Covent Garden Theatre, 208
de Coverley, Roger, 103-104,
Craftsman, The, 88n,
Crassus, M. Licinius, 352n
Critical History of the Celtic Religion and
Learning, A, 95
Crito, 293-295, 297
Croker, Thomas Crofton, 299
Popular Songs of Ireland, 299
Crow Street Theatre, 166
Croxall, Samuel, 332
The Innocent Adultery, 332
Cuffe, Grace, 382
Cuffe, Hon. Martha, 380, 381
Cumberland, Richard, 11,
Crow Street Theatre, 208
Curll, Edmund, 86
Curran, John Philpot , 2, 322, **323-325**,
347, 349
'The Deserter's Lamentation', 323
Speech Defending Archibald Hamilton
Rowan, 323-325
'Curse of Doneraile, The', **349-351**
Damiens, Robert, 232n
Davy, Humphry, 301
Dawson, Bully, 103
Day, Thomas, 301
The History of Sandford and Merton, 301
Debelle, Jean François Joseph, 366
Defenders, 379
Delany, Mary, 187, 192
Delany, Patrick, 27, 43, 133-134, 173, 176,
192-196
Eighteen Discourses, **134-138**
Life and Writings of King David, 134
News from Parnassus, 134
Observations upon Lord Orrery's Remarks
on the Life and Writings of Dr Jonathan
Swift, 134
Social Duties of Life, 134
Demosthenes, 105
Dermody, Thomas, 1, **376-379**
Harp of Erin, The, 376
'John Baynham's Epitaph', **376-379**
'Description of a City Shower, A', **39-41**
'Description of an Irish Feast, The', **52-55**
Deserted Village, The, 16, 245, **253-263**

'Deserter's Lamentation, The', **323**
Diary of Theobald Wolfe Tone, **363-374**
Dingley, Rebecca, 5, 27, 41n
Diogenes, 146
Doneraile, Anne St. Leger (née Blakeney),
Lady, 349
Draper, Elizabeth, 197
Drennan, William, 322, 346, **347-349**
Fugitive Pieces, 347
Letter to his Mother, **348-349**
'The Wail of the Women after the Battle',
347
'The Wake of William Orr', 347
'When Erin First Rose', 347
Drury Lane Theatre, 103, 111, 208, 226n,
325
'Dry Be That Tear', **326**
Dublin Gaelic Society, 19
Dublin Philosophical Society, 320n
Duck, Stephen, 88,
Dunkin, William, **190-191**
The Art of Gate-Passing: or, The
Murphæid, 190
'Carbery Rocks in the County of Cork',
190
'The Modish School-Master', **190-191**
'On the New Bridge Built on the Eastern
Side of Dublin', 190
'The Parson's Revels', 190
The Poetical Works of William Dunkin,
190
Selected Poetical Works, 190
Edgeworth, C. Sneyd, 354
The Memoirs of the Abbé Edgeworth, 354-
363
Edgeworth, Henry Essex, the Abbé, **354-363**
Letters from the Abbé Edgeworth to his
Friends, 354
The Memoirs of the Abbé Edgeworth, 354-
363
Edgeworth, Maria, 308, **309-314**, **379-380**
The Absentee, 379
Castle Rackrent, 379
Ennui, 379
Essay on Irish Bulls, 13, 308
Essays on Professional Education, 308
Letter to Mrs Ruxton, **380**
Memoirs of Richard Lovell Edgeworth,
301, **302-308**, 309, 379
Ormond, 379
Practical Education, 308, **309-314**, 379
Edgeworth, Richard, 305-306
Edgeworth, Richard Lovell, 301, **302-308**,
308, **309-314**, 354, 379
Essay on Irish Bulls, 13, 308
Essays on Professional Education, 308
Memoirs, 301, **302-308**, 309, 379
Practical Education, 308, **309-314**, 379
Edgeworth, Rev. Robert, 354

General Index